Photoshop® CS6

FOR

DUMMIES®

by Peter Bauer

WILEY

John Wiley & Sons, Inc.

Photoshop® CS6 For Dummies®

Published by
John Wiley & Sons, Inc.
111 River Street
Hoboken, NJ 07030-5774
www.wiley.com

Copyright © 2012 by John Wiley & Sons, Inc., Hoboken, New Jersey

Published by John Wiley & Sons, Inc., Hoboken, New Jersey

Published simultaneously in Canada

For general information on our other products and services, please contact our Customer Care Department within the U.S. at 877-762-2974, outside the U.S. at 317-572-3993, or fax 317-572-4002.

For technical support, please visit www.wiley.com/techsupport.

Wiley publishes in a variety of print and electronic formats and by print-on-demand. Some material included with standard print versions of this book may not be included in e-books or in print-on-demand. If this book refers to media such as a CD or DVD that is not included in the version you purchased, you may download this material at http://booksupport.wiley.com. For more information about Wiley products, visit www.wiley.com.

Library of Congress Control Number is available from the Publisher.

ISBN: 978-1-118-17457-9 (pbk); ISBN 978-1-118-22706-0 (ebk); ISBN 978-1-118-24010-6 (ebk); ISBN 978-1-118-26471-3 (ebk)

Manufactured in the United States of America

10 9 8 7 6 5 4 3 2 1

WILEY

About the Author

Peter Bauer is a member of the Photoshop Hall of Fame, an award-winning fine-art photographer, the Help Desk Director for the National Association of Photoshop Professionals (NAPP), and an adjunct professor of design at the University of Notre Dame. He has authored more than a dozen books on Adobe Photoshop, Adobe Illustrator, computer graphics, and photography. Pete is also the host of video-training titles at Lynda.com and a contributing writer for *Photoshop User* magazine. He appears regularly as a member of the Photoshop World Instructor Dream Team, hosting *Help Desk Live!* As NAPP Help Desk Director, Pete personally answers thousands of e-mail questions annually about Photoshop and computer graphics. He has contributed to and assisted on such projects as special effects for feature films and television, major book and magazine publications, award-winning websites, and fine art exhibitions. He serves as a computer graphics efficiency consultant for a select corporate clientele, and shoots exclusive photographic portraiture. Pete's prior careers have included bartending, theater, broadcast journalism, professional rodeo, business management, and military intelligence interrogation. Pete and his wife, Professor Mary Ellen O'Connell, of the University of Notre Dame Law School, live in South Bend, Indiana.

Dedication

I have written (and John Wiley & Sons has published) this book for you — the many who learn and live by the written word. Whether on paper or tablet, these words and illustrative figures were put here for you. There is no irony in the fact that you'll use these words to produce pictures.

Author's Acknowledgments

First, I'd like to thank Bob Woerner and Linda Morris and the rest of the superb crew at John Wiley & Sons that put the book together. I'd also like to acknowledge Scott and Kalebra Kelby, Jean Kendra, Larry Becker, and Dave Moser of the National Association of Photoshop Professionals (NAPP). With their support, I'm the Help Desk Director for NAPP, and get to share my Photoshop knowledge with tens of thousands of NAPP members — and with you. I also thank my Help Desk colleagues Nicole S. Young (Nicolesy) and Rob Sylvan (who served as technical editor on this book) for their support during the development of this project.

Another great group from whom I continue to receive support are my colleagues on the Photoshop World Instructor Dream Team. If you haven't been to Photoshop World, try to make it — soon. Rather than "Photoshop conference," think "Photoshop festival." Where else can you see suits and slackers, side by side, savoring every single syllable? It's more than just training and learning: It's a truly intellectually invigorating environment. And, of course, I thank my wife, the wonderful Professor Mary Ellen O'Connell of the Notre Dame Law School, for her unwavering support during yet another book project.

Publisher's Acknowledgments

We're proud of this book; please send us your comments at http://dummies.custhelp.com. For other comments, please contact our Customer Care Department within the U.S. at 877-762-2974, outside the U.S. at 317-572-3993, or fax 317-572-4002.

Some of the people who helped bring this book to market include the following:

Acquisitions and Editorial

Project Editor: Linda Morris

Executive Editor: Bob Woerner

Copy Editor: Linda Morris

Technical Editor: Rob Sylvan

Editorial Manager: Jodi Jensen

Editorial Assistant: Amanda Graham

Sr. Editorial Assistant: Cherie Case

Cover Photo:
   Cover images created by Peter Bauer

Cartoons: Rich Tennant (www.the5thwave.com)

Composition Services

Project Coordinator: Patrick Redmond

Layout and Graphics: Claudia Bell, Joyce Haughey, Corrie Niehaus

Proofreader: Evelyn Wellborn

Indexer: Potomac Indexing, LLC

Publishing and Editorial for Technology Dummies

   Richard Swadley, Vice President and Executive Group Publisher

   Andy Cummings, Vice President and Publisher

   Mary Bednarek, Executive Acquisitions Director

   Mary C. Corder, Editorial Director

Publishing for Consumer Dummies

   Kathleen Nebenhaus, Vice President and Executive Publisher

Composition Services

   Debbie Stailey, Director of Composition Services

Table of Contents

Introduction

Adobe Photoshop is one of the most important computer programs of our age. It's made photo editing a commonplace thing, something for the everyperson. Still, Photoshop can be a scary thing (especially that first purchase price!), comprising a jungle of menus and panels and tools and options and shortcuts as well as a bewildering array of add-ons and plug-ins. And that's why you're holding this book in your hands. And why I wrote it. And why John Wiley & Sons published it.

You want to make sense of Photoshop — or, at the very least, be able to work competently and efficiently in the program, accomplishing those tasks that need to get done. You want a reference that discusses how things work and what things do, not in a technogeek or encyclopedic manner, but rather as an experienced friend might explain something to you. Although step-by-step explanations are okay if they show how something works, you don't need rote recipes that don't apply to the work you do. You don't mind discovering tricks, as long as they can be applied to your images and artwork in a productive, meaningful manner. You're in the right place!

About This Book

This is a *For Dummies* book, and as such, it was produced with an eye toward you and your needs. From Day One, the goal has been to put into your hands the book that makes Photoshop understandable and useable. You won't find a technical explanation of every option for every tool in every situation, but rather a concise explanation of those parts of Photoshop you're most likely to need. If you happen to be a medical researcher working toward a cure for cancer, your Photoshop requirements might be substantially more specific than what you'll find covered here. But for the overwhelming majority of the people who have access to Adobe Photoshop, this book provides the background needed to get your work done with Photoshop.

As I updated this book, I intentionally tried to strike a balance between the types of images with which you're most likely to work and those visually stimulating (yet far less common) images of unusual subjects from faraway places. At no point in this book does *flavor* override *foundation*. When you need to see a practical example, that's what I show you. I worked to ensure that each piece of artwork illustrates a technique and does so in a meaningful, nondistracting way for you.

You'll see that I used mostly Apple computers in producing this book. That's simply a matter of choice and convenience. You'll also see (if you look closely) that I shoot mostly with Canon cameras and use Epson printers. That doesn't mean that you shouldn't shoot with Nikon, or that you shouldn't print with HP or Canon. If that's what you have, if it's what you're comfortable with, and if it fulfills your needs, stick with it! You'll also find that I mention Wacom drawing tablets here and there (and devoted one of the final chapters to the subject). Does that mean you should have one? If you do any work that relies on precise cursor movement (like painting, dodging, burning, path creation and editing, cloning, healing, patching, or lassoing, just to name a few), yes, I do recommend a Wacom Cintiq display or Intuos tablet. Next to more RAM and good color management, it's the best investment just about any Photoshop user can make.

One additional note: If you're brand new to digital imaging and computers, this probably isn't the best place to start. I do indeed make certain assumptions about your level of computer knowledge (and, to a lesser degree, your knowledge of digital imaging). But if you know your File⇨Open from your File⇨Close and can find your lens cap with both hands, read Chapter 1, and you'll have no problem with *Photoshop CS6 For Dummies*.

How This Book Is Organized

Photoshop CS6 For Dummies is primarily a reference book. As such, you can check the Table of Contents or the index for a specific subject, flip to those pages, and get the information you need. You can also start at the beginning and read cover to cover (just to make sure you don't miss a single tip, technique, or joke). To give you an indication of the type of information in each chapter, I organized the book into parts. Here's a quick look at what sort of content you can find in each part.

Part I: Breezing through Basic Training

The first set of chapters presents the basic operation of Photoshop, what you need to know to get around in the program, and the core process of getting images into Photoshop and back out again. If you're new to digital imaging, and particularly unfamiliar with Photoshop, make sure to read Chapter 1 through Chapter 3. If you've worked with Photoshop or another image editing program and aren't quite sure about the concept of resolution or which file formats are best for which purposes, don't overlook Chapter 2. Chapter 4 is the meat and potatoes of Photoshop: scanning and downloading images from cameras, cropping to fit specific print and frame sizes, and printing or posting your images on the web. All in one nice, tidy package.

Part II: Easy Enhancements for Digital Images

In Chapters 5 through 9, you discover ideas and techniques for improving the appearance of your images. You read about *tonality* (the lightness and darkness of the image), *color correction* (making the image's color look natural), and making selections to isolate individual parts of your image for correction. Part II also includes a full chapter on the Raw file format for digital cameras — what it is, why it's important, and how to determine whether it's right for you. At the end of this part, I include a chapter on the most common problems in digital photos: red-eye, wrinkles, and unwanted objects. And, yes, that chapter includes what to do about those problems, too!

Part III: Creating "Art" in Photoshop

The chapters in Part III take a walk on the creative side. Although not everyone wants to use Photoshop as a digital painting program, everyone should understand how to get around in the complex and daunting Brush panel. *Compositing* images (making one picture from two or more), adding text (whether a simple copyright notice or an entire page), using paths, and adding layer styles are all valuable skills for just about all folks who work with Photoshop, even if they don't consider their work to be "art." You'll also find info about how to integrate your iPad into your Photoshop workflow.

Part IV: Power Photoshop

The two chapters in Part IV are more specialized than the rest of the book. If you don't work in a production environment (even regularly cropping to the same size for printing on your inkjet printer can count as production), you might not need to use Actions in Photoshop. But there's far more to Chapter 16 than just Actions and scripting! It also shows you how you can use Adobe Bridge's Output panel to create an on-screen presentation that anyone can view, generate a single page with small thumbnail images of all your photos, and save paper by printing multiple copies of a photo on a single sheet. Chapter 17 explores Photoshop's new and improved video editing capabilities (now available in the non-Extended version of Photoshop). With more and more digital cameras and smart phones capturing video, here's an introduction to working with both video and animation in Photoshop.

Part V: The Part of Tens

The final part of this book, The Part of Tens, was both the easiest and most difficult section to prepare. It was easy because, well, the chapters are short. It was incredibly tough because it's so hard to narrow any Photoshop-related list to just ten items. Photoshop is such a beautifully complex and deep program that I had a very hard time restricting myself to just ten things to know about the Extended version of Photoshop, just ten reasons a Wacom tablet can be your best friend, and just ten things you need to know about high dynamic range (HDR) photography.

Conventions Used in This Book

To save some space and maintain clarity, I use an arrow symbol as shorthand for Photoshop menu commands. I could write this:

> Move the cursor onto the word Image at the top of your screen and press the mouse button. Continuing to press the mouse button, move the cursor downward to the word Adjustments. Still pressing the mouse button, move the cursor to the right and downward onto the words Shadow/Highlight. Release the mouse button.

But it makes more sense to write this:

> Choose Shadow/Highlight from the Image➪Adjustments menu.

Or even to use this:

> Choose the Image➪Adjustments➪Shadow/Highlight command.

You'll also note that I include keyboard shortcuts (when applicable) for both Mac and Windows. Generally the shortcuts are together, with Mac always first, and look like this:

> Move the selection to a separate layer with the shortcut ⌘+Shift+J/Ctrl+Shift+J.

Icons Used in This Book

You'll see icons in the margins as you read this book, icons that indicate something special. Here, without further ado, is the gallery:

This icon tells you I'm introducing a new feature, something just added to the program with Photoshop CS6. If you're brand new to Photoshop yourself, you can ignore this icon — it's all new to you. If you're an experienced Photoshop user, take note.

When I have a little secret or shortcut to share with you — something that can make your life easier, smoother, more convenient — you see the Tip icon.

This icon doesn't appear very often, but when it does, read carefully! I reserve the Warning icon for those things that can really mess up your day — things that can cause you to lose work by ruining your file or prevent Photoshop from fulfilling your wishes. If there were to be a quiz afterward, every Warning would be included! (Actually, they do appear on my exams — ask my students!)

The Remember icon shows you good-to-know stuff, things that are applicable in a number of different places in Photoshop, or things that can make your Photoshop life easier.

You might notice this icon in a place or two in the book. It's not common because I exclude most of the highly technical background info: you know, the boring techno-geek concepts behind Photoshop. But when you do see the icon, it indicates something that you probably should know.

How to Use This Book

This is a reference book, not a lesson-based workbook or a tips-and-tricks cookbook. When you have a question about how something in Photoshop works, flip to the Table of Contents or the index to find your spot. You certainly can read the chapters in order, cover to cover, to make sure that you get the most out of it. Nonetheless, keep this book handy while you work in Photoshop. (Reading cover to cover not only ensures that you find out the most about Photoshop, but it guarantees that you don't miss a single cartoon or joke.)

Unless you're borrowing a friend's copy or you checked this book out of the library or you're reading it on your iPad, I suggest you get comfortable with the thought of sticky notes and bent page corners. Photoshop is a very complex program — no one knows everything about Photoshop. And many concepts and techniques in Photoshop are hard to remember, especially if you don't use them often. Bookmark those pages so they're easy to find next time because you're sure to be coming back time and again to *Photoshop CS6 For Dummies*.

Where to Go from Here

Occasionally, we have updates to our technology books. If this book does have technical updates, they will be posted at www.dummies.com/go/photoshopCS6fdupdates.

Part I
Breezing through Basic Training

A solid understanding of certain basic concepts and techniques makes learning Photoshop much easier. Heck, it's difficult to understand a discussion of feathered selections when you don't know your pixels from a hole in the ground, right?

In Chapter 1, I introduce you to Adobe Photoshop. Chapter 2 focuses on the basic concepts of digital imaging and offers a look at the primary file formats in which you save Photoshop images. Chapter 3 makes sure we're all reading from the same menu as we discuss Photoshop's various commands, tools, and features — and provides some critical troubleshooting procedures. Finally, Chapter 4 covers bringing images into Photoshop from digital cameras or scanners, organizing those files, and basic output through printing.

Welcome to Photoshop!

Adobe Photoshop is, without question, the leading image-editing program in the world. Photoshop has even become somewhat of a cultural icon. It's not uncommon to hear Photoshop used as a verb ("That picture is obviously Photoshopped!"), and you'll even see references to Photoshop in the daily comics and cartoon strips. And now you're part of this whole gigantic phenomenon called Photoshop.

Before I take you on this journey through the intricacies of Photoshop, I want to introduce you to Photoshop in a more general way. In this chapter, I tell you what Photoshop is *designed* to do, what it *can* do (although not as capably as job-specific software), and what you can *get* it to do if you try really, really hard. I also review some basic computer operation concepts and point out a couple of places where Photoshop is a little different than most other programs. At the end of the chapter, I have a few tips for you on installing Photoshop to ensure that it runs properly.

Exploring Adobe Photoshop

Photoshop is used for an incredible range of projects, from editing and correcting digital photos to preparing images for magazines and newspapers to creating graphics for the web. You can also find Photoshop in the forensics departments of law-enforcement agencies, scientific labs and research facilities, and dental and medical offices, as well as in classrooms, offices, studios, and homes around the world. As the Help Desk Director for the National Association of Photoshop Professionals (NAPP), my team and I solve problems and provide solutions for Photoshop users from every corner of the computer graphics field and from every corner of the world. People are doing some pretty amazing things with Photoshop, many of which are so far from the program's original roots that it boggles the mind!

What Photoshop is designed to do

Adobe Photoshop is an image-editing program. It's designed to help you edit images — digital or digitized images, photographs, and otherwise. This is the core purpose of Photoshop. Over the years, Photoshop has grown and developed, adding features that supplement its basic operations. But at its heart, Photoshop is an image editor. At its most basic, Photoshop's workflow goes something like this: You take a picture, you edit the picture, and you print the picture (as illustrated in Figure 1-1).

Figure 1-1: Basic Photoshop: Take photo, edit photo, print photo. Drink coffee (optional).

Whether captured with a digital camera, scanned into the computer, or created from scratch in Photoshop, your artwork consists of tiny squares of color, which are picture elements called *pixels.* (I explore pixels and the nature of digital imaging in-depth in Chapter 2.) Photoshop is all about changing and adjusting the colors of those pixels — collectively, in groups, or one at a time — to make your artwork look precisely how you want it to look. (Photoshop, by the way, has no *Good Taste* or *Quality Art* button. It's up to you to decide what suits your artistic or personal vision and what meets your professional requirements.) Some very common Photoshop image-editing tasks are shown in Figure 1-2: namely, correcting red-eye and minimizing wrinkles (both discussed in Chapter 9); and compositing images (see Chapter 10).

New features to help you do those jobs

The new version of Photoshop has lots of new features to help you perform those tasks more efficiently and more easily. For example, the non-Extended version of Photoshop can also work with video (Chapter 17), Color Range now offers Skin Tones in the Select menu with a Detect Faces option, working with type now includes both character and paragraph styles (Chapter 13), and you now have the option to enable Automatically Save Recovery Information, which protects your work in case Photoshop crashes.

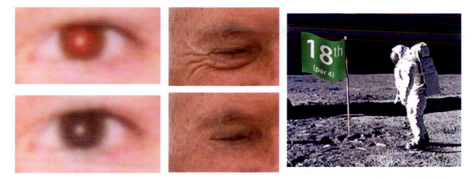

Astronaut image courtesy of NASA

Figure 1-2: Some common Photoshop tasks.

For photographers, perhaps the biggest new thing is the addition of content-aware technology to the Patch tool and the new Content-Aware Move tool. Content-aware patching is perhaps even more powerful than Content-Aware Fill, thanks to five levels of *adaptation*, which is how much free rein you offer the program to replicate the surrounding area.

The Content-Aware Move tool (nested with the Patch tool, the Healing Brush, and the Spot Healing Brush) works its magic in two ways, with a Move mode and an Extend mode. Make a selection and drag in Move mode, and the area from which you moved is filled (content-aware style) to match the surrounding image detail and color. The area to which you drag gets the selected pixels, blending into the new surrounding. In Figure 1-3, you can see the original to the left and the result of using the Content-Aware Move tool in Move mode on the right. As you can see in the Layers panel, I first added an empty layer for non-destructive editing — I've put both the moved pixels and the replacement pixels on their own layer, just in case I need to touch up or even delete the change. The Extend mode is great for flattening bellies or making buildings taller and other such tasks. Make a selection of the pixels you want to extend (or contract) and drag up or down, in or out.

You don't need to make the selection with the Content-Aware Move tool — you might, for example, get a better initial selection with the Magnetic Lasso tool — you just need to do the dragging with the Content-Aware Move tool. In the example shown in Figure 1-3, I painted the selection as an alpha channel and used the Select⇨Load Selection command before dragging with the Content-Aware Move tool. (Selections and alpha channels are discussed in Chapter 10.)

Figure 1-3: The Content-Aware Move tool is another way to seamlessly blend pixels.

In the past few updates, Photoshop has developed some rather powerful illustration capabilities to go with its digital-imaging power. Now Photoshop joins Adobe Illustrator in working with actual vector shapes. Photoshop also has a very capable brush engine, including the new erodible brush tips (they wear down and need to be re-sharpened) and new airbrush and watercolor brush tips, further extending the fine art painting capabilities of the program. Figure 1-4 shows a comparison of raster artwork (the digital photo, left), vector artwork (the illustration, center), and digital painting (right). The three types of artwork can appear in a single image, too. (Creating vector artwork is presented in Chapter 11, and you can read about painting with Photoshop in Chapter 14.)

Figure 1-4: You can use Photoshop with raster images, vector shapes, and even to paint.

Photoshop includes some basic features for creating web graphics, including slicing and animations (but web work is best done in a true web development program, such as Dreamweaver). Photoshop's companion program Adobe Bridge even includes the Output panel to help you create entire websites to display your artwork online and PDF presentations for on-screen display, complete with transition effects between slides. (Read about Bridge's Output panel's capabilities in Chapter 16.)

Photoshop CS6 and Photoshop CS6 Extended

Adobe is once again offering two different versions of Photoshop. Photoshop CS6 and Photoshop CS6 Extended both have all of Photoshop's powerful image-editing, vector-drawing, painting, video editing, and type capabilities. Photoshop CS6 Extended also includes some very specialized, highly technical features for use in science, research, and for use with 3D modeling programs. (I briefly introduce these features in Chapter 18.)

So, if you have Photoshop CS6 rather than Photoshop CS6 Extended, should you feel cheated or like a second-class citizen? Nope! Unless you specifically need those extended features, there's no real reason to purchase them. But what if you got Photoshop CS6 Extended as part of a Creative Suite or Adobe Bundle package of software — did you pay for something you don't need? Well, sort-of-yeah-but-not-really. The folks who're really paying

extra for the extended features are those who purchase Photoshop CS6 Extended as a stand-alone program. The additional cost they pay funds the research and development of the extended features.

So why didn't you get to choose between Photoshop CS6 and Photoshop CS6 Extended when you ordered your Bundle or Suite? Buying software shouldn't be as complicated as, say, ordering a cup of coffee. *(Caf, de-caf, half-caf? Latte, espresso, cappuccino? White, brown, or raw sugar? Cream, half-and-half, milk, or skim? Small, medium, largo, supor, or el grosso maxmo?)* It could get quite confusing. Imagine trying to wade through all of the thousands of products if Adobe marketed every possible combination as a separate Bundle or Suite or Studio! You'd spend so much time trying to *find* your perfect bundle, you'd never get to *use* the software.

Other things you can do with Photoshop

Admittedly, Photoshop just plain can't do some things. It won't make you a good cup of coffee. It can't press your trousers. It doesn't vacuum under the couch. It isn't even a substitute for iTunes, Microsoft Excel, or TurboTax — it just doesn't do those things.

However, there are a number of things for which Photoshop isn't designed that you *can* do in a pinch. If you don't have InDesign, you can still lay out the pages of a newsletter, magazine, or even a book, one page at a time. (With Bridge's Output panel, you can even generate a multipage PDF document from your individual pages.) If you don't have Dreamweaver, you can use Photoshop to create a website, one page at a time, sliced and optimized and even with animated GIFs. And while you're probably not going to create the next block-buster on your laptop with Photoshop, the new video editing capabilities can certainly get you through the family reunion or that school project.

Page layout in Photoshop isn't particularly difficult for a one-page piece or even a trifold brochure. Photoshop has a very capable type engine, consider-ing the program is designed to push pixels rather than play with paragraphs.

(It even has spell check — not bad for an image editor!) Photoshop can even show you a sample of each typeface in the Font menu. Choose from five sizes of preview (and None) in Photoshop's Type menu. However, you can't link Photoshop's type containers, so a substantial addition or subtraction at the top of the first column requires manually recomposing all of the following columns. After all, among the biggest advantages of a dedicated page layout program are the continuity (using a master page or layout) and flow from page to page. If you work with layout regularly, use InDesign.

Dreamweaver is a state-of-the-art web design tool, with good interoperability with Photoshop. However, if you don't have Dreamweaver and you desperately need to create a web page, Photoshop comes to your rescue. After you lay out your page and create your slices, use the Save for Web command to generate an HTML document (your web page) and a folder filled with the images that form the page (see Figure 1-5). One of the advantages to creating a web page in Dreamweaver rather than Photoshop is HTML text. (Using Photoshop, all the text on your web pages is saved as graphic files. HTML text not only produces smaller web pages for faster download, but it's resizable in the web browser.)

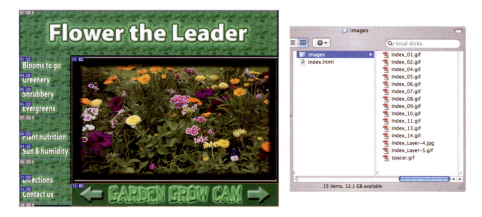

Figure 1-5: You can create an entire web page in Photoshop.

Adobe Premiere (and the budget-conscious Premiere Elements) and Adobe After Effects are the tools for video and related effects. But now Photoshop (and not just the Extended version of Photoshop) offers a more highly-developed video capability, including audio tracks. Adobe Illustrator is the state-of-the-art vector artwork program, but Photoshop now offers true vector shapes, not just simulations created with shape layers. If, however, you need to do sophisticated (or *lots* of) vector artwork, consider Illustrator.

Keyboard shortcuts

Keyboard shortcuts are customizable in Photoshop (check out Chapter 3), but some of the basic shortcuts are the same as those you use in other programs. You open, copy, paste, save, close, and quit just as you do in Microsoft Word, your e-mail program, and just about any other software. I suggest that you keep these shortcuts unchanged, even if you do some other shortcut customization. Okay, well, I do recommend *one* change to the standard keyboard shortcuts. See Chapter 3 for my recommendation on shortcuts for the Edit menu's Undo/Redo and Step Backward.

Photoshop's incredible selective Undo

Here's one major difference between Photoshop and other programs. Almost all programs have some form of Undo, enabling you to reverse the most recent command or action (or mistake). Photoshop also has, however, a great feature that lets you *partially* undo. The History Brush can partially undo just about any filter, adjustment, or tool — by painting. You select the History Brush, choose a history state (a stage in the image development) to which you want to revert, and then paint over areas of the image that you want to change back to the earlier state.

You can undo as far back in the editing process as you want, with a couple of limitations: The History panel (where you select the state to which you want to revert) holds only a limited number of history states. In the Photoshop Preferences⊃Performance pane, you can specify how many states you want Photoshop to remember (to a maximum of 1,000). Keep in mind that storing lots of history states takes up computer memory that you might need for processing filters and adjustments. That can slow things down. The default of 20 history states is good for most projects, but when using painting tools or other procedures that involve lots of repetitive steps (such as touching up with the Dodge, Burn, or Clone Stamp tools), a larger number (perhaps as high as 60) is generally a better idea.

The second limitation is pixel dimensions. If you make changes to the image's actual size (in pixels) with the Crop tool, the Image⊃Crop command, the Image Size or Canvas Size commands (both in the Image menu), you cannot revert to prior steps with the History Brush. You can choose as a source any history state that comes *after* the image's pixel dimensions change but none that come before.

Here's one example of using the History Brush as a creative tool. You open a copy of a photograph in Photoshop. You edit as necessary. You use the Black and White adjustment on the image to make it appear to be grayscale. In the History panel, you click in the left column next to a snapshot (a saved history state) or the step prior to Black and White to designate that as the *source state,* the appearance of the image to which you want to revert. You select the History Brush and paint over specific areas of the image to return them to the original (color) appearance (see Figure 1-7). There you have it — a grayscale image with areas of color, compliments of the History Brush!

Photoshop has another very powerful partial Undo in the Fade command. Found in the Edit menu, Fade can be used immediately after just about any tool or adjustment or filter or, well, almost anything that changes the appearance of the image. (You can even fade the History Brush.) The Fade command enables you to change the opacity and/or the blending mode of whatever alteration you most recently made to the appearance of your artwork. You might, for example, use a Sharpen filter and then use the Fade command to change the filter's blending mode to Luminosity. That's the functional equivalent of sharpening the L channel in Lab color mode without having to switch color modes at all. Keep in mind that when I used the word "immediately," I really meant it — you can't even use the Save command between applying a filter and using the Fade command.

Figure 1-7: Painting to undo with the History Brush, with the original in the upper-right.

Installing Photoshop: Need to know

If you haven't yet installed Photoshop (or the Adobe Creative Suite), here are a few points to keep in mind:

✔ **Install only into the default location.** Photoshop is a resource-intensive program. Installing it into the default location ([*harddrive*]⇨Applications on a Mac and `C:\Program Files` for Windows) ensures that it has access to the operating system and hardware as necessary. Installing into any other location or attempting to run Photoshop across a network can lead to frustrating problems and loss of work in progress.

✔ **Disable all spyware and antivirus software before installing.** Antivirus software can intercept certain installation procedures, deeming them to be hazardous to your computer's health. That can lead to malfunctions, crashes, lost work, frustration, and what I like to call *Computer Flying Across Room Syndrome.* If you use antivirus software (and if you use Windows, you'd better!), turn it off before installing any program, especially one as complex as Photoshop. You might find the antivirus program's icon in the Windows taskbar; or you might need to go to the Start menu, use All Programs to locate the antivirus software, and disable it. On Mac, check the Dock. And don't forget to restart your antivirus software afterward! If you already installed Photoshop and antivirus software was running at the time, I urge you to uninstall and reinstall.

✔ **If you use auto-backup software, shut it down, too.** It's best not to run auto-backup software when installing software. Like antivirus software, it can also lead to problems by interfering with the installer.

✔ **Connect to the Internet and activate right away.** It's also best to run the Photoshop installer while your computer is connected to the Internet. That enables Photoshop's activation and registration process to happen right away, making sure you can get started as soon as the installer finishes.

✔ **Photoshop is 64-bit software (and 32-bit, too).** On both Windows and Mac, Photoshop CS6 is a 64-bit program — if you have a 64-bit operating system. (Windows 7, Vista, and XP all offer 64-bit versions; the Mac OS became 64-bit with Snow Leopard, OS 10.6.) 64-bit software generally runs faster and can take advantage of *much* more RAM than 32-bit software. However, in a Windows 64-bit operating system, Photoshop also installs a 32-bit version in `C:\Program Files (x86)`. On the Mac, Photoshop is a 64-bit program. Only. If you have 32-bit plug-ins for Photoshop, check with the manufacturer or distributor to see if 64-bit versions are available.

✔ **If you have third-party plug-ins, install them elsewhere.** Third-party *plug-ins* — those filters and other Photoshop add-ons that you buy from companies other than Adobe — can be installed into a folder outside the Photoshop folder. You can then make an alias (Mac) or shortcut

(Windows) to that folder and drag the alias/shortcut to Photoshop's Plug-Ins folder. Why install outside the Photoshop folder? Should you ever need to (*gasp!*) reinstall Photoshop, you won't need to reinstall all your third-party plug-ins. Just create a new alias/shortcut and move it into Photoshop's new Plug-Ins folder. And don't forget to go to the plug-ins' websites to see if the manufacturers offer updates!

✔ **If you have *lots* of plug-ins, create sets.** Plug-ins require *RAM* (computer memory that Photoshop uses to process your editing commands). If you have lots of plug-ins, consider dividing them into groups according to how and when you use them. Sort (or install) them into separate folders. (***Hint:*** Plug-ins that you use in many situations can be installed into multiple folders.) When you need to load a specific set, do so through the Photoshop Preferences⇨Plug-Ins pane by designating a second plug-ins folder and relaunching Photoshop.

✔ **If you love fonts, use a font management utility.** If you have hundreds of fonts (over the years, I've somehow managed to collect upward of 12,000 fonts), use a font-management utility to create sets of fonts according to style and activate only those sets that you need at any given time. Too many active fonts can choke the Photoshop type engine, slowing performance. The Mac OS has Font Book built right in, or you can use the excellent Suitcase Fusion 3 (Mac and Windows) from Extensis (`www.extensis.com`).

2

Knowing Just Enough about Digital Images

*I*n the early days of photography, some less-advanced cultures viewed a photo with great suspicion and even fear. Was that an actual person, trapped in the paper? Did taking a photo steal a person's soul? You know that a camera doesn't trap anyone inside the paper — and you can be pretty sure about the stolen soul issue — but how much does the average shooter know about digital images? And how much do *you* need to know about digital images to work effectively in Photoshop?

The answers to those two questions are "Not as much as he/she should" and "Not as much as you might fear." In this chapter, I give you some basic information about how digital images exist in Photoshop, a real understanding of that critical term *resolution,* and an overview of the different ways that you can save your images. But most importantly, I help you understand the very nature of digital images by explaining the world of pixels.

Welcome to the Philosophy Chapter!

What Exactly Is a Digital Image?

Whether you take a picture with a digital camera or use a scanner to bring a photo (or other artwork) into Photoshop, you are *digitizing* the image. That is, *digit* not as in a finger or toe, but as in a number. Computers do everything — absolutely everything — by processing numbers, and the basic language of computers is *binary code.* Whether it's a photo of a Tahitian sunset, a client's name in a database, or the latest box score on the Internet, your computer works on it in binary code. In a nutshell, binary code uses a series of zeros and ones (that's where the numbers part comes into play) to record information.

So what does binary code have to do with the wedding photos that you took this weekend or the masterpiece you must print for your thesis project? An image in Photoshop consists of tiny squares of color called *pixels* (*pixel* is short for *picture element*), as you can see in the close-up to the right in Figure 2-1. The computer records and processes each pixel in binary code. These pixels replicate a photo the same way that tiles in a mosaic reproduce a painting.

Figure 2-1: That's not really Hugo the Bulldog; it's a bunch of tiny, colored squares.

A tile in a mosaic isn't *face* or *sky* or *grass;* rather, it's beige or blue or green. The tiles individually have no relationship to the image as a whole; rather, they require an association with the surrounding tiles to give them purpose, to make them part of the picture. Without the rest of the tiles, a single tile has no meaning.

Likewise, a single pixel in a digital image is simply a square of color. It doesn't become a meaningful part of your digital image until it's surrounded by other pixels of the same or different color, creating a unified whole — a comprehensible picture. How you manipulate those pixels, from the time you capture the image digitally until you output the image to paper or the web, determines how successfully your pixels will represent your image, your artwork, your dream.

The True Nature of Pixels

Here are some basic truths about pixels that you really need to know. Although reading this section probably can't improve your love life, let you speak with ghosts, or give you the winning lottery number, it can help you understand what's happening to your image as you work with it in Photoshop.

✓ **Each pixel is independent.** You might think that you see a car or a circle or a tree or Uncle Bob in an image, but the image is actually only a bunch of little colored squares. Although you can read about various ways to work with groups of pixels throughout this book, each pixel exists unto itself.

✓ **Each pixel is square (except on TV).** Really! Each pixel in a digital image is square except when you're creating images for some television formats, which uses nonsquare pixels. It's important that you understand the squareness of pixels because you sometimes have to deal with those pointy little corners.

✓ **Each pixel can be exactly one color.** That color can change as you edit or alter the image, but each pixel consists entirely of a single color — there's no such thing as a two-tone pixel. Figure 2-2, at 3,200 percent zoom, shows each pixel distinctly.

✓ **Smaller is better (generally speaking).** The smaller each pixel, the better the detail in an image. (However, when you are preparing images for the web, you need smaller images that invariably have less detail.) If you capture an image of a house with a cell phone

Figure 2-2: Each pixel is monotone, containing a single color throughout the pixel.

camera and capture the same shot with a professional DSLR (digital single-lens reflex camera — you know, one of the big professional cameras with interchangeable lenses) that captures three or seven or fifteen times as many pixels, it's pretty obvious which image has better detail. Take a look at Figure 2-3, which illustrates how lots more smaller pixels present a better image than do fewer-and-larger pixels.

Smaller pixels also help hide those nasty corners of pixels that are sometimes visible along curves and diagonal lines. When the corners of pixels are noticeable and degrade the image, you call it a bad case of the *jaggies.*

Keep in mind that the size at which an image can be printed — and still look good — depends on the number of pixels available. Sure, these days every digital camera seems to capture at least 10 megapixels, which is fine for 8x10 prints and perhaps even as large as 16x20 inches. But what about those cellphone shots? How about when your 10 megapixel pocket camera doesn't have a long enough zoom to capture little Tommy's exploits on the soccer field up close? That's when you might need to crop and *resample* the image to increase the number of pixels. Resampling is discussed later in this chapter.

Figure 2-3: More pixels (top) means better detail. Note the zoom factors in the lower-left of each shot.

- **Pixels are aligned in a raster.** The term raster appears regularly when you discuss images created from pixels. Raster, in this case, refers to the nice orderly rows and columns in which pixels appear. Each image has a certain number of rows of pixels, and each row is a certain number of pixels wide — the columns. Within the raster, the pixels perfectly align side to side and top to bottom.

- **Every picture created with pixels is rectangular.** Some images might appear to be round, or star-shaped, or missing a hole from the middle, but they aren't unless you print them out and grab your scissors. The image file itself is rectangular, even if it appears round. There are actually pixels in those seemingly empty areas; the pixels are, however, transparent.

How Many Pixels Can Dance on the Head of a Pin?

You hear the term *resolution* a lot when working with digital images. Digital cameras have so-many megapixels of *resolution;* inkjet printers have so-much by so-much *resolution;* to work in Photoshop, your monitor must have a *resolution* of at least 1,024 x 768 pixels; when printing your images, you must use 300 pixels per inch (ppi) as your *resolution* (wrong!), but your web images must have a *resolution* of 72 ppi (again wrong!); and don't forget your New Year's *resolution!*

Resolution revelations

In this wonderful world of digital imaging, you see *resolution* used in four basic ways:

- **Image resolution:** *Image resolution* is the size of your image's individual pixels when you print. I go into greater detail about this concept in the upcoming section, "Picking an image resolution."

- **Camera resolution:** Digital cameras capture each image in a specific number of pixels. Check your camera's user guide or open one of the images in Photoshop and choose Image⇨Image Size. Take a look at the number of pixels that your camera records for the width and for the height. Multiply the numbers together, divide by one million, and round off the result. (If you're in the camera maker's marketing department, make sure that you round up.) That's the megapixel (MP) rating for the camera. Use it as a general guideline when shopping. If you're still working with a camera that captures only 6 megapixels, you might want to consider upgrading to more fully take advantage of Photoshop's capabilities.

- **Monitor resolution:** *Monitor resolution* determines how many pixels are visible on-screen. Whether you use a Mac or a PC, you set the monitor resolution at the system level (as shown in Figure 2-4). When you use a higher monitor resolution, you get a larger workspace, but each pixel is smaller, which might make some jobs tougher. Experiment to find a monitor resolution that works just right for you.

Figure 2-4: Set a Mac's resolution through the System Preferences (left), a PC's resolution through the Control Panel (right).

• *Mac:* Click the Apple menu in the upper-left corner of the screen and choose System Preferences. Then click Displays.

• *Windows 7:* Go to Control Panel⇨Hardware and Sound, and then click on Adjust screen resolution.

✓ **Printer resolution:** Unlike the three preceding terms, printer resolution doesn't involve pixels. Rather, a *printer resolution* tells you how many tiny droplets of ink are sprayed on the paper. Remember that it takes several droplets to reproduce a single image pixel — you certainly don't need an image resolution anywhere close to the printer's resolution! (See the following section for more on this.)

Resolving image resolution

Image resolution is nothing more than an instruction to a printing device about how large to reproduce each pixel. On-screen, when working in Photoshop, your image has no resolution at all. An image that's 3,000 pixels wide and 2,400 pixels tall looks and acts exactly the same in Photoshop whether you have the image resolution at 300 ppi or 72 ppi. Same number of pixels, right? (The one real exception to this rule is type — text is usually measured in points in Photoshop, and that measurement is directly tied to the print size of your document. Type and text are discussed in Chapter 13.)

You can always check — or change — a picture's resolution by choosing Photoshop Image⇨Image Size. The Image Size dialog box (which you can see in Figure 2-5) has two separate but related sets of information about your image. At the top, you see information about the actual image itself, in the Pixel Dimensions area. Below, in the Document Size area, you see instructions for a printing device — that "size" pertains only to printing and has no impact on what you do in Photoshop.

You'll find it very handy to change the pixel dimensions *and* the print size at the same time in the Image Size dialog box. And, much to the delight of math-challenged folks, the Image Size feature does most of the calculations. For example, with the Constrain Proportions option selected, you enter a new Width and Photoshop calculates the new Height automatically!

Changing the size of your artwork with the Image Size command

You have a number of ways to change the size of your photos and other art. In Chapter 4, I introduce you to *cropping* (chopping off part of the artwork to make it fit a certain size or to improve its overall appearance and impact). You can use Photoshop's Image Size command to change the image dimensions or printing instructions without altering the *composition,* which is the visual arrangement of the image or artwork. All the content of the original image is there, just at a different size. Of course, as you can see in Figure 2-6, if you reduce the size of an image too much, some of that original content can become virtually unrecognizable.

Figure 2-5: At the top, real information about your image. Below, merely printing instructions.

Figure 2-6: As the zoomed-in smaller image shows, you can reduce an image too much.

If you know the specific pixel dimensions that you need for the final image — say for a web page — you can simply type a new number in one of the upper fields in the Image Size dialog box and click OK. In most cases, you select all three check boxes at the bottom of the dialog box, enter your desired print width or height (letting Photoshop calculate the other dimension), enter your desired print resolution, and click OK. Of course, you probably want a little more control over the process, don't you? Figure 2-7 gives you a closer look at the Image Size dialog box.

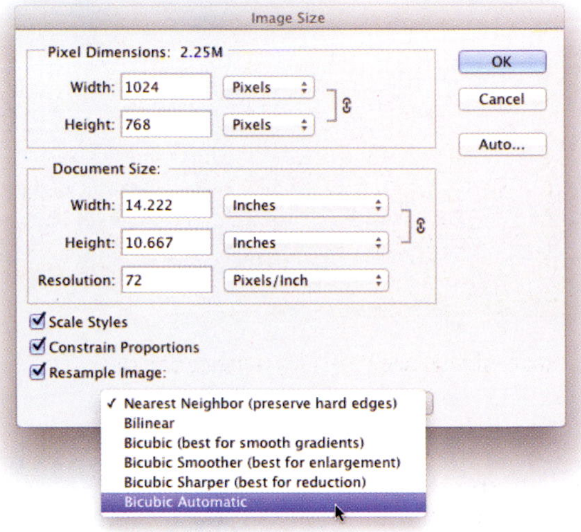

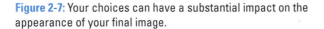

Figure 2-7: Your choices can have a substantial impact on the appearance of your final image.

In the lower part of the Image Size dialog box, you have three decisions to make. The first is rather easy: If you're resizing an image that uses layer styles (see Chapter 12), you want to select the Scale Styles check box to preserve the image's appearance as it shrinks or grows. In a nutshell, layer styles (such as shadows, glows, and bevels) are applied to a layer at a specific size. You can scale the image without changing those sizes, or you can scale the image and change the style sizes proportionally. Not scaling layer styles can dramatically alter the appearance of a resized image, as you can see in Figure 2-8. A slight bevel combined with a small drop shadow produces a subtle 3D effect in the original (upper) image. Below, when the image is scaled down to 1/4 the original size without scaling the effects, your chips change to chumps, and the artwork is ruined.

Figure 2-8: Scaling an image without scaling its layer styles can ruin your image.

The middle check box, Constrain Proportions, should almost always remain selected. Some exceptions might come up, but you normally want to preserve an image's *aspect ratio* (the relationship between height and width) when resizing to prevent distorting the image. Figure 2-9 shows you what can happen when you scale one dimension without constraining the image's proportions.

Figure 2-9: Resizing an image without constraining proportions. Interesting, yes, but useful?

The third check box, Resample Image, is the one that might require the attention of that gray matter within your skull. Not only do you need to decide whether you want to *resample* the image (change its pixel dimensions), but you also need to decide *how* you want to resample. Refer to Figure 2-7 to see that you have six different options for calculating the change (called *resampling algorithms*).

To resample or to crop: That is the question

To better understand the difference between resampling an image and cropping an image, consider this situation:

1. **A painter paints a picture.** He paints it at whatever size he thinks is appropriate. (Or, perhaps, on the only piece of canvas he can afford on that particular day.)

2. **A patron likes the artwork, but the painting is too large for the frame that works best with the dining room table.** Yeah, patrons can be like that, can't they?

3. **The patron asks the artist to make the painting fit the frame.**

4. **The artist decides between cropping and resampling.** He can grab a pair of scissors and cut off some of the painting (cropping), or painstakingly re-create the painting from scratch at a smaller size. Thankfully, Photoshop does the "repainting" for you, using Image Size with its resampling algorithms.

5. **The artist charges the patron for the extra work.** (Don't forget this final, crucial step!)

Cropping cuts away part of the image to meet a target size. Resampling retains all the image, but shrinks or enlarges it to meet the target size.

Before I talk about those choices, let me explain what happens when the Resample Image box is left deselected. The top portion of the Image Size dialog box becomes unavailable — you can no longer make changes in the Pixel Dimension fields (as you see in Figure 2-10). The information is there, but it won't change. When you clear the Resample Image check box, you protect the original pixels, preventing any change to the image itself.

So what's left? When using Image Size without resampling, you're simply changing the instructions recorded in the image for your printing device. When you enter one dimension, either width or height, Photoshop does the math and fills in both the other dimension and the new resolution.

Take a look at Figure 2-11. I cleared the Resample Image check box and entered **10** and **inches** for my new print width in order to print this image to a letter-size (8.5 x 11 inches) sheet of paper. Photoshop fills in the new height (6.667 inches) and a new resolution (307.2 ppi). But what if I want an 8x10 print? If I enter **8** and **inches** for the height, Photoshop recalculates the width to 12 inches and enters a resolution of 256 ppi. If I want a true 8x10, I have to crop some of the image because most digital photos have a different aspect ratio than an 8 x 10. (You can read more about that in Chapter 4.)

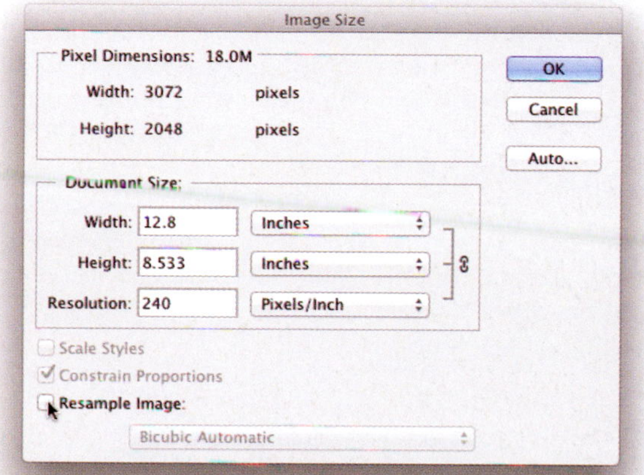

Figure 2-10: Clear the Resample Image check box to change print size, not pixel dimensions.

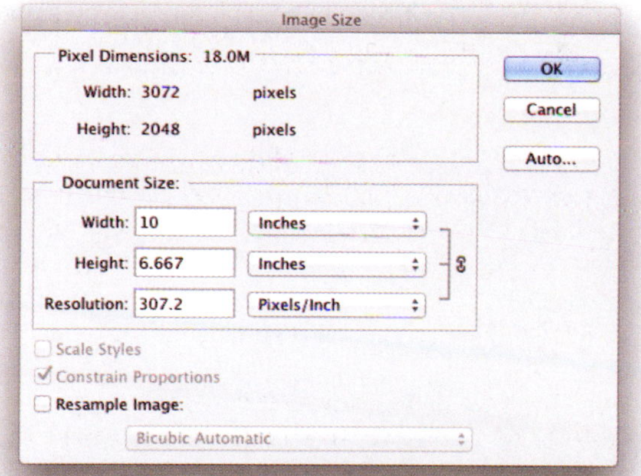

Figure 2-11: Enter a value, and Photoshop recalculates the fields automatically.

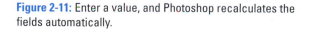

Okay then, back to the subject of resampling! When you resample an image (change the pixel dimensions), Photoshop takes the image and maps it to the new size, attempting to preserve the image's appearances as much as possible at the new size, using the new number of pixels. Of course, if you take an image that's more than 3,000 pixels wide and resample it to 300 pixels wide, you're going to lose some of the detail.

Choosing a resampling method

By default, Photoshop uses Bicubic Automatic as the resampling algorithm. If you're working with photos and downsampling or upsampling as far as 200%, that's fine. Table 2-1 sums up my advice on when you might *not* want to use Bicubic Automatic.

If you'll be resizing a number of non-photographic images in the same way, either upsampling or downsampling, open Photoshop's Preferences⇨General and select the optimal resampling method in the Image Interpolation menu. That algorithm then becomes the default in Image Size, saving you the trouble of changing the algorithm each time.

Table 2-1	Other Resampling Algorithms	
Algorithm Name	*Use It For*	*Results*
Nearest Neighbor	Artwork containing large areas of solid color like a pie chart or a simple logo; avoid using with photos	Maintains pixel color
Bilinear	Artwork having horizontal and vertical lines and blocks of color, such as web page buttons; avoid using with photos	Maintains the sharpness of your edges
Bicubic	General-purpose resampling for minor changes in image size	Calculates the average of surrounding pixels when generating a new pixel
Bicubic Smoother	Increasing the size of photographic images or artwork with gradients and gradual shifts in color	Gives the most pleasing result when increasing the number of pixels (upsampling)
Bicubic Sharper	For reducing the number of pixels in a photo (*downsampling*), also can be used when upsampling beyond 200%	Maintains the crispness of your image

Keep in mind that the resampling method that you select in the Preferences is also used for the Edit⇨Transform commands, which you use to scale, rotate, and otherwise alter individual elements within your artwork. (You can read about the Transform commands in Chapter 10.)

Picking an image resolution

After you have the concept of resampling under your belt, how do you know what size you should be resampling *to?* How many pixels do you need? Here are your general guidelines:

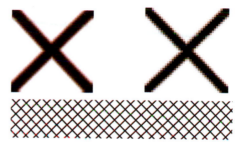

Figure 2-12: The close-up to the left shows inkjet printer droplets and to the right, pixels.

- ✏ **Photos for your inkjet printer:** Inkjet printers are *stochastic* printing devices: That is, they use a series of droplets to replicate each pixel in your image, as shown in Figure 2-12. In theory, the optimal image resolution is one third of the printer's rated resolution. However, most printers don't need an image resolution higher than 300 ppi. (For fine art prints from my high-end Epson printers, I use an image resolution of 360 ppi.)

  If you're printing something that will only be viewed at a distance, such as a banner to be hung above the crowd or a poster that hangs on a wall, you can print at a substantially lower resolution to save ink and print faster. Banners, for example, can often be printed with a resolution of 100 ppi.

- ✏ **Web images:** Ignore resolution. Ignore the entire Document Size area of the Image Size dialog box. Consider only the image's pixel dimensions. Determine what area of the web page the image will occupy and then resize to exactly those pixel dimensions.

- ✏ **Page layout programs and commercial printing:** If your image is to be placed into a page layout program's document and sent to a commercial printing facility, you need to know the *line screen frequency* (the resolution, so to speak) of the printing press on which the job will be run. Ask the print shop or the person handling the page layout. Your image resolution should be either exactly 1.5 times or exactly twice the line screen frequency. (You shouldn't notice any difference in the final printed product with either resolution.)

- ✏ **PowerPoint presentations and word processing documents:** Generally speaking, 72 ppi is appropriate for images that you place into a presentation or Word document. You should resize to the exact dimensions of the area on the page or slide that the image fills.

Content-aware scaling

The Edit➪Content-Aware Scale command is designed to be used when an image needs to be resampled to a new aspect ratio but can't be cropped. It tries (very hard) to keep the subject of the photo undistorted while stretching or shrinking the background. Here's how to use it:

1. **Open an image or make a selection.** Make a selection if you need to scale only part of an image. If you need to resize the entire image, don't make any selection.

2. **Convert the *Background* layer.** If your image has a layer named *Background*, double-click the layer name in the Layers palette and rename the layer. You can't use Content-Aware Scale on a flattened image.

3. **Image➪Canvas Size.** If increasing the pixel dimensions, resize the canvas as required. If you're reducing the size of the image, skip this step.

4. **Edit➪Content-Aware Scale.** Drag the anchor points in the center of the four sides of the bounding box to resize to fill the new canvas, and then press Return/Enter. Hold down the Option/Alt key to scale from the center. If you're resizing an image of one or more people, click the button to the right in the Options bar to protect skin tones. Before selecting Content-Aware Scale, you can also create an *alpha channel* (a saved selection) to identify areas of the image you want to protect. Make a selection, use the Select➪Save Selection command, and then select that alpha channel in Content-Aware Scale's Options bar in the Protect menu. See Chapter 8 for more on alpha channels.

5. **Flatten (optional).** If desired, use the Layer➪Flatten Image command.

In this example, the original image is at the bottom. To the left, the image has been resampled from 6.67x10 inches to 8x10 inches using Image Size (with Constrain Proportions deselected). To the right, Content-Aware Scale does a much better job — in this particular case — of scaling the image to 8x10 inches, minimizing distortion of the subject.

Is Content-Aware Scale a substitute for properly composing in-camera before shooting? Absolutely not! Is it preferable to cropping to a new aspect ratio? Rarely. Is it an incredibly powerful tool for certain difficult challenges? Now we're talking!

File Formats: Which Do You Need?

After working with your image in Photoshop, you need to save the changes. Choosing File⇨Save updates the current file on your hard drive, maintaining the current file format when possible. If you added a feature to the file that isn't supported by the original file format, Photoshop automatically opens the Save As dialog box and shows you which features are not supported by the selected file format. In Figure 2-13, the lower part of the Save As dialog box shows you the yellow warning triangles that identify options being used in the image that are not available when saving as a JPEG.

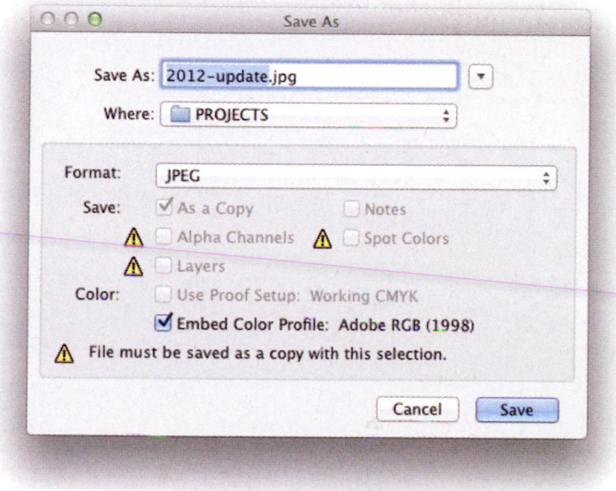

Figure 2-13: Photoshop shows you which image features are not available in your selected file format.

You can go ahead and save the image in that format, but your file will no longer contain those unsupported features. In the example shown in Figure 2-13, I can click the Save button and create a JPEG file, but that JPEG won't have the alpha channel (a saved selection) or the spot channel (a custom printing color); and it will be flattened to a single layer. If I want to retain those features in the file, I need to choose a different file format, such as Photoshop's own PSD format. (Read more about alpha channels in Chapter 8 and about spot channels in Chapter 6.)

No matter which of the file formats you choose, if you add layers, type, adjustment layers, channels, or paths to your image, keep the original as an unflattened/unmerged (all the layers are preserved) Photoshop (PSD) or layered TIFF file. In the future, should you ever need to make changes to the image or duplicate an effect in the image, you won't need to start from scratch.

Formats for digital photos

If you print your images yourself at home or the office, you can stick with the PSD Photoshop format when saving. (Remember that you cannot re-save in a Raw format after opening in Photoshop.) If you send the photos to the local camera shop (or discount store) for printing, stick with JPEG — or, if they accept it, TIFF. Here are the pros and cons of the major formats that you should consider for photos when saving:

✔ **PSD:** Photoshop's native file format is great for saving your images with the most flexibility. Because the PSD format supports all of Photoshop's features, you don't need to flatten your images — and keeping your layers lets you make changes later. If your file size is very large (400MB or larger), make a TIFF or JPEG copy before printing, flattening all the layers. Don't send PSD files to the local shop for prints.

✔ **TIFF:** Although the TIFF file format (as you use it in Photoshop) can save your layers and most other Photoshop features, make sure to choose Layers⇨Flatten Image before sending files out for printing. Layered TIFF files generally are compatible only with programs in the Creative Suite. If you don't flatten the image prior to saving as TIFF or if you elect to include layers when saving as TIFF, Photoshop presents you with a gentle reminder, as shown in Figure 2-14.

Figure 2-14: Flatten layers before saving a TIFF for use in other programs.

✔ **JPG:** JPEG, as it's called, is actually a file compression scheme rather than a file format, but that's not important. What *is* important is that JPEG throws away some of your image data when it saves the file. Save important images in PSD or TIFF and use JPEG only for copies. When should you use JPEG? When sending images to a photo lab that doesn't accept TIFF files and when sending images (perhaps by e-mail or on CD) to people who don't have Photoshop. Unlike PSD and TIFF, you can open JPEG images in a web browser and print from there — and so can Granny, and Cousin Jim, and that overseas soldier you adopted. When saving JPEGs, the lower the Quality setting you choose in the JPEG Options dialog box, the smaller the file, but also the more damage to the image. I discuss saving as JPEG in more detail in the sidebar, "Resaving images in the JPEG format."

✔ **PDF:** It's easy to overlook Adobe's PDF format when talking about photos, but you should consider using this format. Although the local photo lab probably won't accept it, it's a great format for sharing your pictures with folks who don't have Photoshop. Unlike JPEG, your images won't be degraded when saving as PDF; and like JPEG, just about anyone with a computer can view the files. (Either Adobe Reader or the Mac's Preview, which you can also use with PDFs, is found on just about every computer now, just like web browsers for JPEG.) Keep in mind, however, that PDF files are larger than JPEGs.

✔ **Large Document Format (PSB):** Really, really, *really* big pictures — more than 30,000 pixels wide or long or both — need to be saved in the PSB file format. Will you ever need this format? Consider that 30,000 pixels at a photo-quality resolution of 300 ppi is 100 inches long. At a resolution of 85 ppi, more appropriate for a long banner to hang in a hallway, you're talking about artwork that stretches almost 30 feet! Can your printer do that? If not, you probably don't need the PSB file format.

You could theoretically use a number of other available formats, such as DCS or PNG (*never* Photoshop Raw), but there's no real need with the more common and more versatile formats about which you just read.

The JPEG file format doesn't support 16-bit color, but even when working with a 16-bit image (perhaps a Raw image from your digital camera), JPEG is available as a file format in Photoshop's Save As dialog box. The image will automatically be converted to 8-bit color. It's more convenient — saving you a trip to the Image⇨Mode menu to select 8-Bits/Channel — but the JPEG Options dialog box won't give you an estimate of the file size. Don't forget to save in a format that supports 16-bit color, such as PSD or TIFF, before creating the JPEG copy.

Formats for web graphics

Generally speaking, you use Photoshop's Save for Web command rather than Save As to generate copies of your images for use on a website or for use with cellphones, PDAs, and other such devices. Here are the three file formats that you need for the web:

✔ **JPG:** Use JPEG for photos. Remember to resize the photo so that it fits on a web page. When selecting a Quality setting, you need to balance image appearance with file size. A smaller file downloads (and displays in a web browser) faster, but a larger file generally looks better. If you reduce the Quality setting until just before the image doesn't look great, you've hit the *sweet spot* — the compromise between file size and image quality.

✔ **GIF:** GIF is more appropriate for items like web buttons and banners (such as those shown in Figure 2-15) than it is for photos. If you save a photo that's more than perhaps 100x100 pixels in size, you might see some degradation of the image quality as similar colors become one color. When you save an image as GIF, it can contain no more than 256 distinct colors. JPEG and the other common file formats can have thousands of different colors.

✔ **PNG:** PNG comes in two types: PNG-8 (which is a substitute for GIF) and PNG-24 (which is a substitute for JPEG). PNG has a couple of advantages for web designers, such as support for transparency, but not all web browsers can display PNG graphics. Generally speaking, it's safer to use JPEG and GIF.

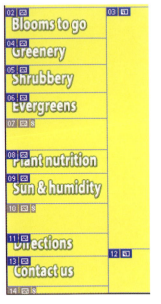

Figure 2-15: Use GIF for web interface items.

Formats for commercial printing

You're the Photoshop master of your office. Everyone knows that you understand everything about digital images. So you're the right person to create the company's new brochure. Except you're a photographer. Or you're a web designer. Or you're actually pretty new to Photoshop. And you don't have a clue about preparing images for a commercial printing press.

Here's what you need to know about file formats for those CMYK (cyan/magenta/yellow/black) color images that you're sending to the print shop:

✔ **TIFF:** TIFF is generally a solid choice. Use TIFF for photographic images that don't contain any type layers.

✔ **EPS:** Choose EPS if your image has type. Don't flatten or merge the type layers before using Save As to create the EPS. In the EPS options, make sure to select the Include Vector Data check box to ensure that your type prints perfectly.

If you reopen an EPS file in Photoshop, your type layers get merged. Don't! Instead, make sure to save your original file as PSD and, should you need to make changes, open the PSD and create a new EPS file when you're done editing.

✔ **PDF:** PDF offers support for spot color channels, alpha channels, and paths — options not supported by EPS. (*Spot channels* are used with custom colors, and *alpha channels* store information about transparency in the image.) If your file uses any of these features, choose PDF over EPS, if your print shop accepts PDFs. When saving as PDF, the PDF

Options dialog box offers you Preserve Photoshop Editing Capabilities. If you select the option, the PDF file will reopen in Photoshop with layers and editable type.

✔ **PSD:** Use PSD only if you're adding the image file to a project in Adobe InDesign. Don't send PSD files to a print shop unless specifically requested to do so by the print shop.

✔ **DCS:** DCS 2.0 is a variation of the EPS file format that supports spot color channels and alpha channels. Use it primarily with QuarkXPress.

Formats for PowerPoint and Word

If the final destination of your image is PowerPoint or Word, use the PNG file format. If your image has areas of transparency in it, PNG is *definitely* the way to go. (Read about the two types of PNG files in "Formats for web graphics," earlier in this chapter.)

And what about all that neat clip art that you have on your hard drive? How do you use those images when Photoshop won't open the vector-based WMF and EMF clip art files? Here's how you get clip art into Photoshop, quick and easy:

1. **Open a new document in Word (or a comparable word processing program).**

2. **Add the clip art.**

    In Word, choose Insert⇨Clip Art (or your word processor's comparable command). Click directly on the artwork and drag the lower-right corner to resize it to the dimensions that you need in Photoshop. (The artwork comes into Photoshop at 300 ppi.)

3. **Choose Edit⇨Copy.**

    This copies the image to the Clipboard (the computer's memory) in Word.

4. **Switch to your Photoshop document.**

5. **Choose Edit⇨Paste.**

    You have your clip art, ready to use in Photoshop! Use the Edit⇨Transform commands to scale, rotate, and otherwise fit the clip art into your design. (See Figure 2-16.)

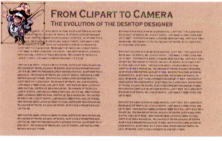

Figure 2-16: Copy vector artwork from Word and paste into Photoshop.

Resaving images in the JPEG format

JPEG uses a *lossy* compression scheme: That is, as part of the compression process, it actually permanently throws away some data when you save your image. The lower the Quality setting, the more image degradation occurs. Take a look at the figure here. The original image is on the left. In the middle is the same image saved in JPEG format with medium quality and then on the right with low quality. Take a look at the inset on the eyelashes (400% zoom). See what I mean by *degradation?*

If you save by using JPEG a second time, even more data is thrown away. Every time you save, your image quality suffers. Yes, indeed, you might sometimes need to open a JPEG image, make some changes, and save as JPEG again (perhaps for the web, perhaps to share with non-Photoshop friends and family). To minimize damage to the image, either use the highest setting (12) for the Quality setting or (if you know it) the exact same setting used last in Photoshop.

3

Taking the Chef's Tour of Your Photoshop Kitchen

I know you're hungry to dive right in and start mixing up some master-pieces, but before you fire up the stove, look around the Photoshop kitchen. Get to know your spoons from your ladles, your pots from your pans, figure out how to turn on the blender . . . that sort of thing.

In this chapter, rather than going through all the Photoshop menus, panels, and tools (which would take several hundred very boring pages), I show you some basic operational concepts. (But don't worry — you can read about how to use specific commands and tools throughout the book, in the chapters most appropriate for them.) Here you discover such things as how to spot which menu commands have dialog boxes, what the little symbol in the upper-right corner of a panel does, and which tools don't use the Options bar. You also read about customizing your Photoshop environment for faster and more efficient work. Next I show you how to set up Photoshop's Preferences and Color Settings. And to wrap up the chapter — perhaps the most important section in this entire book — I explain what to do when Photoshop doesn't seem to be working properly.

Food for Thought: How Things Work

A good understanding of certain fundamental operations and features in Photoshop provides you with the background that you need in order to follow the recipes or get creative and whip up some delicious artwork.

And don't forget about Photoshop's Tool Tips. If you don't know what something or some option does, park your cursor over it for a couple of seconds, and Photoshop provides its information in a little box.

Ordering from the menus

When you're working in Photoshop, you see a horizontal list of menus spread across the very top (Mac) or near the top (Windows) of the screen: File, Edit, Image, Layer, Select, Filter, View, Window, and Help. (If you also see the 3D menu, you have Photoshop CS6 Extended, which you can read about in Chapter 18.) On the Mac, the program also has a menu named Photoshop, just to the left of the File menu.

As with most programs, you click the name of a menu to reveal its commands. For both Mac and Windows, you can click and hold down the mouse button until you're over the command you want; or you can click and release, move the cursor, and then click again. Some commands, such as Crop and Reveal All, are executed immediately after you choose them. When a command name in the menu is followed by an ellipsis (. . .) — the Image Size command shown in Figure 3-1, for example — you know that a dialog box will open so that you can input variables and make decisions. A triangle to the right of a command name, such as that which you see next to Image Rotation, indicates a *submenu.* If you click the command name, another menu appears to the right. The cryptic set of symbols to the right of the Image Size command is the keyboard shortcut for opening the command's dialog box. (I show you how to assign keyboard shortcuts later, in the section "Sugar and spice, shortcuts are nice.")

As you read in the upcoming section, "Clearing the table: Custom workspaces," Photoshop menus are customizable — you don't have to see commands that you never use. You can also color-code your menu commands, making it easier to spot those that you need regularly.

When a specific command appears *grayed out* in the menu (in gray type rather than black), that command isn't available. Some commands, such as Reveal All in Figure 3-1, are available only under specific circumstances, such as part of the image being hidden with the Crop tool. When working with Photoshop's creative filters, you'll find that many aren't available unless you're working with an 8-bit RGB (red/green/blue) image. (Color modes and bit depth are discussed in Chapter 6; filters are explored in Chapter 15.)

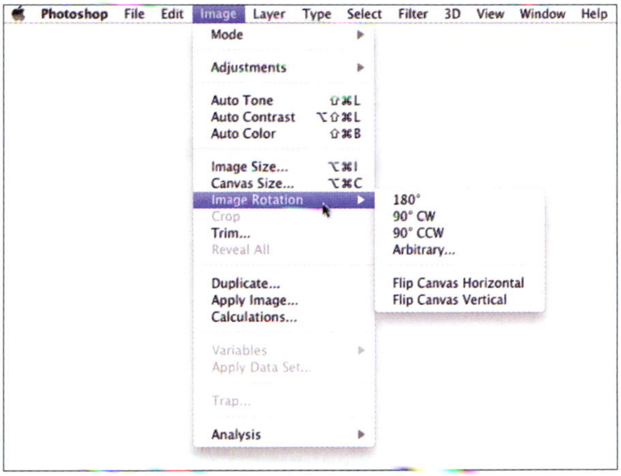

Figure 3-1: Some commands have submenus, and some have dialog boxes.

Your platter full of panels

Photoshop, like the other programs of the Adobe Creative Suite, uses *floating panels.* The panels, many of which you see along the right edge of your screen, usually appear on top of (float over) your image window. (As you drag panels around to customize your workspace, as described later in this section, you'll find that panels can hide other panels.) The Options bar across the top of the work area and the Toolbox (technically, it's called the Tools panel) along the left edge of the screen are also panels.

Panels contain Photoshop features that you might need to access so regularly that using a menu command is inconvenient. (I can't imagine having to mouse to a menu command every time I want to change tools or select a specific layer!) You don't always need to have your panels visible. In Photoshop, press the Tab key to hide all the panels or press Shift+Tab to hide all but the Toolbox and the Options bar. With fewer panels visible, you provide more room for your image. You can selectively hide and show panels via the Window menu.

Photoshop uses expanding/collapsing panel docks. As shown to the right in Figure 3-2, clicking the double-arrow button at the top of a stack of panels collapses that stack to a tidy group of icons. The Color, Adjustments, and Layers panels are fully visible. The Swatches, Styles, Channels, and Paths panels — "nested" with the three visible panels — can be made visible by clicking on the panel tab. The collapsed History and Properties panels together occupy only a tiny fraction of the screen, those two buttons to the left of the Color panel. In Photoshop's Preferences (discussed later in this chapter), you can even elect to have each docked palette automatically collapse when you're done working with it.

Figure 3-2: Nesting and collapsing panels opens up the work area.

By clicking and dragging a panel's tab when the panel isn't collapsed, you can move it to another grouping or pull it out of its grouping and away from the edge of the screen. You might, for example, want to drag the Clone Source panel away from its buddies to make it more easily accessible while performing a complex clone operation. (The Clone Source panel is used with the Clone Stamp tool. You can specify up to five different source locations and easily switch among them.)

Many of the panels are resizable. Like an image window, you drag the lower-right corner of the panel to expand or contract it. Almost all the Photoshop panels have a panel menu from which you select various options. (The Toolbox and Options bar don't have menus.) You open the panel menu by clicking the small button in the upper-right corner of the panel, as shown in Figure 3-3. The panel menu contains such options as thumbnail size (for example, the Layers, Channels, and Paths panels); how to display items in the panel (Swatches, Styles, and Brush among others); or even the size and content of the panel (Info and Histogram).

TIP

You might have noticed in Figure 3-2 that the Photoshop Toolbox is one tall skinny column along the left edge of the screen. If you prefer a shorter, squatter two-column Toolbox, click the Expand/Collapse button (the double arrow) at the top of the column.

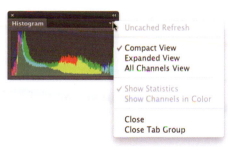

The content of some panels changes automatically as you work with your image. Add a layer, and the Layers panel shows a new layer. Save a selection, and the Channels panel shows a new alpha channel. If you drag a shape tool, the Layers panel gets a new layer, and the Paths panel shows the layer's vector path. You control some other panels by loading and deleting content through the panel menus or with the Edit⇨Presets⇨Preset Manager command. Use the Preset Manager (as shown in Figure 3-4) to save sets of your custom bits and pieces as well as to load and delete items from the panels.

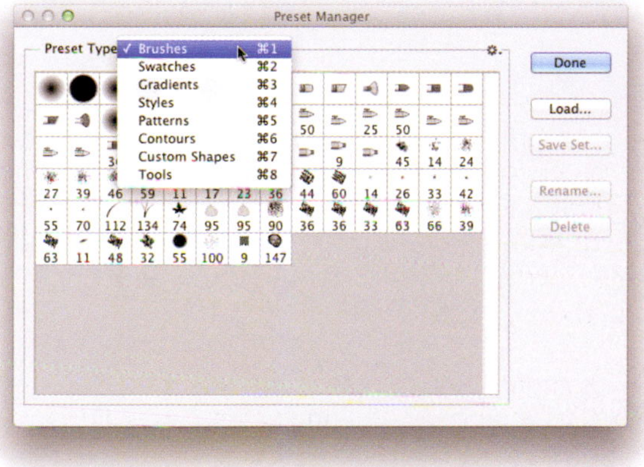

Figure 3-3: Access a panel's menu by clicking the button below the double-arrow. (Clicking the double-arrow expands or collapses the panel group).

Figure 3-4: Use the Preset Manager to control the content of a number of panels.

In addition to the content of the Brush, Swatches, Styles, and Tool Presets panels, you use the Preset Manager with a number of pickers. *Pickers* are sort of mini-panels, available only with certain tools or features. The Gradient and Custom Shape pickers are accessed through the Options bar when those tools are in use. The Pattern picker is found in the Fill dialog box, the Layer Style dialog box, and (with some tools) in the Options bar. The Contour picker is used with six of the effects in the Layer Style dialog box.

If Photoshop CS6 is an upgrade and you have one or more earlier versions of Photoshop on the same computer, you were asked if you wanted to migrate presets when you first opened Photoshop CS6. Picking up presets from earlier versions can save the time it would take to reload (or re-create) presets you use often. If you didn't migrate then, you can do so at any time with the command Edit⇨Presets⇨Migrate Presets.

When you create custom layer styles, brushes, gradients, and the like, use the Preset Manager to protect your work. Create sets of the items and save those sets with the Preset Manager. Then remember to save copies of the sets someplace on your hard drive *outside* the Photoshop folder so that you don't accidentally delete them if you ever *(oh, no!)* have to reinstall Photoshop. Remember that new content of your panels is stored only in Photoshop's Preferences file (introduced later in this chapter) until you create and save sets.

The tools of your trade

You control the behavior of Photoshop's tools through the Options bar. With the exception of a few path-related tools (Add Anchor Point, Delete Anchor Point, and Convert Point), every tool in Photoshop has options. The Options bar changes as you switch tools. The behavior of some tools changes when you add one or more modifier keys (⌘, Shift, and Option for the Mac; Ctrl, Shift, and Alt for Windows). As an example of how modifier keys can affect tool behavior, consider the Rectangular Marquee and Elliptical Marquee tools:

- **Hold down the Shift key while dragging.** Normally the marquee selection tools are *freeform* — you drag however you like. When you hold down the Shift key while dragging, on the other hand, you constrain the proportions of the selection to a square or circle (rather than a rectangle or ellipse).

- **Hold down the Option/Alt key while dragging.** When you hold down the Option/Alt key while dragging a marquee selection tool, the selection is centered on the point where you first clicked. Rather than being a corner of a selection, that starting point is the center of the selection.

✔ **Hold down the Shift and Option/Alt keys while dragging.** You can select from the center while constraining proportions by using the Shift and Option/Alt keys together.

✔ **Use the Shift key to add to an existing selection.** If you already have an active selection in your image, Shift+dragging a selection tool adds to that selection. (Press Shift before you click and drag.)

✔ **Use the Option/Alt key to subtract from an existing selection.** When you have an existing selection and you hold down the Option/Alt key, you can drag to subtract from the selection. Note in Figure 3-5 that the selection tool's cursor shows a small minus sign when subtracting from a selection.

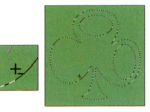

Figure 3-5: Use the Option/Alt key with a selection tool to subtract from a selection.

✔ **"Double-clutch" with the Shift or Option/Alt key.** You can even constrain proportions or select from the center *and* add to or subtract from a selection. Press the Shift key (to add to the existing selection) or the Option/Alt key (to subtract from the existing selection). Click and start dragging the marquee selection tool. While continuing to hold down the mouse button, release the modifier key and press and hold Shift (to constrain proportions), Option/Alt (to center the selection), or both; then continue to drag your selection tool. You might want to use this technique, for example, when creating a donut-shaped selection. Drag the initial circular selection and then subtract a smaller circular selection from the center of the initial circle.

Don't be afraid to experiment with modifier keys while working with tools. After all, you always have the Undo command (⌘+Z/Ctrl+Z) at hand!

Get Cookin' with Customization

Customizing Photoshop not only helps you work faster and more efficiently, but it can also help you work more precisely and prevent tragic errors. Consider using a Crop tool preset to create a 5x7 print at 300 pixels per inch (ppi). Such a preset will *always* produce exactly those dimensions, every single time. Setting up the Crop tool each time you need a 5x7 at 300 ppi doesn't just waste time: It also opens the door for time-consuming or project-wrecking typos. ("Oops! I guess I made a mistake — this image is 5x7 at only *30* pixels per inch!")

Clearing the table: Custom workspaces

One of the easiest ways to work more efficiently is to see your image better. Generally speaking, bigger is better, so the more room you have on the monitor to display your artwork, the better you can zoom in and do precise work. The easiest way to gain workspace? Press the Tab key to hide Photoshop's panels. Pressing Shift+Tab hides all the panels except the Options bar and the Toolbox.

Keep in mind that it's best to use 100% zoom when evaluating your image for banding or moiré and when applying filters. Any other zoom factor is a simulation of the image's appearance. If you have a computer and video card that support OpenGL drawing (take a look in Photoshop's Preferences➪Performance, check the computer's User Guide, or call your tech support folks), you have much better on-screen display. But 100% zoom is safest when making critical decisions.

You can also drag the panels that you need regularly to a custom group of panels. To move a panel, drag it by the tab and "nest" it with other panels. And don't forget that the major panels have keyboard shortcuts assigned to show and hide. Although keyboard shortcuts are customizable (as you can read later in this chapter), here are the primary panels' assigned F keys, the *function keys* that appear at the top of your keyboard:

- **Actions:** Option/Alt+F9
- **Brush:** F5
- **Color:** F6
- **Info:** F8
- **Layers:** F7

Any panels nested with the panel that you show/hide are also shown and hidden. And don't forget that you can always restore all panels to their default locations by choosing Window➪Workspace➪Essentials (Default). If the default workspace is already selected, use the command Window➪Workspace➪ Reset Essentials to get back to the default panel layout.

The most efficient way to customize your work area is to create and save specialized workspaces. Arrange the panels exactly as you need them for a particular job you do regularly, choose Window➪Workspace➪New Workspace (in the Windows menu, visible panels are indicated with a checkmark), and name the workspace for that type of job. Then you can make a specialized workspace for each type of work you do. For example, perhaps when you do color correction, you need to see the Histogram panel (in the expanded view), the Info panel, and the Channels panel. Arrange those panels how you need them and then hide the rest, saving the workspace named as *Color Correction*. Or, perhaps when you create illustrations in Photoshop, you need to see the Layers and Paths panels at the same time. Drag one out of the group to separate it, position them both where convenient, and save the workspace as *Illustration*.

To access a saved workspace, choose Window⇨Workspace and select it from the list at the top of the menu, as shown in Figure 3-6. You can see some preset custom workspaces in the middle sections of the menu, as well.

You can also save the current state of the customizable keyboard short-cuts and menus in your workspace. Although streamlining the menus for the specific work you're doing is a great idea, it's probably not such a great idea to have more than one set of custom keyboard shortcuts. The time it takes to remember which shortcuts go with the current work-space (or to undo a mistake caused by the wrong shortcut) is time wasted.

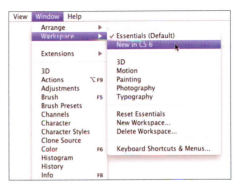

Figure 3-6: Select a workspace from the menu to instantly rearrange your panels.

To customize Photoshop's menus, choose Edit⇨Menus, which opens the Keyboard Shortcuts and Menus dialog box. (Alternatively, choose Edit⇨Keyboard Shortcuts and click the Menus tab.) Here you can find every available menu command listed. (Filters available in the Filter Gallery cannot have individual keyboard shortcuts unless, in Photoshop's Preferences⇨Plug-Ins, you have elected to list all filters in the Filter menu.) You also have the option of hiding a command or assigning a custom color to make it easier to identify in the menu. You might, for example, hide the blur filters that you never use, and color-code the others according to how you like or use them (see Figure 3-7).

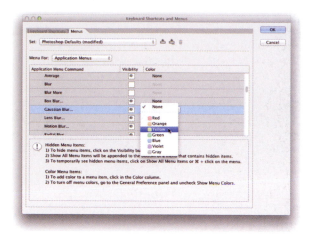

Figure 3-7: You can hide menu commands and color-code the visible commands.

In addition to the application menu commands (from the menus at the top of the screen), you can switch the Menu For pop-up to Panel menus and customize those menus, too. Don't forget to save your customized menu arrangements with the button directly to the right of the Settings pop-up. Your saved menu set appears in that Settings pop-up for easy access. Keep in mind, too, that while customizing shortcuts, you can drag the lower-right corner of the window to expand it, making it easier to find specific items for which you want to assign shortcuts.

Sugar and spice, shortcuts are nice

The Photoshop keyboard shortcuts can save a bunch of time. Rather than mousing to the Toolbox to select the Brush tool, just press the B key. To open the Levels dialog box, press ⌘+L/Ctrl+L instead of mousing to the Image menu, down to the Adjustments submenu, and then over and down to Levels.

Photoshop has customizable keyboard shortcuts. Because the default set of shortcuts is pretty standard — not only throughout the Adobe Creative Suite but also with other major programs — you're probably best served by making only a few changes. Open Keyboard Shortcuts and Menus dialog box (shown in Figure 3-8) through the Edit menu to make one major change and then any changes for personal preferences. Change ⌘+Z/Ctrl+Z to use Step Backward. In most programs, pressing ⌘+Z/Ctrl+Z keeps *undoing* — reverting through a series of previous actions in the program. In Photoshop, however, that shortcut toggles an Undo/Redo function; that is, press once to undo and press a second time to reverse the undo. Bah! Make Photoshop conform to the undo-undo-undo behavior common to other programs. In Keyboard Shortcuts, under Edit, change ⌘+Z/Ctrl+Z to Step Backward and then use ⌘+Option+Z/Ctrl+Alt+Z to toggle between Undo and Redo.

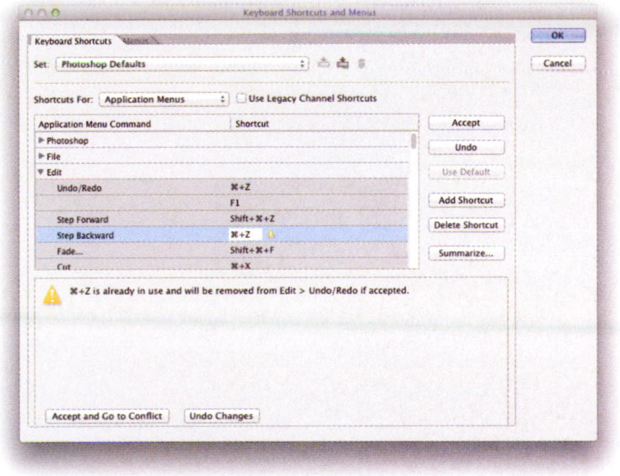

Figure 3-8: Assign custom keyboard shortcuts to speed your work.

Spoons can't chop: Creating tool presets

One of the keys to efficient, accurate work in Photoshop is using the right tool for the job. The Patch tool, for example, copies texture only. If you need to cover a spot on a client's face, changing both texture and color, you may need the Clone Stamp tool rather than the Patch tool. (You can read about how the tools work throughout this book.)

You can ensure that you're using not only the correct tool but also the correct settings for that tool by creating *tool presets,* which store your settings from the Options bar. You can then select the preset tool (and, of course, that's where the catchy name comes from) from the Tool Presets panel or from the left end of the Options bar, as shown in Figure 3-9.

Although just about any tool is a good candidate for tool presets, some are just plain naturals. Consider, if you will, the Crop tool. As I explain in Chapter 4, a photo from a high-end digital camera has an *aspect ratio* (relationship between width and height of the image) of 2:3, and common print and frame aspect ratios include 4:5 for 8x10 prints; 5:7; and 13:19 for large prints. (Some digital cameras shoot in different aspect ratios.) You'll often find a need to crop an image to a specific size to meet your printing requirements. And, don't forget resolution — printing in the correct size at the wrong resolution is simply a waste of paper and ink! Set up a number of Crop tool presets for your typical print sizes and relax, knowing that you'll always be cropping correctly.

Figure 3-9: Tool presets help you work faster and more accurately.

Another logical candidate for tool presets is the Type tool. When you consider all the options for the Type tool in not only the Options bar but also in the Character and Paragraph panels, you have quite a bit to select and track. To ensure consistent text from project to project, consider creating tool presets for each project, including (as appropriate) headline and body text, special effects and accent type, and even your copyright information. Keep in mind, too, that you can use Type tool presets in conjunction with the Character Styles and Paragraph Styles panels (which are discussed in Chapter 13).

 Using the Preset Manager (opened through the Edit menu), you can drag the tools presets up and down to rearrange them. Sort them in a logical order or move the presets you use most often to the top of the panel. The changes are for both the Tool Presets panel and the picker at the left end of the Options bar.

Season to Taste: The Photoshop Settings

The program-level Preferences and the Color Settings flavor all your work in Photoshop. The options that you choose in Photoshop's Preferences (or simply the *Prefs*) control many facets of the program's basic behavior. Choices made in the Color Settings dialog box determine how your work looks, both on-screen and in print. And when you get down to brass tacks, that's what it's all about — the appearance of your artwork.

Standing orders: Setting the Preferences

Photoshop's Preferences file stores a whole lot of information about how you use the program. Whether you prefer to measure in inches or pixels, how you like the grid and guides displayed, what size thumbnails you prefer in your panels, which font you used last — all sorts of data is maintained in the Prefs. Much of the info in the Preferences is picked up automatically as you work (such as the size and color mode of the last new document you created, whether the Character panel was visible when you last shut down the program, and which tool options were selected in the Options bar), but you must actively select a number of options in the Preferences dialog box, as shown in Figure 3-10.

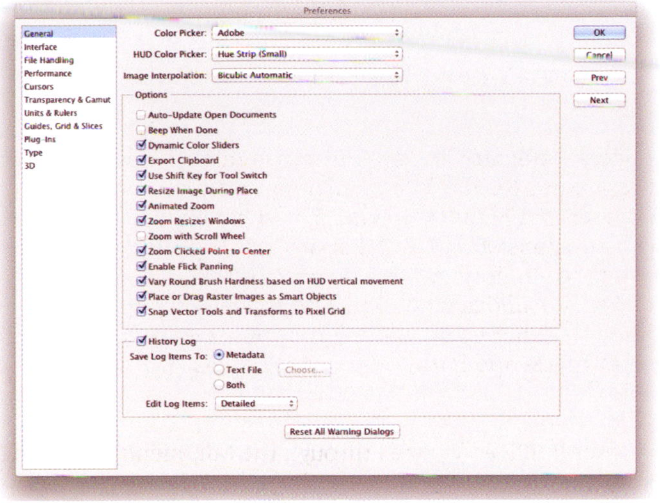

Figure 3-10: Use Photoshop's Preferences to establish many program behaviors.

Your custom styles, brushes, Actions, and the like are recorded only in Photoshop's Preferences until you actually save them to your hard drive. That makes them vulnerable to accidental loss. Use the Actions panel menu command Save Action to save sets of Actions (not individual Actions) and use the Preset Manager (under the Edit⇨Presets menu) to save sets of your other bits and pieces. And make sure to save them in a safe location *outside* the Photoshop folder — you wouldn't want to accidentally delete your custom items if you should ever have to (*oh, no!*) reinstall Photoshop, would you?

Open the Prefs on a Mac with the keyboard shortcut ⌘+K or choose Photoshop➪Preferences to select one of the eleven specific subsets of Preferences to change. The shortcut for Windows users is Ctrl+K, and the Preferences submenu is under the Edit menu. The default settings are perfectly acceptable (after all, they are the defaults for a reason), but the following sections cover some changes to the Prefs to consider, listed by the section of the Preferences dialog box in which you find them.

Preferences➪General

The History Log maintains a record of what you've done to a specific image. You can record when you opened and saved a file with the Sessions option, a summary of what you did with the Concise option, or you can keep track of every command, every feature, and every *setting* you used with the Detailed option! And the log can be recorded to a text file or stored in an image's metadata for retrieval with Photoshop's File➪File Info command.

One option not selected by default that you may find very handy is Zoom Clicked Point to Center. When you click with the Zoom tool, this option automatically centers the view on the point where you clicked.

If the options Animated Zoom and Enable Flick Panning (visible in Figure 3-10) are not available, your computer doesn't support OpenGL drawing. If you *do* see these options, they're worth a try — zooming in and out is smooth and a short, quick jerk of the Hand tool can send a zoomed-in view shooting across the screen.

Also note the button named Reset All Warning Dialogs at the bottom of the General pane. Many of Photoshop's handy reminder messages include a Don't Show Again option. If you someday decide that you do indeed need to start seeing one or more of those reminders again, open the Prefs and click this button.

Preferences➪Interface

The Interface panel of the Preferences offers several options of note:

- **Color Theme:** You may find that Photoshop's new "dark interface" is not to your taste. (Try it for a while — it'll likely grow on you.) You can select from among two lighter (and one even darker) interface appearances.

- **Screen Modes:** You can easily customize the look of Photoshop's three screen modes.

- **Auto-Collapse Iconic Panels:** If you prefer an uncluttered workplace, here's a great option for you! When selected, panels in icon mode (click the upper bar of a group of panels) collapse to buttons. To open a panel, you click its button. When Auto-Collapse is selected, the selected panel automatically closes when you click elsewhere in Photoshop. If you need to keep a specific panel open while you work (perhaps Histogram or Info), drag it out of its group and away from the edge of the screen, and it will stay open until you close it.

- ✔ **Auto-Show Hidden Panels:** Position the cursor over a collapsed panel and it springs open.

- ✔ **Open Documents as Tabs:** Photoshop, by default, opens each document as a tab across the top of the work area. You click on a tab to bring that image to the front. If you find that you're constantly dragging tabs off to create floating windows, deselect this option in the Preferences. And if you disable tabbed image windows, you'll likely also want to disable the option Enable Floating Document Window Docking. This prevents image windows from docking as you drag them around onscreen.

- ✔ **Show Channels in Color:** When only one channel is active in the Channels panel, it normally shows a grayscale representation of the image. If you prefer to have the active channel appear in its own color, select this option. Keep in mind, however, that after you get comfortable working with individual channels, the default grayscale is easier to see.

- ✔ **Show Menu Colors:** As I discuss earlier in this chapter, you can assign colors to specific commands in the Photoshop menus. That might make it easier for you to quickly spot and select often-used commands. Use this option to disable the color coding without having to deselect each assigned color.

- ✔ **Show Tool Tips:** Pause the cursor over just about any tool or option in Photoshop and a little yellow box appears, telling you what that feature does. This is a great feature while you're learning about Photoshop, but might be distracting after you master the program. Disable the Tool Tips if you decide you no longer need or want to see them.

- ✔ **Show Transformation Values:** When using the transform commands, Photoshop shows you numerically precisely what you're doing. A small display will show the new dimensions (when scaling) or the angle (when rotating or shearing). You may find that to the top-right of the cursor isn't a good location (perhaps while using the stylus in your right hand on a Wacom Cintiq tablet). Change the location — or select Never to hide the info completely.

- ✔ **UI Font Size:** If you find yourself squinting to read panel names and such, change the UI Font Size to Large and restart Photoshop. If you *still* have problems reading the screen, reduce the monitor's resolution (see Chapter 2, "Resolution revelations").

Preferences⇨File Handling

Image previews add a little to the file size, but in most cases, you want to include the preview. On Macs, you have the option of including a file extension or not (or having Photoshop ask you each and every time). Even if you don't plan on sharing files with a Windows machine, I strongly recommend that you always include the file extension in the filename by selecting the Always option. Likewise, I suggest that you always maximize PSD and PSB file compatibility. This ensures that your Photoshop files can be opened (with as many features intact as possible) in earlier versions of the program and that they'll function properly with other programs in the Creative Suite. Maximizing compatibility is also critical if you also work with Adobe's Lightroom.

Adobe has finally included an auto-recovery feature in Photoshop, one that doesn't compromise the creative process. If, as with some programs, your open file was simply saved to your hard drive at specific intervals, overwriting the original, your artistic experimentation could be limited to that specified time frame. Say, for example, that you tried a specific artistic filter, took an important phone call, and later found out that the program had rewritten the file on your hard drive and that experimental filter has become a permanent part of your artwork. But you decided you don't like it after all. Bummer! Rather than taking such risks with your creativity, Photoshop now can save recovery information, which doesn't affect the original file in any way, at intervals specified in the Preferences. Or you can disable the feature by deselecting the check box.

Preferences⇨Performance

The Performance panel contains options related to how Photoshop runs on your computer:

- ✔ **Memory Usage:** If you have 2GB or less of RAM, leave the memory allocation set to the default (70% for Mac, 55% on Windows). If you have more than 2GB of RAM, especially when working with a 64-bit version of Windows or with Mac 10.6 or later, try bumping the memory allocation to 100%. If things seem slower rather than faster, back off the memory allocation to perhaps 85%. In a 64-bit environment, Photoshop can take advantage of all the RAM you can cram (into the computer).

- ✔ **Scratch Disks:** Photoshop's *scratch disks* are hard drive space used to support the memory. Use only internal hard drives as scratch disks — never an external drive, a network drive, or removable media! If you have multiple internal hard drives, consider a dedicated partition (perhaps 15–50GB) on the second drive — not the drive on which the operating system is installed. Name the partition Scratch and use it exclusively as a scratch disk for Photoshop (and perhaps Adobe Illustrator). If you have a couple of extra internal drives, each can have a scratch partition. (On a Windows computer, you might see a message warning you that the scratch disk and the Windows paging file, which serves the same basic purpose at the system level, are on the same drive. If you have only one internal hard drive, ignore the message.) To re-order the scratch disks, click on the scratch disk in the list and then, rather than dragging, use the arrows keys to the right.

✔ **History States:** This field determines how many entries (up to 1,000) appear in the History panel. Storing more history states provides more flexibility, but at a cost — storing too many history states uses up all your available memory and slows Photoshop to a crawl. Generally speaking, 20 or 30 is a good number. If, however, you do a lot of operations that use what I call "little clicks," such as painting or dodging/burning with short strokes, that History Panel fills up quickly. For such operations, a setting of perhaps 50 or even 60 is more appropriate.

✔ **Cache Levels:** The image *cache* stores low-resolution copies of your image to speed on-screen display at various zoom levels. Although this process speeds up screen redraw, the price is accuracy. Unless your video card has trouble driving your monitor at your selected resolution and color depth, you might be better served by Cache Levels: 1. That gives the most accurate picture of your work. (But remember to make critical decisions at 100% zoom, where one image pixel equals one screen pixel.)

✔ **Graphics Processor Settings:** This area displays information about your computer's video card. If your system has the capability, you'll see a check box for Use Graphics Processor. This provides smoother, more accurate views at all zoom levels and other enhancements, including the capability to rotate the image on screen — not rotate the canvas, but rotate just the on-screen image. And that's too cool for words when painting a complex layer mask!

Preferences⇨Cursors

Photoshop offers you a couple of ways to display cursors for painting tools. You can show the tool icon (Standard), a small crosshair (Precise), or a representation of the tool's brush tip, indicating the size and shape of the brush (Brush Size). With soft-edged brushes, the brush size cursor shows where the tool will be applied at 50% strength or higher. Alternatively, select the Full Size Brush Tip option, which always shows the full extent of the brush tip, regardless of the Hardness setting.

You also have the option of adding a crosshair in the middle of either brush-size cursor. The crosshair option is great for keeping a brush centered along an edge or path, and it just about eliminates the need for the Precise cursor option. As you can see in Figure 3-11 when working with a soft brush, showing all the pixels that are changed even a little (to the right) might not give you an accurate view of your work. (The Normal Brush Tip cursor is shown at the top center and with the Show Crosshair in Brush Tip option to the lower left.)

Figure 3-11: When working with a low Hardness setting, Normal Brush Tip is usually best.

When the Show Only Crosshair While Painting option is selected in the Preferences, the brush cursor appears at the selected diameter display (Full Size or Normal) until you press the mouse button (or press the stylus to the tablet). It then automatically switches to the crosshair and remains as a precise cursor until you release the mouse button (or lift the stylus). Experienced brush tool-using Photoshoppers might want to experiment with this option — if you know the diameter, you might want to better focus on the center of the brush when you are, for example, painting or dodging or burning along a distinct edge.

When you're sure that you have a brush-size cursor selected in the Preferences but Photoshop shows you the precise cursor, check the CapsLock key. Pressing CapsLock toggles the painting cursors between precise and brush size.

Also found in the Cursors panel is the Brush Preview color. Click the color swatch to open the Color Picker and assign a color to use when dynamically resizing your brushes. (If you don't have OpenGL drawing capability, the brushes can still be resized, but the color preview will not be visible.) With a brush-using tool active, press and hold down the Option+Control keys on Mac and drag left or right; on Windows, Alt-right-click and drag left or right to resize the brush — on the fly! Want to change the brush hardness? Hold down those same keys and drag up or down rather than left or right.

Preferences⇨Transparency & Gamut

If you work in grayscale regularly, you might want to change the color of the transparency grid to something that contrasts with your image; perhaps pale blue and pale yellow. If you find the gray-and-white checkerboard pattern distracting in images with transparency, you can set Grid Size to None, which gives you a plain white background in transparent areas of your artwork.

Preferences⇨Units & Rulers

If you create web graphics rather than print images, you probably want to change the unit of measure from Inches to Pixels. Keep in mind that you can change the unit of measure on the fly by right-clicking the rulers in your image (which you show and hide with the shortcut ⌘+R/Ctrl+R). If you regularly print at a resolution other than 300 ppi, you might also want to adjust the default resolution for print-size new documents.

Preferences⇨Guides, Grid & Slices

Photoshop offers *Smart Guides,* which appear and disappear automatically as you drag the content of one layer into and out of alignment with the content of other layers. Smart Guides (magenta in color by default) show when the content of the layer you're dragging aligns perfectly with the edges or center of other layers' content. See Figure 3-12. (Show/hide Smart Guides through the View⇨Show menu.)

Figure 3-12: The magenta guides show how the layer aligns with other layers.

The one thing you might want to change in this panel of the Preferences is the Show Slice Numbers option. The slice numbers appear in the upper-left corner of each slice when you're subdividing web graphics. Unless you intend to edit the images individually later, you probably don't need to know which slice is which, so slice numbers are generally not necessary. Clear the check box to remove the distractions.

Preferences⇨Plug-Ins

If you have third-party plug-ins, filters, and such that you purchased separately for use in Photoshop, consider using a second folder for the plug-ins, outside the Photoshop folder, and designate that folder as the Additional Plug-Ins Folder in the Preferences. Having your extra plug-ins outside the Photoshop folder means you won't have to reinstall them if you have to replace Photoshop.

The creative filters of the Filter Gallery are no longer listed individually in the Filter menu. Now you open the Filter Gallery, and then select the filter you need. If you would rather have the Filter Gallery open directly to the filter you need, select Show All Filter Gallery Groups and Names option and restart Photoshop.

Preferences⇨Type

Photoshop has a panel in the Preferences that you can use to select some type-related options. But don't look here for the option to select a font preview size — that's moved to the Type menu so that you can change on the fly.

Photoshop's Preferences menu also provides you with direct access to the Camera Raw plug-in's Preferences. In Camera Raw's Preferences you can, among other things, determine whether JPEG and TIFF files open into Camera Raw.

Ensuring consistency: Color Settings

If one term strikes fear deep in the heart of a typical Photoshop user, it's *color management*. Few aspects of the program are so misunderstood. Yet without wise color management decisions, your images won't print accurately. For most Photoshop users, color management can be implemented with a few key choices in the Edit⇨Color Settings dialog box, which can then be saved for future use:

- **Select an RGB working space.** Open the Color Settings dialog box (under the Edit menu) and select your *RGB working space* — the color space in which you edit and create. If you primarily create web graphics, shoot in the JPEG format, send your images to a photo lab for printing, or print with an inkjet printer that uses only four ink colors (cyan, magenta, yellow, and black), choose sRGB as your color space. If you shoot Raw and print to an inkjet printer that uses six or more inks, or you prepare artwork that will be converted to a CMYK color space, choose Adobe RGB. (If you have hardware and software to create a custom profile for your computer's monitor, use that profile at the system level so that it's available to all programs.)

- **Elect to convert images to your working space.** In the Color Management Policies area of the Color Settings dialog box, choose RGB: Convert to Working RGB. This ensures that the images you see onscreen actually use your working profile.

- **CMYK and Grayscale settings:** CMYK (cyan/magenta/yellow/black) color mode is used exclusively with images intended for output on commercial printing presses and some color laser printers. (Don't be fooled by the inks you purchase for your inkjet printer — the printer's driver expects to convert from RGB, so sending CMYK color to an inkjet will produce substandard output.) Likewise, you'll use Grayscale very rarely. If, in fact, you have an inkjet printer that is capable of printing grayscale (such as the magnificent Epson Stylus Pro 7900), you may still want to have an RGB image and let the printer's print driver handle the grayscale conversion. If, however, you *are* preparing an image for output on a commercial press (in CMYK or Grayscale color mode), speak directly with the person who will place the image into the page layout or with the print shop to find out what settings to use for that particular job.

- **Turn off the mismatch warnings.** Clear the check boxes for those annoying and time-wasting warnings that pop up on-screen any time you open an image with a profile other than your working space. You're intentionally converting to your working space — you don't need to reaffirm the decision every time.

When it's time to print, you'll get the most accurate and pleasing color prints when you let Photoshop (rather than the printer) control color. In the Print dialog box's Options area, choose Color Handling: Photoshop Manages Colors and select the printer's own profile for the specific paper on which you're printing as the Printer Profile. Use Relative Colorimetric as the rending intent and leave the Black Point Compensation check box marked. (Note: If your prints are too dark, try deselecting Black Point Compensation.) Click the Print Settings button to open the printer's own options. Make sure to deactivate the printer's built-in color management and select the same paper you chose to the right in Photoshop's Print dialog box.

The preceding guidelines are appropriate for most, but not all, Photoshop users. You might fall into a special category. If you *exclusively* create web graphics, set the RGB color management policy to Off. In the Save for Web & Devices dialog box, when saving images in the JPEG file format, don't embed ICC profiles. (*ICC profiles* make specific adjustments to the appearance of your images to compensate for vagaries of the hardware. I discuss color profiles in Chapter 4.) When you eliminate color profiles from the equation, you're creating web graphics that any web browser can show properly (or, more accurately, "as properly as the viewer's uncalibrated monitor can display").

If color in your images needs to be absolutely perfect because merely accurate won't do, consider purchasing hardware and software to calibrate and profile all the devices in your workflow. GretagMacbeth and X-Rite (www. xrite.com), Datacolor (www.datacolor.com), and PANTONE (www. pantone.com) are three sources to explore.

When Good Programs Go Bad: Fixing Photoshop

Sometimes things happen. Bad things. Tools don't work right. Simple commands take ages to execute. Photoshop (gasp!) *crashes*! Don't give up, and please don't toss the machine through the window. (Hey, I might be walking past at the time.) Start with the easy fixes and work your way up as necessary:

✔ **Check the panels and selection.** If a tool isn't working as expected or isn't working at all, check whether you're inadvertently preventing it from doing its job. See whether you have an active selection elsewhere in the image or press ⌘+D/Ctrl+D to deselect. Look at the Layers panel: Are you working on the correct layer? Is the layer itself active or a layer mask? Is there no higher layer hiding the area in which you're trying to work? Check the Channels panel: Are the color channels active? At the left end of the Options bar, right-click (Control+click for an older trackpad) on the tool icon and select Reset Tool. Open a flattened 8-bit RGB image and try the tool or technique in that image. If it works there, the problem isn't Photoshop but rather the specific image. Check the Image➪Mode menu to ensure that you have an appropriate color mode and bit depth.

✔ **Reset Photoshop's Preferences file to the defaults.** Before replacing the Prefs, open Photoshop's Preset Manager (through the Edit menu) and save any custom styles, gradients, brushes, and so forth. Save them in a safe place, outside the Photoshop folder. Open the Actions panel and save any sets of custom Actions with the panel menu Save Actions command. (Remember that you must click a set of Actions — not an individual Action — to use Save Actions.) Open the Preferences and Color Settings and make notes about any special settings you're using. Quit Photoshop and restart the program with the ⌘+Option+Shift keys pressed (Mac); or in Windows, position your fingers over the Ctrl+Alt+Shift keys and immediately after launching the program (not before), press and hold down the three keys. When asked whether you want to delete the Settings file, release the modifier keys and confirm the deletion; allow Photoshop to finish starting. Reset your Preferences and Color Settings and reload your custom bits and pieces.

✔ **Reinstall Photoshop.** If replacing the Prefs doesn't solve the problem, try reinstalling Photoshop. Save all your custom items (as described earlier) and then uninstall Photoshop. Insert the Photoshop DVD and launch the installer, and then opt to uninstall. After uninstalling, restart your computer (not always necessary, but a good practice) and reinstall.

If reinstalling Photoshop doesn't solve the problem, the source might be at the operating system level or perhaps a hardware problem. Call in the big guns by contacting Adobe tech support at `www.adobe.com/support/contact`.

4

Getting Images into and out of Photoshop

You could, theoretically, open a new empty Photoshop file, paint in it, save the file, and drive from house to house to show the artwork on your computer to friends and family. However, you have lots of ways to share your images that are *much* easier. You can print them, post them on your website, or even e-mail them. And e-mailing an image file across the country is much more convenient (and, of course, more eco-friendly) than driving hither and yon with your computer in the trunk.

In this chapter, I show you how to get images into Photoshop from your digital camera and your scanner and then how to keep those images organized on your hard drive and CDs/DVDs. I discuss the basics of printing your images on inkjet printers (and alternatives) and tell you some things you need to know to make sure you get the prints you expect. I also explain how to prepare images for sending by e-mail.

Bringing Images into Photoshop

Artwork in Photoshop originates in one of three ways:

- ✔ You open an image using Photoshop's File⇨Open dialog box (as shown in Figure 4-1) or through Bridge (discussed later in this chapter). If you own the Creative Suite, you also have the option of using Version Cue, the Creative Suite's workgroup management program. (Read about Version Cue in Bridge's Help.) In Figure 4-1, note that Windows does not provide previews or thumbnails of PSD files (or many Raw formats), which is one of the reasons you have Bridge available.

- ✔ You import an image (typically through a scanning device).

- ✔ You create an image from scratch by choosing File⇨New.

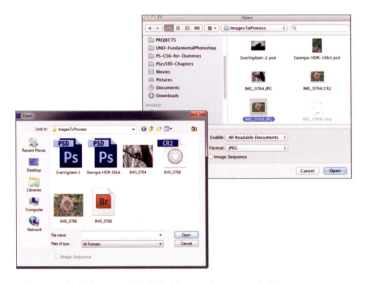

Figure 4-1: Windows on the left, Mac to the upper-right.

If you double-click a file and Photoshop doesn't launch or the wrong program launches, you need to associate the file format with Photoshop:

- ✔ **Adobe Bridge file association**

    a. Open Bridge's Preferences with the shortcut ⌘+K/Ctrl+K.

    b. In the column to the left, click File Type Associations.

    c. In the lower right, click the Reset to Default Associations button.

✔ **Mac file association**

   a. In the Mac Finder, right-click (Control+click for a trackpad or two-finger click on a trackpad set up for Gestures) on a file of the type that you want to open in Photoshop.

   b. From the contextual menu, choose Get Info.

   c. In the Get Info dialog box, expand the Opens With area, choose Photoshop from the pop-up menu, and click Change All.

   d. (Optional) Repeat for any additional file formats.

   If you double-click a file and Photoshop launches but the image doesn't open, you've likely made a change to the Mac OS and should reinstall Photoshop.

✔ **Windows 7 file association**

   a. Click on the Start button in the lower-left corner of the screen.

   b. From the menu, select Computer.

   c. Navigate to a folder that holds one or more files of the format you need to associate with Photoshop.

   d. Right-click on the image file, and in the Open With submenu, select Choose default program, and then choose Photoshop.

   e. (Optional) Repeat for any additional file formats.

Downloading from your digital camera

Adobe Bridge offers the File⇨Get Photos from Camera command, which opens Adobe Photo Downloader and offers you the options of organizing with subfolders, renaming, and automatically converting Raw files to the DNG file format. Alternatively, you can use the software that comes with your digital camera to transfer photographs from it to your computer's hard drive. On Macs, Photoshop's File⇨Import menu offers Images from Device, discussed later in this chapter, which can be used to import photos from cameras as well as control a scanner.

If you have the hardware, you can remove your camera's memory card, memory stick, or other media from the camera and use a *card reader,* which is a small device designed to read camera storage media. Transferring via the Mac Finder or Windows is often faster than and usually just as reliable as transferring using the camera manufacturer's software.

Purchasing commercial images

Some projects require images that you can't run out and shoot yourself. Say, for example, that you're preparing a poster or brochure about a ski trip to Japan. In your office or studio. In the United States. In July. Pretty tough to shoot what you need, eh? Turn to stock photography. You can purchase or license stock images (photos, illustrations, video, and even audio) from a wide variety of sources, including Internet-based services and collections on CD/DVD.

When you consider using stock images, keep in mind the difference between royalty-free and rights-managed images. *Royalty-free images* are yours to use as you see fit (within the terms of your agreement — no resale as stock photos,

no defamatory or pornographic use, and so on). You can use the images when you need them, as often as you need them. *Rights-managed images,* on the other hand, are licensed for a specific use, in specific media, for a specified time. Rights-managed artwork does have one advantage over royalty-free: Because usage is controlled, you can license *exclusive* rights to the image for that period of time so that the image you use won't appear in some competitor's advertising at the same time. Royalty-free images, on the other hand, are available to anyone who pays for them, and usage is not controlled.

Never open an image into Photoshop directly from a camera, Flash card, or CD/DVD. Doing so can slow down your work, and you also risk losing your work if Photoshop isn't able to immediately and efficiently read the original file while you work. And, of course, you can't save from Photoshop back to most removable media, so you need to create a new file (on a writable drive) anyway. Open images from a network drive only when working with Adobe's Version Cue, the Adobe Creative Suite's project management software.

After the images are safely stored on your local hard drive (or a high-speed external hard drive), you can open them in Photoshop by using one of the methods that I describe earlier in the chapter. Depending on your color settings, you might see a warning that the image's color profile and the profile that you selected as your RGB working space don't match. You'll see the embedded profile and the working profile, and you're given three options (as well as a Cancel button, which won't open the document):

- ✔ Use the embedded profile (instead of the working space)
- ✔ Convert the document's colors to the working space
- ✔ Discard the embedded profile (don't color manage)

Generally speaking, you want to convert to your working space so that you see the most accurate color on your monitor. You might want to preserve the embedded profile if you'll be returning the image to the originating computer after looking at or working on it. The third option disregards all color profiles and works with uncorrected color. This is a good choice when working with images that you'll later use with a non-color-managed program, such as a web browser or presentation program. (Without color management, you see the image as it will appear in the other program.) You can disable the color mismatch warnings in Photoshop's Color Settings dialog box.

When opening an image that includes text, you might also get a message warning you that the type layers need to be updated. Generally speaking, you want to update them unless the image contains fonts that aren't available on your computer.

Scanning prints

You place a photo (face down) on the glass of your scanner. You push a button. It automatically appears on your computer screen. That's scanning at its most basic. You can save that file to your hard drive and use Photoshop's File⇨Open command to bring it into Photoshop for editing.

On Macs, Photoshop's File⇨Import⇨Images from Device enables you to scan right from Photoshop, right into Photoshop. (Windows users have WIA Support in the File⇨Import menu.) The scanned image can open in Photoshop as a separate file or as a layer in the currently-active document. The Import Images from Device dialog box is shown in Figure 4-2.

Figure 4-2: Access your scanner directly from Photoshop on a Mac, scanning right into Photoshop.

To the right in Figure 4-2, you see a column of options available when scanning. You can elect to scan as color or grayscale (the Black & White option), set the resolution and print dimensions, rotate the image, and elect to identify separate photos placed on the scanner's glass. In addition to JPEG, available file formats include TIFF and PDF (as well as a number of other formats you'll likely not use for scanning). Other available options include manual color correction (do it in Photoshop instead), three levels of sharpening (again, a task to be done in Photoshop), descreening to remove moiré patterns (discussed later in this chapter), Backlight Correction (not applicable to scanning prints), dust removal (another in-Photoshop task), and color restoration for faded photos (give it a shot — it might work for the specific image you're scanning).

When you've finished scanning, use the menu command File⇨Close or the shortcut ⌘+W/Ctrl+W to close the window — there's no Quit or Cancel button.

Determining scan resolution

Before scanning an image, you need to make some decisions:

- How you want to use the image
- What its final size will be
- What resolution you need

By determining how many pixels you need beforehand, you eliminate the need to resize the image in Photoshop (and the resulting image degradation). Many scanner interface windows let you input the final size and resolution you need right in the scan window. If you find the need to calculate scan resolution manually, here's how:

1. **Determine the required pixel dimensions.**

   - *For print:* If you'll be printing the image, determine the size at which you want to print (in inches) and the resolution at which you want to print (typically 300 ppi [pixels per inch] is a good choice). Multiply the print width and height by the resolution to determine pixel dimensions.

   - *For the web:* If the image is destined for your website, determine how much of your page the image will occupy (in pixels).

2. **Measure the original.**

   Before placing it on the scanner's glass, measure the original image. If you're using only part of the image, measure that part. (Be careful not to scratch the original with your ruler!)

3. Do the math.

Divide your required pixel dimensions (Step 1) by the physical dimensions of the original (Step 2). The result is your *scan resolution.* (If you get different numbers for the width and height, use the larger and expect to do some cropping in Photoshop.)

Many flatbed scanners (scanners designed for use with documents and photos) have *transparency adapters* that let you scan film and slides. However, if you have a lot of negatives or slides to scan or if the best possible quality is required, consider a dedicated film scanner from Nikon, Minolta, or Kodak.

Notice to the left in Figure 4-2 the list of available devices from which you can bring images into Photoshop using Images from Device. In addition to the Epson GT-20000 scanner, two camera storage cards (inserted into a card reader) and a directly-connected camera can be accessed. When downloading images, you simply select which images on the device you want to download, choose a location, and download. Although you don't have all the options available when downloading with Bridge's Get Photos from Camera (automatic subfolders, converting to DNG, renaming, and so on), using Import Images from Device does offer one huge advantage — it's "sticky." In other words, the dialog box doesn't go away after the first import.

Say, for example, that you have images on a single flash card from three different projects or locations and you want to download them into three different folders. When using Get Photos from Camera, you wait for Adobe Photos Downloader to examine the entire card, you select the first batch of photos, you download, and then Adobe Photo Downloader goes away. To download the second set, you start from scratch (including re-examining the entire card and waiting for thumbnails to generate). When importing directly from Photoshop, you select the first set of images, choose a location, download; select the second set, choose a different location, download; select the third set, choose a third location, download, close the window. But if you want to create DNG copies, rename while downloading, separate into subfolders by date, and so forth, Bridge's Get Photos from Camera is the way to go.

Preventing moiré patterns

Unless you spent thousands of dollars on your scanner, you probably want to forget about the scanner software's color and tonal correction capabilities — Photoshop gives you more control. However, here is one thing that scanner software does much better than Photoshop, and it's a capability that you should use when appropriate: moiré (pronounced, roughly, *mwah-RAY*) reduction. A *moiré pattern* is a visible rosette pattern created by the pattern of dots placed by the printing press to reproduce color.

When you need to scan a color image or artwork that comes from a book, magazine, or newspaper (or other material printed on an offset printing press, such as product packaging or signs), you want to use the scanner's software to reduce moiré. When you let the scanner know the pattern is there, the scanner's software compensates for the pattern and smoothes the scanned image (as you can see in Figure 4-3).

Figure 4-3: Scanning without (left) and with the scanner's moiré reduction option.

The moiré reduction feature in your scanner's software might not be immediately recognizable. It might be labeled Descreening, or it could be a choice between Color (Photo) and Color (Document). As always, refer to your hardware's User Guide for specific guidance.

If rescanning is out of the question and you have a moiré pattern to reduce in Photoshop, blur the image enough to disguise the problem, and then paint with the History Brush to restore areas of critical detail in the image.

Here's an important announcement from *The Department of an Ounce of Prevention is Worth a Pound of Cure:* A minute or two spent cleaning the scanner could save hours of touch-up in Photoshop. Before doing any scanning, use a can of compressed air to make sure that the scanner's glass is clean and free of dust. Likewise, check the inside of the scanner's lid. (What good does it do to clean the glass if dust from the lid is going to contaminate it again as soon as you close it?) If necessary, eliminate fingerprints or smears with appropriate glass cleaner. (Check the scanner's User Guide for cleaning instructions and be careful when using liquid glass cleaner with an electrical device! I like to use the same premoistened wipes I use for my eyeglasses.)

You can use a burst of compressed air on the original image, too, before placing it on the glass. Just be careful — first spray a quick burst away from the photo to clear the nozzle, hold the can of air some distance away from the photo, and spray at an angle so that you don't damage the surface of the print.

Keeping Your Images Organized

Because digital photography doesn't have a significant per-shot cost (as does shooting film), people certainly have a tendency to shoot more. And more. And more. Experimental shots, this-might-be-interesting shots, special effects shots, and (at least in my case) the same shot over and over and over again. They build up on your hard drive.

It's pretty easy to stay organized after you choose a system. The hard part is actually deleting those digital photos that you really don't need to keep — you know, out-of-focus, shot at a bad angle, Aunt Betsy's eyes were closed and her mouth was open, the 400th shot of the dogs sleeping all curled up, the 401st shot of the dogs sleeping all curled up, and the like. It takes discipline! (Or an optical drive that can burn CDs and/or DVDs.)

Creating a folder structure

I generally recommend using a subject-based organization scheme, such as the one shown in Figure 4-4. For example, inside the main folder named AllVacationPhotos, you might have subfolders with names such as London-Feb2012, NHL_30CityTour, or perhaps BackyardCamping_Sept_2011. (Notice that none of the folder names use empty spaces or characters other than letters, numbers, a dash, and an underscore — that minimizes the possibility that Photoshop or another program won't be able to find a file.)

Figure 4-4: Organize with subfolders.

Don't overload your folders! If you find that your computer is slowing down when it tries to display the content of a folder, you have too many files in the folder. Create a second folder of the same name and add -01 and -02 to the folder names. Generally speaking, 500MB is probably as large as you want in a single folder.

You can use your computer's CD/DVD drive (if it has the capability) to burn folders of images to disc. This not only provides you with a reliable backup (assuming you store the discs correctly and handle them carefully), but it can free up space on your hard drive. Your folder/subfolder structure can also be used when creating your discs.

Using Adobe Bridge

Adobe Bridge, the asset-management program for Photoshop and the Creative Suite, is installed at the same time you install Photoshop or the Creative Suite. Bridge has its own folder on your hard drive, inside the Applications folder on the Mac and in C:\Program Files for Windows — and also the Program Files (x86) folder if you're running a 64-bit version of Windows. (The Photoshop/Bridge you see in the x86 folder is the 32-bit version.) You can open Bridge independently, or you can use the Photoshop File⇨Browse command to launch Bridge, which you see in Figure 4-5. If you choose Bridge's Preferences⇨Advanced, you can elect to have Bridge launch automatically whenever you log in to your computer.

Figure 4-5: Adobe Bridge is a separate program for managing and organizing your image files.

Here are a few tips for working with Adobe Bridge:

- **Use keywords and categories.** Using the Keywords tab (shown in Figure 4-6), to the lower-right in Bridge's default layout, you can assign keywords and categories to images. *Keywords* and *categories* are descriptive terms that you assign to individual images. Down the road, you can use the File⇨Find command to find all images with a specific assigned keyword. A checkmark to the left of a keyword indicates that all of the files currently selected in Bridge's Thumbnails pane have that keyword assigned, a dash indicates that some, but not all, selected images have been assigned that keyword.

METADATA	KEYWORDS	
Assigned Keywords: Birthday; Hugo; Nelson; Paris		
▼ ☐ Events		3
☐ Birthday		
☐ Graduation		
☐ Wedding		
▼ ☐ People and Animals		3
▼ ☐ Dogs		3
☑ Hugo		
☐ Nelson		
☐ Oscar		
☐ Matthew		
☐ Ryan		
▼ ☐ Places		5
▶ ☐ Georgia-0709		5
☐ Lake Michigan		
☐ New Buffalo		
☐ Paris		
☐ San Francisco		
▼ ☐ Things		1

Figure 4-6: Assign keywords and categories to help organize (and locate) images.

- **Select multiple images in Bridge.** You can have multiple images active by clicking and Shift+clicking (or ⌘+clicking/Ctrl+clicking) on the image thumbnails. You might want to select multiple images and then assign the same keywords to all the selected images at once.

- **Use labels, ratings, and filters.** Under the Label menu, you can assign a star rating to each image and assign colors to organize by subject or project. Use the View⇨Sort menu to arrange images in the thumbnails area of Bridge according to either the label or the rating. In the lower-left of the default workspace, you find the Filter tab. Use that feature to locate specific files by showing as thumbnails only those files that meet the selected criteria. Want to find a specific JPEG file? Click on that format in the Filter tab to hide the thumbnails of all non-JPEG files.

- **Add folders to the Favorites.** You invariably will visit some folders on a regular basis. Choose File⇨Add to Favorites to get back to that folder faster and more easily. In the upper-left corner of the Bridge window, click the Favorites tab for one-click access. Keep in mind, too, that you can add a folder to the Favorites while working on a specific project, and then choose File⇨Remove from Favorites when the project is finished.

- **Change your view and workspace.** Use the View menu to customize what the Bridge window shows, and use the Window⇨Workspace menu to determine how it is displayed. You might find that Compact Mode fits your needs better in some circumstances than does Full Mode. And don't overlook Bridge's Slideshow feature — it can be a great way to show off your work!

✔ **Use Stacks to organize images.** Select similar images or variations on the same shot and use Bridge's menu command Stacks➪Group as Stack. All of the selected images are piled into one spot as a single thumbnail, with a number in the upper-left corner to indicate how many images are stacked together. When you have images in a stack, you can scroll through the thumbnails with a slider that appears when you move the cursor over the stack.

✔ **Export directly to Facebook or Flickr.** After you have perfected your images in Photoshop, use Bridge's menu command File➪Export To to upload images directly to Facebook or Flickr.

✔ **Zoom with the Loupe.** Click in the Preview (in the upper-right corner of the default workspace) to zoom in. Drag the cursor to inspect the preview up close and personal.

Mini Bridge is a panel that provides a Bridge-like tool right in Photoshop. You open it with Photoshop's command File➪Browse in Mini Bridge or through the Window➪Extensions menu. Mini Bridge provides a quick and easy way for you to work with files and thumbnails without leaving Photoshop (see Figure 4-7).

Figure 4-7: Mini Bridge is an even faster and easier way to access folders of images and special features.

Renaming image files easily

All right, then, you've arranged a hierarchy of folders and subfolders. You've sorted your images into those folders. You've assigned rank and label to the images. However, you still have no idea which is which in the File➪Open Recent menu. Filenames such as _MG_1907.CR2 and PB270091.jpg don't tell you much about the image content, do they? Use Bridge's Tools⇨Batch Rename command (as shown in Figure 4-8) to assign more meaningful (and informative) names to your files. Select content from each field from the pop-up menu or type in a field. Click the + button to the right to add more elements or variables to each name.

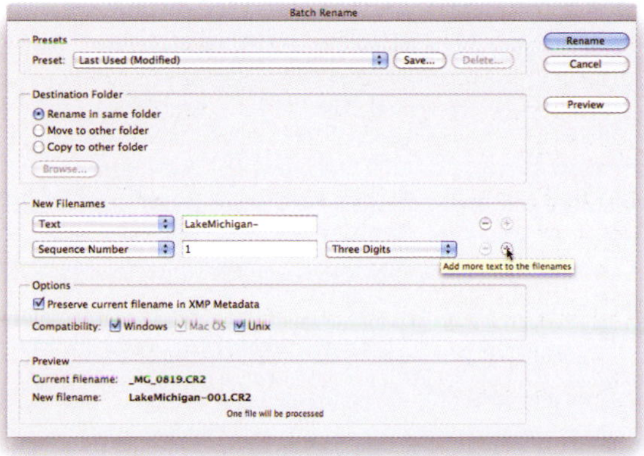

Figure 4-8: Use Batch Rename to assign informative names to files.

So that each of your original images gets a unique name, you *must* include a variable when using Batch Rename. (If you did try to rename all the images in a folder to say, `picture.jpg`, you would end up with only one image file in the destination folder — each would overwrite the previous.) Therefore, when using Batch Rename, you must choose one of the variables for one of the fields via the pop-up menu, be it the original document name or a sequence number/letter.

Also keep in mind that you shouldn't type a period (.) into any field. That character should be used only before the file extension. And, as a wonderful keep-us-from-creating-problems-for-ourselves improvement, Batch Rename automatically adds the file extension for you.

Printing Your Images

In the very recent past, the subject of printing images from Photoshop required a huge number of pages. Thankfully, improvements in hardware and software make printing much easier. Monitors are well calibrated out of the box, printers reproduce color more accurately, and inks and papers last for decades. Yes, things have come a long way in a short time. But before you click the Print button, you should make sure that your image is ready to print. Will it fit properly on the page and in the frame? Are the pixels small enough that they blend evenly into the overall picture? Will the colors you envision be the colors that appear on paper?

Cropping to a specific aspect ratio

Aspect ratio is the relationship between the width and height of your image. An image in *landscape* aspect ratio is wider than it is tall, and an image in *portrait* aspect ratio is taller than it is wide. Although digital cameras capture in a variety of aspect ratios, including 3:4 and 4:5, DSLR (digital single lens reflex) cameras typically use a 3:2 aspect ratio: One side is 1.5 times the size of the adjoining sides. Typical print (and picture frame) sizes are 8x10 inches (a 4:5 aspect ratio), 5x7 inches (5:7), 4x6 inches (3:2), and 3x5 inches (3:5). In Figure 4-9, the 3:2 aspect ratio is outlined in green, 5:7 is shown in yellow, and 4:5 is red.

Figure 4-9: Different print sizes encompass different amounts of your image.

Although an 8x10 print is physically larger than a 4x6 print, it may print less of your original image because of cropping. The 4x6 print, with a 3:2 aspect ratio, includes all of the original image; the 8x10 print (with its 4:5 aspect ratio) is missing 2 full inches of the image's longer dimension. To print 8 inches wide and retain the entire image, you'd be printing at 8x12. Of course, if your camera captures in a 4:5 aspect ratio, the problem is reversed — the original image fits perfectly into an 8x10 print, but won't fill a 4x6 print without cropping.

In Photoshop, you can change the aspect ratio of your image with the Canvas Size command (if one dimension is already correctly sized), the Crop tool, or the Rectangular Marquee tool with the Image⇨Crop command. With the Crop tool selected, you can enter specific dimensions and a target resolution on the Options bar. Drag the tool, position and adjust the bounding box, and then press Return/Enter to execute the crop. Whatever is within the bounding box is resampled to the exact size that you specify on the Options bar. If you crop with Canvas Size or Crop commands, you may need to use Image⇨Image Size to specify the desired print resolution. (And see Chapter 2 for information on Photoshop CS6's Content-Aware Scale command.)

As soon as you activate the Crop tool (with the tool shortcut C or by clicking on the tool icon in the Toolbox), a bounding box appears around your image. You'll also see a variety of options in the Options bar (see Figure 4-10). The top inset shows the various preset aspect rations available in the Options bar. Note the option Size and Resolution — select it to crop to a specific size and resolution. The middle inset shows the variety of overlays available, including Grid, visible over the image in Figure 4-10. The lower inset, opened by clicking the gear-shaped button in the Options bar, provides options on basic Crop tool behavior.

Also notice in the example that the crop has been straightened, but it's the image, not the crop bounding box, that's rotated. To the right in the Options bar is the Delete Cropped Pixels option. When selected, the pixels outside the bounding box are deleted, but when selected, those pixels are hidden and can be restored with the command Image⇨Reveal All.

The first time you drag an anchor point of the Crop tool's bounding box you're likely to say "Whoa!" (or something stronger) — dragging an anchor point not only moves the bounding box, it shifts the image itself. Quite disorienting at first! Until you get used to this behavior (and when you do, you're likely to love it), I suggest that you drag the side anchor points rather than the corner anchor points. And drag slowly. Remember, too, that you can click the gear-shaped button in the Options bar and select Use Classic Mode to restore the old-fashioned Crop tool behavior.

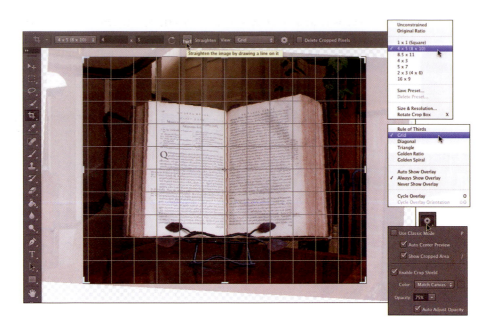

Figure 4-10: The Crop tool overlays can help when composing an image.

When cropping, Photoshop uses the resampling algorithm that you specify in Preferences➪General as the Image Interpolation method. When set to Bicubic Automatic, the Crop tool uses Bicubic Smoother when increasing an image's pixel dimensions and Bicubic Sharper when decreasing the size.

When creating a cropping selection with the Rectangular Marquee tool, you can change the tool's Style pop-up menu (on the Options bar) from Normal to Fixed Ratio or Fixed Size. Generally speaking, use Fixed Ratio and drag the marquee to encompass that part of the image you want to retain. When the selection marquee is how and where you want it, choose Image➪Crop.

Keep in mind that the Image➪Crop command doesn't resample the image — you've just changed the aspect ratio so far — so you need to also choose Image➪Image Size (which is discussed in Chapter 2).

Remembering resolution

Chapter 2 presents you with an in-depth look at resolution as it pertains to digital imaging. As a quick refresher, keep these points in mind when thinking about printing your images:

- **Images themselves have no resolution.** Whether in your camera, on your hard drive, or open in Photoshop, your images consist only of tiny colored squares called *pixels.* The image looks and acts the same within Photoshop (except for adding type), regardless of resolution. An image of 3,000x2,000 pixels at 300 ppi is handled in Photoshop exactly as an image of 3,000x2,000 pixels at 72 ppi.

- **Resolution is an instruction to a printing device.** The resolution value that you assign to an image in your digital camera or in Photoshop's Image Size dialog box is recorded with the image strictly as an instruction to the output device.

- **Resolution measures the size of individual pixels.** A resolution of 300 ppi really means that each pixel will print at a size exactly 1/300 of an inch square. Likewise, 72 ppi equates to each pixel printing at 1/72 of an inch square.

- **Web images use only pixel dimensions.** Web browsers aren't capable of reading the resolution information embedded in your simple graphics by Photoshop. Each image is displayed in the web browser strictly according to the number of pixels in the image.

Controlling color using File⇨Print

In the past few years, reproducing accurate color from monitor to printer has become much easier. Although the process of color management still strikes fear into the hearts of many, the actual need for complex hardware and software to control color is greatly reduced. Why? Simply because computer manufacturers recognized that we, the consumers, wanted better color. Monitors ship from the factory calibrated and accurate. Printers use smaller droplets and better inks. Software does a better job of communicating color.

For most Photoshop users, accurate color is important. After spending hours tweaking an image's appearance on-screen, surely you want the print to look exactly like the monitor. Here's how to get that great color:

1. **When you're ready to output your image, choose Photoshop's File⇨ Print command.**

   A large, one-stop-shopping Print Settings dialog box opens (see Figure 4-11).

2. **Select your printer and the number of copies you want to print.**

   In the Position and Size section, you can center the image within the printer's margins or offset the print. You can also elect to scale the image to fit the paper rather than printing at the image's actual size.

(The Printing Marks, Functions, and PostScript Options sections of the Print Settings dialog box are used almost exclusively by print shops.)

Figure 4-11: Photoshop's Print Settings dialog box offers resizing and color management options.

3. **Set up color management.**

   • In the Color Handling pop-up menu, select Photoshop Manages Colors.

   • In the Printer Profile pop-up menu, choose the printer's profile for the paper on which you're printing. If the Send 16-Bit Data option is available, and your image is in 16-bits/channel mode, you should take advantage of that feature.

   • Select Normal Printing (rather than Hard Proofing), for Rendering Intent, choose Relative Colorimetric, and select the Black Point Compensation check box. (If your prints are too dark, deselect this last option.)

4. **Click Print Settings to disable the printer's color management and to select the proper paper.**

   Because you're doing all your color management in Photoshop, you want to disable all printer-level color management in the printer's own Print dialog box. (Check your printer's User Guide for specific instructions.) You'll also want to make sure that the same paper specified in Photoshop is selected in the printer's Print Settings dialog box.

5. **Print.**

   Clicking the Print button in Photoshop's Print dialog box sends the image to the printer and starts the actual process of putting ink on paper. The Done button saves the choices you've made and closes the Print dialog box.

Don't forget that Bridge offers you a couple of different ways to save paper (and time and money) by printing multiple images on a single sheet of paper. See Chapter 16 for full information.

Considering color management solutions

If your prints don't match your monitor, first evaluate your monitor's settings. Open an image with known color values (you know what the image should look like) in a non-color-managed program. You might, for example, open Microsoft Word and choose Insert⇨Photo⇨Picture from File to add the image `Ducky.tif` from the Samples folder (inside the Photoshop folder) or a downloaded color chart to a blank document. Use the monitor's controls to make that image look the best possible, and then print. If the image prints accurately, great — you're all set.

If the monitor looks great but the print is strange, first try cleaning and calibrating the print head, and then print from Photoshop. And take another look at the Print dialog box to make sure that you're selecting the proper paper and color settings. (Again, refer to the User Guide for your printer for specific instructions.)

If your work (or play) requires extreme color fidelity, a number of companies offer hardware and software that regulate color. You can create custom profiles for monitors, printers, and even scanners and digital cameras. Although not inexpensive, skillful handling of these tools (in accordance with the User Guides!) not only results in better prints, but also reduces the amount of aw-shucks wasted paper and ink from bad output. If you fall into this category, explore the current offerings from X-Rite (`www.xrite.com`), PANTONE (`www.pantone.com`), and Datacolor (`www.datacolor.com`).

Keep in mind that all the color management hardware and software in the world doesn't do you a bit of good if you're not controlling your environment. If your work requires perfect color — not *good,* but *perfect* — you need to take some additional steps. In the office or studio, you need to regulate ambient light so that you have a consistent color-viewing situation, day in and day out, rain or shine, summer and winter. If you have windows, you need shades or drapes that you can close before doing color-critical work. The walls visible behind the monitor and the immediate work area should be neutral in color. (And that means no brightly colored sticky notes on the bezel of your monitor!) You probably need a hood for your monitor and perhaps a D50 (or D65) viewing station in which to evaluate your prints under optimal lighting conditions.

Printing alternatives

Many Photoshop folks use an inkjet printer to put their photos on paper. Although inkjet printers are the most popular and perhaps the most practical, you do have alternatives. If, for example, your work consists mainly of brochures and flyers rather than photos, a color laser printer might better fit your needs. The initial cost of a high-quality color laser printer is generally higher than all except wide-format inkjets, but the cost per page is much lower. Color laser printers generally don't print photographs as well as a mid- to high-end inkjet, and the prints aren't archival (they won't last for a whole lot of years without fading), but such prints might be just fine for sharing snapshots among friends and family. The print options for a color laser printer differ from an inkjet's options. Compare the inkjet options, to the left in Figure 4-12, with those of a color laser printer. Take a look at the User Guide for the specific printer you use to set up your job correctly.

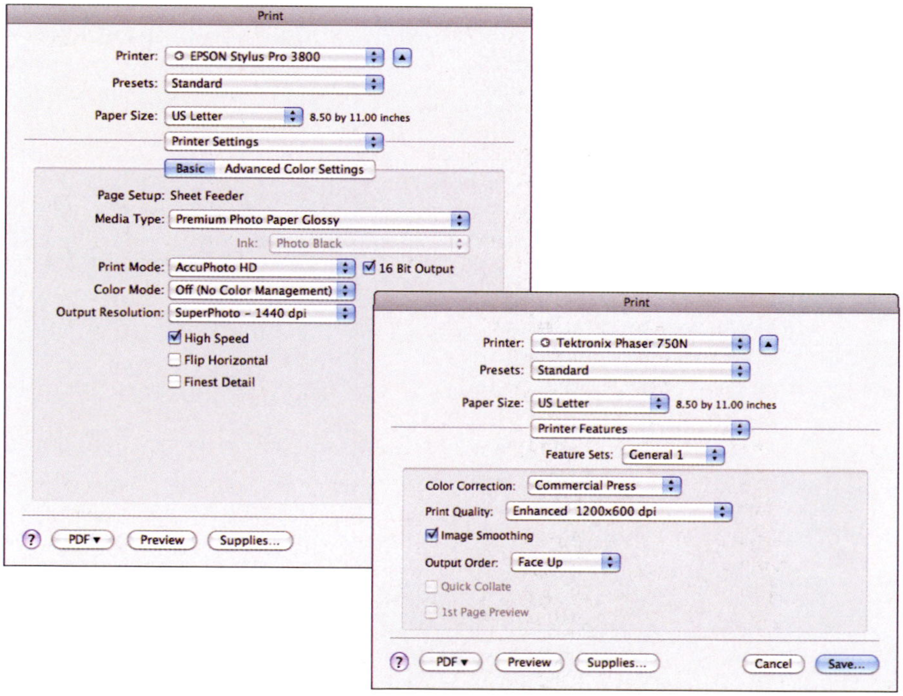

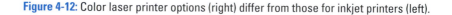

Figure 4-12: Color laser printer options (right) differ from those for inkjet printers (left).

Dye sublimation printers use rolls of film impregnated with dyes to reproduce prints. Prices for these printers range from less than $200 to several thousand dollars. The quality and longevity of the prints is generally tied to the price.

Here's another output alternative available to virtually all Photoshop users. Burn your images in JPEG format (highest quality, 300 ppi) onto a CD and take the CD to the local photo lab. Alternatively, use an online service with which you upload your JPEGs to the service's web service to order prints. (Check with the lab or service to see if you need to use the sRGB color profile for your images.) You'll get back glossy or matte prints at the size(s) requested. And the cost per print can be substantially less than using your inkjet printer. The local photo lab is often a great alternative for stacks of vacation photos and family reunion shots that need to be sent to a whole passel of kin.

Unless your inkjet printer is specifically designed to handle grayscale images, you might want to use a photo lab for such prints. Inkjet printers designed with grayscale in mind output using black ink plus one or more supplemental gray (or "light black") inks to increase the tonal range and ensure adequate detail in your shadows. Inkjets that aren't designed to print grayscale can either print using only black ink (which severely limits the detail and tonal range) or they print with all of the installed inks (which invariably leads to some color tint or color cast in the supposedly neutral grayscale images).

Sharing Your Images

Photoshop and Bridge offer a number of nifty ways to make it easy to share your images with others. Bridge's File⇨Export To command enables you to upload directly to Facebook or Flickr. You could also simply send a CD of JPEG files to a friend or client with instructions to double-click each one to view the images. However, there are certainly more elegant ways to showcase your talents.

Creating PDFs and websites

Portable Document Format (PDF), the native file format of Adobe Acrobat, has become an incredibly useful and near-universal format. It's hard to find a computer that doesn't have Adobe Reader (free software to open and view PDF files) or another PDF-capable program (such as the Mac's Preview), and that helps make PDF a wonderful format for sharing or distributing your images.

You can use Bridge's Output panel to create PDF presentations and multi-page PDFs to send to others for review or to simply show off your magnificent imagery. You can also create stand-alone websites to post to a web server using the Output panel. You'll find more information on these sharing features in Chapter 16.

E-mailing your images

Remember, too, that you can send images via e-mail. Keep in mind, however, if you like these folks enough to send them your images, you probably want to keep their friendship. And to that end, you want to be a responsible e-mailer — you don't want to send out an e-mail attachment so large that it disrupts service for the recipient. ("Hi Marge. You know those images from your vacation that you e-mailed me on Tuesday? They're still trying to download. Yeah, today is Saturday. Anyway, why don't I drive up to Maine and look at the snapshots — it's probably faster than waiting for the e-mail.")

As a general rule, your attached images should rarely if ever total more than 1MB in size (unless you verify through direct communication that everyone on your To list can handle large attachments). Each image should be no more than 550 pixels tall so that it can be viewed in a web browser on most computer (and the most popular tablet) screens. You can certainly use your computer's compression utility to compress one or more images before sending. But if you do compress your attached images, make sure to include instructions to save the compressed file to the hard drive and double-click to expand.

Part II
Easy Enhancements for Digital Images

The 5th Wave   By Rich Tennant

@RKHTENNANT

"Hey— let's put scanned photos of ourselves through a ripple filter and see if we can make ourselves look weird."

*S*ome photos can be printed straight from
the camera without ever seeing the light of
Photoshop. However, most images need at least
some adjustment, and many need a *lot* of adjustment. Here's where you discover how to work
magic on your images.

The range of brightness from black to white is critical for most images. In Chapter 5, you read how
to maximize and adjust that tonal range in your
photos, and how to maximize your use of the
Histogram palette. And there's more to a great
photo than shadows and highlights. Chapter 6
looks at adjusting the color in your images,
making them look as natural as possible. More
and more digital photographers are switching to
the Raw file format because of the control it provides over the final image. Read Chapter 7 for the
Raw lowdown.

Sometimes only part of an image needs to be
adjusted. The key to making precise adjustments,
as you can read in Chapter 8, is to tell Photoshop
where to work with selections and masks. Chapter
9 examines many of the most common problems
in Photoshop (and what to do about them). You
can read about eliminating red-eye, reducing wrinkles, whitening teeth, and minimizing digital noise.

5

Adding Dark Shadows and Sparkling Highlights

*I*t's the difference between an Ansel Adams print and the snapshot of your backyard. It's the difference between premium cable channel shows on your HD television and on your smart phone. It's the difference between a Ferrari and a minivan. It's that *thing* — that special *something* — that tells you that you're looking at the real deal, the genuine article, all that it can be. And it's something that you can do for your images.

When an image really *pops* — when it jumps off the page at you — it's generally because the shadows are dark, the highlights are light, and the colors are rich. I'm sure it's no surprise to you that Photoshop can handle the job. (That's one of the reasons why you bought the program, right?)

In this chapter, I introduce you to the concept of *tonality,* which is the range of brightness in your image. I also introduce to you the various commands that Photoshop offers for you to adjust your image's tonality. A couple of tools even give you pin-point control of shadows and highlights. And along the way, I offer you a look at the Histogram panel — what it tells you, what it *doesn't* tell you, and how to use it best.

Adjusting Tonality to Make Your Images Pop

Most photos look better with a little tweaking. For pictures that look good to begin with, you might still want to perk them up a little with a tonal adjustment. Making the shadows a little darker and the highlights a bit lighter increases your image's perceived *tonal range,* which is sort of the distance between black and white. Take a look at Figure 5-1. It's a pleasant enough snapshot, with decent composition and an interesting subject. But it lacks pizzazz.

With Photoshop, you can darken the shadows and lighten the rest of the image to make it more interesting. By intensifying the difference between what the eye sees as dark and what the eye sees as light in the image, you add some semblance of depth to this simple picture. Comparing Figure 5-1 with Figure 5-2, you can see that one basic tonal adjustment can also make the colors seem richer and even produce a perceived increase in detail and sharpness.

Figure 5-1: A nice snapshot, but not *art.*

You might hear a number of words used for the same concept: the lightness and darkness of your image. Tonality, luminosity, and even brightness can be used virtually interchangeably when you're talking about the general subject. However, you generally use *brightness* when talking about specific pixels and *tonality* when referring to the image as a whole.

Figure 5-2: One simple tonal adjustment darkens, lightens, enriches color, and brings out detail.

Histograms Simplified

In most photographs of general subject matter, your eye sees the darkest neutral (gray) tone as black and the lightest neutral as white. (If the darkest color is obviously purple and the lightest a bright yellow, you probably wouldn't classify the photo's subject matter as "general.") In a given image, the shadow under the shoe might be just a dark gray, and the shirt looks like it might need some bleach, but your mind (in cooperation with your eye) compensates to some degree and lets you see black and white.

For a more accurate look at the tonal range of your image, Photoshop offers the Histogram panel, which displays the distribution of the pixels in your image at various luminosity values. The darker pixels *(shadows)* are stacked at the left end, the lighter pixels *(highlights)* are stacked at the right end, and the rest of the brightness values *(midtones)* are stacked between. The taller a column in the histogram, the more pixels at that luminosity value. Figure 5-3 shows an image with what some semi-experienced folks would call a near-perfect histogram distribution because of the beautiful bell curve centered in the graph.

Figure 5-3: This image has a very even distribution of pixels through the midtones.

As you look at histograms in this chapter and in your own work, keep in mind that the color coding in the histogram shows where there are preponderances of pixels of specific color at certain luminosity values. Where the histogram shows red or green or blue, the pixels at that brightness level are primarily in one channel of an RGB image. The cyan and magenta and yellow areas of the histogram show pixels in two of the RGB channels. When pixels in a specific tonal range appear in all three RGB channels, you'll see gray in the histogram.

Do not be seduced by a histogram distribution! Not every properly exposed image has a bell curve such as that in Figure 5-3. Many perfect images have wildly different histograms. The correct distribution in the histogram depends on two things: the image content and the artistic aims of the image's maker.

Consider, if you will, an image that consists primarily of white pixels, perhaps a beautiful Alpine snow scene or an ugly creepy-crawly thing on porcelain (as you can see in Figure 5-4). Either image has a histogram skewed dramatically to the right — what you call a *high-key* image. Nothing is wrong with the image (despite the histogram); it just happens to have a huge number of light-colored pixels.

Figure 5-4: The histogram is skewed to the right because of the many white pixels. Or maybe it's trying to escape the spider.

Likewise, a *low-key* image has a preponderance of dark pixels, which skews the histogram to the left. Just about any night scene has a very large number of very dark pixels, pulling the distribution to the left in the histogram. But many night scenes also include lights, which produce a spike at the far right end.

Keep in mind, too, that the heights of the individual columns in the histogram area are relative: The tallest goes all the way to the top of the box, and the others are scaled accordingly. For example, an image on a black background — say, a large black background — might have so many pixels in the left-most column that the other columns in the image appear tiny and almost unreadable, like the histogram shown in Figure 5-5.

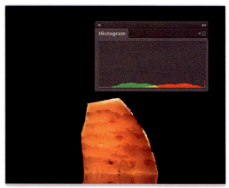

Figure 5-5: Too many pixels in the left-most column make the distribution for the midtones hard to see.

If the histogram is skewed to one end or the other, making it hard to read, you can make a selection within the image and the histogram updates to show information for only the selected area. (Read about making selections in Chapter 8.) If the image has multiple layers or adjustment layers, the little pop-up menu below the histogram (when in Expanded View mode) enables you to specify what layer to calculate.

If you see a little warning triangle to the upper-right of the histogram data in the panel, you're not necessarily seeing accurate information. The histogram is using information from the image cache rather than the image. Click the triangle to update the histogram. And, if you choose Preferences⇔Performance, you can set the Image Cache to 1 (and restart Photoshop) to ensure accurate onscreen display and histograms.

Sometimes a histogram seems to tell you almost nothing worthwhile. For example, take the histogram in Figure 5-6. The image doesn't have a bell curve distribution, with a gentle sloping to either side of the center peak. It's not a high-key image because the pixels aren't mashed together at the right. The image is somewhat low-key, but the histogram doesn't have a huge stack at the left end. It does tell you, however, that there are three distinct ranges of tonality in which you find most of the image's pixels.

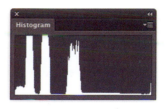

Figure 5-6: This histogram shows only luminosity values rather than distribution by color channel.

Using the menu, opened with the button in the upper-right corner of the Histogram panel, you can change the panel's configuration. (So far in this chapter, I've shown the Compact View in Colors mode, whereas Figure 5-6 shows RGB mode.) In this case, switching to the All Channels View, which shows you a histogram for each color channel, helps solve *The Mystery of the Wacky Histogram*, especially when seen with the image itself, as shown in Figure 5-7. The image contains a large number of pixels of a rather consistent color. If you mixed that color in the kitchen, the recipe would call for one part red, two parts green, and four parts blue.

As you read later in this chapter (in the section "Level-headed you!"), you can use the histogram to help avoid degrading your image while making adjustments, and (as you can read in Chapter 7) it's very important for working with the Camera Raw plug-in. But don't forget about your eyeballs — you don't need the Histogram panel to spot a low-key or high-key image.

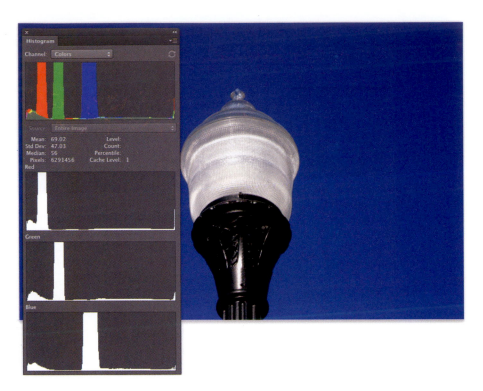

Figure 5-7: The All Channels View shows individual histograms for each color channel.

Using Photoshop's Auto Corrections

Adjusting the tonality of your image can be as simple as selecting one of the Auto commands from Photoshop's Image menu. With many photos, the tonality (and even the color) jump to just the right look for your image. No muss, no fuss — just a great-looking picture with a single command. Auto Color usually does the best job for most images that are close-but-not-perfect. If you don't like the result, simply Undo and use one of Photoshop's more powerful tools.

Although Auto Color (and, to a lesser extent, Auto Tone and Auto Contrast) might do a good job with images that need simple corrections, take an extra few seconds and try the new and improved Auto buttons in Levels and Curves. In the Image⇨Adjustments menu, choose Levels or Curves, click on the Auto button and the new algorithm will search for an adjustment that, when applied, improves both brightness and contrast in all three channels in an RGB image.

If, for some reason, you prefer one of the older algorithms for Levels and Curves, open either dialog box, click the Options button, select your desired algorithm, and then click OK (see Figure 5-8).

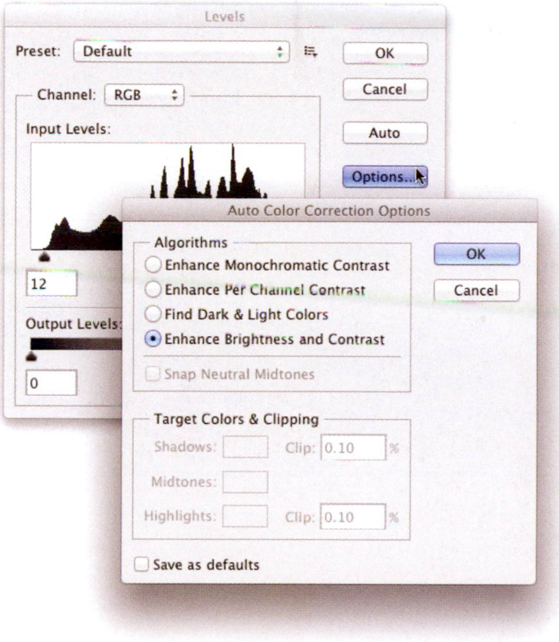

Figure 5-8: The new Enhance Brightness and Contrast algorithm is selected by default.

Levels and Curves and You

Sometimes you need (or simply want) more control than what's offered by the Auto commands. You might have a more demanding problem or a more expansive artistic vision. You might need to make major corrections or create stupendous effects. Photoshop, not surprisingly, offers that sort of control over your image. In fact (and also not surprisingly), you have several features at your disposal to manipulate the tonality of your images. Two of the most commonly used are Levels and Curves, both found in the Adjustments menu at the bottom of the Layers panel (see Chapter 8), the Layer⮆New Adjustment Layer menu, and the Image⮆Adjustments menu.

Defining white and black

The Options button in the Levels (and Curves) dialog box opens a door through which you might never need to walk. However, should your path lead you to that door, I want you to know what lies behind. Neither pit nor tiger awaits you, only the possibility of controlling your highlights and shadows — or making a total mess of your image, of course. (Adobe does a good job of hiding those it-could-cost-me-a-fortune-if-I-screw-it-up features.) The Options button gives you control over the behavior of the Auto button in both Levels and Curves. (I suggest that you leave the algorithm to set the Enhance Brightness and Contrast.) The Options button also lets you define what colors Photoshop should use for the lightest pixels and for the darkest pixels.

That's right: White and black are not always white and black.

Generally speaking, if you print to an inkjet, you want the full tonal range of the printer, so you should leave white and black set to the extremes, as far apart as possible. However, if you're creating gallery prints, you might want to change the definition of "white" from RGB 255/255/255 to RGB 245/245/245 to ensure that you produce 100 percent ink coverage, with no paper showing through in the highlights. Remember that, rather than changing overall the definition of "white" and "black" when preparing a print, you can use a Levels adjustment or adjustment layer, setting the Output Levels slider in the lower-right to 245.

Before I introduce you to those two commands, let me quickly explain and dismiss a couple of other available options, one at the very top of the Adjustments menu, the other at the very bottom. Since the early days of Photoshop, the Brightness/Contrast command has lurked among the Image⇨Adjustments commands. In fact, it was *the* image adjustment command way back when. Now, however, the feature is somewhat lacking in control and sophistication and is perhaps of most use when fine-tuning an alpha channel or layer mask. Although its behavior is *vastly* improved from the early days, it is still a two-slider adjustment. But if you're an old-timer and absolutely *love* that old-time behavior of the Brightness/Contrast adjustment, click on the Use Legacy box to restore the older adjustment performance. (Alpha channels are discussed in Chapter 8, and layer masks appear in Chapter 10.) In both alpha channels and layer masks, you use a grayscale representation to identify specific areas of your image. Brightness/Contrast is perfectly adequate for many adjustments that you might make to those channels.

Also of limited use is the Equalize adjustment. It finds the lightest pixel in the image and calls that *white* and also finds the darkest pixel and calls that *black.* The rest of the pixels in the image are distributed between those values, creating an extended tonal range. In practice, you'll find that the adjustment results in extreme highlights and extreme shadows, with a rather garish image overall as well as a lack of details in the midtones.

Always keep in mind that you don't have to make changes to the *entire* image. If only part of an image needs repair, make a selection of that area before opening the particular adjustment dialog box you want to use. (Read about making selections to isolate areas of your image in Chapter 8.) Say, for example, that you take a beautiful photo of a room in your house — "beautiful" except that the view out the window is far too bright. Isolate the window with a selection, and then use one of your image adjustment commands to tone it down.

Level-headed you!

The Image⇨Adjustments⇨Levels command (⌘+L/Ctrl+L), or adding a Levels adjustment layer (discussed in Chapter 8), gives you control over shadows, highlights, and your image's overall tonality individually. Using a slider with three controls, you adjust the picture both to suit your eye, and with an eye on a histogram for reference. You even have numeric fields in which you can type exact values, should you find the need.

To perform the basic Levels correction, spreading the image's tonality over the full range of values available, you simply drag the slider controls under the histogram in the Levels dialog box inward until they're under the point where the histogram begins to rise in a mountain shape. Ignore those little flat tails that extend outward — they represent individual stray pixels — and drag the little pointers under columns that are at least a few pixels tall. The histogram in the Levels dialog box (as shown in Figure 5-9) is for reference as you make changes, showing changes to the overall luminosity of each pixel. Note, however, that while you work in Levels, the Histogram panel also updates, showing you the changes that will be made to each color channel.

Dragging the middle slider in Levels to the right moves the bulk of the histogram toward the left, making the overall appearance of the image slightly darker. Dragging the middle slider to the left lightens the overall image.

Also note the Output Levels slider in Figure 5-9, which you generally use only when preparing an image for a gallery print or for a commercial printing press that requires you to compress the image's tonal range. Otherwise, ignore Output Levels. And make a mental note of that pop-up menu at the top of the Levels dialog box — you can apply Levels to each color channel of your image individually, changing this tonal adjustment tool to a color correction feature. (Fixing the color in your image is covered in Chapter 6.)

When you're working in Levels (or just about any dialog box), remember that holding down the Option/Alt key changes the Cancel button to Reset. When you click Reset, all values in the dialog box are restored to the defaults, letting you start over without having to cancel and reselect the command.

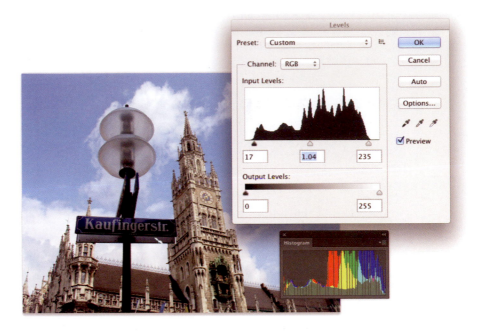

Figure 5-9: Compare the Levels histogram and the Histogram panel.

Earlier in this chapter, I mention that you can use the Histogram panel to avoid introducing problems into the image. Note in Figure 5-9 that the Histogram panel shows slight gaps appearing among the columns. Technically called *posterization,* these gaps represent tonal values that are being squished together into a single value. The pixels at one brightness level are being shifted to the next higher or the next lower value, leaving that empty column in the Histogram. Is this a problem? No, as long as you don't see wide gaps, representing a number of consecutive tonal values not in use. (Extensive posterization ruins the subtle transitions between colors in your image.) And *that's* why you want to keep an eye on the Histogram panel — to make sure you're not creating wide gaps in the histogram and noticeable posterization in your image.

Posterization is rarely a problem with an image captured in and processed in 16-bit color, such as a Raw photo brought into Photoshop through Camera Raw. If, however, you shoot JPEG (which requires 8-bit color), here's an easy way to minimize that posterization, one that lets you make your Levels adjustment, but keep a pretty histogram that doesn't show posterization. Immediately after using Levels, choose Edit⇨Fade Levels and change the blending mode from Normal to Luminosity. As you see in Figure 5-10, the posterization is greatly reduced with a minimal change in the effect of the

Levels adjustment. Remember that the Fade command is available only *immediately* after applying an adjustment (or filter or tool) — you can't even use the Save command between. (Read more about the Fade command in Chapter 15.)

Figure 5-10: Change the Levels adjustment blending mode to Luminosity with the Fade dialog box.

Tonal corrections with the eyedroppers

The Levels dialog box (and the Curves dialog box, too) offers another way to make tonal corrections to your image — sort of a half-automated technique, using the three eyedroppers in the right side of the dialog box. Open your image, open the Levels dialog box, and correct both tonality and color in your image with three little clicks:

1. **Click the left eyedropper on something that should be black.**

   This might be a shadow, a piece of clothing, or the tire of a car. Generally, you click something in the image that's already quite dark.

2. **Click the right eyedropper on something that should be white.**

   A cloud, the bride's dress, perhaps an eye . . . all are likely targets for the highlight eyedropper. You usually click something that's already quite light.

3. **Click the middle eyedropper on something that should be gray.**

   Click something that should be neutral in color (*should be*, not *already is*). It doesn't have to be mid gray, just something that should be neutral.

This reduces or eliminates any unwanted color cast in the image. If you don't like the result, click somewhere else in the image. Keep clicking until the colors in the image look right.

In Figure 5-11, the shadow under the bridge, the splash of water, and the weathered wood of the bridge itself provide excellent targets for the three eyedroppers.

Figure 5-11: Use the eyedroppers in Levels to set the black and white points; then neutralize your image's colors.

Here's another way to adjust color using Levels. Duplicate the image layer and apply the Blur⇨Average filter. The layer becomes a solid color. Open the Levels dialog box. Click in the layer with the middle eyedropper and click OK. Delete that blurred layer. This technique doesn't work with every image (such as extremely bright, super-saturated images), but it does a great job on most.

Adjusting your curves without dieting

One step up from Levels in complexity, and about five steps ahead in terms of image control, is Image⇨Adjustments⇨Curves (⌘+M/Ctrl+M). The Curves dialog box has a pair of slider controls (similar to the left and right sliders in Levels) to easily control the endpoints of your shadows and highlights. The curve line itself gives you control over various parts of the tonal range independently. Curves also offers eyedroppers for tonal and color correction. They're used the same way you use the eyedroppers in Levels.

At the very beginning of this chapter, I show you how a simple tonal adjust-ment can add some drama and some interest to a rather bland image. Figure 5-12 shows you the simple Curves adjustment that I applied to that image. Dragging the curve downward in the shadows makes them darker; dragging upward for the highlights makes them brighter. The *midtones* (that section of the tonal range between shadows and highlights) have improved contrast using this adjustment.

Figure 5-12: A simple S-curve adjustment makes the image more dramatic.

When you first open the Curves dialog box or add a Curves adjustment layer, you see a graph with a diagonal line running from an anchor point in the lower left to another in the upper right. You can click and drag that line up or down (not sideways) to add anchor points and make changes in the curve (and in your image). By default, the shadows are in the lower left, so drag-ging down will darken, and dragging up will lighten. (In the Curves Display Options area, switching from Light to Pigment/Ink will reverse the shadows/highlights. Use this option when preparing CMYK images for page layout programs.) You can add more than a dozen anchor points to the curve — although you generally need only between one and three new points.

Most snapshots can benefit from a slight tweak in Curves. Click at the inter-section of the first vertical and horizontal gridlines in the lower left (the *three-quarter tones*) and drag down slightly. The Input field should read 64, and the Output field should be somewhere between 55 and 60 for a shot that looks pretty good to start. Next, click at the intersection of the grid lines in the upper right (the *quarter tones*) and drag up slightly. The Input field should show 192, and the Output field can be anywhere from 195 to 205. This is called a basic *S-curve*.

Both the Curves and Levels dialog boxes offer you the Load and Save options using the menu button to the right of the Preset menu. If there's a correction that you'll use more than once or a correction that needs to be precise time after time, use Save. Then, later, you can click Load to apply that adjustment to another image. If, for example, you used the wrong setting in your camera while taking a series of shots all under the same lighting conditions, they probably all need the same correction. Make the adjustment once, save it, and then apply it to the other images with the Load button.

If you want to correct a specific area in the image, move the cursor into the image window (where it appears as the Eyedropper tool). Hold down the mouse button and you'll see a circle on the curve, telling you where those pixels fall in the tonal range. To add an anchor point there ⌘+click/Ctrl+click in the image.

Curves offers the option to adjust the curve by clicking and dragging right in the image window. Activate the on-screen adjustment option by clicking the tool to the lower-left of the grid in the Curves dialog box (or to the upper-left of the grid when adding a Curves adjustment through the Properties panel). With the on-screen adjustment option active, click in the image window on an area that needs improvement and drag upward to lighten or downward to darken (see Figure 5-13). The adjustment is applied to the entire image or selection, not just the area where you click. (Working with adjustments layers in the Properties panel is discussed in Chapter 8.)

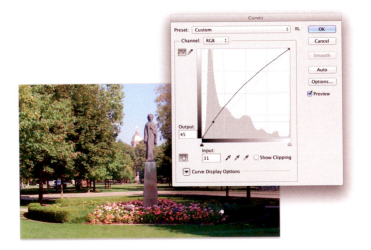

Figure 5-13: Drag up to lighten, down to darken. Adjustments are applied throughout the image.

When your curve has multiple anchor points, the active anchor point shows as a filled-in square. Deselected anchor points are hollow squares. For precision, you can use the arrow keys on your keyboard to move the active anchor point, or you can type specific values in the Input field (starting position for the anchor point) and Output field (where you want the anchor point to go).

Option+click/Alt+click in the grid area to toggle between a 4x4 grid and a 10x10 grid or expand the Curve Display Options and use the two grid buttons to switch back and forth. And, rather than clicking and dragging on the curve, you can activate the Pencil tool and draw your curve by hand (as shown with a Curves adjustment in the Adjustments panel in Figure 5-14). When hand-drawing your curve, the Smooth button is available, too, to ensure that the transitions in your tonal adjustments aren't too severe.

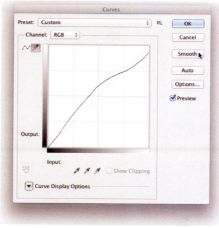

Figure 5-14: Hand-draw a curves adjustment with the Pencil tool.

Grabbing Even More Control

The Image⇨Adjustments menu in Photoshop includes a couple more extremely powerful ways to work with tonality in your images. You can use the Shadow/Highlight adjustment to isolate and change whatever range of dark and light pixels you want. By specifying what range of tonal values that you want to be considered dark or light, you control how broadly or narrowly your change is applied. The Exposure feature lets you change the overall tonality of the image, much as if you'd taken the photo with a different camera setting. And don't forget about making spot corrections with the Dodge and Burn tools!

The Image⇨Adjustments⇨HDR Toning command is designed — like the Exposure adjustment — to be used with 32-bit/channel high dynamic range images. You can read about HDR (and HDR Toning) in Chapter 20.

The Shadow/Highlight and Exposure adjustments are *not* the same as working with Raw images in the Camera Raw plug-in (see Chapter 7). Camera Raw works with unprocessed image data, the so-called *digital negative.* Using Photoshop's Adjustment commands, you're working with image data that has already been manipulated in the camera, in Photoshop, or both. When working with unprocessed data in Camera Raw, you truly have control over the exposure, the shadows, the highlights, and much more.

The Shadow/Highlight adjustment is not available as an adjustment layer. Changes that you make with the Shadow/Highlight command are a permanent part of your image. However, if you convert the layer to a Smart Object, Shadow/Highlight can be applied as a Smart Filter. (Smart Objects are introduced in Chapter 10 and Smart Filters are discussed in Chapter 15.)

Using Shadow/Highlight

The Shadow/Highlight adjustment is designed to rescue two specific sorts of images — you've seen them (and maybe taken them): The background is perfectly exposed, but the subject in the foreground is in horrible shadow. Or, equally bad, the background looks great, but the subject is washed out by a strong flash. (See both examples in Figure 5-15.) By controlling the shadows and highlights separately from the rest of the image, this feature helps you restore more balance to the image.

Figure 5-15: Shadow/Highlight does a rather good job with these very common problems.

The default settings in Shadow/Highlight are intended to repair backlighting problems, as you see on the left in Figure 5-15. When the foreground lacks detail because of flash (as you can see in the top dog image on the right), minimize changes to the shadows and drag the Highlights slider to the right. And, as shown in Figure 5-16, with Show More Options selected, Shadows/ Highlights gives you incredible control over images that have problems at *both* ends of the tonal range.

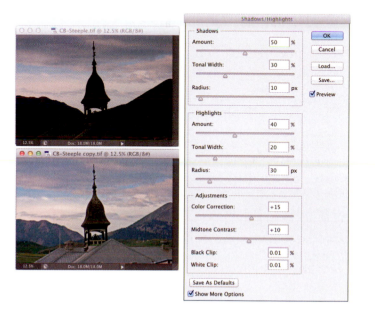

Figure 5-16: Some images need help for both shadows and highlights.

In the Shadows/Highlights dialog box, the Shadows slider lightens the darker areas of your image, and the Highlights slider darkens the lighter areas. Generally, you'll use one slider or the other to fix a specific problem in an image, but you can use both if you need to lighten shadows and tone down highlights in the same image.

When you enable the Show More Options check box, Shadow/Highlight has a rather intimidating set of controls. Not to worry! It's actually pretty simple:

✔ **Amount:** For both Shadows and Highlights, the Amount slider is how much of a correction you're making. This is the nuts and bolts of the Shadow/Highlight adjustment. For a backlit subject, you'll use the Shadows slider a lot and not the Highlights slider. When working with a washed-out subject, you'll probably move the Shadows slider to 0% and work with the Highlights slider.

- **Tonal Width:** Use the Tonal Width sliders to specify how much of the image's tonal range you want to include as shadows or highlights. If you drag either Tonal Width slider to 100%, you're working on the entire tonal range of the image — not a particularly appropriate job for Shadow/Highlight (use Curves instead). The default of 50% is rather too high most of the time. Instead, start your adjustment with a range of perhaps 20% and fine-tune from there.

- **Radius:** You adjust the Radius sliders to tell Shadow/Highlight which pixels should be identified as being in the shadow or highlight. With too low a Radius setting, an individual black pixel stuck in the middle of a light area in your image might get classified as a shadow area. Too high a setting has a tendency to apply the adjustment to the entire image. Generally speaking, start with a Radius of perhaps 10 pixels for very small images and 30 pixels for large digital photos. After adjusting your Amount and Tonal Width sliders, move the Radius slider back and forth while watching some of the smaller patches of shadow or highlight (whichever you're correcting) to make sure that those areas are being included in the adjustment.

- **Color Correction/Brightness:** This slider changes its name to match your image's color mode. When working with a color image, you see Color Correction. When you apply Shadow/Highlight to a grayscale image, the slider's name changes to Brightness. Don't bother with this slider until you make your Amount adjustment. In a color image, lightening the shadows or darkening the highlights shows the actual color of the pixels in those areas. Use this slider to increase (drag to the right) or decrease (drag to the left) the saturation of those pixels. Remember that Color Correction works only on the pixels that you identify with the Tonal Width and Radius sliders. (If you set both sets of Tonal Width and Radius sliders to 0%, Color Correction has no effect on the image at all.) When you correct a grayscale image, on the other hand, the Brightness slider affects all pixels except those that are already pure white or pure black.

- **Midtone Contrast:** You can increase or decrease the contrast throughout the image with the Midtone Contrast slider. Much like clicking in the middle of the curve in the Curves dialog box and dragging up or down, you adjust the whole range of your image, including the shadows and highlights. When the overall appearance of your image needs improvement, start with Midtone Contrast and then work with your shadows and highlights individually.

✔ **Clip:** Most of the time, you don't want to change the clipping values. *Clipping* takes pixels that are *almost* black and forces them to pure black, or it takes pixels that are *almost* white and forces them to pure white. Clipping your shadows or highlights reduces those subtle differences in color that provide the detail in the shadows and highlights. When would you want to clip shadows or highlights? When you don't care about detail in those areas of your image and need more contrast through the midtones.

Changing exposure after the fact

Photoshop also offers the Exposure feature in the Image⇨Adjustments menu. It simulates how the image would have looked if you changed the exposure setting on your camera before clicking the shutter. Think of it as an across-the-board adjustment of tonality in the image or within a selection in the image. The Offset and Gamma Correction sliders are designed primarily to work with very high-bit images (the special 32-bit/channel high dynamic range images), and you likely will find them too sensitive to be of much use for most images.

Using Photoshop's toning tools

You have a couple more ways to work with tonality in Photoshop — the toning tools. These two brush-using tools let you paint corrections on your image, giving you incredible control over the appearance. Select the Burn tool to darken or the Dodge tool to lighten. Select a brush tip in the Options bar and drag the tool in your image to apply the correction. (You can read about controlling the brush-using tools and that incredibly powerful Brush panel in Chapter 14.) In Figure 5-17, you see the Burn tool darkening a specific area of the fence on the right.

The Dodge tool is great for minimizing (without removing) shadows in an image. You'll find it particularly useful for reducing wrinkles in faces and other such jobs that require lightening specific areas of an image. Figure 5-18 compares the original (left) with a working copy in which I'm using the Dodge tool to reduce the appearance of the wrinkles. By reducing rather than eliminating those wrinkles completely, I retain the character of the man's face as well as prevent that phony, just-out-of-plastic-surgery look.

Figure 5-17: "Painting" the fence with the Burn tool. Where is Tom Sawyer when I need him?

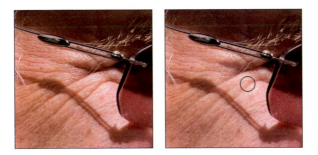

Figure 5-18: Use the Dodge tool to minimize wrinkles without removing them.

In almost all circumstances when working with the Dodge and Burn tools, you should activate the Protect Tones option in the Options bar. With this option selected, the tools do a much better job of protecting color and retaining detail in shadows and highlights. To the right in the Options bar is a button you can use to enable pressure sensitivity when you're working with a Wacom tablet, overriding any pressure-sensitivity setting in the Brush panel.

For most of the work that you do with the Dodge and Burn tools, the default Exposure setting of 50% is *way* too strong. In the Options bar, reduce the Exposure to about 15–20% for most work. And unless you're specifically working on lightening shadows or toning down highlights, set the tools' Range to Midtones in the Options bar.

6

Making Color Look Natural

*I*n the end (and the middle and the beginning), your image in Photoshop is nothing but little squares of color. Each square — each pixel — can be exactly one color. Which color for which square is up to you. I'll say it again: There is no car or circle or tree or Uncle Bob in your Photoshop image — just a bunch of little squares of color.

In this chapter, I explain how those squares of color are formulated, how Photoshop works with those formulations, and — most important — how you can manipulate the colors of those squares. Toward the end of the chapter, you read about one of the biggest color-related challenges in Photoshop: achieving accurate skin color.

What Is Color in Photoshop?

Photoshop works with digital images (including digital photos, images that have been digitized with a scanner, and artwork that you create from scratch in Photoshop). The *digits* are the computer code used to record the image's information. The number of pixels, the color of each pixel, and any associated information are all recorded in a series of zeros and ones on your hard drive. Color, therefore, is nothing more than numbers — at least as far as Photoshop and your computer are concerned. For you and me, however, color is far more than binary code on a hard drive. It's the image, the artwork, the message. The artwork is the color, and color is the artwork, pixel by pixel.

Color modes, models, and depths

Photoshop records the color of each pixel in your image in any of several different ways. Every pixel in any given image has all color recorded in a single *color mode,* which is the actual color format for the image file. While working with your image, however, you can define specific colors in any of a variety of *color models,* which are sort of the formula or recipes with which you mix color. And an image can have only one *color depth,* which is the limitation on the number of colors in an image.

Before I get into too many details, you need to understand one of the basic concepts of color: *gamut.* Consider gamut to be the range of colors that can be theoretically reproduced in a specific color mode or with a specific color profile. A wide gamut, therefore, has many more colors available than does a limited gamut. Those extra colors are generally the brighter, more vibrant colors . . . the ones that make an image come alive. The red/green/blue (RGB) color mode generally offers you a wider range of colors than does cyan/magenta/yellow/black (CMYK). See, for example, the comparison in Figure 6-1, paying particular attention to the purples, oranges, and yellows. And keep in mind that the specific *color profile* (the working space that you select; see Chapter 4) also has an impact on the colors in your image.

Which color mode should you choose?

If you'll be printing to an inkjet printer, sending photos to a lab for prints, or posting your image on the web, you need RGB color mode. (Despite the CMYK inks that you load into your inkjet printer, the printer's software expects and must receive RGB color data.) If you're prepping an image for inclusion in an InDesign document destined for a commercial offset press, you need CMYK. You select the image's color mode from the Image⇨Mode menu. That's the simple summary. Here's a bit more detail, presented in the order in which you're likely to need the various color modes:

- ✔ **RGB:** RGB is the color mode for digital photos, computer monitors, the World Wide Web, and inkjet printers. All colors are recorded as proportions of the three component colors, red, green, and blue. RGB color is recorded in the three color channels (described a bit later in this chapter). RGB is an *additive* color mode — that is, the more of each component color you add, the closer you get to white.

- ✔ **CMYK:** CMYK is used primarily for printing on a commercial offset press, but you might need it for a color laser printer or a high-end inkjet printer with which you use a RIP (*raster image processor,* which is a specialized bit of hardware or software that lets your inkjet pretend it's a printing press). CMYK is the color mode of magazines, books, and other mass-produced printed material, such as the example in Figure 6-2. CMYK is a *subtractive* color mode — that is, the less of each component color you have, the closer you are to white.

Figure 6-1: A wide-gamut image (on the left) and the same picture with a smaller gamut.

✔ **Grayscale:** When most people talk about a black-and-white photo, they really mean grayscale. The image does contain black and white but also a wide range of grays in between. You might use grayscale mode for web-based images or for prints. Keep in mind that unless your inkjet printer is designed to reproduce grayscale images with black and gray inks (or black and light-black inks), you probably won't be happy with

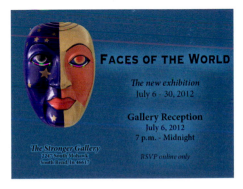

Figure 6-2: You typically use CMYK images for bulk-print materials.

grayscale output. Using just one black ink doesn't reproduce the full range of grays in the image. Using the color inks adds a tint to the image. You do have an alternative for grayscale images: Send them to the local photo lab for printing.

✔ **Indexed Color:** Using a *color table,* or a list of up to 256 specific colors, Indexed Color mode is for the web. You save GIF and PNG-8 images in Indexed Color, but only those file formats require such a limited number of colors. Things like buttons on your web page, which need only a couple of colors, should be created as GIFs using Indexed Color mode. That keeps the file size down, reducing the amount of space the image requires on your web server and also speeding the *download time* (how long it takes for the image to appear on your site-visitor's monitor).

✔ **Lab:** Also known as *L*a*b* and *CIELAB* (and pronounced either *lab,* as the dog or a research facility, or verbally spelled out, as *el-ay-be*), this is a color mode that you might use when producing certain special effects or using certain techniques in Photoshop, but it's not one in which you'll save your final artwork. The three channels in a (or "an") Lab image are

   • *Lightness,* which records the brightness of each pixel

   • *a,* which records the color of the pixel on a green-to-red axis

   • *b,* which records each pixel's color value on a blue-to-yellow axis

You shouldn't try to print Lab images on an inkjet or post them on your web site. You might see (not in *this* book!) a tip that you should convert your RGB or CMYK images to Lab mode before using one of Photoshop's Sharpen filters. Bah! Apply the Sharpen filter, choose Edit➪Fade Unsharp Mask (or Fade Smart Sharpen — the Fade command changes its name to match the last-used filter), and change the blending mode from Normal to Luminosity. Same result, less work, and less potential for degradation of your image.

✔ **Duotone:** Duotone (including tritone and quadtone) is a very specialized color mode, exclusively for commercial printing, that uses only two (or three or four) inks spread throughout your image. Although that might sound good for an inkjet printer, in fact, Duotone is not an acceptable color mode for inkjets. Duotone images require that specific premixed inks are poured into the printing presses, which isn't something that you can do to your inkjet.

✔ **Multichannel:** Like Duotone, the Multichannel color mode is restricted to commercial printing because it depends on specific premixed colors of ink that are applied to the paper. Unlike Duotone, in which the inks are generally spread across the page, Multichannel images use certain inks in certain areas. You might need Multichannel mode when creating a logo for a client.

✔ **Bitmap:** Bitmap color mode is *true* black and white (as you see in Figure 6-3). Each pixel is either black or white. The placement of the black and white pixels produces shading, but the image doesn't really have any gray pixels. You might use Bitmap mode to create images for some wireless devices, use on the web, or commercial print, but that's about it.

Figure 6-3: Bitmap images contain only black and white pixels; no grays, no colors.

Converting between color modes or gamuts (done with the Image⇨Mode menu) can reduce the quality of your image by compressing variations of a color into a single color value. You would not, for example, want to convert from RGB (which has a comparatively large number of colors available) to CMYK (with a more restricted color gamut) and then back to RGB. After colors are compressed by a conversion, you can't restore their original values by converting back to a wider gamut.

Does a color model make a difference?

Although the image itself has a single color mode, you can use any of the available color models when defining a color in Photoshop. Say, for example, that you're preparing to use the Brush tool to paint some artistic elements for your latest project. The project is in RGB mode because you'll be printing it with your inkjet printer. You can use the Color panel to define your foreground color any way you please — RGB, CMYK, Grayscale, Lab, or even HSB (hue/saturation/brightness, which isn't available as a color mode, just a color model). It doesn't matter how you set up the Color panel, which you do through the panel's menu, as shown in Figure 6-4. When you add the color to your image, Photoshop uses the nearest RGB (or CMYK) equivalent.

Figure 6-4: Choose your preferred color model from the Color panel menu.

Notice that the Color panel menu in Figure 6-4 doesn't list Duotone or Multichannel. Those are color modes only, not color models. A couple of other things to note about working with the Color panel: The warning triangle visible in Figure 6-4 in the lower-left corner of the panel indicates that the selected color is outside the CMYK color gamut. (Clicking the swatch to the right would select the nearest equivalent color. If, that is, you were actually working in CMYK mode.) Also note that the background swatch is selected in the panel, highlighted with a black outline — click the foreground swatch to make changes to the foreground color.

You can also select or define a color using the Color Picker, which you open by clicking the foreground or background color swatches near the bottom of the Toolbox or in the Color panel. The Color Picker is explained in detail in Chapter 14.

Why should you worry about color depth?

Color depth is the actual number of different colors that you have available. (Remember that each pixel can be only one color at any time.) When you work in *8-bit per channel* color, simply called *8-bit color,* each of the component colors is recorded with exactly 8 bits of information per pixel in the computer file. (At the beginning of this chapter, I mention digits. These are the actual numbers — the zeros and ones recorded on the hard drive to track each pixel's color.) In an 8-bit RGB image, each pixel's color is recorded with three strings of eight characters. When you work with *16-bit per channel,* or *16-bit color*, each of the component colors is recorded with 16 characters. The larger numbers mean more possible ways to record each color, which means more possible variations of color (as well as files that take up more space on your hard drive).

What that means to you, in practical terms, is possibly a better-looking image when working in 16-bit color. You'll have smoother transitions between colors throughout your image, no *banding* in gradients (those annoying areas in a gradient where you can actually see one shade of a color stop and the next shade of that color start), and no splotchy shadows. *Posterization,* which I explain in Chapter 5, is the degradation of your image's appearance when similar colors are forced to the same color, making transitions between colors more abrupt. Many tonal and color corrections that produce posterization in your 8-bit images won't harm a 16-bit image in the least. Take a look at Figure 6-5. To the left, the Histogram panel shows the result of a Levels adjustment. When the same adjustment is applied to an 8-bit version of the image, posterization becomes visible in the Histogram panel (represented by the gaps in the histogram).

Some of the top inkjet printers, when printing on a Mac, can process and use 16-bit color — but unless Photoshop's Print dialog box offers the Send 16-Bit Data option (shown in Figure 6-5), you won't be using more than 8 bits of color data.

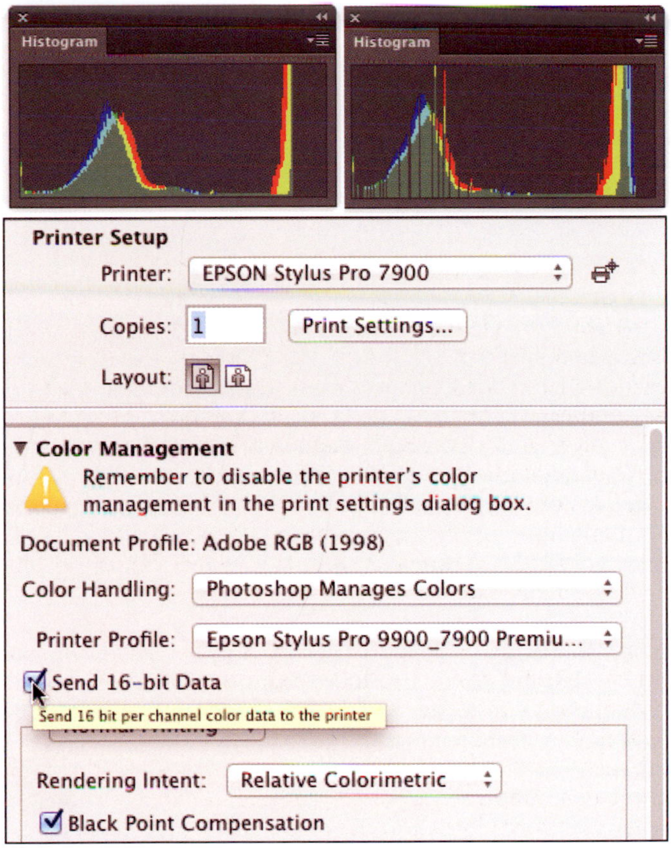

Figure 6-5: Compare the Histogram panels to see posterization (right).

So, should you use 16-bit color all the time? No. You can't post a 16-bit image on the web, and 16-bit color is rarely used for CMYK images. Digital photos taken in JPEG format are 8-bit because that file format doesn't support 16-bit color. And unless you're using a 16-bit capable inkjet printer, you won't see any improvement in the final print. If you shoot in 16-bit color, typically using a Raw file format, it makes sense to keep the image in 16-bit color. Do all the processing in 16-bit color, save the file as a 16-bit image, and send the 16-bit data to your inkjet printer. If you'll be sending the file off to a print lab or eventually posting the image on a website, create a copy of the file and convert the copy to 8-bit/channel color through the Image⇨Mode menu.

You might consider converting an 8-bit image to 16-bit color as part of a larger project, perhaps one that includes a large gradient as part of the artwork. But, generally speaking, if the image was captured in 8-bit color, keep it in 8-bit color; if the image was captured in 16-bit color, keep it in 16-bit color.

One other note on color depth: Photoshop can work with 32-bit/channel images. These monstrous files are called *high dynamic range* (HDR) images and are typically constructed by combining different exposures of the same photo. Chapter 20 takes a look at HDR.

Recording color in your image

All your image's color data is saved in the Channels panel. When you're working with RGB or CMYK images, each color channel holds information for one of the component colors (red, green, blue or cyan, magenta, yellow, black). Each channel is a grayscale version of the image as a whole, using shades of gray, from white to black, to indicate where that channel's color appears (and how strongly) in the image. In RGB images, the lighter the pixel in a channel, the more of that color. When you work with a CMYK image, the light-dark in a channel is reversed, with darker areas showing where more of that color is applied.

Note that the Blue channel of an RGB image and the Yellow channel of a CMYK copy of that image will be nearly identical — "lots of blue" in an RGB image is comparable to "a lack of yellow" in a CMYK image. Similar RGB/CMYK relationships hold true with the Red/Cyan channels and the Green/Magenta channels.

Making Color Adjustments in Photoshop

Sometimes you have an image that needs some help in the color department. It might have been shot with an incorrect camera setting, it might have a *color cast* (an unwanted tint of a specific color), or it might just be dull and dingy. Photoshop provides you with an incredible array of commands and tools to make the colors in your images look just right. You'll hear the term *color correction* being tossed about, but not all images have incorrect color. Some have very good color that can be *great* color. Instead of color *correction,* I like to think in terms of color *improvement.* And just about every image can use a little tweaking to improve its color.

"Here, Spot!": What is a spot color?

Spot colors in your image are printed by using premixed inks of exactly that color. (I'm talking commercial printing press here, not your run-of-the-mill inkjet printer.) To properly prepare a spot color for press, it needs to be in its own *spot channel,* which is a separate color channel in which you show where and how the ink will be applied. (Channels in your image are eventually used to create the actual printing plates that pick up ink and put it on paper.) Because spot channels are used with CMYK images, *dark* represents *more.* Where you need the spot color at 100% strength, the spot channel should be black. In areas where you want only a light tint of the spot color, use a light gray.

You create your spot channel by selecting the Spot Channel command from the Channels panel menu. Click the color swatch in the New Spot Channel dialog box to open the color libraries. (If you see the regular Color Picker, click the Color Libraries button.) Select the appropriate *book* (collection of colors; see the figure here) for your project, and then select your color. Click OK in the New Spot Channel dialog box to accept the color, do *not* change the name of the spot channel, and then click OK. You can now paint, fill, or copy/paste into that new channel.

When saving images with spot channels, you can use the PSD file format (if the image will be placed into an InDesign document), PDF, TIFF, or DCS 2.0. Check with the person handling the layout or the print shop to see which is required.

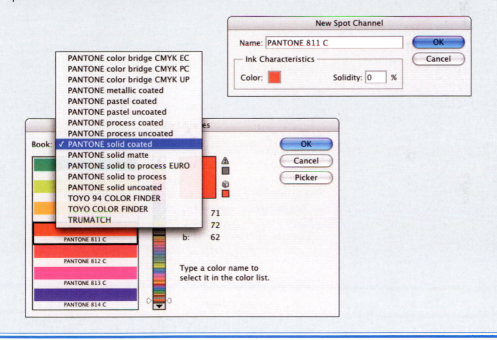

How do you know when the color is right? Your primary tool for the job is in your head. Literally. Make your decisions based primarily on what your eyes tell you. Sure, you can check the Info panel and the Histogram panel to make sure that your shadows are black and your highlights are white, but adjust your images until they look good to you — until you're satisfied with the color.

That little bomb symbol to the left of this paragraph is a little scary, but it does get your attention, doesn't it? This isn't a your-computer-will-blow-up sort of warning but more of a you-don't-want-to-waste-your-time-and-effort warning. Do your tonal adjustments before you start working with the image's colors. Go through the procedures in Chapter 5 first and then use the techniques here. Why? If you get perfect hue and saturation and then start making tonal adjustments, you're likely to knock your colors out of whack again. And, of course, there's also the possibility that adjusting your image's tonality will make the colors look perfect!

Watching the Histogram and Info panels

As you work with your various color adjustments in Photoshop, a couple of panels can help you track the changes you're making. You show the Info and Histogram panels by selecting them in Photoshop's Window menu. Keeping an eye on your Info and Histogram panels while you're dragging sliders and entering numbers into various fields can help you spot potential problems as they develop.

The Histogram is useful for tracking changes in the distribution of pixels at various tonal ranges. You can read more about it in Chapter 5. The Info panel, while you've got an adjustment dialog box open, shows you "before" and "after" color values. Wherever you move the cursor in the image window, the Info panel shows you the result of the adjustment — the consequences of your action, so to speak. You can click in the image with the Color Sampler (or Shift-click with the Eyedropper tool) to add up to four markers in the image. The color values under those color samplers appear in the Info panel and, like the cursor location, show before/after values as you're making changes, as shown in Figure 6-6. (Take a look at the end of this chapter for more info on the Info panel.)

Choosing color adjustment commands

Photoshop offers almost two dozen different commands that you can use to improve the appearance of your images, all of which are easily accessed through the Image➪Adjustments menu (as you see in Figure 6-7). Some have specialized purposes, and some are extremely versatile, but all are worth understanding so that you choose the most appropriate feature for the problem staring at you from the screen. Most (but not all) of the commands that I discuss here can be added to your images as an *adjustment layer,* which gives you added flexibility. (Adjustment layers are discussed in detail in Chapter 8.)

Figure 6-6: Each of the crosshairs in the image is tracked in the Info panel, as is the location of the cursor.

Auto Tone, Auto Contrast, Auto Color

The three "auto" adjustments, found in the Image menu rather than Image➪Adjustments, are one-click solutions to many image problems. However, the improved algorithms used by the Auto buttons in the Levels and Curves dialog boxes are usually worth the additional couple of clicks.

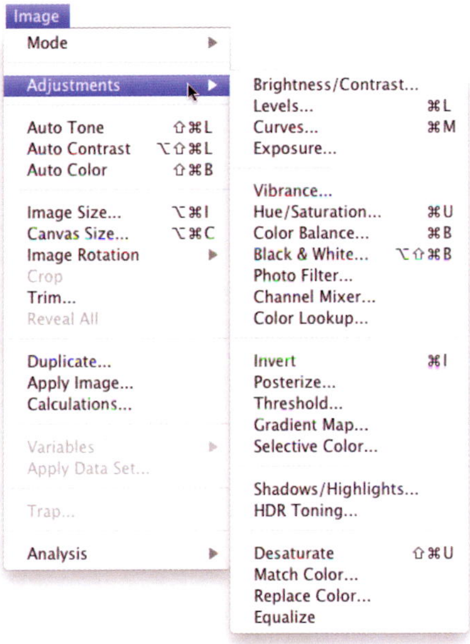

Brightness/Contrast, Levels, Curves, Exposure

These commands are generally used to work with tonality rather than color (see Chapter 5). However, you can select an individual channel in Levels or Curves, as shown in Figure 6-8, to adjust color in an image. Keep in mind that changes to an individual color channel are reflected throughout all colors in an image.

Figure 6-7: Photoshop's flexibility is truly evident in the Image➪Adjustments menu.

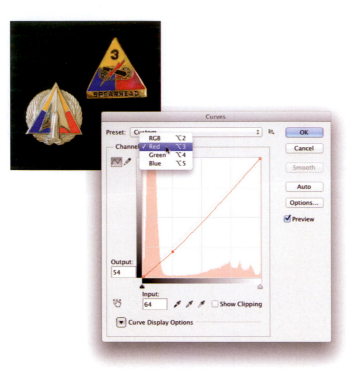

Figure 6-8: Correct each channel individually with Curves to adjust color in your image.

Vibrance

The Vibrance adjustment gives you control over both vibrance (the saturation of near-neutral colors) and saturation (the saturation of colors throughout the image). You can increase Vibrance to make the near-neutral colors more saturated, or you can reduce Vibrance to make those colors even more neutral, while increasing Saturation to make the brighter colors in your image stand out even more.

Hue/Saturation

Often overlooked and rarely exploited to the fullest, Hue/Saturation is a very powerful tool. Using the three sliders together, you can adjust the hue to eliminate a color cast, increase saturation so that your colors appear richer and more vibrant, and adjust lightness to improve your image's tonality. (See Figure 6-9.) Keep in mind that when you adjust something that's very dark, start with the Lightness slider so that you can evaluate the other changes (Hue and Saturation) properly. Remember, too, that you can apply Hue/

Saturation (like a number of other adjustments) to a specific range of colors in the image, selected in the pop-up menu at the top of the dialog box or at the top of the Properties panel when adding an adjustment layer.

Figure 6-9: Hue/Saturation can cure three problems at once.

Using the pop-up menu, you can elect to apply an adjustment to only a certain part of the color in your image. After a color is selected, the eyedroppers become active, to add to or subtract from the range of color being adjusted, and sliders become active between the gradients at the bottom, giving you yet another way to control the range of color being adjusted.

Visible in Figure 6-9 are the Adjustments and Properties panels, which you use to add adjustment layers to your images. Select the type of adjustment in the Adjustments panel, or in the menu at the bottom of the Layers panel, or through the Layer➪New Adjustments Layer menu. Make the actual adjustment in the Properties panel. (Adjustment layers are discussed in more detail in Chapter 8.) The content of the Properties panel offers the same options as the Image➪Adjustments➪Hue/Saturation dialog box, but the Preview check box is replaced by the eyeball icon you see at the bottom of the panel in Figure 6-9, which toggles the visibility of the new adjustment layer on and off.

Use the Adjustments panel to add adjustment layers for the 16 commands you saw in the top three sections of the Adjustments menu (Figure 6-7).

Color Balance

The Color Balance command (as shown in Figure 6-10) presents you with three sliders that you use to make changes to the balance between your color opposites. If the image is too blue, you drag the third slider away from Blue and toward Yellow. (This is also a great way to remember which colors are opposite pairs!)

Figure 6-10: Color Balance gives you direct control over opposites.

You can control the highlights, midtones, and shadows of your image individually by using radio buttons in the Color Balance dialog box and the Adjustments panel. And, in almost all cases, you'll want to leave the Preserve Luminosity check box marked so that the brightness of the individual pixels is retained.

You can also use Color Balance to throw an image out of whack for special effects or (getting back to the adjustment's roots) compensating for a color cast being introduced by the printing device.

Black & White

The Black & White adjustment creates outstanding grayscale copies of your color images. As you can see in Figure 6-11, you can control the amount of each major range of color used to create the grayscale copy. In this particular example, the original consists primarily of greens and browns, so the top three sliders are key. Reducing Reds and increasing Yellows both lighten the browns and greens and increases contrast among the brown tones. When adding a Black & White adjustment layer, you have an on-screen adjustment tool available, which you click in the image and drag up or down to adjust the brightness of a color throughout the image.

Figure 6-11: Black & White enables you to determine grayscale tones by mixing color values.

Note the Tint check box, with which you can easily create sepia or Duotone looks for your images. If you'll be printing on an inkjet printer (rather than sending the file to your photo lab), you'll want to use a Black & White adjustment layer rather than the menu command. Your inkjet printer may introduce an unwanted color shift. If so, you can reopen the adjustment layer and work with the sliders to compensate. Keep in mind, however, that the Black & White adjustment you open through the Image➪Adjustments menu offers Hue and Saturation sliders when adding a tint.

Photo Filter

Photoshop's Photo Filter is actually an image adjustment rather than a filter. The filter in the name refers to those physical photographic filters that you screw onto the end of a lens. This adjustment is a great way to correct problems with *temperature* in an image — the perceived warmth or coldness of an image. When the camera takes a picture under unexpected lighting conditions, a color problem is apparent. (Say, for example, that the camera is set to Daylight when shooting indoors.) When an image is too blue, it's too *cool;* conversely, an image that's orangey is too *warm.* (Remember that these are perceptual evaluations — blue light is technically hotter than yellow or red light.)

In Photo Filter, you select a preset filter from a pop-up menu or select a color of your choice. As you can see in Figure 6-12, both preset filters and custom colors can be effective in neutralizing a color cast. (You could, of course, also use these filters to add a color cast . . . if you wanted to, that is.)

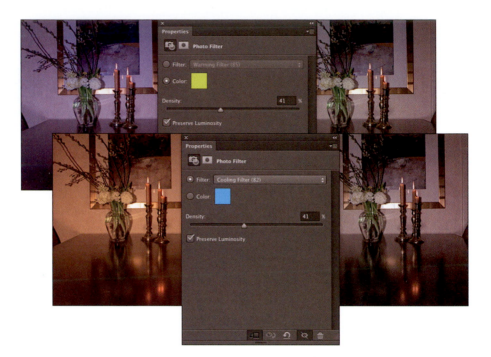

Figure 6-12: Neutralize a color cast with a filter of the opposite color in Photo Filter.

Channel Mixer

Designed to repair a defective channel in an image, Channel Mixer lets you use sliders to replace some or all of the intensity of one color channel with content from the others. Should you come across an image with damage in one channel, you can certainly use the Channel Mixer adjustment to work on it (with some degree of success). You reduce the value of the target channel by dragging the slider to the left. You then drag one or both of the other sliders toward the right. Generally speaking, you want to add an amount (combined between the two other channels) just about equal to what you subtract from the target channel.

If you drag a slider to the left past 0 (zero), you invert the content of the channel. You can produce some incredible (and incredibly weird) effects with this technique, partially inverting one or two channels. When you get a chance, give it a try. Using the Monochrome check box in Channel Mixer gives you an alternative to the Black & White adjustment for a controlled grayscale effect.

Color Lookup

A color lookup table is, at its most basic, a formula for applying color changes. Color Lookup takes the image's original colors and maps them to new colors based on the table you select in the dialog box (see Figure 6-13). Typically used with video, it may have some applicability to your work (depending on what lookup tables — "LUTs" — you find online). The "3D" in "3DLUT," by the way, refers to three color channels (RGB) and has nothing to do with three-dimensional objects.

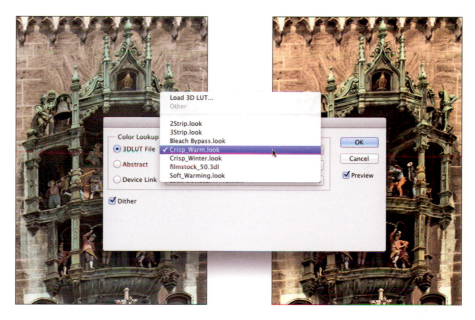

Figure 6-13: Color lookup tables are often used to match lighting in computer-generated scenes to live-motion video or film.

Invert

More creative than corrective, the Invert command (no dialog box) simply reverses the colors in your image or the selected area. Although inverting areas of an image (like desaturating) can draw attention to the subject of the image, it's an edgier technique and generally requires touch-up after inverting. You'll find that any *specular* highlight — a pure-white area (mainly reflections) — becomes a distracting black spot.

Posterize

The Posterize command forces your image's broad range of colors into a few selected colors. You automatically get black and white, and then a limited number of additional colors, based on the content of the original. You pick the number of colors that you want to use, and Photoshop picks which colors to use. You can use as few as two colors (plus black and white) or as many as 255, which pretty much gives you your original image. Posterize can create a rather pleasing rendering of a photo with very few colors.

When experimenting with Posterize, click in the Levels field and use the up- and down-arrow keys to preview different numbers of colors. Start low and work your way up. If you see something that you like, you can stop or you can keep going and come back to that number later — the image will look exactly the same when you try that number again.

Threshold

Threshold converts each pixel to either black or white (no colors, no grays). You adjust the border between black and white with a slider or by entering a value in the Threshold Level box. For an eye-catching special effect, open a color image and make a selection of the background (or the subject!) and apply Threshold, mixing color and black and white.

Sometimes, when adjusting color in an image, you need to find the darkest and lightest pixels in an image (for use with the eyedroppers in the Curves dialog box, for example). Open Threshold, drag the slider all the way to the left, and then slowly back to the right. The first black spot you see is the darkest in the image. Add a color sampler (so you can find the spot again) by Shift+clicking in the image. Drag the slider all the way to the right and then slowly back to the left to find and mark the lightest pixels. After placing your color samplers, click Cancel.

Gradient Map

Again, more creative than corrective, the Gradient Map feature re-creates your image by using a gradient. The leftmost color stop (the anchor points where a gradient color is assigned) in the gradient is mapped to the shadows, the right-most to the highlights, and any color stops in between are appropriately assigned to the rest of the tonal range. In Figure 6-14, you can see how a two-color gradient (upper left) lacks detail compared with the four-color gradient being created for the lower image.

Figure 6-14: Using more colors in your gradient produces more detail.

Generally speaking, you use darker colors for the color stops on the left and lighter colors for the color stops on the right (although you can create extremely interesting effects by mixing things up). Using a black-to-white gradient produces a grayscale image.

To edit the gradient, simply click directly on the sample gradient in the Gradient Map dialog box. Click to add color stops, drag to move color stops, and click the color swatch near the bottom to change the color of the selected stop. (You can find more detailed information on creating and working with gradients in Chapter 14.)

Selective Color

Although designed to help you compensate for the vagaries of printing presses, Selective Color can do other great things for you! The command's dialog box, shown in Figure 6-15, has a pop-up menu that offers the six basic colors of Photoshop, as well as Whites, Neutrals, and Blacks. You select which range of colors to adjust and then drag the sliders. You can work on one set of colors, switch to another and make adjustments, switch to another, and so on without having to click OK in between. For example, you can adjust the reds in the image and leave the blues untouched, or you can adjust the reds and then tweak the blues without having to exit the dialog box.

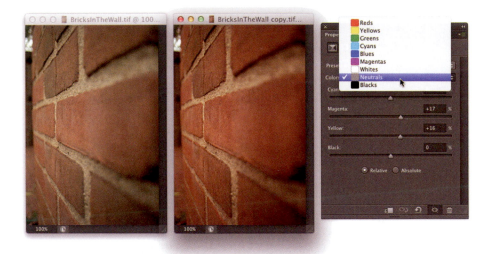

Figure 6-15: Tweaking the Neutrals can adjust the overall appearance of an image.

When you have reasonably small adjustments to make and are using the Selective Color adjustment (not an adjustment layer), select the Relative radio button at the bottom. If you have substantial changes — rather radical alterations — select the Absolute radio button.

Shadow/Highlight

The Shadow/Highlight adjustment is discussed at length in Chapter 5 as a tonal-correction tool, the job for which it was designed. However, keep in mind that the Shadow/Highlight dialog box also includes the Color Correction slider. After you lighten shadows or tone down highlights, you can increase or decrease the saturation of the colors in the adjusted areas of your image with the Color Correction slider.

Although Shadow/Highlight is not available as an adjustment layer, you can use the menu command Layer➪Smart Objects➪Convert to Smart Object, and then add Shadow/Highlight as a Smart Filter. (Smart Objects and Smart Filters are explained in Chapter 10.)

HDR Toning

Designed for use with high dynamic range images (32-bits/channel), the HDR Toning adjustment provides a different way to adjust color. It can be used with flattened images in 8-bit or 16-bit color, but keep in mind that small adjustments are usually required. HDR Toning is examined in Chapter 20.

Desaturate

The Photoshop Desaturate command creates a grayscale representation of a color image without changing the color mode. However, with no dialog box or adjustments, it doesn't offer the control you get by using a Black & White adjustment.

Match Color

Now *this* is a feature to savor! There you are, adding Cousin Joe to the family reunion photo because he wasn't bailed out in time, and you see that the lighting is all kinds of different and he sticks out like a sore thumb (or bum). Or you return from a major shoot only to find that something wasn't set correctly in the camera, and *all* your images have a nasty color cast.

Match Color lets you adjust one image to another (and you can even use selections to identify areas to adjust or areas of the images to use as the basis for adjustment), but keep in mind that you get better results with images that are already rather similar. You can also fix one shot and use that shot as a standard by which others are corrected. (Like most image adjustments, you can record a change in an Action and use Photoshop's Batch command to apply that adjustment to a series of images. Read more about Actions in Chapter 16.) Take a look at Figure 6-16 to see the Match Color dialog box.

Because Match Color is such a powerful tool, it's worth taking at look at what's going on in the dialog box:

- ✔ **Ignore Selection when Applying Adjustment:** If you have an active selection in the target layer or image (for calculating the adjustment, see the upcoming bullet on that) and you want the adjustment to be applied to the entire target, select this check box. If the box is left clear, the adjustment is applied only within the selection. Note that you can use selections to apply Match Color to only a portion of your image, such as flesh tones, or you can adjust sections of the image one at a time.

- ✔ **Luminance:** After the preview shows in your image window, you can tone down or brighten up the target area with the Luminance slider.

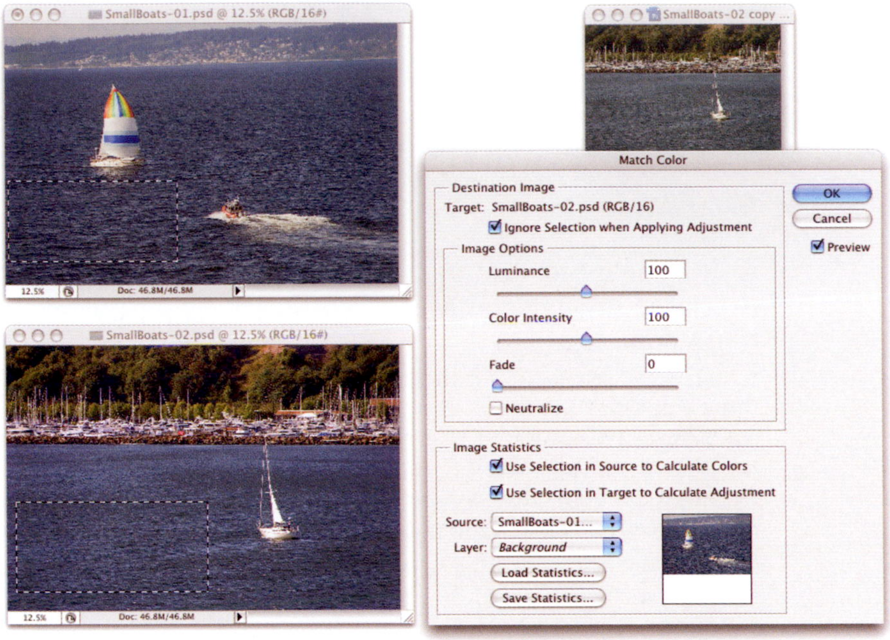

Figure 6-16: The small image to the upper-right shows the before image.

- **Color Intensity:** Think of this slider as a saturation adjustment.

- **Fade:** Using Fade lets you blend the adjustment, reducing its intensity.

- **Neutralize:** If a color cast is introduced by the adjustment, selecting the Neutralize check box often eliminates it.

- **Use Selection in Source to Calculate Colors:** You can make a selection in the image to which you're trying to match (the *source*) and use the colors within that selection as the basis for the Match Color calculation.

- **Use Selection in Target to Calculate Adjustment:** You can make another selection in the target layer or image that presents Match Color with a sample of those pixels to use for calculating the adjustment.

- **Source:** The Source pop-up menu lists all the open images that can be used as a basis for adjustment. Only images of the same color mode and color depth get listed. Think of *source* as the image whose colors you're trying to match. (The selected image or the active layer within an image is what you're adjusting.)

✔ **Layer:** When a multilayer image is selected in the Source pop-up menu, you can designate which layer (or a merged copy of the layers) is the actual source.

✔ **Load Statistics/Save Statistics:** If you're doing a series of images and you want to speed things up, click the Save Statistics button to record the adjustment you're making and then use the Load Statistics button with other images.

In Figure 6-16, an area of water is selected in the target image and a comparable area of water is selected in the source image. (The selection in the source image is visible in Figure 6-16 for illustrative purposes only — a selection in an inactive image window isn't normally visible.) With the two selections, I tell Match Color to adjust the target image based on the difference between the water color in the two images. Using selections prevents any skewing of the adjustment that would be caused by the colors in the sail (source image) and the trees (target image). But with the Ignore Selection When Applying Adjustment check box enabled as well, I make sure the entire target image is adjusted, not just the areas within the selection.

Replace Color

Sort of a cross between the Select➪Color Range command (see Chapter 8) and the Hue/Saturation adjustment, Replace Color is an outstanding tool for swapping out one color for another. It's truly great in a production environment where, for example, a certain blouse is available in several colors. Shoot one color and then use Replace Color to produce the additional product shots.

The Replace Color dialog box, as shown in Figure 6-17, has two separate parts: Selection and Replacement. Click with the left eyedropper in either the preview area or in the image windows and adjust the Fuzziness slider (how much variation counts as "selected") to make your initial selection. Use the middle eyedropper to add colors or shades of your initial color, and use the right eyedropper to subtract from the selection. Choose only variations of one color. Then drag those Hue, Saturation, and Lightness sliders in the Replacement section of the dialog box to produce your new look.

Rather than switching eyedroppers back and forth, use the left eyedropper and the Shift key (to add) or the Option/Alt key (to subtract). You can also hold down the Shift key and drag through an area to select all the colors in the area. If you accidentally select some colors you don't want, release the Shift key and click once to start over.

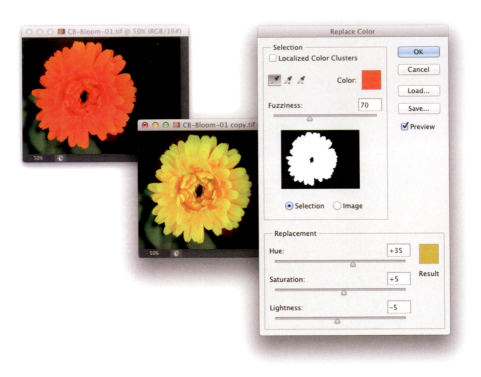

Figure 6-17: Make a selection and change the selection's hue, saturation, and lightness.

When the Localized Color Clusters option (to the upper-left of the Replace Color adjustment in Figure 6-17) is active, Replace Color looks at each range of color you add to the selection as a separate entity. This enables much better technical control over the colors selected, but may not be appropriate for most uses of Replace Color, in which you generally want smooth and complete transformation of all of the selected colors.

Equalize

When you select the Equalize adjustment, Photoshop finds the darkest pixel in the image and maps it to black, maps the lightest pixel to white, and distributes the rest of the tonal values between. You can pretty much skip Equalize — use Auto Color or — even better — the Auto button in Curves or Levels.

Manual corrections in individual channels

Sometimes different areas of an image require different corrections or adjustments. You can, for example, "paint" corrections into specific areas of a channel by using the toning tools in Photoshop's Toolbox. The image in Figure 6-18 has a distinct problem (okay, well, maybe a few problems). In the lower left is a light-green blob that needs to be eliminated if there's any chance of salvaging this photo. By using the Burn tool on one channel at a time, you can darken that specific area of each channel — each channel according to its needs.

Figure 6-18: The problem is only in one area of each channel, but you can fix it manually.

On the left, you can see the distinct light area in the thumbnail of the Red and Green channels. On the right, after using the Burn tool, those lighter areas are gone in the Green channel and a similar adjustment to the Red channel eliminates the problem completely.

In addition to the Burn tool, you can use the Dodge, Blur, Sharpen, and Smudge tools. You can use the Brush tool and paint with black, white, or gray. You can use Levels or Curves on an individual channel or even a selection within one or more channels. When fine-tuning (or salvaging) an image, don't be afraid to work in one channel at a time, perfecting that channel's contribution to the overall image.

Take another look at the two Channels panels shown in Figure 6-18. Obviously that's a composite image because there's only one Channels panel in Photoshop, right? On the right, the Green channel is active (you can tell because it's highlighted), and only the Green channel is visible (only it shows the eyeball icon to the left). The other channels are invisible, and you see only the grayscale representation from the Green channel in the image window. On the left, however, only the Red channel is active, but *all* the channels are visible. Any change I make to that image in that state is applied only to the Red channel. But because all channels are visible, I can see the overall impact on my image.

Sometimes you want only one channel visible, such as when you're trying to balance the tonal range throughout the channel, for example. But most of the time, you want to see what's going on in the image as a whole. Click the one channel (or Shift+click two channels) in which you need to work. Then click in the left column next to the composite channel at the top to make all channels visible.

The People Factor: Flesh Tone Formulas

One of the toughest and yet most important jobs in Photoshop is making sure that skin looks right. People come in a wide variety of colors and shades and tints, and all people vary in color in different places on their bodies and at different times of the year. (The top and bottom of your forearm are likely different colors, and the difference is generally much greater in summer than in winter.) There are even some exceptions to those broad generalities. Making skin tones look great is often a major, yet often critical, challenge.

When you have skin in your image, it's generally part of the focus of the image — the person whom you're photographing. And even when a person isn't the subject of the image, skin attracts attention in the image. The eye naturally goes to people in just about any image (perhaps not first, but eventually).

You'll also find that unnatural variations in skin color are *very* noticeable. Consider how often you think to yourself that someone looks a little pale, or flushed, or sunburned, or tanned, or just plain sick. You're making that judgment call based to a large degree on the appearance of the skin.

Keeping in mind that the numbers shown in Figure 6-19 are general guidelines and that real people vary quite a bit, I've prepared for you some target values for skin tones. Use these formulas loosely when using the techniques in this chapter to adjust the color in your images, keeping in mind the individual you photographed and the lighting at the time.

Flesh Tone Formulas

	Pale Caucasian	Dark Caucasian	Afro-American	Asian
Highlights	C:4 - M:17 - Y:15 - K:0	C:11 - M:35 - Y:42 - K:0	C:5 - M:14 - Y:22 - K:0	C:3 - M:11 - Y:13 - K:0
Midtones	C:14 - M:35 - Y:35 - K:0	C:14 - M:38 - Y:49 - K:0	C:23 - M:50 - Y:63 - K:5	C:12 - M:35 - Y:42 - K:0
Shadows	C:31 - M:63 - Y:71 - K:31	C:35 - M:64 - Y:73 - K:27	C:35 - M:67 - Y:72 - K:52	C:29 - M:60 - Y:56 - K:25

Figure 6-19: These are guidelines only, not absolute values!

Note that the numbers are CMYK, even for use with RGB images. Open the Info panel menu, choose Panel Options, and set the Second Color Readout to CMYK Color (see Figure 6-20). Remember, too, that you can use the Color Sampler tool to add placeholders in the image, monitoring the changes that you're making in the Info panel. Set the color sampler readings to CMYK in the Info panel itself by clicking the eyedropper symbol to the left of the color mode listed for each sampler.

Promise me that you'll keep in mind that these numbers are for reference only, okay? Your individual image determines what the correct adjustment should be. You can use these numbers as a starting point, but trust your eyes and evaluate your image as you work.

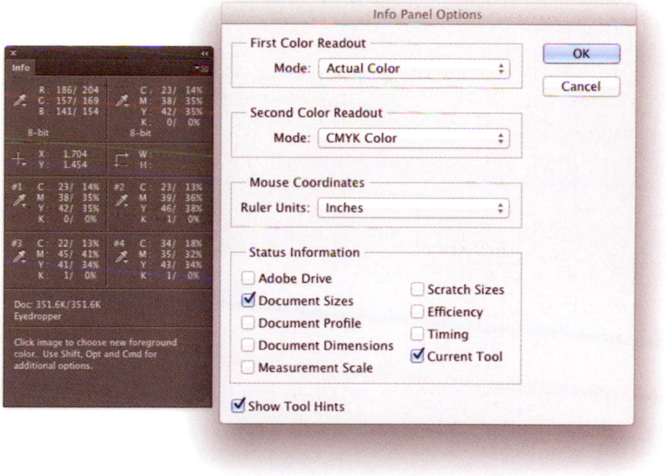

Figure 6-20: Use the panel options to set up the Info panel.

In the Status Information section of Info Panel Options, you can elect to have the panel display quite a bit of useful information. If you're new to Photoshop or are exploring Photoshop in more depth these days, the Current Tool option can be very helpful — select it and the Info panel gives you tips about how to work with the currently-active tool. Of course, you'll need to keep the Info panel open to take advantage of all that helpful information.

7

The Adobe Camera Raw 7 Plug-In

In This Chapter

▶ Taking advantage of the Raw file format

▶ Evaluating your Raw capabilities

▶ Using the Camera Raw plug-in

*T*here was a time, not so long ago in people years (but a couple of generations ago in computer years), when capturing digital photos in a Raw file format required you to spend tens of thousands of dollars. The wonderful thing about the Raw file format is that you use it to record unprocessed image data, which gives you incredible control over the final appearance of your image. These days, however, cameras that cost only a few hundred dollars can capture images "in the Raw." If you don't have a Raw-capable camera now, after reading this chapter, you might decide that you *need* to have Raw capability.

In this chapter, I explain how Raw differs from other image file formats and why those differences can be important. I show you how to determine whether you have what you need to capture in Raw and whether Photoshop's Adobe Camera Raw plug-in is capable of handling your camera's image files. Most of the rest of the chapter looks at the Camera Raw interface and what all those sliders do for you and your image.

Understanding the Raw Facts

The Raw file format at its heart is nothing but unprocessed image data. It comes in a number of variations — one or several for each camera manufacturer. Each has its own file extension (such as `.crw`, `.cr2`, or `.nef`), and many have their own special features that are totally incompatible with each other and even incompatible with Raw images from different camera models that use the same file extension. And those camera manufacturers love to tinker with their proprietary formats, changing them regularly. But each of the formats, at the basic level, is Raw. (Check your camera's User Guide to see whether it's capable of recording image data in a format other than JPEG or TIFF. If so, it's probably a variation of Raw.)

Thankfully, Adobe updates the Camera Raw plug-in for Photoshop (as shown in Figure 7-1) on a regular basis, adding the capability to work with the newest cameras shortly after they're available. (Plug-ins, like Camera Raw and most of Photoshop's filters, extend the program's capabilities. Updating your plug-ins regularly ensures you have the greatest capabilities.) Be warned, however, that purchasing a new camera model the day it comes on the market might mean using the camera's own software for a while until Camera Raw is updated.

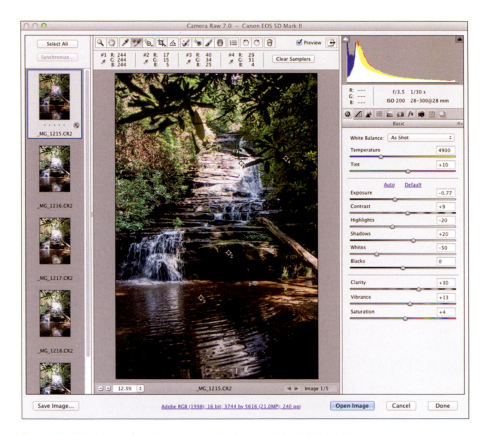

Figure 7-1: The impressive Camera Raw window, explained fully in this chapter.

In the Camera Raw window in Figure 7-1, notice the thumbnails stacked to the left. Select multiple Raw images in the Photoshop File⇨Open dialog box or in Bridge and they all open in Camera Raw together. Click a thumbnail to work on that particular image. If you open images that all need a similar correction, adjust one and then click the Select All and Synchronize buttons in the upper-left corner.

Adobe also offers the free DNG Converter software for converting supported Raw files to the open source DNG file format. (Open source means that anyone can freely use it. The DNG format is also known as "digital negative.") Although some camera manufacturers have adopted the DNG format for their cameras, it's more commonly used as "insurance for the future" — if support for a specific Raw format is dropped in the future, the DNG copies of the image can still be processed. However, because Adobe doesn't plan on dropping support for any Raw formats in Camera Raw, you really don't need to make DNG copies at this time. If there is a problem with one of your Raw formats in the future, it *will* make sense to download DNG Converter and make DNG copies of the no-longer-supported files at that time.

What's the big deal about Raw?

Cameras that record images using the Raw format save *unprocessed* image data. When recording as JPEG or TIFF, the camera manipulates the image data, processing it in a variety of ways. So what's the big deal with unprocessed — Raw — image data? Assuming that you're as hungry for food as for knowledge, I'll use a cooking analogy.

Say you purchase frozen lasagna and heat it up in your microwave oven. It probably tastes good and fulfills your needs ("Food!"). However, the chef who designed this prepared meal and the good folks who churn it out use a specific recipe designed to appeal to a large number of people, hopefully offending very few. When you reheat your lasagna in the microwave, you have some choices. For example, you decide how warm to make it (generally following the package's reheating instructions). Perhaps you'll add some pepper or hot sauce.

What you *can't* do with that frozen lasagna is take out some of the salt or fat in it from the recipe designed by the chef and prepared by the good folks. You *can't* substitute olive oil for butter. You *can't* cut back on the garlic a bit (just in case your date goes well). You're pretty much restricted by what the original chef and his good folks prepared. Sure, you could pour a half-bottle of blue food coloring over it, creating a special effect, but you're not likely to turn that microwavable lasagna into a gourmet dinner. So if you're just hungry and your demands aren't too severe, no problem — shoot JPEG (the digital photo equivalent of a microwave meal).

The gourmet dinner is what Raw is all about! If you consider yourself a gourmet chef of the camera, creating art from light, Raw is the format for you. Avoid the limitations put on your image editing by preprocessing and dive right in with the greatest flexibility. (And you don't even have to go down to the farmers' market for fresh tomatoes.)

Working in Raw

There's one critical difference between working with Raw images and working with JPEGs or TIFFs: You never actually make changes to the Raw file. Instead, you record your adjustments in the image's *metadata* (non-image data recorded with the image data) or in a *sidecar* file (a separate file in which Camera Raw records any information that can't be recorded in the metadata). Because adjustments are recorded separately rather than applied to the images, the original image data remains unchanged, waiting for you to create again and again, all from the same unprocessed, undegraded image data.

Sidecar files have the same name as the image file, but they use the .xmp file extension. Keep each sidecar file in the same folder as the image with which it is associated. If you move the image file without taking the sidecar file along for the ride, the information stored in the sidecar file won't be available when you reopen the image file, so you'll need to adjust the image's appearance all over again.

When capturing in Raw, you can basically ignore all the camera's settings other than aperture, shutter speed, ISO, and (of course) focus. Everything else can be adjusted in the Camera Raw plug-in. However, because Raw devotes significantly more resources to recording highlights than shadows, it's not a bad idea to concentrate on those highlights when shooting. When the highlights are great to start with, you can reallocate some of the image's tonal range to the deprived shadows, thus reducing unwanted digital noise and increasing detail.

Keep in mind that in addition to the Photoshop Camera Raw plug-in, you also have available the software that came with your camera. (And you might even have additional software packages available, such as Aperture from Apple and Adobe Lightroom, depending on what camera make and model you use.) Which package is best? As usual, "best" is a relative term. For example, Nikon's proprietary software does a great job with sharpness when processing .nef files, but it lacks some of Camera Raw's features. If sharpness is your overriding requirement, you might prefer the Nikon software. (Remember that your Raw file can't be processed by both the camera's software and then by Camera Raw, but you can process the data with either and then further refine your image in Photoshop itself.)

While working in Camera Raw, keep in mind that what happens when you move the image from Camera Raw to Photoshop (or save your adjustments and close with Camera Raw's Done button) is governed by Camera Raw's Workflow Options. Discussed later in this chapter, Workflow Options controls the color space, color depth, pixel dimensions, and resolution of the image after you're done in Camera Raw. Workflow Options is where you also control whether the formerly-Raw file opens into Photoshop as an image or a Smart Object and whether a sharpening preset is applied.

Photoshop's Save As dialog box offers you the option of the Photoshop Raw file format. Photoshop Raw is *not* compatible with the Camera Raw plug-in and does not provide you with the benefits of using the Raw format with your digital camera. It is, however, necessary for certain high-end graphics and animation programs into which someone, somewhere, sometimes places images from Photoshop.

Do You Have What It Takes?

To capture images in the Raw format requires only a camera that shoots Raw. To work with those images in Photoshop, however, you need both a camera and software that can process the Raw files. To work with images in the Camera Raw plug-in, you need a camera on the supported cameras list for Camera Raw — and, of course, Photoshop with Camera Raw. Adobe updates the Camera Raw plug-in regularly to ensure compatibility with the latest cameras as well as with the latest nit-picky changes that camera manufacturers have made to their proprietary versions of Raw. Use Photoshop's Help⇨Updates command or check for the latest Camera Raw update and list of supported cameras here:

www.adobe.com/products/photoshop/extend.html

Working with images in the Raw format requires one other thing that you might not have: additional time. Opening the Camera Raw plug-in, making the necessary adjustments to your image, and then transferring the image into Photoshop all take time. Granted, making changes in Camera Raw eliminates the need for many of the adjustments that you'd be making in Photoshop, but working in Camera Raw could seem to be slower. (Actually, depending on your system, Camera Raw might speed things up because tonal adjustment, color correction, sharpening, and noise reduction are all in one place — there's no waiting for adjustments and filters to be applied and then for the next dialog box to open.)

Camera Raw with JPEG and TIFF

Camera Raw also offers the capability to work with JPEG and TIFF in the Camera Raw dialog box. Although not a substitute for shooting Raw (JPEG and TIFF image data has already been processed by the camera), it's a huge step forward in terms of flexibility. When you do your initial processing in Camera Raw, the adjustments are recorded as instructions in the file metadata rather than actually making changes to the pixels in your image. You can later go back and make changes to those adjustments — the changes are applied to the original pixel data fresh and clean rather than making changes to changes.

To open a JPEG or TIFF File in Camera Raw, open the Camera Raw Preferences (which you can open through the Photoshop Preferences menu) and elect to open all JPEG and TIFF files into Camera Raw. Later you may decide to change that Preference setting to only open JPEG and TIFF files that already have settings associated with them, or you may elect to not open JPEG and TIFF files into Camera Raw at all. After changing the Preferences, you can simply use any of Photoshop and Bridge's open commands, or double-click the file in Bridge to open into Camera Raw.

Keep in mind that after you adjust a TIFF or JPEG file in Camera Raw, that image will *always* open into Camera Raw. If, down the road, you decide that you want to bypass Camera Raw and make those adjustments a permanent part of the image's appearance, use Photoshop's Save As command to create a new copy of the file, or disable JPEG and TIFF support in Camera Raw's Preferences.

Working in the Camera Raw Plug-In

The cornerstone of Photoshop's Raw capability is the Camera Raw plug-in. After an image is open in Photoshop itself, you manipulate the pixels directly, rather than manipulating the metadata. When you work in the Camera Raw plug-in, you never change the image itself, only the adjustments recorded in the file's metadata (or in a sidecar file). As shown previously in Figure 7-1, the Camera Raw window is filled with tools and sliders. Even though you might not work with all the Camera Raw features, here's the lowdown on the features there.

Tools and preview options

In the upper-left corner of the Camera Raw window are almost a dozen tools (as shown in Figure 7-2) for manipulating your image and the workspace. From the left, the tools are Zoom, Hand, White Balance, Color Sampler, Targeted Adjustment, Crop, Straighten, Spot Removal, Red Eye Removal, Adjustment Brush, and Graduated Filter. To the right of the tools are buttons to open Camera Raw's Preferences and two rotation buttons.

When multiple images are open in Camera Raw, you also have the Trash icon to the right of the rotation buttons. With one or more image thumbnails selected, click the Trash button to mark the files for deletion. When you click the Done or Open Images button, marked images are sent to your computer's Trash or Recycle Bin. Mark images for deletion only when you're *sure* you have no use for them.

#1 R: 244	#2 R: 17	#3 R: 40	#4 R: 29	Clear Samplers
G: 244	G: 15	G: 34	G: 31	
B: 244	B: 5	B: 25	B: 4	

Figure 7-2: Camera Raw offers 11 tools for perfecting your images and up to nine color samplers.

The Zoom and Hand tools function as you would expect — they zoom in and out and reposition a zoomed-in image in the window. Click with the White Balance tool on something in the image that should be gray (not something that is already gray, but that should be gray) to automatically adjust the Temperature and Tint sliders. It's a one-click way to neutralize any color cast and correct the color balance. If you get an unexpected result, click elsewhere. And, of course, afterward you can still tweak the Temperature and Tint sliders as desired.

When you add color samplers (a maximum of nine) to the image preview area (click with the Color Sampler tool), their values are displayed below the tools, as you see in Figure 7-2. When you haven't added color samplers, that area is collapsed, leaving more room for the preview area. Color samplers in Camera Raw function the same as they do in Photoshop (see Chapter 6). Color samplers are visible earlier in Figure 7-1 as numbered targets in the preview area, strategically located in critical areas of the photo. You can use the Color Sampler tool to drag existing color samplers to new locations or delete them by Option/Alt+clicking on the sampler. Clicking the Clear Samplers button deletes all existing color samplers. Remember, too, that the position of the cursor can function as an additional color sampler — the RGB values are shown below the histogram.

Designed for on-image adjustments, you click on the Targeted Adjustment tool (shown in Figure 7-3), hold down the mouse button, select the type of adjustment you want to make, and then click directly in the image preview. Drag up or down and left or right to adjust the image's appearance. Whether you elect Parametric Curve, Hue, Saturation, Luminance, or Grayscale Mix, the appropriate pane opens to the right so that you can monitor (and fine-tune) the adjustment. If you select Parametric Curve and click in a light area in the image, Highlights or Lights are adjusted; if you click in a dark area,

Shadows or Darks are adjusted. With the other four options for the Targeted Adjustment tool, you're adjusting a specific range of color — based on the color on which you click — as you drag.

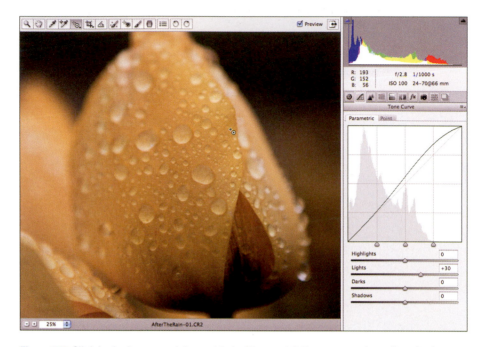

Figure 7-3: Click in the image and drag with the Targeted Adjustment tool to adjust the image.

Click and hold the Crop tool icon to select an *aspect ratio* (relationship between width and height), as shown in Figure 7-4. Drag the Crop tool to create a bounding box, which will automatically adjust to Landscape or Portrait orientation as you drag. You can then adjust the size of the bounding box by dragging its anchor points. You can also rotate an image while cropping: Position the tool just outside the bounding box and drag to rotate. If you drag the Straighten tool along a line in the image that should be horizontal or vertical, perhaps the intersection of two walls or the horizon, a crop bounding box is created with that alignment. Using the Crop tool's Custom option enables you to specify the resulting image's dimensions in aspect ratio, pixels, inches, or centimeters.

When you have the Crop tool's bounding box just right and you've finished adjusting the image's appearance, click the Open or Done button. Should you change your mind about cropping, click the Crop tool, hold down the mouse button to show the menu, and select Clear Crop. Or you can eliminate the bounding box (when the Crop tool is active) by pressing Delete (Mac) or Backspace (Windows).

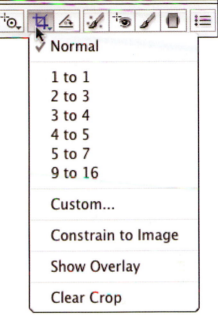

The Straighten tool can be used in conjunction with the Crop tool. Select the tool and drag along any line in the image that should be vertical or horizontal. A crop bounding box is automatically created that encompasses as much of the image as possible while rotating to straighten the image. Keep in mind that the Straighten tool uses the aspect ratio currently selected for the Crop tool, so make that selection before dragging the Straighten tool.

Figure 7-4: The Crop tool can ensure perfect aspect ratio.

The Spot Removal tool gives you the ability to make minor corrections right in the Camera Raw dialog box. As shown in Figure 7-5, it offers capabilities similar to the Healing Brush and the Clone Stamp, including an Opacity slider. However, the Spot Removal tool's behavior is quite different. To use the Spot Removal tool, follow these steps:

1. **Click the area you want to heal or clone over.**

2. **Drag to expand the tool's diameter.**

   You can also set the diameter using the Radius slider to the right, in the area below the histogram.

Figure 7-5: Camera Raw's Spot Removal tool offers both healing and cloning modes.

3. **Position the source (green) and destination (red) circles.**

   When you release the mouse button after setting the tool's diameter, a pair of circles appears. Click within the green circle and drag it over the element from which you want to clone or heal. You can also drag the red circle to fine-tune the location of the destination. You can click the edge of either circle and drag to resize them both (or use the Radius slider).

4. **Repeat, accept, or clear.**

   Clicking outside the circles accepts the change and starts the next healing/cloning process. Changing tools and continuing with your adjustments accepts the changes. Clicking the Clear All button (just above Camera Raw's Done button) deletes the changes you made with the Spot Removal tool.

To use the Red Eye Reduction tool, drag a rectangle around the entire eye, including some surrounding skin (see Figure 7-6). It automatically tries to hunt down and eliminate any suspicious red eye in the rectangle. You might need to adjust the Pupil Size and Darken sliders (in the area to the right, under the Histogram) to fine-tune the adjustment, but you can also simply click and drag the edges of the box created by the Red Eye Removal tool.

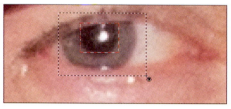

Figure 7-6: Minimize the haunted red eye effect right in Camera Raw.

To make localized adjustments in specific areas of your image, select the Adjustment Brush (shown in Figure 7-7), drag the sliders, and paint in the image. You can paint a number of different adjustments (use the New button) or paint the same adjustment in different areas (use the Add button). And remember that these adjustments are only recorded in the metadata, and therefore can be changed any time down the road. It's not quite the same as duplicating layers and using layer masks in Photoshop, but a great non-destructive way to paint adjustments!

The Graduated Filter tool enables you to set the adjustment in the area to the right, and then drag the tool in the image window. The adjustment is applied at full strength in the area before your first click, and gradually faded through the area where you dragged (see Figure 7-8). You can add more than one graduated adjustment if necessary.

To the right of the tools are Camera Raw's buttons to quickly open Camera Raw's Preferences (the same as using the keyboard shortcut ⌘+K/Ctrl+K) and to rotate the image in 90 degree increments in either direction.

Figure 7-7: Paint to make adjustments to exposure, brightness, contrast, and more.

Here are some options in the Preferences that you might want to consider:

✔ **Save settings in sidecar files.** This is already the default, and it's a good one. When Camera Raw can't record data directly to the image file's existing metadata, you can either save everything in one central location — which means you lose *everything* if that database is damaged or lost — or each image you adjust can have its own .xmp file to hold your adjustments.

✔ **Set defaults for each camera.** If you shoot with more than one camera, use separate defaults for each of them. You can also make defaults that change based on the ISO setting with which each image was captured.

✔ **Update DNG previews.** If you work with Adobe's DNG Converter and make DNG copies of your images, doesn't it make sense that you'd want the latest adjustments reflected in the file's preview? (The JPEG preview is used by your computer's operating system and other programs that can't read DNG files.) And those previews might as well be full-size, eh?

Figure 7-8: Like using a graduated filter when shooting, but with more control!

You'll also find options in Camera Raw's Preferences for opening JPEG and TIFF files into Camera Raw. Keep in mind that after you open an image in either format using Camera Raw, you'll have to go through Camera Raw *every* time you open that image (unless, of course, you disable all support for JPEG and TIFF files in Camera Raw's Preferences). If you ever decide you don't want to open a particular image through Camera Raw again, use Photoshop's Save As command to create a new copy of the picture.

The histogram

Because of the unprocessed nature of Raw images, the histogram you see in the top-right corner of the Camera Raw window (also shown in Figure 7-9) is generally far more important than the Histogram panel in Photoshop itself.

By keeping an eye on the histogram while you adjust sliders, you can ensure that you're not blowing out the highlights (when the very right end of the histogram starts crawling up the edge) or clogging the shadows (the left edge gets too tall). The RGB values that you see just below the histogram represent the values of the pixel directly under the cursor when the cursor is in the preview area of the window.

Figure 7-9: Consult the histogram to make sure you don't wreck your highlights and shadows.

The histogram in Camera Raw shows you not only the distribution of tonal values but also the distribution by channel. In Figure 7-9, you can see that the Blue channel has a *lot* of dark pixels: The blue column climbs the left edge of the histogram. This could indicate any of a number of situations. However, because you also see a generally good distribution of blue throughout the histogram (in part shown by the areas of white, which indicate that all three channels have comparable values), you can be pretty sure that the column of blue to the left simply indicates a lot of bright yellow in the image. (Blue and yellow are color opposites in RGB.) As always, remember that what you see in the preview area — what your eyes tell you — trumps any information from a histogram.

To toggle a preview of any "clipping" in your image, click the triangles in the upper-left (shadows) and upper-right (highlights) of the histogram. Any place where the shadows are being forced to pure black, losing detail that you could retain, you see a bright blue overlay. Use the Shadows and Blacks sliders to correct the problem. Anywhere that the highlights are being blown out to pure white, again losing valuable detail, you see a bright red overlay. Use the Highlights and Whites sliders to bring the problem under control. (Using the individual sliders is discussed later in the chapter.) You can hide these *gamut warnings* by again clicking the triangles. The triangles change color to tell you what's wrong or which colors are causing the problem. You might want to hide the overlays when creating special effects. (I readily admit that I often intentionally clog shadows and blow out highlights to produce special effects and to focus attention on the subject of my photos.)

The preview area

As shown previously in Figure 7-1, the bulk of the Camera Raw window is filled with the image preview, giving you the best possible view of your work. Remember that you can drag a corner or edge of the Camera Raw window to resize it. The preview area benefits/suffers from the changes that you make as you enlarge/shrink the window. To the lower left are a pop-up menu with preset zoom factors as well as a pair of buttons to zoom in or out. (Don't forget about the Zoom tool!) Unlike Photoshop, Camera Raw's maximum zoom percentage is 400%.

Above the top-right corner of the preview area is the Preview check box, which you can toggle off and on to see the difference between the current adjustments and the Camera Raw defaults (or earlier adjustments made in Camera Raw). To the right of the Preview check box is a handy button that expands Camera Raw to Full Screen mode. The only Camera Raw–related information that disappears is the title bar, containing the name of the camera from which the images came. Note to Mac users: In Full Screen mode, you may not have access to the hidden Dock. Simply click the button again to toggle back to Normal mode or use the Mac's shortcut ⌘+Tab to switch programs. (Pressing the F key also toggles to and from Full Screen mode.)

Workflow Options and presets

Just below the preview area in Camera Raw is a line of information in blue. That tells you the current color space, color depth, pixel dimensions, and resolution. Click that line to open the Workflow Options dialog box.

Here are your workflow options:

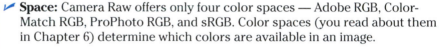

- ✔ **Space:** Camera Raw offers only four color spaces — Adobe RGB, Color-Match RGB, ProPhoto RGB, and sRGB. Color spaces (you read about them in Chapter 6) determine which colors are available in an image.

  Using the ProPhoto RGB color space gives you the widest *gamut* (the largest number of possible colors), which minimizes the chance of colors getting squished into each other as you work with your image. If your image has extreme colors, use ProPhoto and 16-bit color in Camera Raw, and then, if your printer can't handle ProPhoto as a color space, choose Edit⇨Assign Profile to change to your required profile (Adobe RGB for inkjet printers or sRGB for images being sent to a photo lab). Select Relative Colorimetric as the rendering intent.

- ✔ **Depth:** Because a greater color depth means more possible variations in color, generally you want to select 16-bit color and either keep the image in that color depth or switch to 8-bit color later in Photoshop by choosing Image⇨Mode⇨8-Bits/Channel. Use 8-bit color for any image that must be saved in JPEG format (including web images), for CMYK (cyan/magenta/yellow/black) images, or when the file size overwhelms your printer. You might also opt for 8-bit color if storage space is limited. (Chapter 6 includes a detailed explanation of color depth.)

- ✔ **Size:** You can choose from a number of pixel dimensions for your image in Camera Raw. The camera's native pixel dimensions for the image is the default, but you can also downsize or upsize to various preset sizes (which vary from one camera model to the next). Camera Raw uses a variation of the Bicubic Sharper algorithm for *resampling* (calculating the colors of the new pixels). If you crop the image in Camera Raw, the pixel dimensions are proportionally scaled.

✓ **Resolution:** *Resolution* is simply an instruction to a printing device about what size to make each pixel. It can be assigned in Camera Raw or later in Photoshop's Image Size dialog box (with Resample unselected). If your camera embeds a resolution that Camera Raw can read, it will be used. Generally speaking, 300 ppi is an appropriate resolution for images that will be printed.

✓ **Sharpen For:** The Sharpen For menu provide you with presets designed for specific purposes, including on-screen presentation, inkjet prints on glossy paper, and prints on matte paper. Each category includes Low, Medium, and High options. This sharpening is in addition to the sharpening you add in Camera Raw's Detail tab. (Generally I leave this set to None and sharpen each image according to the image's content.)

✓ **Open in Photoshop as Smart Objects:** This option enables you to automatically open your Raw image into Photoshop as a Smart Object. Smart Objects, which are discussed in Chapter 10, can be scaled and transformed multiple times with minimal degradation of the image quality. And, as explained in Chapter 15, you can apply Smart Filters — re-editable filters — to Smart Objects.

On the subject of workflow, let me also suggest two ways that you can save *loads* of time when working with Camera Raw: Create your own defaults and use saved settings. Figure 7-10 shows the menu commands available to you. (Not all commands are available all the time.) The most important is perhaps Save New Camera Raw Defaults.

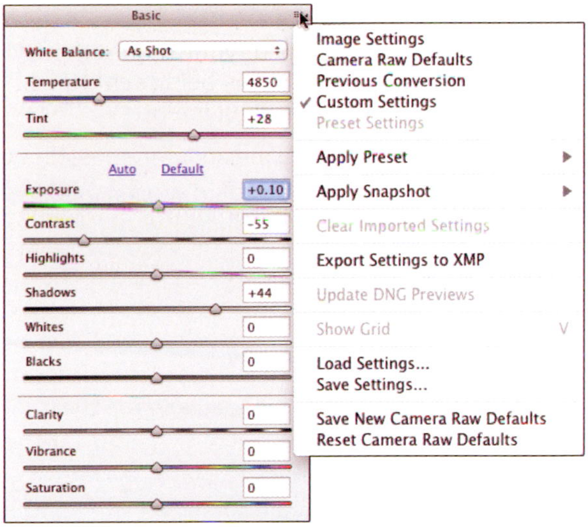

Figure 7-10: Camera Raw permits you to save, export, and import settings, as well as establish custom default settings.

Here's my recommendation:

1. **Open one of your typical images.**

   Open an image that's well exposed and typical for what and how you shoot. *Don't* open some wild image that's three-quarters wrecked and in need of emergency surgery.

2. **Adjust the image to make it look perfect.**

   The various adjustments are discussed in the following sections. Make all the necessary adjustments, including noise reduction and camera calibration if required.

3. **Save as your new defaults.**

   Open the menu and select Save As New Camera Raw Defaults.

Now when you open one of your images into Camera Raw, you'll already have a good correction established and you'll need to tweak the settings only a bit to adjust for the peculiarities and vagaries of that particular shot.

Remember, too, that you can save settings for each individual shoot by using the Save Settings command. Say, for example, that you shot on-location under difficult lighting circumstances. Rather than adjusting each image, adjust one, save the settings, and load (or apply) those settings for each additional image from that shoot that needs to be processed.

The Basic panel

When it comes to actually correcting your images in Camera Raw, the meat-and-potatoes portion is the Basic panel. Click on the leftmost of the eight tabs directly below the histogram area to open the Basic panel, which is shown in Figure 7-11.

Here are some general guidelines for working in the Basic panel (but remember that each image has its own particular requirements):

- **Adjust the white point.** Generally, you adjust the white point (the Temperature and the Tint sliders) by clicking with the White Balance tool (which looks like the Eyedropper tool, shown here in the margin) in some area that should be neutral and close to white. If the image doesn't look right, click elsewhere or manually adjust the Temperature and Tint sliders.

- **Adjust the Exposure.** Drag the Exposure slider right or left to spread the histogram across most of the space available. (Remember, these are general guidelines for *typical* images, not "rules.")

✔ **Fine-tune the shadows and highlights**. Use the Highlights and Shadows sliders to adjust the relationship between the brightest pixels and the midtones and between the darkest pixels and the midtones. You can fine-tune the highlights a bit more with the Whites sliders and touch up the shadows with the Blacks slider.

✔ **Fine-tune the contrast.** Drag the Contrast slider to the right to increase contrast or to the left to flatten out the image's contrast.

✔ **Make the image "pop" with the Clarity slider.** Drag the Clarity slider to the right to increase the contrast among neighboring areas of color. Somewhat akin to sharpening, this slider can do a great job of adding life to most images.

✔ **Tweak the colors.** Using the Vibrance slider in conjunction with the Saturation slider, adjust the appearance of the color in your image. Remember that the Saturation adjustment is applied to all colors in the image, while Vibrance works primarily with the near-neutral colors.

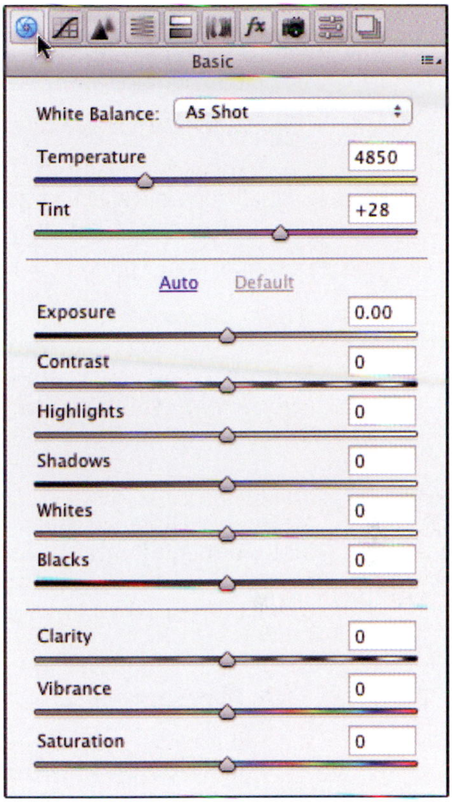

Basic		
White Balance:	As Shot	
Temperature		4850
Tint		+28
	Auto Default	
Exposure		0.00
Contrast		0
Highlights		0
Shadows		0
Whites		0
Blacks		0
Clarity		0
Vibrance		0
Saturation		0

Figure 7-11: The Basic panel is where you do the bulk of your image correction.

Double-click any slider control to reset that slider to its default value. This works not only for sliders in the Basic panel, but also for sliders anywhere in Camera Raw.

As you work, the best adjustments are those that make the image look great to you and meet your creative goals. The order of adjustments and the histogram suggestions here are *not* appropriate for all images. Let your artistic sense be your guide.

Vibrance and Saturation

Both the Vibrance and the Saturation sliders in Camera Raw adjust the intensity of colors in your image. So what's the difference? The Saturation slider changes all color in the image, whereas the Vibrance slider works its magic primarily on those pixels that are least saturated. To see how this works, open an image in Camera Raw and adjust the sliders to make the image look great. Drag the Saturation slider all the way to the left. Grayscale, right? Move the Saturation slider all the way to the right. Over-saturated, right? Drag the Vibrance slider slowly to the right while keeping an eye on areas of the image that are close-to-but-not-quite gray. Watch how they increase in saturation, gradually going from near gray to almost colorful. Now here's the coolest trick of all: With Saturation still at +100, drag the Vibrance slider all the way to the left, to −100. Starting with an appropriate image, this can be a *very* interesting effect.

The second tab in Camera Raw, just to the right of the Basic tab, presents you with a pair of ways to adjust the histogram using curves (see Figure 7-12). In the Tone Curve panel, you have two tabs: Parametric and Point. The first thing to know about the Tone Curve adjustments is that they are *in addition to* changes you make in the Basic tab. All changes are cumulative — dragging sliders in the Parametric panel, for example, won't change the sliders on the Basic tab.

In the Parametric panel, you adjust four sliders to control various parts of the tonal range. The three sliders immediately below the curve itself govern the *pivot points* around which the sliders bend the curve. The two outer sliders govern what part of the tonal range is affected by the Shadows and Highlights sliders, and the middle slider controls the relationship between the Darks and Lights sliders.

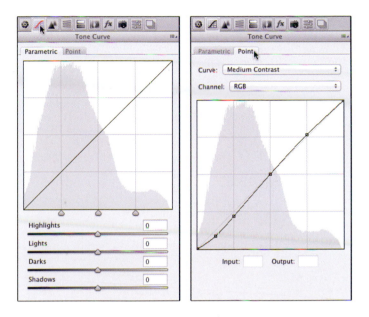

Figure 7-12: You make changes to tonality in the Tone Curve tab.

The Point panel of the Tone Curve tab is quite similar to the Curves adjustment in Photoshop: Click the curve to add an anchor point; drag up and down to adjust that part of the tonal range. You can add up to 14 separate points to the curve. Click an anchor point to make it active (it appears as a solid point rather than hollow) and you can use the Input and Output fields to adjust the point numerically, or use the arrow keys to change the point's location. You can also choose a preset from the Curve menu as a starting point and, if desired, adjust each of the RGB channels individually.

So, you might ask yourself, "Should I use the Basic tab, the Tone Curve tab, or both?" And the answer is "Yes, you should use the Basic tab, or the Tone Curve tab, or both." You might find that you're more comfortable using one curve or the other rather than the Blacks, Brightness, and Contrast sliders in the Basic tab. Or you might find that for one particular image, you want to make large adjustments with one set of sliders and fine-tune with the other.

The Detail panel

Nine sliders on the Detail tab (as shown in Figure 7-13) control sharpness and noise in your image. I suggest that as soon as you click the Detail tab, you zoom in to 200% or even 400% on an area of shadow in your image and drag the sliders all the way to the left, setting them to 0 (zero). Rather than working from the top down, as you do in most Camera Raw panels, I generally suggest reducing noise before sharpening. Drag the Color Noise Reduction slider slowly to the right until all red/green/blue specks in the shadows disappear. Next, drag the Luminance slider to the right until the bright specks in your shadows are reduced but not so far to the right that detail in your image is damaged. Use the Luminance Detail, Luminance Contrast, and Color Detail sliders in conjunction with the Luminance and Color sliders to minimize the loss of detail.

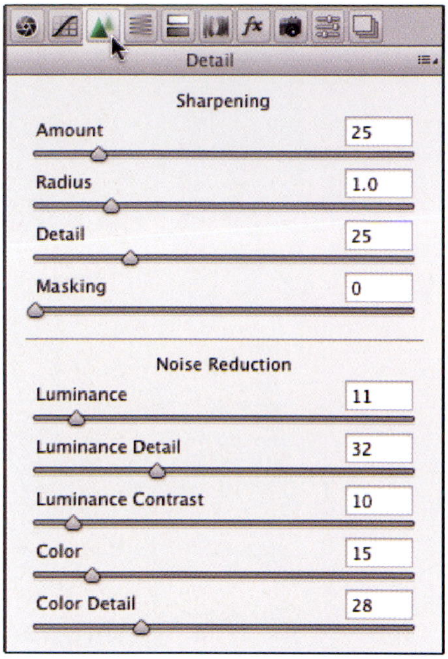

Sharpening in Camera Raw has developed so much that it's perhaps better than sharpening in Photoshop. Rather than a single slider, you now have four sliders with which to perfect your images:

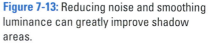

Figure 7-13: Reducing noise and smoothing luminance can greatly improve shadow areas.

- ✔ **Amount**. The Amount slider is the basic how-much-sharpening-am-I-adding slider. You might consider "sharpening" to be creating bright and dark "halos" along edges in the image. Amount refers to the brightness/darkness of those halos. The slider ranges from zero to 150.

- ✔ **Radius.** The Radius slider controls the width of the "halos" along the edges. Higher is wider, up to a maximum of 3 pixels.

- ✔ **Detail.** Use the Detail slider to control how large an edge has to be to get included in the sharpening process. Leave it at zero and only major edges in the image are sharpened. Drag the slider all the way to the right, to 100, and everything in the image gets sharpened, every pore, each grain of sand — even the remains of any digital noise you want to hide.

- ✔ **Masking.** The Masking slider, used in conjunction with the Detail slider, can help protect the smallest detail in the image from becoming over-sharpened and garish. The farther to the right you drag the slider, the more tiny detail is excluded.

Here's the coolest part: Zoom in to at least 100% and hold down the Option/Alt key while dragging any of the Sharpening sliders — you'll see a grayscale preview of what you're actually doing to your image!

Figure 7-14 shows three views of the same image: The unsharpened original (top); the Sharpening sliders set to Amount–85, Radius–1.0, Detail–55, and Masking–5 (middle); the preview of the Detail adjustment (bottom).

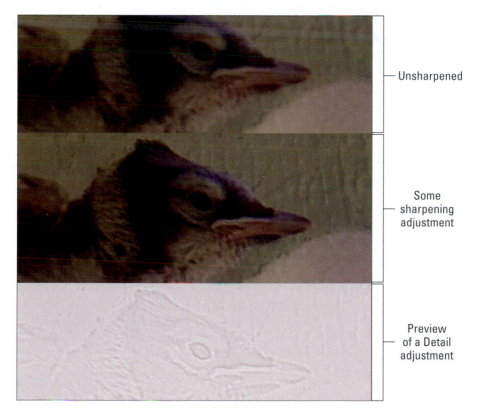

Unsharpened

Some sharpening adjustment

Preview of a Detail adjustment

Figure 7-14: Hold down the Option/Alt key while dragging to preview the sharpening.

HSL, grayscale, and split toning

Working with options in three tabs, Camera Raw's HSL/Grayscale feature gives you incredible control over hue, saturation, and luminance of specific color ranges in your image. Need to perk up the reds in your image? Not a problem — boost the Reds slider in Saturation and Luminance! Yellows a bit too garish? Tone 'em down with the Yellows slider. Maybe the green grass looks a bit yellow. Drag the Greens slider halfway to the right in the Hue tab. You can control each of the eight major color ranges independently (as shown in Figure 7-15).

Figure 7-15: Grayscale greenery contrasts nicely with highly saturated blooms.

A fourth panel, Grayscale Mix, appears only when the Convert to Grayscale box is selected. With the Convert to Grayscale option selected, you control the contribution of each range of color to the final grayscale image. Use the Basic tab's Exposure, Blacks, Brightness, and Contrast sliders to control the overall appearance of the image.

The Saturation tab also enables you to create partial grayscale images quite easily. Drag some sliders to the left to make those areas of color grayscale; drag others to the right to enhance the remaining colors. Figure 7-15 shows an excellent candidate for this partial-grayscale technique.

The Split Toning tab is generally used in conjunction with the Convert to Grayscale option HSL/Grayscale tab. (Although you can use it to make adjustments to highlights or shadows, you would generally remove or introduce a color cast in the Basic tab with the Temperature and Tint sliders.) Think of split toning as creating a sepia or Duotone version of an image. As you can see in Figure 7-16, you have separate controls for adjusting the highlights and shadows. Select a different hue for each and adjust the saturation independently. The Balance slider allows you to control what part of the tonal range is considered highlight or shadow.

To create a sepia effect, start with a value of 40 in both of the Highlights fields and perhaps +30 for Balance. Use a Shadow saturation value of 0 (and because saturation is set to 0, it doesn't matter what value you select for the Hue slider). Remember, too, that you can select the same hue for both Highlights and Shadows to create a monochrome effect.

Figure 7-16: A photo of a bland building in front of an overcast sky is improved with split toning.

Compensating with Lens Corrections

Use the Lens Corrections tab's controls (as shown in Figure 7-17) to compensate for certain undesirable characteristics of your lens. Click on the Profile tab within Lens Corrections, select the option Enable Lens Profile Corrections and let Camera Raw fine-tune your image based on a database of lenses. You can further adjust for pin cushioning (the center of the image looks too far away) and barrel distortion (the center seems to be bulging) with the Distortion slider. The Vignetting slider is used for excessive shadowing or brightening in the corners of the image. (Use this slider only to correct for unwanted vignetting. If you want to add a vignette, use the Post Crop Vignetting section of the Effects pane, discussed in the next section.)

Don't overlook the Remove Chromatic Aberration box! Zoom in on an area of angled lines in a corner of your image — perhaps tree branches in front of a bright sky — and look for colorful halos or fringes along edges. Select/deselect Remove Chromatic Aberration to see how it magically removes the fringe. (And don't forget to re-select.) Figure 7-17 shows an example of before and after.

The Manual tab in the Lens Corrections panel (visible to the right in Figure 7-17) can be used when there's no profile available. It can also supplement auto corrections made in the Profile tab. You might find the Vertical, Horizontal, and Rotate sliders very handy. The Scale slider zooms in (drag to the right) and out (drag to the left). It doesn't change the pixel dimensions of the image, but it does change how much of the image is displayed within those pixels. Zooming in on the center of the image crops to that area, whereas zooming out will add a gray frame around the image when opened.

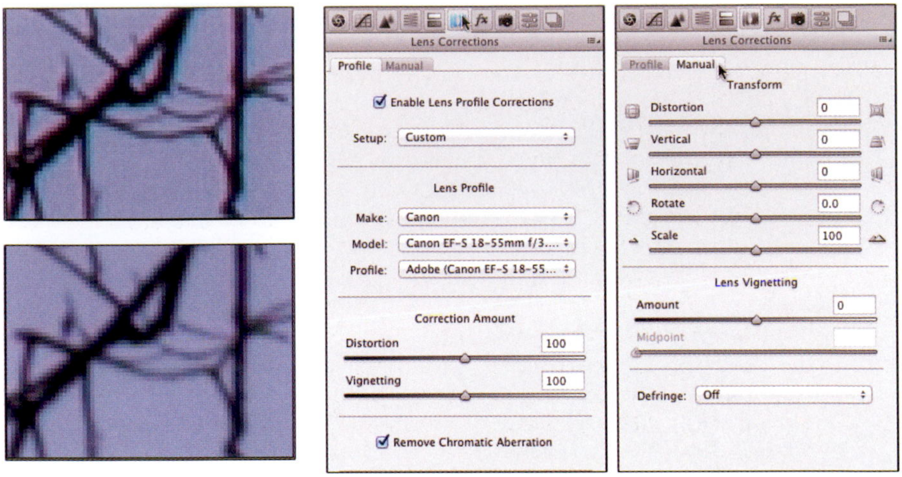

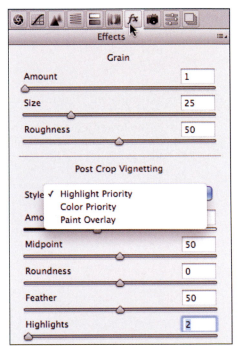

Figure 7-17: Chromatic aberration (top) and then removed (bottom); to the right, the automated and manual Lens Corrections panels.

Adding special effects

The Effects pane of Camera Raw, shown in Figure 7-18, is used to add simulated film grain and vignette effects. Instead of using Photoshop's Artistic⇨Film Grain or Texture⇨Grain filters, you may choose to simulate grain in Camera Raw. (Or perhaps you won't add any film grain. Ever. Especially after you worked so hard to minimize noise in your images. Your *digital* images.) The Post Crop Vignetting sliders are used to add a dark or light vignette effect (unlike the Vignette slider discussed in the preceding section, which is used to remove a vignette.) You can add a vignette before or after working with the Straighten and Crop tools. For both Grain and Post Crop Vignetting, adjust the Amount slider first to activate the other sliders. Experiment with the three options in the Style menu to see which type of vignette best suits your artistic vision.

Figure 7-18: Simulate film grain and vignettes in the Effects panel.

Camera profiles, presets, and snapshots

Generally you'll skip the Camera Calibration tab completely, with one exception: Make sure the Process menu is set to "2012 (Current)" to take advantage of the improvements in this version of Camera Raw. You might, however, want to use the Camera Calibration tab to compensate for what you perceive to be regular and consistent deviation in your particular camera's behavior. You might, under some circumstances, want to use the sliders on the Camera Calibration tab to reduce a *color cast,* an unwanted color tint in the image. Use very small adjustments!

If your particular camera model has had multiple profiles created, you'll see them listed in the Name menu. These camera profiles correlate to the in-camera settings you may have selected when capturing the image. (The content of the menu varies from one camera model to the next.)

Camera Raw's Presets and Snapshots tabs provide handy ways to streamline your work. If you think you'll need one particular set of adjustments again with other images (perhaps a series of similar images, or a favorite special effect), you can use Camera Raw's menu command Save Settings (refer to Figure 7-10) to create a preset. Saved settings are listed by name in the Presets panel. Use the Snapshots panel to save and restore to points in your development process of a single image. Saved snapshots, unlike their History panel counterparts, are saved with the image and can be accessed at any time in the future.

The Camera Raw buttons

In the lower-left and lower-right corners of Camera Raw are four buttons, three of which have hidden features that you access by pressing the Option/Alt key:

- **Save Image . . ./Save Image:** After making your adjustments, click the Save Image . . . button to save a copy of the image as a DNG, JPEG, TIFF, or PSD file. Option/Alt+click to bypass the Save Options dialog box and simply save the image using the most recently selected options.

- **Open Image/Open Copy (or Open Object/Open Copy):** After making your adjustments, click Open to update the file's metadata and open the image in Photoshop itself. Holding down Option/Alt changes the button to Open Copy, which opens the image without updating the metadata. You might use Open Copy when creating a second version of the image while preserving your exactingly precise original adjustments. (Remember that a simple change in the Workflow Options — which you open by clicking the blue information line under the preview — enables you to automatically open an image from Camera Raw into Photoshop as a Smart Object.)

- **Cancel/Reset:** Clicking Cancel closes the Camera Raw window without making any changes to the image's metadata. Holding down the Option/ Alt key changes the button to Reset, which restores the settings seen when you first opened the image in Camera Raw.

- **Done:** The Done button, with or without the Option/Alt key, simply updates the image's metadata with the adjustments you've made and closes Camera Raw without opening the image.

8

Fine-Tuning Your Fixes

*T*here you are, repainting the bedroom — all by yourself, saving money, being productive — and it's time to do the windows. Now, you probably don't want to paint over the glass, right? Just the frame, the sash, the sill, those little whatch-ya-call-its between the panes, right? (Okay, technically the dividers between the panes are called *muntins*.) There are several ways you can avoid painting the glass. You can use a little brush and paint *very* carefully. You can use a larger brush, paint faster, and scrape the excess from the glass afterward. You can grab the masking tape, protect the glass, and paint as sloppily as you like — when the tape comes off, the glass is paint-free.

Those are unbelievably similar to the choices that you have in Photoshop when you need to work on only a part of your image. You can zoom in and use tools, dragging the cursor over only those pixels that you want to change (just like using a tiny paintbrush). You can use the History Brush feature (which I introduce in Chapter 1) to restore parts of the image to the original state (like scraping the glass). You can isolate the area of the image you want to change with a selection (much like protecting the rest of the image with masking tape).

In this chapter, you read about getting ready to make changes to your image rather than actually making those changes. You can isolate groups of pixels in your image in a variety of ways. For example, you can select pixels that are in the same part of the image (regardless of color), or you can select pixels that are the same color (regardless of location in the image). This is *power:* the ability to tell Photoshop exactly which pixels you want to alter. After you make that selection, you can manipulate the pixels in a variety of ways — everything from making color and tonal adjustments to working with Photoshop's creative filters to simply copying them so you can paste them into another image.

I discuss "taping the glass" first by making selections and then by using *masks* — channels that actually store selection information. After that, I tell you about working with *adjustment layers,* which are special layers that help you apply certain color and tonal adjustments without actually changing any pixels in the image. An adjustment layer even lets you restrict the change to one or several layers in the image.

What Is a Selection?

When you make a *selection* in your image, you're simply isolating some of the pixels, picking them (*selecting* them) so that you can do something to those pixels without doing it to all the pixels in your image. Photoshop shows you what part of the image is within the selection with a flashing dashed line. (Now that you're part of the Photoshop Inner Circle, you call that selection boundary the *marching ants.*)

Say, for example, that part of your image looks great, but part of the image looks, well, just plain wrong. Figure 8-1 is an excellent example.

Figure 8-1: Sometimes only part of the image needs changes.

By making a selection and applying an adjustment, I can make this image look much, much better. Of course, you might choose to make a different selection and apply a different adjustment, but you can see what I chose to do in Figure 8-2. By selecting the rails (in this case, with the Polygon Lasso tool, which I explain later in this chapter), I isolate those areas from the rest of the image, enabling me to change the color of those pixels without changing anything else. (Rather than selecting and darkening the rails to make them appear to be in front of a glow, I could have selected the lighter area and created a uniform sky color. But this is visually more interesting.)

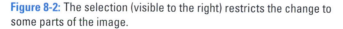

Figure 8-2: The selection (visible to the right) restricts the change to some parts of the image.

The tonal and color adjustments that I discuss in Chapters 5 and 6 are often applied to an image as a whole. You can, however, apply them to specific areas of an image. Much of the rest of the work that you do in Photoshop is not global in nature, but rather is done to only restricted areas of your image. You use selections to do that restricting.

You can also use selections for a variety of other jobs in Photoshop. One of the most common is copying from one image and pasting into another. You can see one example in Figure 8-3. The subject of one image (upper left) is selected. You can see a close-up of the selection to the right. Choosing Edit⇨Copy copies the selected pixels to the Clipboard. You can then switch to another image and use the Edit⇨Paste command to drop those pixels into a second image (lower left). You can adjust the size by choosing Edit⇨Transform⇨Scale, adjust the position by dragging with the Move tool, and perhaps add some shadows by using the Brush tool. The composited picture is ready for whatever nefarious purpose you might have in mind!

Figure 8-3: Make a selection, copy, switch to another image, and paste.

Any pixel in your image can be selected, deselected, or partially selected. For example, if you have a selection and fill it with red, the selected pixels turn red, the deselected pixels don't change, and the partially selected pixels get a red tint. How much tint depends on the level of selection. (Photoshop generally uses 8-bit grayscale for selections, so there are 256 different levels of "selected.")

Feathering and Anti-Aliasing

You need to keep in mind a couple of very important terms as you read about the various tools and commands with which you make selections. Both *feathering* and *anti-aliasing* make the edges of your selections softer by using partially transparent or differently colored pixels. That, in turn, helps blend whatever you're doing to that selection into the rest of the image.

Don't forget that all pixels in your image are square, aligned in neat, orderly rows and columns. (That's the *raster* in raster artwork.) When you create a curve or diagonal in your artwork, the corners of the pixels stick out. Feathering and anti-aliasing disguise that ragged edge. You can also use feathering to create larger, softer selections with a faded edge. Generally speaking, use anti-aliasing to keep edges looking neat and use feathering to create a soft, faded selection.

Nothing illustrates the power of feathering quite like a simple black-on-white demonstration, as you see in Figure 8-4. In the upper-left, I made an unfeathered selection and filled it with black. To the upper-right, the filled selection is exactly the same size but has a 2-pixel feather. Below, I used a 15-pixel feather when making the selection.

Note that there's feathering on both sides of the selection border. And don't be fooled by the amount that you enter in the Feather field on the Options bar — that's a general guideline, not a precise value. A 15-pixel feather for the Elliptical Marquee tool might give you 50 or 60 partially transparent pixels, half on either side of the selection border. Even a 1-pixel feather gives you a selection with several "soft" pixels on either side.

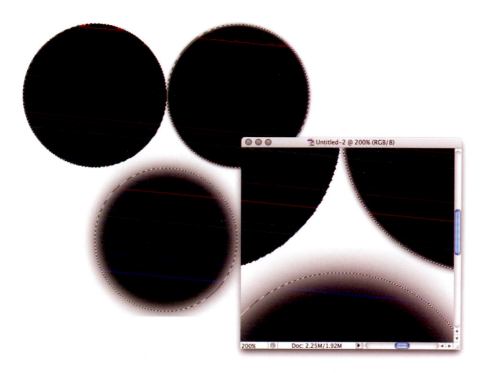

Figure 8-4: A close-up look at no feathering, feathering, and lots of feathering.

Anti-aliasing is similar to feathering in that it softens edges: It's designed to hide the corners of pixels along curves and in diagonal lines. You use anti-aliasing with type (as I explain in Chapter 13). You'll often find that anti-aliasing is all you need to keep the edges of your selections pretty; feathering isn't required. Anti-aliasing is a yes/no option, with no numeric field to worry about. Figure 8-5 compares a diagonal with no anti-aliasing, with anti-aliasing, and with a 1-pixel feather.

Figure 8-5: Anti-aliasing helps smooth the appearance of curves and diagonals.

At 100 percent zoom (to the upper left), the first line looks bumpy along the edges (it has a case of the *jaggies,* you would complain to a friend or co-worker). The lower line looks soft and mushy, out of focus. And the middle line? To quote Goldilocks, "It's just right!" When zoomed to 600 percent, you can really see those jaggies and that softening. And in the middle, you see that the anti-aliasing uses light gray and mid-gray pixels interspersed along the edge among the black pixels. At 100 percent zoom (upper left), your eye is fooled into seeing a straight black edge.

Making Your Selections with Tools

Photoshop offers you nine tools whose whole purpose in life is to help you make selections. You also use those tools to alter your selections by adding to, subtracting from, and intersecting with an existing selection. The nine selection tools are divided into three groups:

- ✔ Four marquee tools
- ✔ Three lasso tools
- ✔ The Quick Selection tool and the Magic Wand

Marquee selection tools

You have four marquee selection tools, although you'll generally use only two of them. Figure 8-6 shows the marquee selection tools, along with each tool's Options bar configuration. (Note that the Refine Edge button is only available when you have an active selection in your image.)

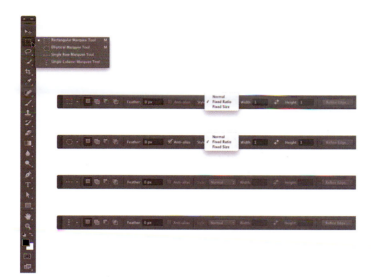

Figure 8-6: Marquee selection tools come in four flavors, two of which are tasty.

You drag the very useful Rectangular Marquee and Elliptical Marquee tools to make selections. Click and drag in any direction to make your selection. After you start dragging, hold down the Shift key (while still dragging) to constrain proportions. When you constrain the proportions of a selection, you create a square or circle rather than a rectangle or an ellipse. If you start dragging a selection and press the Option (Mac)/Alt (Windows) key, the selection centers itself on the point where you click. The Shift and Option/Alt keys can be used together. Holding down the Shift key *before* you click and drag adds the selection to any existing selection. Holding down the Option/Alt key *before* dragging subtracts the new selection from any existing selection.

The Single Row Marquee and Single Column Marquee tools are simply clicked at the point where you want a 1-pixel selection, running from side to side or from top to bottom. These tools create selections that extend the full width or full height of your image. You might use these tools to create a gridlike selection that you can fill with color. Or you might never use them at all.

Take another glance at the Options bars in Figure 8-6. The four buttons to the left in the Options bar, which you can use with any of the tools, determine how the tool interacts with an existing selection.

✔ **New Selection:** When you select the first button, any selection that you make replaces an active selection (deselecting any previous selection). If, with a selection tool, you click inside an active selection when the first option is active, you can drag that selection in your image without moving any pixels. When you haven't already made a selection, these tools always make a new selection, regardless of which button is active.

✔ **Add To:** When you have an active selection and need to add to that selection, use the second button or simply press and hold down the Shift key while dragging.

✔ **Subtract From:** When you have a selection and need to deselect part of it, use the third button. Say, for example, that you make a round selection and want to chop out the middle to make a donut shape. Click the third button and then drag within the original selection to deselect the donut hole.

✔ **Intersect With:** You have a selection, but you want to keep only part of the selection. You could set your selection tool to subtract from the existing selection, or you could intersect with that original selection and deselect a number of areas at once.

Figure 8-7 presents a visual explanation of how all four buttons work. On the left, you see the selected option for the active marquee selection tool. Next is an original selection. In the third column, you see another selection being made (with the selection tool dragged from the lower right to the upper left). Finally, on the right, you see the result of combining the two selections.

In the bottommost example, you could do a whole series of subtractions from the existing selection to chop off the "points," but using the intersect option takes care of the job with a single drag.

While you're dragging a selection with the Rectangular Marquee or the Elliptical Marquee tool, you can hold down the mouse button and press and hold the spacebar to reposition the marquee. When you have it where you want it, release the spacebar and continue to drag.

Take another look at the four views of the Options bar shown earlier in Figure 8-6. Take note of these variations among them:

✔ Anti-aliasing isn't available for the Rectangular Marquee tool. That's because all four edges of the selection will align perfectly with the edges of the pixels — no need to disguise corners of pixels. (You can, of course, soften the selection with feathering.)

✔ Both the Rectangular Marquee and the Elliptical Marquee tools offer the options of Normal (unconstrained, just drag as necessary), Fixed Aspect Ratio (the relationship between width and height you specify in the Options bar is maintained as you drag), and Fixed Size (just click in the upper-left corner of your intended selection).

✔ The Single Row Marquee and Single Column Marquee tools offer the four buttons to determine how the tool will interact with an existing selection and the Feather field. Although feathering a 1-pixel wide or tall selection seems a little strange . . .

Figure 8-7: The buttons at the left on the Options bar control selection interaction.

Lasso selection tools

Three lasso selection tools are available in Photoshop. On the Options bar, all three of the lasso selection tools offer you the same basic features that you find in the marquee selection tools, as you can see in Figure 8-8. You can add to, subtract from, or intersect with an existing selection. You also have the feathering and anti-aliasing options available. The Magnetic Lasso tool offers three additional settings that help determine how it identifies edges as you drag.

Figure 8-8: The basic options for the lasso selection tools match those for the marquee selection tools.

So what makes lasso tools different from a marquee tool? Read on to find out:

- **Lasso tool:** The Lasso tool is a true *freeform* tool; that is, you click and drag it wherever you want the selection to go. You can drag around and return to the starting point, or you can release the mouse button anywhere, and your selection is finished along a straight line from that point to the spot where you start your selection. If you press and hold the Option/Alt key while dragging, you'll temporarily switch to the Polygon Lasso tool.

- **Polygon Lasso tool:** Rather than dragging, you click-click-click to make straight selection segments, at any angle, for any distance. When you position the cursor directly over your starting point, a little circle appears to the lower right of the cursor to indicate that you're back to the start. Or simply double-click to finish the selection. If you press and hold the Option/Alt key while dragging, you'll temporarily switch to the regular Lasso tool, which lets you drag your selection any way you want. Using the Option/Alt key lets you switch back and forth between the freeform drag of the Lasso tool and the perfectly straight selection borders of the Polygon Lasso tool.

- **Magnetic Lasso tool:** When you need to select around a subject that has good contrast with its background, the Magnetic Lasso tool can do a great job. The perfect candidate for this tool is a simple object on a very plain background. You can, however, use it with just about any image where the edges of the area you want to select differ substantially from the rest of the image. Click and drag the tool along the edge of your subject. If the tool misses the edge, back up and drag along the edge again. If the edge makes a sudden change in direction, click to add an anchor point. If the tool places an anchor point in the wrong spot, back up and then press Delete/Backspace to remove the point. (By the way, if you have a Wacom pressure-sensitive tablet hooked up, you can set the Magnetic Lasso tool to vary its width according to pen pressure. Use the button just to the right of the Frequency field on the Options bar.)

The Magnetic Lasso tool works by identifying the difference in color along the edges, using all available color channels. From the Options bar, use the Width field to tell the tool how wide an area it can look in to find an edge. The edge Contrast field tells the tool how much the edge must differ while searching. Use the Frequency field to choose the number of anchor points the tool sets while outlining the selection.

The Quick Selection tool

Consider the Quick Selection tool to be sort of a color-based-selection-in-a-brush. You drag the tool through an area of color and, based on the color variations under the brush and the brush size, the tool automatically selects similar colors in the surrounding area. Keep in mind that you can adjust the brush size as you work by using the square bracket keys, [and]. (When working with a Wacom tablet, this tool works great with brush size set to pen pressure.) The Auto-Enhance option in the Options bar may slow down the performance of the Quick Selection tool a bit, but the great job it does analyzing edges usually produces a better selection. With just a little practice, you'll likely find the Quick Selection tool to be quite simple to use, even for rather complex selections (see Figure 8-9).

Figure 8-9: Drag through an area of color to select the pixels under the brush and nearby pixels of similar color.

Controlled selections

Lurking within the Options bar Style drop-down menu are two options worth noting: Fixed Aspect Ratio and Fixed Size. Using the Fixed Aspect Ratio option with the Rectangular Marquee or the Elliptical Marquee tool forces the selection to the height and width relationship that you specify in the Options bar. This is great for composing an image that you need at a specific size, say to fit in a standard 5 x 7-inch picture frame. The selection tool won't resize the image for you, but you can make the selection and choose Image⇨Crop and then choose Image⇨Image Size to resize to your required dimensions and resolution. (Read about resizing and cropping your images in Chapter 4.)

The Fixed Size option changes the behavior of the tools. After you enter an exact width and height in the Options bar, position the cursor in the upper-left corner of the area that you want to select and click once — the selection is created to the lower right of that point. Don't worry about being exact because you can drag the selection marquee into position afterward. (You'll want to have the leftmost of the four buttons on the Options bar selected to reposition your selection.) And take a look at the button between the Width and Height fields on the Options bar: When you're using the Fixed Aspect Ratio or Fixed Size styles, click that button to swap the values in the two fields.

The Magic Wand tool

The Magic Wand tool selects pixels similar in color to the pixel on which you click with the tool. Like the other selection commands, you can add to, subtract from, or intersect with an existing selection, and you can select anti-aliasing. *Tolerance* determines how closely pixels must match your target color to be included in the selection. When you enable the Contiguous check box and then click a spot, only pixels connected to the spot by pixels of the same color are selected. The Sample All Layers option lets you make a selection of similarly colored pixels on every visible layer in your image, not just the currently active layer.

When you use a low Tolerance setting, you select only those pixels in the image that are very similar to the pixel on which you click. A high Tolerance setting gives you a much wider range of color, which might or might not be appropriate for the selection you're making.

Refine Edge

You may have noticed the Refine Edge button in Figures 8-6, 8-8, and 8-9. It sits quietly to the right of the other options in the Options bar, waiting for you to click. Take a gander at Figure 8-10 to see the Refine Edge dialog box.

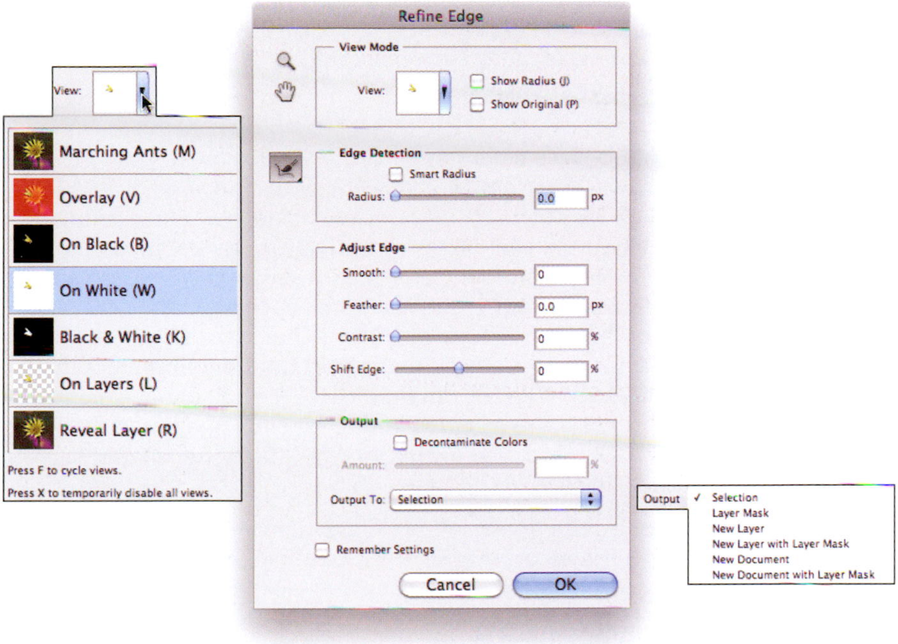

Figure 8-10: Refine Edge is a very powerful feature for fine-tuning selections.

Here's what you need to know about each of the options in Refine Edge:

- **View Mode:** Click on the downward-pointing triangle to select from among several different ways to view the selection you're refining. Using a black or white or red mask is great for many images, but the new On Layers option shows you the content of the selection as if it was floating on a separate layer. Show Radius and Show Original are great for a quick preview of what you're doing, but you'll generally take a look and then disable those options. The keyboard shortcuts for the various views are also handy, especially X to disable all views and show the original and F to cycle through the view modes to see which is most appropriate for the current task.

- **Edge Detection:** The Radius slider determines how much an area surrounding the initial selection will be refined. The Smart Radius option enables Refine Edge to differentiate between hard edges and soft edges — think in terms of the edge between the subject's shirt and the background (usually a well-defined "hard" edge) versus the subject's hair and the background (usually a fuzzy "soft" edge).

- **Adjust Edge:** Smoothing the selection edge minimizes any jagged areas. Feathering (as described earlier in this chapter) softens the edge. Contrast makes the selection edge more distinct. (You rarely use Feather and Contrast together.) Shift Edge expands or contracts the selection edge.

- **Output:** Here's where Refine Edge really rocks! You can click OK and see a newly-refined selection marching around some pixels in your image, but you also have the options of clicking OK and producing a layer mask (background layers are automatically converted), a new layer with only the content of the refined selection, a new layer using a layer mask to reveal the content of the selection, a new document with only the content of the selection, *or* a new document consisting of a layer using a layer mask to reveal the content of the selection! Decontaminate Colors can do a great job of eliminating that fringe of background color that sometimes appears when you're making complex selections. (With this option selected, you output to a new layer or document, with or without a layer mask.)

- **Tools:** To the upper-left in Refine Edge are the usual Zoom and Hand tools for inspecting your work up close. Below them is the Refine Radius tool, with which you can selectively expand the area in which Refine Edge looks for edges of the selection. Drag over areas where you see omissions along edges in the selection, hold down the Option/Alt key, and drag the tool to eliminate areas from the selection.

- **Remember Settings:** If you hit upon a sweet set of refinement settings that look like they are a sure-fire answer to most of your selection challenges, by all means make sure to select the Remember Settings box before you click OK. Refine Edge then starts with those preferred settings each time you open the dialog box.

Refine Edge does double duty as Refine Mask, which can be used to tweak an existing layer mask. In the Layers panel, click on the layer mask thumbnail to make it active. From the Select menu, choose Refine Mask. Use the options discussed in the previous list, elect to output to a layer mask, and click OK. The selected layer mask is updated to reflect the changes you specified in Refine Mask.

Your Selection Commands

You have 17 menu commands at your service when selecting pixels in your artwork. Some, like those near the top of the Select menu, are rather simple and aptly named. See Figure 8-11 for a list of the Select commands. (The All Layers, Deselect Layers, and Similar Layers commands are not used to select pixels, but rather to change the activation of layers in the Layers panel. The New 3D Extrusion command is available only in Photoshop CS6 Extended — see Chapter 18 for a look at the Extended features.)

The primary selection commands

The commands near the top of the Select menu are features that you're likely to use regularly. (Okay, maybe not the Reselect command.) Memorizing their keyboard shortcuts and using them regularly is a timesaver.

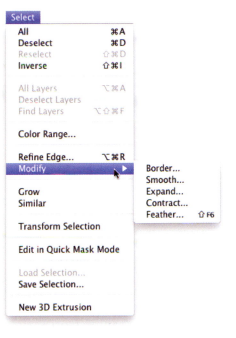

Figure 8-11: The Deselect or Reselect command — or both — are always grayed out, depending on whether there's an active selection in your image.

- ✔ **Select All (⌘+A/Ctrl+A):** Select All does exactly what the name implies — it makes a selection of all the pixels in your image on the active layer (or in an active layer mask).

- ✔ **Deselect (⌘+D/Ctrl+D):** Use the Deselect command to make sure that no pixels are selected. This is a handy command when it seems that a tool, or a filter or adjustment command isn't working. There could be an unnoticed selection in the image, preventing the command from appearing how — or where — you expect.

- ✔ **Reselect (⌘+Shift+D/Ctrl+Shift+D):** This is a great little command for those times when you're making a complex selection, and a little slip accidentally deselects. Just use Reselect to restore the most recent selection. Or use the Undo command.

- ✔ **Inverse (⌘+Shift+I/Ctrl+Shift+I):** The Inverse command reverses the selection. What was selected is deselected, and what wasn't selected becomes selected. (Don't forget to include the Shift key — without it, you invert the colors in your image rather than your selection!)

The Color Range command

In its own little group, right in the middle of the Select menu, is the incredibly powerful Color Range command. Rather than dragging the Quick Selection tool or Shift+clicking with the Magic Wand, you can select by color quickly and easily with the Color Range command. In Figure 8-12, I clicked and dragged through some orange areas in the image with the middle Eyedropper tool. You

Figure 8-12: The Color Range feature selects by color.

can also click once with the left eyedropper and use the other eyedroppers to add and subtract colors from the selection. The Fuzziness slider near the top of the dialog box determines how close a color must be to those through which you dragged to be included in the selection.

Here are a couple of ways that you can get a better look at your selection as you create it. In Figure 8-13, you see the options available from the Selection Preview menu. The Grayscale (upper left) and Black Matte (upper right) do a good job of showing that the background will be partially selected if you click OK. You can lower the Fuzziness or use the eyedropper on the right to click in those areas of

the fence that shouldn't be selected. The White Matte (lower left) does an excellent job of showing that the tips of some leaves below the blooms will also be selected. (Ignore that and Option+drag/Alt+drag with the Lasso tool later to deselect that area.) Because of the color of this image's subject, the red Quick Mask preview (lower right) is almost worthless for this image, although it is often good with other images that don't have red and orange.

Figure 8-13: Color Range offers four ways to preview — five, if you include None.

The Localized Color Clusters option looks for distinct areas of the selected color and tightens up edges along those "clusters" of color. When your target color appears distinctly in different areas of the image, this option is a plus. When selecting a range of color with subtle transitions, deselect this option. (Think "leopard's spots" compared to "blue sky.")

When the Localized Color Clusters option is active, Color Range also offers Detect Faces. If you have people in the image that you want to select, Detect Faces does a rather good job of identifying them. You'll still need to Shift-drag through the rest of the person to make the selection, but faces are a good starting point. And don't overlook the Skin Tones option in the Select menu — it's a great way to start selecting flesh tones in an image.

Also available only when the Localized Color Clusters option is active, the Range slider determines how far from the point where you clicked in the image Color Range should look for similar colors. When set to 100%, Color Range looks at the entire image for similar colors. If you want to restrict the area in which you want to create a selection, you can reduce that value.

The pop-up menu at the top of the Color Range dialog box lets you pick among the RGB (red/green/blue) and CMY (cyan/magenta/yellow) colors, as well as the image's highlights, midtones, or shadows, and even any *out-of-gamut* colors in the image (colors that can't be reproduced within the selected color space). When you choose one of the presets from the top menu (other than Skin Tones), the Fuzziness slider isn't available, limiting that feature's value.

Selection modification commands

The next group of commands in the Select menu actually holds six separate commands, including Refine Edge (discussed earlier in this chapter), and the five Modify commands (shown in Figure 8-11), each of which has a single numeric field.

The Border option creates a selection of your specified width, centered on the original marching ants visible in the image window. It's great for creating borders or vignettes and can also be used to delete pixels along a selection edge to neaten it up. The other four commands are poor cousins to the control you have in the Refine Edge dialog box — none of them offers a slider or a preview. However, if you know exactly how many pixels you need to smooth or expand or contract or feather, these commands are quick and simple.

As you make your way down the Select menu, you come across the Grow and Similar commands, which are somewhat like the Magic Wand with Contiguous (Grow) and without Contiguous (Similar) selected on the Options bar. (In fact, they use the Magic Wand's Tolerance setting.) Grow adds to your selection any adjacent pixels of the appropriate color, and Similar looks throughout the entire image for similarly colored pixels. Use Grow and Similar when your initial selection consists primarily of a single color. Using these commands with a selection that contains lots of different colors generally results in most of your image being selected.

Transforming the shape of selections

As you work with selections, you might find times when the selection capability doesn't match your need. For example, the Elliptical Marquee tool can certainly make oval selections, but those ovals are either vertical or horizontal. What if you need an oval selection at an angle? That's where the Select⇨Transform command comes into play. Make your initial selection, choose the Transform Selection command, and then manipulate the selection to fit your needs, as shown in Figure 8-14.

Here's what you see in Figure 8-14:

- **Top left:** This is the original selection.

- **Top center:** Click an anchor point on any side of the bounding box and drag to change the height or width of the selection.

- **Top right:** Position the cursor outside the bounding box and drag to rotate.

- **Middle left:** Drag any corner anchor point to manipulate the selection's width and height at the same time.

- **Middle center:** Hold down the Shift key while dragging a corner anchor point to avoid distorting the selection while changing size.

- **Middle right:** Hold down the Option/Alt key while dragging a corner anchor point, and you end up scaling the image based on that crosshair in the center of the bounding box. (You can drag that crosshair anywhere, even outside the bounding box, to change the point of transformation.) You can use the Shift key with Option/Alt, too.

- **Bottom left:** Hold down the ⌘/Ctrl key and drag any side anchor point to skew.

- **Bottom center:** Hold down the ⌘/Ctrl key and drag a corner anchor point to distort.

- **Bottom right:** If you ⌘/Ctrl+drag two or four corner anchor points, you can add perspective to the selection. I might, for example, fill this transformed selection with color, move the selection, scale it down a bit, fill again, and repeat a number of times to create a series of paw prints marching into the distance.

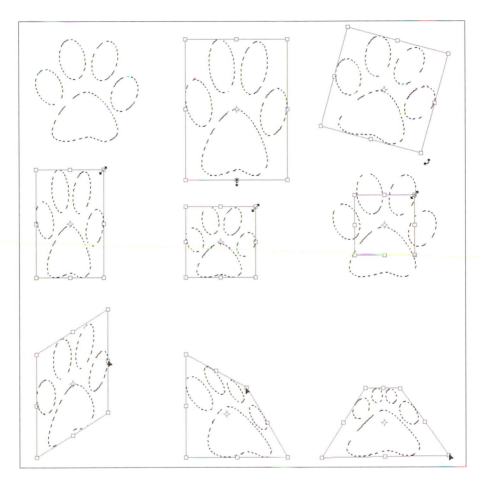

Figure 8-14: The many faces of transformations.

Edit in Quick Mask mode

With Photoshop's Quick Mask mode, you make a basic selection, enter Quick Mask mode (by using the Select➪Edit in Quick Mask Mode command, clicking the button at the bottom of the Toolbox, or by pressing Q on the keyboard), edit the selection as if it were a mask, and then exit Quick Mask mode (by deselecting this command in the Select menu, by clicking again on the button in the Toolbox, or by pressing Q again). Heck, you don't even have to start with a selection! In Quick Mask mode, your mask appears on-screen as a red overlay, just like the red overlay for Refine Edge or Color Range (see the Overlay preview in Figure 8-10). Paint, apply filters or adjustments, or make selections — anything you can do to a grayscale image, you can do in Quick Mask mode. (The following sections go into further details on working in masks.)

If you're more comfortable with the Brush tool than the Lasso tool, you might want to use Quick Mask mode to make all your selections. You might find it faster and easier to "paint" a selection in Quick Mask mode rather than to drag a selection with a lasso tool or use the selection commands. Enter Quick Mask mode, paint the mask, exit Quick Mask mode, and you have your selection. You can also enter and exit Quick Mask mode by clicking the button at the bottom of the Toolbox. Double-clicking the button opens the Quick Mask Options dialog box (as shown in Figure 8-15). You can reverse the behavior of the overlay, making it show selected areas instead of the deselected areas, and you can change the color and opacity of the overlay.

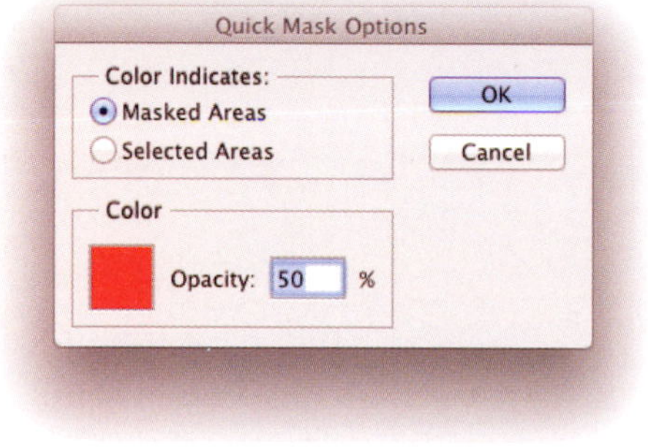

Figure 8-15: You can change the opacity and color of the Quick Mask overlay.

By default, you paint with black in Quick Mask mode over areas that you don't want selected, paint with white over areas that you do want selected, and paint with shades of gray over areas that you want partially selected.

The mask-related selection commands

At the bottom of the Select menu, you see a pair of commands that you use to store your selections for future use and to actually reuse them. When you save a selection, you create an alpha channel in the image. The *alpha channel,* like a color channel, is a grayscale representation of the image. White areas in the alpha channel represent areas that are selected when the channel is loaded as a selection. Black areas in the channel show you deselected areas. Gray represents feathering and other partially selected pixels.

I discuss channels in greater depth in the next section of this chapter. While you're exploring selection commands, the key points to remember are that you can use the Save Selection command to save any selection as an alpha channel, and then later you can use the Load Selection command to reactivate the selection without having to re-create it from scratch.

Masks: Not Just for Halloween Anymore

In Photoshop, a *mask* is a channel (in the Channels panel) that stores information about a selection or about layer visibility (or that can be used with certain filters as a *bump map*, a grayscale representation of 3D in the image). When you talk about selections saved as masks, you can refer to them as *alpha channels.* Any time you make a complex selection, consider saving it as an alpha channel, just in case. So what exactly counts as *complex?* That depends on how much time you have on your hands. If it takes me more than a minute or two to do *anything* in Photoshop, I want to save it. And what counts as *just in case?* You might need to return to the image at some later date to make changes, you might need to shut down for the day, or maybe you'll even (fingers crossed against!) have a crash. Save your selections, just in case . . .

Saving and loading selections

Creating an alpha channel from a selection is as simple as choosing Select⇨Save Selection and selecting a name for the new channel. If you have more than one document *of exactly the same pixel dimensions* open in Photoshop, you can select any of the available documents for the new channel. If you already saved a selection as an alpha channel, you can elect to have the two selections interact in a single channel.

When you need to work with a saved selection, choose Select⇨Load Selection or simply ⌘+click/Ctrl+click the alpha channel's thumbnail in the Channels panel — either activates the selection. As you see in Figure 8-16, when loading a selection, you can add to, subtract from, or intersect with an active selection. You can also invert a selection when loading by selecting the Invert check box. Using

Figure 8-16: When you already have an active selection, an alpha channel can replace, add to, subtract from, or interact with it.

that check box produces the same result as loading the selection and choosing Select⇨Inverse, but it's faster and easier.

Editing an alpha channel

Alpha channels, like color channels, are grayscale representations. As such, you can edit them like you would any grayscale image. Click the channel in the Channels panel to make it active and visible. You see it in the image window as a grayscale (or black and white) representation of the saved selection. If you want to see the image while you work on the channel, click in the left column (the eyeball column) to the left of the RGB (or CMYK) channel. The alpha channel then appears as a red overlay on top of the image, just like working in Quick Mask mode or using the red overlay in Refine Edge or Color Range. Figure 8-17 shows you what the screen looks like with just the alpha channel visible (left) and how it appears when the alpha channel is active and the RGB channel is also visible. Also take a look at the difference in the Channels panel. See the eyeball column on the left?

Figure 8-17: You can see just the alpha channel itself (left) or as a red overlay (right).

Here are some of the things that you might want to do to an active alpha channel:

- **Blur the alpha channel.** Blurring an alpha channel (Filter⇨Blur commands) is much like feathering a selection — it softens the edges. One of the big differences is that you can see a preview of the blur, which is much better than guessing how much feathering you need while dragging a selection tool.

- **Sharpen the alpha channel.** Sharpening a saved selection (Filter⇨Sharpen commands) makes the edges cleaner and more precise.

- **Paint in the alpha channel.** Painting with the Brush tool using black, white, and gray in the channel changes the selection. Paint with white to add areas to the saved selection; paint with black to remove areas from the selection; paint with shades of gray to partially select areas of the image. You can edit an alpha channel with the Brush tool very precisely, adding and eliminating stray pixels, as well as creating precise edges.

✔ **Use Levels or Curves on the alpha channel.** If the saved selection has feathering or other areas of partial selection (grays in the alpha channel), you can manipulate them with a Levels or Curves adjustment (from the Image⇨Adjustments menu). The Levels adjustment is particularly appropriate for controlling the feathering along an edge.

✔ **Apply one or more filters to an alpha channel.** Use artistic filters on a saved selection to create special effects, such as borders and frames. Chapter 15 covers filters.

Adding masks to layers and Smart Objects

When your image has multiple layers (as I discuss in Chapter 10), including Smart Objects, you can partially hide the content of the layer or Smart Object with *layer masks*. Layer masks and alpha channels have much in common: Layer masks are selections saved as channels, you can paint in the layer mask, you can apply filters and adjustment to the layer mask, and so on. Just keep in mind that a layer mask appears in the Channels panel only when you select its layer in the Layers panel. (In the Layers panel, you'll see the layer mask thumbnail to the right of the layer's thumbnail.) If you want to edit a layer mask, click its thumbnail in the Layers panel and then edit it as you would an alpha channel or use Select⇨Refine Mask to edit the mask as you would edit a selection with Refine Edge. Remember to click the layer thumbnail afterward to reactivate the layer itself.

The easiest way to add a layer mask is to make a selection of the pixels that you want visible on that layer and then click the Add Layer Mask button at the bottom of the Layers panel (third button from the left). You can also make a selection and choose Layer⇨Layer Mask⇨Reveal Selection or Layer⇨Add Layer Mask⇨Hide Selection. That menu also offers Reveal All and Hide All as well as commands to *disable* (hide) or delete the layer mask. You can also *apply* the layer mask, which deletes any hidden pixels on that layer.

You can adjust the density and feathering of a mask in the Properties panel. (Properties has taken the place of the Masks panel — and it changes features based on what sort of layer or layer mask is active in the Layers panel.) You can also access Refine Mask and Color Range from the Properties panel to fine-tune a mask. There's also a handy Invert button to reverse the mask.

By default, the layer mask is *linked* to the layer or Smart Object. If you drag the layer, the mask comes right along, staying in alignment. If you like, you can unlink the mask from the layer content by clicking on the Link icon between the two thumbnails in the Layers panel. Re-link the mask to the layer content by clicking in the empty space between the thumbnails.

A layer named *Background* (in italics) in the Layers panel can't have any transparent areas, so you can't add a layer mask. Not a problem! Simply double-click the layer name in the Layers panel and rename the layer. That converts it to a regular layer, which would be more than happy to accept your layer mask.

Masking with vector paths

A layer or Smart Object can also be masked with a vector path. (Paths are explained in Chapter 11.) Vector masks can have very precise edges, and you can edit them as a path with the Direct Selection tool. A layer (other than a Background layer) can have both a regular pixel-based layer mask and a vector mask. To show up in your artwork, pixels on that layer must be within both the layer mask and the vector mask. When a layer has both a layer mask and a vector mask, the vector mask thumbnail appears to the right in the Layers panel.

Vector masks no longer *have* to have those very precise boundaries defined by a path. You can change the density and feathering of a vector mask in the Properties panel, just as you would a pixel-based mask (although Refine Edge, Color Range, and Invert are not available for path-based masks).

Adjustment Layers: Controlling Changes

Photoshop gives you the capability of making tonal and color adjustments that you can later refine, change, or delete. Most of the adjustment commands (discussed in Chapters 5 and 6) are available as *adjustment layers*. An adjustment layer applies the selected change to color or tonality just as the comparable command would, but using an adjustment layer offers a few major advantages:

- **Adjustable adjustments:** You can reopen an adjustment layer's dialog box at any time to change the settings.

- **Reversible adjustments:** You can delete an adjustment layer, removing the change from your image.

- **Hidden adjustments:** Click the eyeball column to the left of the adjustment layer in the Layers panel to temporarily hide that change.

- **Tweakable adjustments:** You can change the opacity and blending mode of adjustment layers to fine-tune the effect.

- **Limitable adjustments:** You can add layer masks and vector masks to your adjustment layers to restrict their effect to only some of the pixels below. And you can later edit the masks as necessary.

Because of the added flexibility, you'll generally want to use adjustment layers rather than adjustment commands in your images. Of course, you still need the Image⇨Adjustments menu for those several commands that can't be added through an adjustment layer.

Adding an adjustment layer

Photoshop uses the Adjustments and Properties panels (shown in Figure 8-18) as a quick and easy way to add adjustment layers to your images. Open the panel, select a preset or, for a custom adjustment, click on the button for the type of adjustment layer you want to add. The Properties panel changes to a small version of that particular adjustment's dialog box, presenting you with the same options you have when using the Image⇨Adjustments menu.

When an adjustment layer is selected in the Layers panel, several buttons appear at the bottom of the Properties panel (to the right in Figure 8-18):

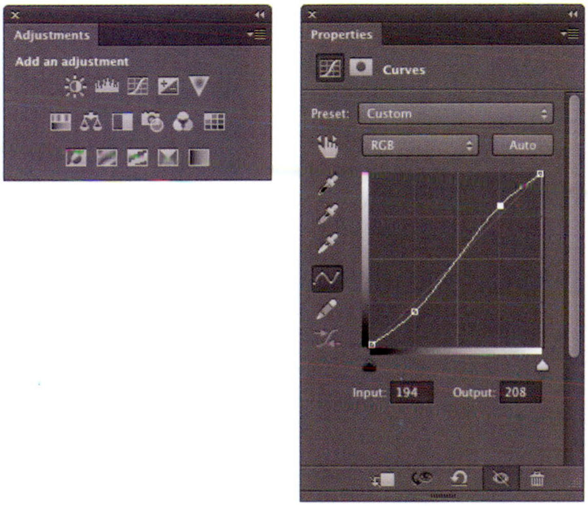

Figure 8-18: To the left, the Adjustments panel; to the right, a Curves adjustment layer being added to the image using the Properties panel.

✔ **Clip the adjustment layer to the layer immediately below:** Click the button to toggle between the adjustment layer being applied to only the one layer immediately below in the Layers panel and it being applied to all layers below. (Clipping adjustment layers is explained more completely in the next section.)

✔ **Review previous adjustment:** Click and hold down the mouse button to see the image as adjusted prior to returning to the adjustment layer. Say, for example, that you have added a Curves adjustment layer and later return to the Adjustments panel to tweak the curve a bit. To see the difference between the current appearance of the image and the appearance of the image with the original Curves adjustment, use this button. If you prefer the untweaked version, use the Undo command.

- **Reset adjustment:** Click the curled arrow button toward the right to reset the current adjustment to the adjustment's default settings.

- **Toggle adjustment layer visibility:** Click on the eyeball button to hide the current adjustment layer; click again to show it. Use this button to preview the adjustment as you work.

- **Delete adjustment layer:** Click the Trash icon to the far right at the bottom of the Adjustment panel to delete the current adjustment layer.

You can also add an adjustment layer through the menu at the bottom of the Layers panel (click the fourth button from the left) and then move the cursor to the type of adjustment layer that you want to add and through the Layer⇨New Adjustment Layer submenu. The choices are the same. When you select the particular adjustment that you want to add from the bottom of the Layers panel, that specific adjustment's options appear in the Properties panel. (Selecting the adjustment through the Layers menu presents you with the New Layer dialog box first.)

The top three options in the menu that you open from the Layers panel are *fill layers* — layers completely filled with a color, gradient, or pattern. You can add a new empty layer and choose Edit⇨Fill to do the same thing, or you can add such a layer through the Layer⇨New Fill Layer menu. (Note that these three options are not available through the Adjustment panel.)

Limiting your adjustments

When your image has multiple layers and you want to apply an adjustment layer to only one layer, the new adjustment layer must be *clipped* — restricted to the one layer immediately below it in the Layers panel. (That's the layer that's active when you add the adjustment layer.) You can clip it to the layer below by Option+clicking/Alt+clicking the line between the two layers in the Layers panel (which is also how you unclip a pair of layers). When working in the Properties panel, click the left-most button at the bottom of the panel to clip the new adjustment layer to the layer below. Figure 8-19 shows the difference between a clipped adjustment layer (left) and an unclipped adjustment layer (right). When unclipped, the adjustment is applied to all the layers below rather than to the one layer immediately below. When adding an adjustment layer through the Layers menu, select the option Use Previous Layer to Create Clipping Mask.

On the left side of Figure 8-19, the Hue/Saturation adjustment is applied only to the upper layer — the layer named Symbol. On the right, the adjustment layer isn't clipped, so it changes both the Symbol layer and the *Background* layer. By the way, the thumbnail in the Layers panel shows the Symbol layer's original copper color prior to the addition of the Hue/Saturation adjustment layer.

Among the beauties of using adjustment layers is the joy you might feel when the client says, "Yup, you were right — let's go back to the original design."

Figure 8-19: Restrict an adjustment to one layer by clipping it to the layer.

In the Layers panel to the right in Figure 8-19, you can see the icon that indicates you're holding down the Option/Alt key and about to clip the upper layer to the layer immediately below.

But what if you want an adjustment layer to change, say, three of the layers in your image? Create a layer group from the layers (click the New Group button at the bottom of the Layers panel and drag the layers into the Group icon in the panel), add the adjustment layer within the group and above the layers in the group, and change the layer group's blending mode from Pass Through to Normal at the top of the Layers panel. The adjustment layer, within the layer group and at the top of the layer group, is applied to all your layers in the group and only the layers in that group.

Because they're layers, you can use a layer mask to apply the adjustment layer to only part of your layer. You may find it easier to make a selection of the area where you want the adjustment before selecting the adjustment layer — the mask will be automatically created from the selection.

9

Common Problems and Their Cures

Sometimes you take perfect photos of imperfect people, and sometimes you take imperfect photos of, well, imperfect people. (Even the top models benefit from a little Photoshopping.) Although capturing absolute reality is the goal of some artists and most photojournalists, the people in your photos probably prefer to look as good as you (and Photoshop) can make them look.

In this chapter, I present you with some basic techniques for curing many of the most common problems that you encounter as a photographer. I show you how to remove that spooky *red-eye* effect that appears when your camera's flash reflects off the blood vessels in the back of a subject's eyes. I also show you tricks for removing wrinkles, whitening teeth, and tightening waistlines. Digital *noise* (those distracting red, green, and blue pixels scattered in your image's shadows) is easy to minimize when you use the tricks here. I cover how to remove some larger problems from images using the almost-magical Content-Aware Fill and introduce you to Puppet Warp. At the end of the chapter you'll learn how to fix problems with perspective, rotation, and barrel distortion in photos. Throughout this chapter, I use real-world examples — the types of photos with which you're most likely to work. (After all, you probably don't get to shoot beautiful models *all* the time.)

Making People Prettier

You can do lots of things in Photoshop to improve your images, but few are appreciated as much as fixing a person's photographed flaws (the appearance kind, not their bad habits). Whether it's a studio portrait or a snapshot, the people in your images generally can benefit from a little touching up.

Although you can theoretically make almost anyone look truly beautiful and glamorous using Photoshop, remember to balance *improving* with *reality.* Always work on a copy of your image. I also recommend saving separate copies at different stages during the editing process. The client might say that he wants the braces removed from his teeth, but after you present the finished product, he might just (gasp!) change his mind.

Getting the red out . . . digitally

When a subject looks directly into the camera and the camera-mounted flash fires, the result is often red-eye. This result is caused when light (such as a flash) bounces off the blood vessels at the back of an eye, and it gives the subject a spooky vampire look. Among the many ways to minimize this problem is with the Red Eye tool, nested in the Toolbox with the healing and patch tools. Zoom in and drag a small rectangle over the iris and pupil to watch the red disappear, leaving the natural highlights and a perfect eye. As you see in Figure 9-1, the default settings are good for typical cases of red-eye.

Figure 9-1: To the left, the Red Eye tool being dragged; to the right, the result.

The Red Eye tool finds red and not green. For *green-eye* (in photos of animals), for too-bright white reflections from eyes, and for those times when you're not happy with the performance of the Red Eye tool, use the Brush tool (as you see in Figure 9-2). Set the foreground color to black; in the Options bar, select the Normal blending mode and an Opacity of about 75%. Use a brush diameter just slightly larger than

Figure 9-2: When the Red Eye tool won't work, use the Brush tool.

the pupil and a brush hardness of about 85%. Click once and evaluate the result; if necessary, reduce the Opacity to 20% and click again.

Here's one more red-eye/green-eye trick: Use the Sponge tool to desaturate, followed by the Burn tool (Midtones, 25% exposure). You'll find the Sponge tool nested in the Toolbox with the Dodge and Burn tools.

The digital fountain of youth

At the end of Chapter 5, I show an example of using the Dodge tool to fade wrinkles without removing them completely. Photoshop, being a complex and capable animal, has lots of other ways to minimize or eliminate wrinkles. Among the most powerful tools for this job are the Healing Brush, the Spot Healing Brush (especially with the Content-Aware option), the Patch tool (also now with the Content-Aware option), and the Clone Stamp.

Both the Healing Brush and the Patch tool work by copying texture from one area to another. You can, for example, overlay smooth skin texture onto a wrinkled area, smoothing the wrinkles while retaining the area's general tonality and color. To work with the Healing Brush, Option+click (Mac)/Alt+click (Windows) the area from which you want to copy texture, and then click and drag over the area that you're fixing. When you select the Aligned option from the Options bar, you maintain the relationship between the point from which you're healing and the area over which you drag. No matter where you move the cursor, the source point retains the same distance and direction. When repairing areas of a face, however, you might find it easier to clear the Aligned check box. Every time you release the mouse button, you start over from the same source point. By using short strokes, you can heal from the same source area to any area of your image.

To work with the Patch tool, make a selection with the Patch tool (or with any of Photoshop's selection features) and then drag with the Patch tool. Depending on which option you select from the Options bar, you can either select and drag the damaged area to a good area (select Source from the Options bar), or you can select a good area and drag to the damaged area (select Destination). You can use both the Healing Brush and the Patch tool to apply a predefined pattern, too. That can be handy for adding a texture where one doesn't already exist in your image.

Like the Healing Brush, you Option+click/Alt+click with the Clone Stamp to set the area from which you're copying and then paint over an area to make a change. The Healing Brush copies texture, but the Clone Stamp copies pixels, completely replacing the area over which you drag. (That is, of course, subject to the blending mode and opacity that you select from the Options bar.) Like the Healing Brush, the Clone Stamp offers the Aligned option. Figure 9-3 shows a comparison of wrinkle reduction using the Clone Stamp (set to Normal and 100 Opacity) and using the Healing Brush. (If you use the Clone Stamp to repair skin, reduce the opacity and make sure to select a source area that has similar skin color and lighting.)

Original photo

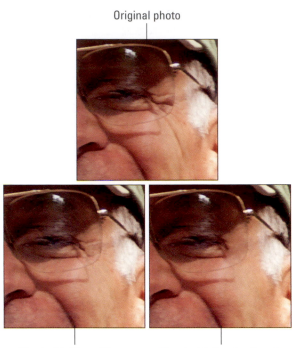

Fixed with Clone Stamp   Fixed with Healing Brush

Figure 9-3: The Clone Stamp (lower left) covers wrinkles, whereas the Healing Brush (lower right) melts them away.

Dieting digitally

You can certainly use the Clone Stamp tool to reduce a bit of a bulge at the waistline or below an upper arm, but you might find it easier (and more natural-looking) to make a selection and rotate the outer edge inward a bit. Take a look at Figure 9-4. Although this subject hardly has what you'd call a "spare tire," that bit of extra sticking out above her skirt isn't particularly flattering. Make a selection with the Lasso tool that includes some of the background and some skin (or shirt or dress). Copy the selection to a new layer with ⌘+J/Ctrl+J. Press ⌘+T/Ctrl+T to enter Free Transform (or choose Edit⇨Transform⇨Rotate). Drag the *point of rotation* (the little crosshair symbol in the middle of the bounding box) to the top of the bounding box, and then position the cursor slightly outside the bounding box and drag to rotate. When you're satisfied, press Return/Enter to accept the

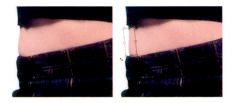

Figure 9-4: Rotate a selection to pinch in a waist.

transformation and merge the layers with ⌘+E/Ctrl+E. (With complex backgrounds, you might need to do a little cloning to even things out.)

When working with double chins, your best bet is usually to minimize rather than eliminate. Putting a skinny neck under a fleshy face looks unnatural. You can certainly tuck in the sides of the second chin a bit by using the rotate method, but rely on the Burn tool to darken. By darkening the excess flesh under the chin, you make it appear to be in shadow — and, therefore, under the actual chin (see Figure 9-5). Use the Dodge tool or the Clone Stamp (if necessary) to hide any creases or wrinkles associated with the excess chin. Redefine a natural-looking jaw line and chin — but once again, remember that the result must not only be acceptable to the client, it must also look natural.

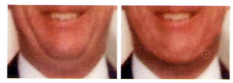

Figure 9-5: Burning and dodging can reduce even a very prominent double chin.

TIP

When working with the Burn and Dodge tools, don't forget to reduce the Exposure setting in the Options bar — 15% to 20% is plenty strong for this type of work. You'll also want to juggle between Highlights and Midtones (the Range setting in the Options bar) when creating an artificial shadow on a double chin with the Burn tool. Zoom in when doing this sort of work, but also open a second window via Window➪Arrange➪New Window for [filename] to keep an eye on the overall impact of your changes.

You can use the Filter➪ Liquify feature to push, pull, twist, pucker, bloat, and otherwise manipulate pixels into the shape and position you need. There's really nothing more powerful when it comes to reconfiguring a figure. In Figure 9-6, you see how leveling off a beltline in Liquify is sometimes all that's needed to restore that trim-man-she-married look. And a little touch-up with the Healing Brush or Dodge and Burn tools can eliminate the wrinkles

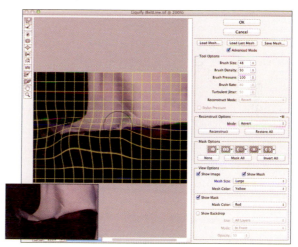

Figure 9-6: The original beltline is shown to the lower-left.

in the shirt, helping improve the overall appearance of the image by reducing distraction. (Chapter 15 has full info on using Liquify.) Make sure to click on the Advanced Mode box when working with Liquify in order to access all of the features shown in Figure 9-6.

De-glaring glasses

Although hindsight is usually 20/20, many people need spectacles. Unfortunately, those eyeglasses can be a photographer's nightmare! The reflections off glass are usually *specular highlights* — that is, areas of pure white with absolutely no detail in them. To properly evaluate flash reflections in eyeglasses, open the Info panel and move the cursor through the area. If you see a noticeable variation among the RGB values in the Info panel, you might be able to restore the area with the Burn tool.

If the Info panel shows RGB values of 255/255/255 or close to it, the area has no detail. Zoom in close and use the Clone Stamp tool to copy over the area from another part of the image. In severe cases of glare, you might need to copy from another photo of the same person. When possible (say, in a portrait sitting), try to take one shot of the subject without eyeglasses, just in case.

Whitening teeth

Teeth generally aren't truly white (unless somebody has spent a lot of time and money getting ready for a portfolio shoot). Instead, you see shades of ivory and yellow in teeth, but they don't necessarily have to be unattractive or distracting shades of yellow. The Sponge tool is great for desaturating teeth, moving them from yellow to gray. Use the Dodge tool to lighten teeth. From the Options bar, set the tool to Midtones (not Highlights) and an Exposure of perhaps 30% for front teeth. Paint over each tooth individually, making sure that you don't eliminate the shadows that differentiate the individual teeth. Then switch to Shadows and lighten those molars visible in back. Don't overdo it — remember that folks who don't make their living in Hollywood or on TV generally don't have snow-white teeth. Figure 9-7 shows normal people teeth, "improved" normal people teeth, and Hollywood teeth. Balance your judgment with the client's needs.

Figure 9-7: Coffee and caps; Dodge tool digital correction; show-biz-white teeth.

Reducing Noise in Your Images

The move from the darkroom to digital may have saved you thousands of dollars in film and processing costs (not to mention a reduction in possible environmental pollution), but has added a new set of challenges to the art and business of photography. Perhaps foremost among the problems presented by digital photography is *noise.* Those pesky red, green, and blue (or light and dark) specks in an image can ruin a digital photo. Noise is generally most prominent in shadow areas and against dark colors in your images.

The higher the ISO setting on your camera, the more digital noise it will record. Use the lowest ISO setting that's suitable for the environment in which you're shooting. When you *must* use a high ISO (low light, moving subject), be prepared for digital noise. Using a tripod can also help keep the problem to a minimum.

Decreasing digital noise

If you shoot Raw, reduce noise in Camera Raw, as described in Chapter 7. If you shoot Jpeg, use the Reduce Noise filter (under the Filter➪Noise menu). As you see in Figure 9-8, it does a very good job of neutralizing the random red, green, and blue pixels while preserving detail in the image.

Notice that Reduce Noise also offers a Remove JPEG Artifact option. When saving in the JPEG file format, you compromise between image quality and smaller file size. The smaller the file, the greater the likelihood of compression damage to your image. That damage generally shows itself as visible lines between blocks of pixels measuring eight pixels square.

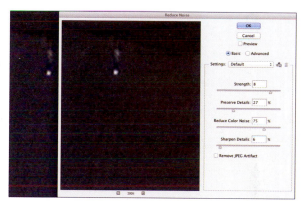

You'll also find the Color Replacement tool very handy for noise reduction, especially in areas of rather uniform color. Option+click/Alt+click right in the area to set the foreground color; then

Figure 9-8: The Reduce Noise filter keeps your image sharp while eliminating RGB noise.

simply paint away the digital noise. As you move from area to area in your image, Option+click/Alt+click to pick up a new foreground color.

Eliminating luminance noise

In addition to the red, green, and blue specks of digital noise, you might face *luminance noise,* the bright and dark specks sprinkled throughout your photo. Under the Filter➪Noise menu, you can find the Despeckle command. No dialog box appears and you have no options to choose from: You simply run the filter two or three times. For more challenging noise, try Photoshop's Blur⇨Smart Blur filter. (If Smart Blur is grayed out in the Filter⇨Blur menu, convert the image to 8-bit color through the Image⇨Mode menu.) For supreme control over blurring, Smart Blur even lets you enter fractions for both the Radius and Threshold values (as shown in Figure 9-9).

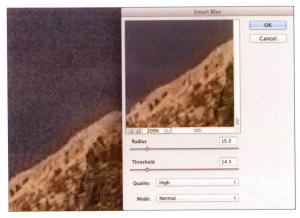

Figure 9-9: The Smart Blur filter is a good choice for luminance noise reduction.

Fooling Around with Mother Nature

Sometimes a very nice photo has something in it that you want gone . . . a piece of litter, telephone lines in the distance, or perhaps a building that distracts from the composition. Other times, everything in the image is fine, but the image looks wrong because of the angle at which it was taken, or you want to change the angle of something *in* the photo. Photoshop offers you quite a variety of tools and techniques for cutting out, copying over, cleaning up, and even correcting perspective.

Removing the unwanted from photos

Perhaps the easiest way to remove something from an image is to *crop* the photo: that is, cut off that part of the picture. This technique is easy enough if that piece of litter or whatever happens to be at the edge of the image and cropping won't ruin your composition. (Of course, picking up that piece of litter and disposing of it prior to taking the photo is the best solution.) When you must cover up rather than crop out, consider the very powerful Content-Aware option for Edit⇨Fill.

Content-Aware Fill analyzes the pixels within a selection and compares them to pixels elsewhere in the image, and then re-creates the area within the selection. (Making selections to isolate part of an image is discussed in Chapter 8.) In Figure 9-10, the waterfall within the selection is both natural and normal.

However, it does visually water down (pun intended!) the message of "Motion: Horizontal and Vertical." With a single waterfall, the single railroad train is better balanced.

Figure 9-10: The original photo (left); using Content-Aware Fill in the selected area (right).

When you're not satisfied with Content-Aware Fill, undo and try changing the size of the selection, perhaps including a bit more (or less) of the surrounding image.

If you're still not pleased with what Content-Aware Fill has produced, you can undo again and either copy/paste pixels over the unwanted area or use the Clone Stamp tool. To work with the Clone Stamp, first tell Photoshop what pixels you want to copy — Option+click (Mac)/Alt+click (Windows) in that area — then move the cursor to the problem area and drag. Like the Healing Brush, the Aligned option for the Clone Stamp maintains the angle and distance relationship between the source point and the cursor's current location. Deselecting that option sends the source point back to where you Option+clicked/Alt+clicked when you release the mouse button. Also in the tool's Options bar, you have the choice of working on the active layer (ignoring pixels on other layers), the active layer and the layer immediately below (which you'll choose when you add an empty layer to hold your cloned pixels), or to use all layers in the image (helpful in layered images with areas of transparency and adjustment layers).

The Spot Healing Brush works much like the Healing Brush to repair and replace texture. However, instead of designating a source point by Option+clicking/ Alt+clicking, the Spot Healing Brush samples from the immediate surrounding area, which makes it perfect for repairing little irregularities in an area of rather consistent texture. The Content-Aware option for the Spot Healing Brush makes it a "smart" tool — it looks at the surrounding area and tries to replicate both the texture and the content.

You can also move something in your image to a new location to create a new look in the shot. As shown in Figure 9-11, copy the entire image, reposition it, use a layer mask to hide parts of the upper layer, and clone to remove anything not needed on the exposed areas of the lower layer. In Figure 9-11, the background layer is copied and moved upward (after using the Image⇨Canvas Size command to expand the canvas), and a layer mask hides everything except the boy, his racket, and the ball. On the lower layer, the boy is cloned out. (The look of surprise from the boy in the red hat in the background is simply a fortuitous coincidence that seems to add credibility to the adjusted image.)

Figure 9-11: One small step for Photoshop, one giant leap for mankind!

The Edit⇨Puppet Warp feature, like Liquify (presented in Chapter 15), enables you to very easily produce complex distortions on an image. Here's the workflow I recommend for most jobs using Puppet Warp:

1. **Make a selection of the area of the image you want to alter.**

   You can use whatever selection technique works best for the part of the image that needs to be selected — Lasso tool, Color Range command, or any of the selection tools and techniques described in Chapter 8.

2. Copy to a new layer.

Use the keyboard shortcut ⌘+J/Ctrl+J to put the selected pixels on their own layer.

3. Remove the selected pixels from the lower layer.

Hide the upper layer by clicking the eyeball icon to the left of the layer name in the Layers panel. Click on the lower layer in the panel to make it the active layer. Clone or copy/paste over the selected pixels using the techniques in the preceding section. (This stage of the workflow is shown to the upper-right, next to the original shot, in Figure 9-12.)

Figure 9-12: The original in the upper-left; layered and cloned in the upper-right; Puppet Warping and the left part of the Options bar below.

4. Make the upper layer visible and active.

Click in the eyeball column to the left of the upper layer's name to make the layer visible, and then click on the layer name or thumbnail to make the layer active.

5. Activate the Puppet Warp feature.

Select Puppet Warp from the Edit menu.

6. Set pins.

Click in two or more places along the axis that you want to change to set anchor points known as *pins*. If you're manipulating an arm, you would generally place pins at the shoulder, elbow, and wrist. When manipulating a leg, place pins at the hip, knee, and ankle.

7. Select your options.

In the Options bar, choose a mode. Normal is usually appropriate, Distort enables you to change perspective while dragging pins, and Rigid helps maintain special relationships. You can also change the density of the now-visible mesh and use the Expansion slider and field to expand or contract the content within the mesh.

8. Drag the pins and accept the warp.

Click on a pin to make it the active pin; drag as desired. You can switch among pins as often as necessary, and you can remove a pin by clicking on it and pressing Delete/Backspace. To the right in the Options bar on your screen you'll see three buttons that remove all pins, cancel Puppet Warp, and accept the transformation. When you're happy with the new look of your "puppet," click that third button or press the Return/ Enter key.

Eliminating the lean: Fixing perspective

When you take a photograph at an angle, perhaps shooting upward at a building, you get *foreshortening,* with the upper part of the subject shrinking into the distance. If you shoot Raw, you can work in Camera Raw's Lens Correction tab (see Chapter 7). With JPEG images, Photoshop's Filter➪Lens Correction does a great job of fixing perspective. If you shoot on a recent model high-end DSLR, you can use custom profiles created for your camera/ lens combination to correct many lens-related vagaries. Use these automatic corrections when the perspective is acceptable and you just need to compensate for the tendencies of the lens itself. You can even search online at Adobe Labs for profiles created and posted by other photographers. (If you have the technical inclination and time, you can even create your own custom profiles and post those online for others shooting your same camera and lens.)

In the Custom panel of Lens Correction, drag the Vertical Perspective slider to the left to correct images shot from below, or to the right for shots from above. In Lens Correction, as shown in Figure 9-13, you can also adjust horizontal perspective, barrel distortion (when the center of the image bulges out), pin cushioning (when the center of the image bulges in), chromatic aberration (blue/yellow or red/cyan fringing along edges), and add a vignette.

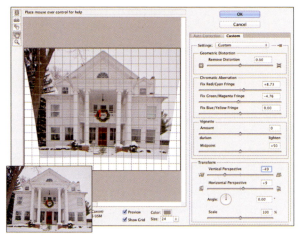

Figure 9-13: The original is shown to the lower-left.

Before entering Lens Correction, double-click the layer name *Background* in the Layers panel and rename the layer. Use Image➪Canvas Size to add some empty area all around the image. That way, you won't chop off any of the photo when dragging the perspective sliders. Notice in Figure 9-13 that a generous amount of extra canvas was added, which can easily be cropped off after correcting perspective.

You can also use Photoshop's Edit⇨Transform⇨Perspective command, but that usually produces some foreshortening of the image, requiring you to scale it upward a bit afterward. The Crop tool can also fix perspective. Mark the Perspective check box on the Options bar before dragging a bounding box. For best results, position the four corners of the bounding box on visible corners of something in the image that should be rectangular or square; drag the side handles outward to expand the bounding box to encompass your image. Press Return/Enter when you're done.

Also found in the Filter menu is Adaptive Wide Angle, another way to compensate for vagaries of specific wide-angle and fisheye lenses. When Lens Correction's Remove Distortion slider isn't enough to correct barrel distortion, try Adaptive Wide Angle. If the camera model and lens information can be read from the image's metadata, the Auto adjustment is applied. When the camera and/or lens is unknown, you'll see the Focal Length and Crop Factor sliders (shown in Figure 9-14), which you use to manually adjust the image. Start, however, by selecting the type of adjustment you need to make in the Correction menu.

Whether working automatically or manually, you can assist the filter by using Constraint and Polygon Constraint tools in the upper-left. Use

Figure 9-14: Adaptive Wide Angle is another filter for adjusting photos.

the first tool to drag along lines that should be vertical or horizontal. Use the second tool to click rectangles around shapes that should be square or rectangular in the image. The Scale slider can be used to shrink or enlarge the image to fit on the original canvas size. (Alternatively, rename the background layer and expand the image with Canvas Size before opening Adaptive Wide Angle.) The Move tool (third from the top) can be used to reposition the image in the canvas after scaling. The Hand and Zoom tools function as usual, repositioning the image on-screen and changing the zoom factor.

Rotating images precisely

Buried under the Eyedropper in the Photoshop Toolbox is the little-known Ruler tool. Generally, you use it in conjunction with the Info panel or Options Bar to find distances and angles in your image. You can also use it to make sure that you apply the exact amount of rotation needed for your image. Select the Ruler tool, drag it along any line in your image that should be vertical or horizontal and then choose Image⇨Image Rotation⇨Arbitrary. The angle of the Ruler tool will already be waiting for you in the dialog box, so you need only click OK to precisely rotate your image.

One final thought for this chapter: When you come across an image that requires more fixing than you have time for, or one with such severe luminance noise that smoothing removes too much detail, or just a problem photo in general, head for the Filter Gallery. It's amazing how many flaws you can hide with a few artistic effects. Creating an artistic rendering of an image is often preferable to deleting a lousy photo. Blur away the noise and add a canvas texture with the Texturizer filter. Blown out highlights? Try the Colored Pencil filter. (Read more about the Filter Gallery in Chapter 15.) When faced with lemons, think of the Filter Gallery as your own personal lemonade stand.

Part III
Creating "Art"
in Photoshop

hotoshop is far more than just a pixel-pushing image editor. More than merely perfecting excellent photography, you can create art in Photoshop. And Photoshop includes a very powerful painting engine. You need to understand the extremely complex Brush panel and painting tools, all covered here.

Chapter 10 introduces you to *compositing* (combining images into a piece of artwork) and working with layers. You also see how to use color channels as the basis for selections, enabling you to move elements from one image to another. Chapter 11 introduces you to Photoshop's *shapes* and *vector paths,* which are illustration tools used to add specific elements.

In Chapter 12, I show you how to work with the Styles palette and how to create your own custom styles — and make sure you don't lose them by mistake! Chapter 13 looks at the many tools, palettes, and commands you have available in Photoshop to add text and type. Chapter 14 introduces you to painting in Photoshop and provides a few tips on how to integrate your iPad into your Photoshop workflow. Chapter 15 introduces you to those filters you need on a near-daily basis, and then shows you how to work in the Filter Gallery and in Liquify.

Combining Images

A pharaoh's head on a lion body. A lion with the head, talons, and wings of an eagle. As evidenced by the sphinx and the mythological griffin, compositing elements has been around a lot longer than Photoshop, but Photoshop certainly makes it easier! Take part of one image, drop it onto another image, and sell the composite to the tabloids for thousands of dollars. (One of the more infamous misuses of image compositing occurred during the 2004 U.S. presidential campaign, with the publication of a fake photo of candidate John Kerry with actress and antiwar activist Jane Fonda.) Photoshop offers you incredible power — use it wisely!

In this chapter, I show you some basic techniques for *compositing* (combining two or more images into a single picture), how to use channels to select part of an image for compositing, the Vanishing Point feature, and then wrap up the chapter with a look at combining images automatically to create panoramas.

Compositing Images: 1 + 1 = 1

You make a selection in one image, copy, switch to another image, and paste. There you have it — the basic composite! Pretty simple, isn't it? Whether you're putting together two images or creating complex artwork involving dozens of elements, the trick is making the composited image look natural. The key techniques are blending the edges of your selections and matching color among the elements.

Understanding layers

When you put together images, you work with *layers*. Think of layers in Photoshop as stackable elements, each of which holds part of your image. Where an upper layer is transparent, the lower layer or layers show through. Where the upper layer has pixels that aren't transparent, those pixels either block or interact with pixels on the lower layer. (You control that interaction with blending modes and opacity, explained later in this chapter.)

Take a look at Figure 10-1 (which reveals how Figure 13-3 is created). The Layers panel shows the individual layers and their content. The individual elements come together to create a single image.

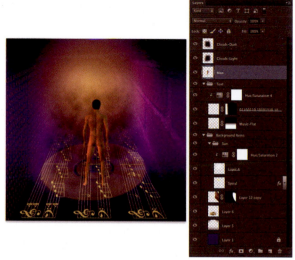

You can manipulate the content of each layer independently — moving, resizing, erasing, painting, or adjusting color and tonality — to suit your needs and artistic vision. Remember to click a layer in the Layers panel to make that layer active for editing. The Move tool's Options bar offers

Figure 10-1: Elements on different layers form a single image.

the option Auto-Select, which enables you to make a layer or group active by clicking any visible pixels on that layer or in that group.

You can *link* two or more layers so that they maintain their positions relative to each other as you move them. (⌘/Ctrl+click to select the layers; then click the Link button at the bottom of the Layers panel — a Link symbol appears to the right of linked layers when active in the layers panel.) Linked layers can be moved together without knocking them out of alignment.

The left column in the Layers panel, known as the *eyeball column* (for an obvious reason) allows you to hide a layer, making the content of the layer invisible. The pixels are still there; they're just not visible. Click the eyeball icon to hide the layer and then click the empty space in the left column to make the layer visible again. You can hide and show adjustment layers, too, which lets you see their impact on the image. (Read about adjustment layers in Chapter 8.)

One key concept about layers is well illustrated in Figure 10-1. The higher a layer is in the *stacking order* (the order of layers in the panel from the top down), the more "in front" it will be. The layers Clouds-Dark and Clouds-Light are on top of everything in the image. The layer Man is in front of everything except the clouds. Because of the stacking order, the man appears to be standing on top of the musical notes, and the notes appear to be on top of the compact disc.

You can also create *groups,* which are two or more layers packaged together in the Layers panel so that you can show or hide them together. As you can see in the Layers panel in Figure 10-1, you can have *nested groups:* a group within a group. The group named Background Items includes another group, named Sun, as well as several layers that aren't part of the Sun subgroup.

Video layers are available in both Photoshop CS6 and Photoshop CS6 Extended. Generally speaking, you're more likely to add regular pixel layers, type layers, shapes, and adjustment layers to a video project than to add video layers to another sort of project. Working with video is discussed in Chapter 17.

Seldom used — actually, seldom even noticed — are the layer-related commands in the Select menu. The Select⇨All Layers and Deselect Layers commands are pretty obvious, but the Select⇨Similar command deserves a little attention. With a layer active in the Layers panel, this command selects all layers of the same category. All type layers, shape layer, and adjustment layers can be selected quickly with this command. You can also select all layers of a particular type using the menu and buttons in the top row of the Layers panel. When would you use this capability? You might, for example, select all of the type layers before working with the Character Style or Paragraph Style panel.

Why you should use Smart Objects

Smart Objects provide you with even more flexibility in Photoshop. When working with Smart Objects, you preserve your editing options without risk to the image quality. For example, you can transform a Smart Object as often as you like because each time you rotate or scale or otherwise manipulate a Smart Object, Photoshop goes back to the original pixels and resamples again. This prevents the sort of image degradation you would see if you were to shrink, enlarge, or rotate a regular layer's content numerous times.

When working with Smart Objects, you can apply a filter to a selection in Photoshop and then later go back and change the filter settings or even remove the filter entirely. But this feature is available only when you're working with Smart Objects. Again, it goes back to Photoshop's ability to return to the original source pixels when working with Smart Objects. (Filters are discussed in Chapter 15.) In the Layers panel, Smart Filters very much resemble layer styles: You can click an eyeball icon to temporarily hide a filter's effect, and you can double-click the filter name to re-open the dialog box so that you can make changes (see Figure 10-2).

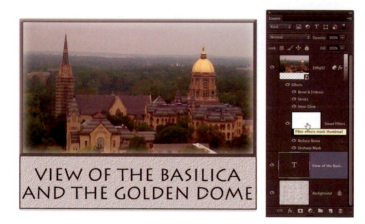

Figure 10-2: Filters applied to the Smart Object are listed under Smart Filters.

If you want to apply a Smart Filter to only a section of a Smart Object, make a selection before selecting the filter. In keeping with the whole concept of "smart," the filter is applied to the entire Smart Object but the filter's visibility is controlled with a mask. (An empty filter mask is visible to the left of the words Smart Filter in the Layers panel in Figure 10-2.) And, of course, you can — at any time — paint in the mask with black, white, and shades of gray to alter where the filter is visible. (Painting in masks is discussed later in this chapter.) Note, too, that a Smart Object can have both Smart Filters and a layer style.

When you choose File➪Place, a Smart Object is automatically created. To create a Smart Object from an existing layer (even a background layer), choose Layer➪Smart Objects➪Convert to Smart Object. When working with Raw images, hold down the Shift key and Camera Raw's Open Image button changes to Open Object. If you want Open Object to be Camera Raw's default, click the blue line of info below the preview to open Workflow Options.

Using the basic blending modes

The pop-up menu at the top-left corner of the Layers panel offers more than two dozen different *blending modes*. A layer's blending mode determines how the pixels on that layer interact with the visible pixels on the layers below.

Because a layer named *Background* can't have any layers below it, you can't change the blending mode of background layers. Convert a background layer to a regular layer by changing the layer's name in the Layers panel. Simply double-click a layer name in the Layers panel and type to rename the layer.

In Figure 10-3, the black-white and rainbow strips of gradients overlaid on the garden photo below each use the blending mode shown by the text outline. (You can see the original gradients in the Normal stripe.) Normal, Multiply, Screen, Overlay, and Luminosity are the blending modes you're most likely to use regularly.

 When working with layer blending modes, always keep in mind that you can use the Layers panel's Opacity and Fill sliders to help determine the layer's visibility and appearance. The Opacity slider controls the visibility of the layer's content and any layer style applied to the layer. The Fill slider controls the visibility of the layer content without hiding any layer style. For a practical example of the difference between the two sliders, take a look at the section "Opacity, fill, and advanced blending" in Chapter 12.

Figure 10-3: Blending modes control the interaction between the gradients and the photo.

The Layers panel blending mode pop-up menu is divided into six sections, based loosely on how the pixels on the upper layer affect the pixels on the lower layer. Here's a quick look at how you use the key layer blending modes:

- **Normal:** Photoshop picks Normal by default. Pixels on the upper layer completely hide the pixels on the lower layers (subject, of course, to the Opacity and the Fill settings). Use Normal to show the content of the layer without any interaction with lower layers.

- **Multiply:** The Multiply blending mode darkens where your upper layer is dark and ignores white. Use Multiply when you want the upper layer to darken but not obscure the lower layer and also for shadows and dark glow effects.

- **Screen:** The Screen blending mode — the opposite of Multiply — uses lighter pixels to lighten the pixels below. Use it for highlights and light-colored glows.

- **Overlay:** Overlay works like a combination of Multiply and Screen. Use it when you're working with an upper layer that includes both dark and light pixels that you want to interact with pixels on layers below.

- **Soft Light:** Soft Light is a subtle blending mode. Like Overlay, where your upper layer's pixels are dark, the lower layer is darkened; where they're light, the lower layer is lightened. Soft Light is like adding a diffused spotlight to the lower layer — useful for adding a little drama to the lower layer.

- **Hard Light:** The Hard Light blending mode is much like a more vivid version of Soft Light. Use it to add a *lot* more drama to the lower layer. Hard Light works well with colors that aren't overwhelmingly bright.

- **Difference:** Where the upper layer (using the Difference blending mode) and the lower layer are exactly the same, you see black. Where the two layers are different, you see brightness or color. For example, use Difference (temporarily) when trying to align two overlapping photos. Set the upper layer to Difference, move the upper layer until the areas of overlap show black, and then switch the upper layer's blending mode back to Normal.

- **Color:** When the upper layer is set to Color, the lower layer's brightness and saturation are retained, and the upper layer's color is used. If you want to create a color picture from a grayscale picture, convert the image to RGB (Image⇨Mode⇨RGB), add a new layer, change the upper layer's blending mode to Color, and paint on the upper layer (as shown in Figure 10-4).

- **Luminosity:** When the upper layer is set to Luminosity, the color and saturation of the lower layer are retained, and the brightness (luminosity) of the upper layer is applied. Because the luminosity (dark and light) generally provides texture, use this blending mode to produce detail in the lower layer.

Photoshop also offers two pairs of blending modes that you might find useful, but confusing. Lighten and Lighten Color compare a pixel on the upper layer to the pixel immediately below to determine the resulting color. Lighten chooses the higher (brighter) value in each of the RGB color channels and produces a new color based on those three independent lightness values. Lighten Color, on the other hand,

Figure 10-4: Paint on a layer set to Color to retain the detail of the layer below.

looks at the color on the upper layer created by all three channels, compares it to the color on the lower layer, and makes visible whichever of those two colors is lighter overall. The Darken and Darker Color blending modes work similarly, but choose the darker values.

Opacity, transparency, and layer masks

Blending modes help determine how pixels on an upper layer interact with pixels on a lower layer, but those upper pixels have to be *visible* before they can do any interacting at all. When looking at any pixel on a layer, you have to consider four factors about transparency:

- Whether the pixel has any color to start with
- The Opacity value
- The Fill value
- Whether there's a layer mask

When you add a layer and paint on it, for example, you color some of the pixels yet leave other pixels transparent. (Every layer in every image is completely filled with pixels, whether visible or not.) If nothing is done to color some pixels, they remain transparent, and the lower layers can be seen through that part of your upper layer. In Figure 10-5, the words *upper layer* are on a separate layer above the layer containing the words *LOWER LAYER.* Where the upper layer has transparent pixels, the lower layer shows through.

Figure 10-5: Where you see the lower layer, the upper layer is transparent.

A layer named *Background* in the Layers panel can have no transparent pixels.

Lowering the Opacity or the Fill slider in the Layers panel (or the Layer Style dialog box) makes all visible pixels on the layer partially transparent: The pixels on layers below can be seen through the upper layer's pixels. (The Opacity slider controls the pixels on the layer and any layer style; the Fill slider works only on the pixels, not the layer style.)

Chapter 8 discusses layer masks and vector masks. Remember that any pixel inside the mask is at least partially visible, and any pixel outside the mask is transparent, regardless of whether it has color. But, as you can guess, any completely transparent pixels inside the mask remain completely transparent.

Creating clipping groups

This being Photoshop, here is yet another way to restrict the visibility of pixels on an upper layer: clipping groups. *Clipping* an upper layer to the layer below, in effect, creates a mask for the upper layer. The opacity of the pixels on the lower layer is applied to the pixels on your upper layer. Where the lower layer is transparent, the upper layer (regardless of original content) becomes transparent. In the Layers panel, Option+click (Mac)/ Alt+click (Windows) the line between two layers to clip the upper layer to the lower. When you hold down the Option/Alt key, the cursor turns into the icon shown between the two layers in Figure 10-6.

After you Option+click/ Alt+click the line between Layer 1 and the type layer, the upper layer is visible only within the text on the lower layer.

Figure 10-6: Option+click or Alt+click the line between two layers to clip the upper to the lower.

The upper layer is indented to the right in the Layers panel, with a downward-pointing arrow to let you know that it's clipped to the layer below. Note that the upper layer's thumbnail in the Layers panel shows the entire layer,

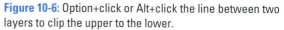

not just the visible area. To unclip a layer, Option+click/Alt+click again on the line between the two layers in the Layers panel. Also note in Figure 10-6 that the layer style is applied to the lower layer rather than the upper layer.

Photoshop lets you show the layer thumbnails in two ways. Normally, the entire layer, including all areas of transparency, shows in the thumbnail. Although that gives you a good indication of how large or small the particular layer's content is in the image, layers with little content have little to show in the thumbnail. By using the Panel Options (from the Layers panel menu) or Control+clicking/right-clicking the empty area below the layers in the panel, you can elect to show a thumbnail that includes only nontransparent areas of the layer. Little things fill the thumbnail, but they also appear out of proportion to the other thumbnails. Your choice.

Making composited elements look natural

One of the keys to compositing two images is a slight fade to the edges of the element you're adding to the original image. That fade, called *feathering,* makes the edges of the image appear to fall off into the distance very slightly rather than having a sharply defined edge that sticks out like a sore thumb. (See Chapter 8 for full information on feathering.) You have a number of ways to feather a selection, including the following:

- ✔ Use the Feathering field on the Options bar before you use a selection tool.

- ✔ Use the Refine Edge button in the Options bar or the Select⟹Refine Edge command after making your selection.

- ✔ Choose Select⟹Modify⟹Feather after you make a selection.

- ✔ Apply a slight blur to a saved selection's alpha channel in the Layers panel (or to a layer mask).

Matching color between two layers is also critical for a natural appearance. Take a look at Chapter 6 for full information on Match Color and Photoshop's other color adjustment capabilities.

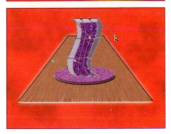

You also need to be aware of *perspective* and *scale.* When an element in your composited image seems to be too large or too small or when it seems to be facing the wrong way or standing on air, rely on the Edit⟹Transform commands. Although the Scale and Rotate commands are self-explanatory, Figure 10-7 shows

Figure 10-7: Drag anchor points to transform.

visually how you can use the other Transform commands, such as Skew, Perspective, and Warp. Drag the bounding box anchor points to transform the selected pixels.

The Edit⇨Transform⇨Warp command adds a simple mesh over the content of the layer or selection. You click and drag the direction lines for the corners of the mesh and at the intersection of mesh lines to distort your artwork. As you see in Figure 10-8, the Warp distortion gives you a level of control second only to Photoshop's Liquify feature (discussed in Chapter 15). You can also use Warp with paths and vector shapes.

Figure 10-8: Use the Warp transformation to distort layers or selections.

Making Complex Selections

In order to combine elements from separate images into a single piece of artwork, you sometimes need to make very complex selections. That's often best done with an alpha channel, which can then be made into an active selection with the aptly-named Select⇨Load Selection command. Among the alpha channel creation techniques available to you are

✔ **Save a selection:** If you already have a selection, perhaps created with the Lasso tool or the Select⇨Color Range command, you can use the Select⇨Save Selection command to create an alpha channel. This saved selection can then be edited as necessary by painting, or can be combined with another selection or additional alpha channels.

✔ **Duplicate a quick mask:** Press Q to enter Quick Mask mode, paint your quick mask (as described in Chapter 8), and then — before exiting Quick Mask mode — drag the Quick Mask channel to the New Channel button at the bottom of the Channels panel to duplicate it.

✔ **Paint from scratch:** Click the New Channel button at the bottom of the Channels panel, and paint with black, white, and shades of gray. White will be included in the selection, black will be excluded from the selection, and gray indicates partial selection.

✔ **Duplicate an existing channel as the basis for a mask:** You can also examine the color channels to see which provides the best contrast between the subject and the background, drag that channel to the New Channel button, and then adjust the duplicate channel.

Duplicating a color channel is often the most effective way to extract a complex subject from a complex background. Here's one way to approach the task:

1. **Examine each channel individually to see which offers the most contrast between subject and background.**

   Open the Channels panel and click on each color channel, one at a time, to see which presents the best contrast between the edges of the subject and the surrounding background.

   Don't forget that you have 10 color channels — that's right, *10* channels — from which to choose! In addition to the Red, Green, and Blue channels in your image, you can use the Image➪Duplicate command and then convert the copy to CMYK or Lab mode. One of the CMYK channels often offers much better contrast between subject and background than do the RGB channels. In Lab mode, the *a* and *b* channels are also worth a try. And after creating your alpha channel, you don't even need to switch back to RGB mode.

2. **Duplicate the selected channel.**

   Drag the color channel of your choice to the New Channel button at the bottom of the Channels panel to create an alpha channel from it.

3. **Maximize the contrast between subject and background.**

   Ideally, you'll end up with a subject that's completely white and a background that's completely black. (If your alpha channel shows a dark subject and a light background, simply use ⌘+I/Ctrl+I or the command Image➪Adjustments➪Invert.) Generally speaking, the first place to start maximizing the contrast is Levels. Drag the end sliders way in under the middle of the histogram, and then adjust the middle slider. After clicking OK, you may want to use Levels again. After Levels has done most of the work, grab the Brush tool and clean up any additional areas, painting directly in the channel with black and white.

As you adjust your duplicated channel, pay attention to the edge between the subject and background. Don't worry about areas away from the edge — those are easy to clean up with the Brush. It's that narrow band that separates the subject and background that's critical.

Figure 10-9 illustrates the steps. To the left, the Red channel shows decent contrast between the subject and background, the Green less so, and the Blue channel is useless for this particular image (too much yellow in the background). After you create a duplicate and convert to CMYK mode, it's apparent that both the Cyan and Black channels are even better starting points than the Red channel. After duplicating the Black channel and using Levels twice, the alpha channel is in pretty good shape (top center). After a few swipes with the Brush using black and then again using white, the alpha channel is ready (top right). Switch back to the original RGB image, use Select⇨Load Selection and load the Black copy channel, and there's a perfect selection of the flower!

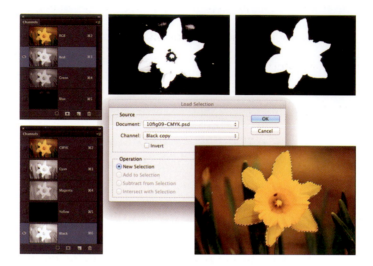

Figure 10-9: Duplicating a color channel is often the fastest way to a great alpha channel.

When working with Raw images, you have another option available. After making the subject look great in Camera Raw, click Open Image to open the image into Photoshop, and then save it as a `.psd` or a `.tif` file. Reopen the original Raw image back into Camera Raw. This time, maximize the differences between the edges of the subject and background in the Basic and HSL/Grayscale panels — without regard for how ugly the image becomes. Hold down the Option/Alt key and click the now-visible Open Copy button (which opens the new copy without overwriting your earlier Camera Raw adjustments). Select a color channel, duplicate the channel, and create your alpha channel as described in the preceding section.

Vanishing Point

When combining images to create a scene, you might find a need to add texture or a pattern along what is supposed to be a three-dimensional object. You might, for example, add a product box to a photo of a kitchen and need to add a logo to the front of the box. Or maybe you will create a room, perhaps in a house high on a hill, and you'll need to add a realistic brick texture to the walls. Use the Vanishing Point feature to "map" a pattern to angled surfaces, such as walls, floors, buildings, and boxes. Vanishing Point, using information that you provide, automatically determines the correct angle, scale, and perspective. (Vanishing Point is rather complex, so for simple jobs, you might want to stick with the Paste and Edit⇨Transform commands.)

To use Vanishing Point, you follow a specific sequence of steps:

1. **Copy your pattern.**

   Open whatever pattern file (or texture or logo or whatever) you're going to add to the walls or sides in your image, make a selection, and then choose Edit⇨Copy. You can now close the pattern file.

2. **Make a selection in your working image.**

   Identify where you want the pattern to be applied. If you're working with walls, for example, make a selection that includes the walls but doesn't include windows and doors.

3. **Open Vanishing Point (Filter⇨Vanishing Point).**

   The Vanishing Point window opens, displaying your image.

4. **Create planes on your image in the Vanishing Point window.**

   a. Select the Create Plane tool (the second tool from the top on the left edge of the window).

   b. Click on your image where you want to place the three corners of your plane and then move the cursor to the fourth corner.

      You see the plane extending along the last two sides.

   c. Click the fourth corner to create the plane.

      If the plane is yellow or red rather than blue, it's not aligned properly. Drag the corners of the plane to realign them, using the Edit Plane tool (the top tool on the left). Drag the side anchor points outward to expand the plane's mesh to cover the whole wall or side.

   d. Create perpendicular planes by holding down the ⌘/Ctrl key and dragging the side anchor point at the point where the two planes should meet. If the second plane should be at an angle other than 90 degrees to the first plane, Option+drag/Alt+drag one of the anchor points to rotate the grid.

      If the second plane's angle is off a little, drag one of the corner anchor points to adjust it. In Figure 10-10, you see two perpendicular planes.

Figure 10-10: Use the Create Planes tool to identify surfaces.

5. **Paste your pattern.**

   a. Press ⌘+V/Ctrl+V to paste your pattern into Vanishing Point.

   Your pattern is pasted into the upper-left corner of the Vanishing Point window.

   b. Select the Marquee tool (third from the top) and drag the pattern into your plane.

   The pattern automatically adopts the orientation of the plane. If necessary, click on the Transform tool (or press T on your keyboard) and then rotate and scale the pattern.

6. **Replicate the pattern.**

   Unless your pattern is an exact fit, you need to replicate it to fill the plane. With the Marquee tool selected, hold down the Option/Alt key. Then click and drag in your pattern to replicate it. Repeat as necessary to fill the plane. As you see in Figure 10-11, you can replicate a relatively small pattern to fill a large area.

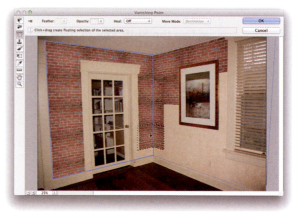

Figure 10-11: Option+drag or Alt+drag with the Marquee tool to copy your pasted selection.

If the lighting in your original image varies, set the Healing pop-up menu (at the top of the window, only with the Marquee tool active) to Luminance. That helps maintain the original lighting on the new pattern or texture.

7. **Click OK to exit Vanishing Point and apply the pattern or texture to your image.**

   After exiting Vanishing Point, you might need to do some touch-up work on your image with the Clone Stamp tool (depending on how precise you were when dragging). You might also, depending on the original image, need to add a layer and paint some shadows or highlights to reproduce the original lighting in the scene.

In Figure 10-11, the pasted and replicated brick pattern doesn't cover the door, window, or artwork because they were not selected prior to opening Vanishing Point. Without that active selection when opening Vanishing Point, it would have been much more difficult to properly align the pattern without covering those areas.

Here are some tips for working with Vanishing Point:

- **Create accurate planes; then drag.** Click in four corners of any identifiable area of your plane — perhaps a window — and drag the side anchor points outward (or inward) to identify the whole plane.

- **Use the X key to zoom.** Pressing and holding the X key on your keyboard makes the preview area zoom to show the area where you're working. Release the X key to zoom back out.

- **Press T to transform.** After pasting your pattern, you can press T on your keyboard and then scale and rotate your pasted pattern.

- **Use the Shift key to drag in alignment.** Hold down the Shift key while Option+dragging/Alt+dragging to replicate your pattern. That keeps the new part aligned to the old.

- **Duplicate elements in the image.** Make a selection with the Marquee tool and ⌘+Option+drag/Ctrl+Alt+drag to the area where you want to place the copy.

- **Paste over objects in Vanishing Point.** Create your plane. Use the Marquee tool to select an area that you want to replace, and then hold down the ⌘/Ctrl key and drag to an area that you want to paste into the marquee selection.

- **Clone in Vanishing Point.** Define your plane, select the Stamp tool, and Option+click/Alt+click at the source point. Release the Option/Alt key and move the cursor to the point where you want to start cloning. When the preview is properly aligned, click and drag to clone.

- ✔ **Paint in perspective.** With a plane identified, the Brush tool in Vanishing Point shrinks or grows in accordance with your perspective plane.

- ✔ **Work on an empty layer.** You can add an empty layer in the Layers panel before entering Vanishing Point. Your result is added to the new layer, which lets you work with blending modes and opacity to merge your pattern into the original.

Creating Panoramas with Photomerge

Sometimes a snapshot doesn't adequately portray a scene. (It's hard to capture the majesty of the Grand Canyon in a single frame.) For those situations, take a series of images and combine them into one large panorama with Photomerge.

The first step in using Photomerge successfully is taking appropriate photos. Here are some tips:

- ✔ **Use a properly leveled tripod.** Use a tripod, making sure that the tripod's head is steady and level so the individual photos align properly. If necessary, set the legs to different heights.

- ✔ **Turn off auto-exposure.** If you use your camera's auto-exposure feature, each image is actually exposed differently because of the lighting in that frame. Instead, expose for the center (or most important) photo and use the same settings for all shots.

- ✔ **Don't use auto-focus with zoom lenses.** Auto-focus can change the zoom factor of the lens. Instead, set the lens to manual focus after using auto-focus on your most important shot.

- ✔ **Overlap by at least 15 percent.** Up to one-quarter of each shot (on each side) should overlap so that Photomerge can properly align neighboring images.

When working with images that are properly exposed and have suitable overlap, Photomerge is fully automated. You open Photomerge, select your images, select how you want the component images to interact (typically Auto, but other options include Cylindrical, Spherical, Collage, and Reposition), and click OK. As you watch, the elements are put into order, aligned, and blended.

After Photomerge completes its mission, you're left with a layered image that uses layer masks to combine individual photos (one per layer) into a unified whole. Each layer is named for the file from which it was created. Typically you'll need to crop the image a bit to neaten up the edges and remove any areas of transparency.

11

Precision Edges with Vector Paths

In This Chapter

▶ Understanding vector artwork

▶ Creating objects with shapes

▶ Making a new path

▶ Changing the shape of an existing path

▶ Editing the shapes of type characters

*M*ost of the images with which you work in Photoshop — digital photos and scanned artwork, layers on which you paint, and filled selections — are created with pixels. There's also another type of artwork: *vector art,* which you create by defining a *path* (an outline) and adding color within and along that path. That path has a very precise edge, enabling vectors (when printed appropriately) to give you very crisp, clean lines in your artwork.

Typically, vector art consists of specific elements (objects) that are uniform in color (although vector art can also include gradients and patterns). You might have, for example, a red triangle, a blue square, and a green circle as your logo (boring!). These three solid-color objects are best defined as *vector artwork.* Vectors, however, are not appropriate for photographic images and other such imagery that include subtle transitions among colors.

In Photoshop, you have tools that create predefined shapes; you have tools that create freeform shapes; you have tools to edit the paths that define those shapes. You also have a shape picker and a bunch of menu commands. You can even bring in artwork from Adobe Illustrator and create your own shapes, too. After reading this chapter, you'll have a solid understanding of all these bits and pieces. I even tell you where to find dozens, or even hundreds, of custom shapes already on your computer — absolutely free!

Pixels, Paths, and You

The vast majority of the artwork with which you work (or play) in Photoshop is raster artwork. *Raster imagery* consists of uniformly sized squares of color *(pixels),* placed in rows and columns (the *raster*). Digital photos, scanned images, and just about anything that you put on a layer in Photoshop consists of pixels. When you edit the image, you're changing the color of the individual pixels, sometimes in subtle ways and sometimes in dramatic ways.

Vector artwork is a horse of another color. Rather than pixels, *vector art* consists of a mathematically defined path to which you add color. Now in Photoshop, as in Adobe Illustrator, the path produces the shape of the object, and you can add color both along the path *(stroke),* within the path *(fill),* to make the shape become an object. (In earlier versions of Photoshop, vector artwork was simulated with shape layers, layers filled with color that used a vector mask to display the "shape.")

Figure 11-1 shows a fine example of vector artwork. Observe that each element in the image consists of a single color. Each section of the image is easily identifiable as an individual object, consisting of a specific color. (Remember, though, that vector objects can be filled with gradients rather than color.)

Figure 11-1: Each element in vector art has a single specific color.

Each element in the artwork is defined by its path, which consists of a number of path segments. In Figure 11-2, you see the path that defines the tongue. (You read about the anatomy of a path later in this chapter, in the section "Understanding paths.")

When artwork is defined by pixels, the little square corners of the individual pixels can be noticeable along curves and diagonal lines. With vector artwork, the path is sharp, and the edges are well defined. However, to truly get the best appearance from vector art or vector type, the artwork must be printed to a PostScript-capable

Figure 11-2: Paths define the outline of an object — the snake's tongue, in this case.

device, such as a laser printer. *PostScript* is a page-description language that takes advantage of the mathematical descriptions of vector art. When you print to an inkjet printer, the vector art is converted to pixels. If you print to such a non-PostScript device, use a high image resolution for best output — 300 pixels per inch (ppi) is usually good. If you know you'll be outputting to a non-PostScript device, before you start creating shapes, go to Photoshop's Preferences⇨General and make sure to select Snap Vector Tools and Transformation to Pixel Grid.

A vector path can be *scaled* (changed in size) almost infinitely without losing its appearance. A vector logo can be used for both a business card and a billboard without loss of quality because the path is mathematically scaled before the stroke or fill is added. Raster art, on the other hand, can be severely degraded by such scaling. For a simple demonstration of the difference between scaling rasterized text and scaling Photoshop's vector type, see Figure 11-3.

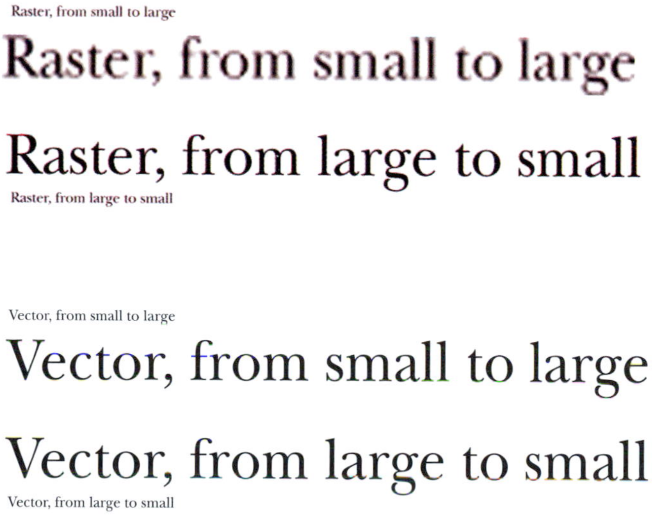

Raster, from small to large

Raster, from small to large

Raster, from large to small

Raster, from large to small

Vector, from small to large

Vector, from small to large

Vector, from large to small

Vector, from large to small

Figure 11-3: Using text as an example shows the advantage of vector artwork when scaling.

Easy Vectors: Using Shapes

If you made it through the preceding section, you're officially an expert on the theory of vector graphics. It's time to see how you can actually create these little darlings in your artwork. The easiest way to create a shape in Photoshop is with the aptly named *shape tools,* which automatically create a vector shape that you can stroke with a solid, dashed, or dotted line, and fill with color, a gradient, or a pattern. Could you have it any easier? Just drag a tool and create a vector-based object!

Your basic shape tools

Rectangles, rectangles with rounded corners *(rounded rectangles),* circles and ovals, multisided polygons, straight lines and arrows, and a whole boatload of special custom shapes are all at your command with a simple click-drag. Select the appropriate tool in the Toolbox, select the desired options in the Options bar, and click-drag to create your object. (The various shape tools are nested in the Toolbox, as shown in Figure 11-4.) Sounds simple, right? It is — no tricks. Here are some additional features to make things even easier for you:

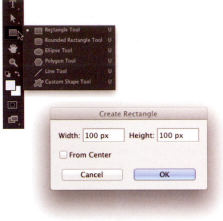

Figure 11-4: The shape tools are collected in one spot in Photoshop's Toolbox.

- ✔ **Use the Shift key.** Pressing the Shift key (both Mac and Windows) while you drag *constrains proportions* (maintains the width-to-height ratio). With the Shift key, the Rectangle tool creates squares; the Ellipse tool creates circles; the Polygon tool creates proportional polygons; the Line tool creates horizontal or vertical lines (or lines at 45° angles). When using custom shapes, pressing the Shift key ensures that the shape retains the width-to-height ratio with which it was originally defined.

- ✔ **Use the Option (Mac) or Alt (Windows) key.** The Option/Alt key creates the object centered on the point at which you click. Without the Option/Alt key, the object is created in whichever direction you drag.

- ✔ **Use the Shift and Option/Alt key.** Pressing the Shift and Option/Alt together helps you create a proportionally constrained object, centered on the point at which you click.

- ✔ **Click the shape tool.** If you click rather than drag, you'll open a small dialog box that allows you to enter precise dimensions for your new shape. Click the OK button and the shape is created to the lower-right of (or centered on) the point where you clicked. The dialog box is visible in Figure 11-4.

🖝 **Use the spacebar.** While you're dragging a shape, keep the mouse button down and press the spacebar. You can then drag to reposition the object while you create it. Still keeping the mouse button down, release the spacebar and finish dragging the object.

🖝 **Check the Options bar.** When you switch from shape tool to shape tool, the Options bar changes to fit your needs. For example, with the Rounded Rectangle tool active, you choose the radius of the rounded corners. The Polygon tool offers a simple field in which you choose the number of sides for the shape. When you're using the Line tool, choose the thickness *(weight)* of the line in the Options bar. Click the button to the left of the Weight field in the Options bar to add arrowheads to the lines.

🖝 **Change the layer content.** With a shape layer selected in the Layers panel, select any shape tool and change the shape's attributes in the Options bar. You can easily change (or remove) both the fill and the stroke.

🖝 **Edit the vector path.** As you can see later in this chapter (in the section "Adding, deleting, and moving anchor points"), you can use the Direct Selection tool to change the course of the path, customizing the appearance of the shape.

🖝 **Create work paths or pixel-filled shapes.** Using the three options in the menu to the left on the Options bar, you can elect to create shapes, work paths, or add pixels in the selected shape to your currently active layer.

You can easily spot a shape layer in the Layers panel — especially when the default layer name starts with the word *Shape*. (You can, of course, change the layer name by double-clicking it in the Layers panel.) You can see in the Layers panel shown in Figure 11-5 that the shape layer thumbnail includes the shape badge in the lower-right corner. When a shape layer is selected in the Layers panel, that shape's path is visible in the Paths panel.

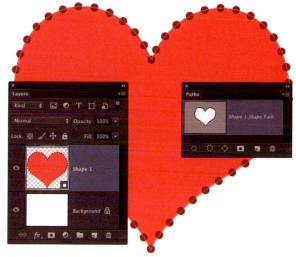

Figure 11-5: Dragging a shape tool creates both a shape layer and the path that defines the shape.

The Custom Shape tool

Although the basic shape tools are great for circles and squares and lines and arrows, you'll probably get the most use out of the Custom Shape tool. With this tool selected, you click the triangle to the right of the sample shape on the Options bar to open the Custom Shape picker, as shown in Figure 11-6. The Custom Shape picker offers a number of ready-to-use shapes. When you click the triangle in the upper-right corner, you can choose from a variety of other sets of shapes listed at the bottom of the Custom Shape picker menu. Also in the Options bar, you click on the Fill field and the Stroke field to open their options, and the More Options button enables you to customize the stroke.

Figure 11-6: The Fill and Stroke options are available for all shape-creation tools.

When you select a set of custom shapes from the menu (or use the Load Shapes command to add a set of shapes not in the menu), you are asked whether you want to add the new shapes to the current content of the Custom Shape picker (Append), replace the current shapes (OK), or not add the shapes after all (Cancel). When you select All from the Custom Shape picker menu and click OK, you'll load over 300 custom shapes, ranging from signs and symbols to animals and cartoon talk balloons.

More custom shapes — free!

The custom shapes already available in Photoshop cover a wide range, but they might not fill all your needs. You can purchase commercial collections of custom shapes from a couple of sources. You can create custom paths and define shapes from them, too. But you've already got bunches of custom shapes on your computer, just waiting for you to use them. Select Photoshop's Type tool and take a look in your Font menu. Check out the fonts already there with names like *Wingdings, Webdings, Symbol,* and *Dingbats.* These are all examples of *symbol fonts,* which are fonts that have shapes and symbols rather than letters and numbers. Many more typical fonts also have special characters available when you use the Shift key, the Option/Alt key, and the Shift key in combination with the Option/Alt key.

Here's how you can define a custom shape from a symbol:

1. **Choose File⇨New to open a new document.**

   The document can be virtually any size and can be either grayscale or color.

2. **Select the Type tool and pick a font.**

   With the Type tool active, choose a symbol font from either the Options bar or the Character panel. The font size doesn't matter much because you're creating a vector-based shape that you can easily scale. The foreground color doesn't matter either because shape tools rely on the foreground color active at the time you create the shape.

3. **Type a single symbol and then end the editing session.**

   Figure 11-7: Name your new shape and click OK.

   Click the check mark button to the right on the Options bar, switch tools in the Toolbox, or press ⌘+Return (Mac) or Ctrl+Enter (Windows) to end the editing session. (The symbol visible in Figure 11-7 can be produced by pressing the V key when using the font Webdings.)

4. **Convert the type character to a shape layer.**

   With the type layer active in the Layers panel, use the menu command Type⇨Convert to Shape. (Note that Type is a separate menu now, rather than a submenu of Layers.)

5. **Define a custom shape.**

   Choose Edit⇨Define Custom Shape, give your new shape a name in the Shape Name dialog box (shown in Figure 11-7), and save it. Your new shape is added to the Custom Shape picker, ready to use.

Later in this chapter, after you master using the Pen tool, remember this section. You can also define a custom shape from paths that you create with the Pen tool — any shape at all!

Remember that your custom shapes aren't truly saved until you use the Custom Shape picker menu command Save Shapes (to save all the shapes in the picker as a single set) or the Edit➪Presets➪Preset Manager command (to save a set of selected shapes). In the Preset Manager dialog box, ⌘+click/ Ctrl+click each of your custom shapes and then click the Save Set button to save them as a set (see Figure 11-8). Until you take this step, the shapes exist only in Photoshop's Preferences file. If the Preferences become corrupt, you could lose all your custom shapes. This holds true, too, for custom brushes, layer styles, swatches, and the like — use the Preset Manager to save all your custom items.

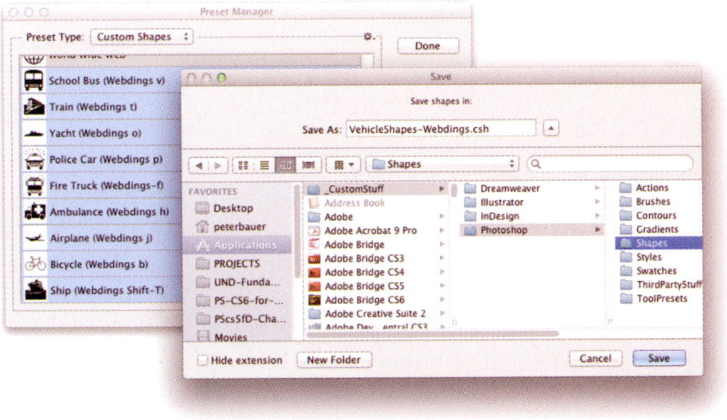

Figure 11-8: Use the Preset Manager to save sets of your custom shapes.

When saving custom shapes (or layer styles or brushes or any of your other custom bits and pieces) with the Preset Manager, save them in a folder outside the Photoshop folder. That prevents accidental loss should you ever need to (*gasp!*) reinstall Photoshop. Figure 11-8 shows one possible folder structure for saving and organizing your custom bits and pieces.

When you installed Photoshop, you were offered the option of migrating presets from earlier versions of the program. If you did not do so then, you can add those older presets to Photoshop's new Presets folders with the Edit➪Presets➪Migrate Presets command.

Changing the appearance of a shape

After you use any one of the numerous shape tools in the Photoshop arsenal to add a shape to your artwork, you have a number of ways that you can enhance, adjust, and simply change its appearance:

✔ **Add a layer style.** Layer styles, such as bevels, glows, and shadows (applied through the Layer➪Layer Style menu), can certainly spice up a shape layer. Compare, for example, the pair of shapes in Figure 11-9. (Layer styles are presented in Chapter 12.) By working with blending modes and opacity, you can combine a Gradient Overlay or a Pattern Overlay effect with a shape's gradient or pattern (or color) fill.

Figure 11-9: A simple layer style makes your shape jump off the page.

✔ **Change the layer content.** As with any shape, you can use a shape tool's Options bar to make changes to fill, stroke, and other custom shape attributes.

✔ **Edit the path shape.** Click a path with the Direct Selection tool and drag to change the path's shape. (This is discussed in more detail later in this chapter.)

✔ **Change the layer blending mode or opacity.** By default, your shape layer's blending mode is Normal, and the Opacity is set to 100%. Your shape layer blocks and hides the content of every layer below. By changing the blending mode or opacity, you can make your shape layer interact with the layers below in interesting ways. Experiment with different blending modes to find one that suits your artistic vision. (Blending modes are covered in more detail in Chapter 10.)

Simulating a multicolor shape layer

Shapes can be filled with a single solid color, a gradient, or a pattern. Sometimes, however, you're better served with a multicolor shape. Take a look at Figure 11-10 and compare the pair of shapes to the left with the same two shapes to the right.

Figure 11-10: Dressing up the shapes can make a world of difference.

In addition to the layer styles applied, *layer masks* hide parts of the more elaborate pair of shapes on the right. A layer mask determines what areas of the layer are visible. You can use layer masks with shapes, as you can see for three of the four layers in Figure 11-11.

Comparing the shapes' color in the left thumbnail in the Layers panel to the artwork helps you identify what you see in Figure 11-11:

Figure 11-11: Layer masks determine layer visibility.

- ✔ **Shape 1 copy:** This is the top layer and would normally hide everything on the layers below. The shape, as you can tell from the left thumbnail in the Layers panel, is green. The thumbnail to the right is the layer mask. By painting with black in the layer mask, you can hide parts of the layer. In this case, only the left part of the shape is visible.

- ✔ **Shape 2 copy:** You can see that the shape is an entire pair of scissors. The thumbnail to the right shows that most of the layer is hidden by a layer mask, leaving only the blades of the scissors shape visible.

- ✔ **Shape 2:** This layer requires no layer mask for this artwork. The shape layer just above hides what would be black scissors blades.

- ✔ **Shape 1:** The layers above partially hide the red shape layer. Notice how because of the order of the layers in the Layers panel, the blades of the scissors appear to be in front of the red part of the object and behind the green part of the object.

Adding a layer mask to your shape is as easy as clicking the Add Layer Mask button at the bottom of the Layers panel (third button from the left), and then painting with black to hide, white to show, and gray to partially hide. You can also make a selection in your image and use the Layer⇨Layer Mask menu commands. You can add layer masks to any layer except those named *Background.* (You can't have transparent areas on a background layer, but you can rename a background layer to convert it to a regular layer.)

Using Your Pen Tool to Create Paths

Even with all the custom shapes available, you might need to create a path that's unique to a specific image. For that, Photoshop offers the Pen tool and its associated tools. Before you start creating paths willy-nilly, you can probably benefit from a little bit of background information about paths.

Understanding paths

As you click and click-drag, you place *anchor points,* which connect the *path segments* that create your path. Path segments can be straight or curved. You control those curves not with diet and exercise but rather with *direction lines* and their *control points.* A straight path segment is bordered on either end by *corner anchor points,* and a curved path segment is bordered by two *smooth anchor points* or one of each type. As you can

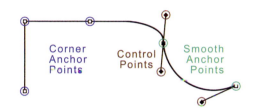

Figure 11-12: Paths have square anchor points and diamond-shaped control points.

see in Figure 11-12, Photoshop helps you differentiate between path segments and direction lines by using squares (hollow and filled) for anchor points and diamond shapes for control points.

Only smooth anchor points have direction lines and control points. The angle and length of the direction line determine the shape of the curve. When you create a curved path segment between a corner anchor point and a smooth anchor point, only the smooth point's direction lines adjust the curve. When you create a curved path segment between two smooth anchor points, both points' direction lines affect the curve.

Here's another important way to classify paths in Photoshop:

- ✔ An **open path** has two distinct and visible endpoints; think of it as a pencil line or piece of string.

- ✔ A **closed path** has no beginning or end — like a circle or an unbroken rubber band.

When you use a shape tool, you're creating closed paths. When you click-click-click with the Pen tool, you create an open path — unless, that is, your final click is back on the very first anchor point.

Clicking and dragging your way down the path of knowledge

All that theory about how paths work is fine, but you'll get a better understanding by playing around with the Pen tool. Open a new document (any size, resolution, and color mode will do) and select the Pen tool. On the Options bar, click the menu to the left (as shown in Figure 11-13) and select Path so that the tool creates work paths rather than shapes, and then start clicking around. Randomly click in various places in the image, adding new straight path segments as you go.

Figure 11-13: Use the menu to the left in the Options bar to determine whether the Pen tool creates a shape or a work path.

The third option in the menu, Pixels, is used only with Shape tools.

I'm sure Picasso would be proud, but it's time to let go of your new artwork and move on — press Delete (Mac) or Backspace (Windows) twice. The first time deletes the most recent anchor point; the second time deletes the rest of the path.

Now, in that same canvas, start click-dragging to create curved path segments. Watch how the distance and direction in which you drag control the segment's curve. Just because it's fun, try a click-drag and, with the mouse button held down, move the mouse around and around in a circle. "Path Jump Rope"! Press Delete/Backspace twice to delete the path.

Now, to get a feel for how to control your curved path segments, try this:

1. **Choose File⇨New to open a new document.**

2. **Choose 1024x768 from the Preset: Web group.**

    A reasonable size to work with, it should fit on your screen at 100% zoom.

3. **Show the Grid.**

    Press ⌘+' (apostrophe; Mac) or Ctrl+' (apostrophe; Windows) to show the Grid in the image. The Grid makes it easier to control the Pen tool as you drag. You can also show the Grid with the menu command View⇨Show⇨Grid. In Photoshop's Preferences⇨Guides, Grid & Slices, the Grid shown in Figure 11-14 is set to Gridline every: 1 inch and Subdivisions: 6.

4. **Select the Pen tool in the Toolbox.**

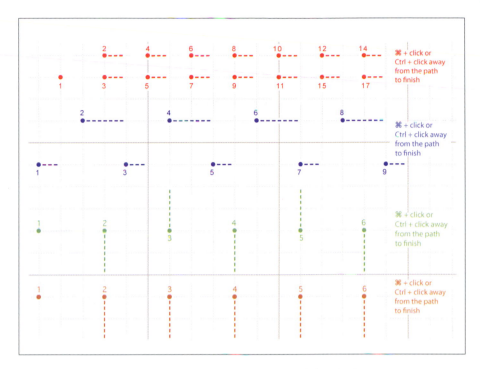

Figure 11-14: You don't need to be precise; just more or less follow the four patterns.

5. **Click and click-drag as shown in Figure 11-14.**

   Don't worry about precision — you won't be creating a work of art this time. Click on the dots in numeric order; where you see a dashed line, click-drag in that direction for approximately that distance.

You've just created four of the more useful scallops and curve sets! These sorts of paths can be used in a variety of ways, including stroking, filling, and creating selections (all of which I discuss later in this chapter) to create decorative borders and artistic elements in your images.

You should know about a couple of other features of the Pen tool before you move on. With the Pen tool active, take a look at the Options bar (or look at Figure 11-15, which shows the Options bar).

Figure 11-15: The Pen tool has a couple of tricks up its sleeve!

With a path active in the Paths panel, the Pen tool's Options bar enables you to load the path as a selection, create a layer mask (as long as there's a layer that supports transparency active in the Layers panel), and to create a shape from the path. Note, too, that when the Freeform Pen tool is active, the Options bar offers a Magnetic option.

When you have the Freeform Pen tool selected in the Toolbox you can click and drag around your image, creating a path as you go. It's much like painting with the Brush tool or drawing lines with the Pencil tool — wherever you drag the tool, the path is created. When you need to make a path (or selection) around the outside of something of uniform color in your image, using the Magnetic option forces the path to look for and follow edges. Take a look

Figure 11-16: Tracing around an object that contrasts with the background is simple when using the Freeform Pen with the Magnetic option.

at Figure 11-16, which shows an example of an appropriate use for the Freeform Pen and the Magnetic option.

A closer look at the Paths panel

You can save, duplicate, convert, stroke, and delete paths via the Paths panel (which, like all panels, you can show and hide through the Window menu). You can even create a path from a selection by using the Paths panel. Without the Paths panel, your paths have no meaning or future and probably won't get into a good university or even a good collage.

Pick a path, any path

The Paths panel can hold as many paths as you could possibly want to add to your artwork. You can also see the seven buttons across the bottom of the panel that you use to quickly and easily work with your paths. You can classify paths in the five different ways, as shown in Figure 11-17.

You might not use them all, but it's good to know the five types of paths:

✔ **Work path:** As you create a path, Photoshop generates a temporary work path, which is not automatically saved. Unless you save your path, it's deleted as soon as you start to create another path or when you close the file. To save a work path, simply double-click the name field in the Paths panel and type a new name.

✔ **Clipping path:** *Clipping paths* are used primarily with some page layout programs, such as QuarkXPress. Much like how a vector path determines what parts of the layer are visible, a clipping

Figure 11-17: The Paths panel is your key to organizing and controlling vectors in your artwork.

path identifies what part of the image as a whole is visible. You won't need a clipping path when you work with Adobe InDesign — simply create your artwork on a transparent background and place that Photoshop file into an InDesign document. To create a clipping path, first make your path, give it a name in the Paths panel (to save it), and then use the Paths panel menu command Clipping Path.

✔ **Saved path:** Much like working in the Layers panel, you can double-click the name of any path and rename it in the Paths panel. (You *must* rename a work path in order to save the path for later use.) After you give the path a name, it's safe from accidental deletion.

✔ **Shape path:** When a shape is active in the Layers panel, its path is visible in the Paths panel. If you want to customize a shape's path, you need to make the layer active first. When a shape path is visible, you can drag it to the New Path button at the bottom of the panel to create a duplicate. (It's the second button from the right.)

✔ **Vector mask path:** When a regular layer has a vector mask assigned and that layer is visible in the Layers panel, the layer's mask path is visible in the Paths panel.

When creating a clipping path, leave the Flatness field completely empty unless your print shop specifically instructs you to use a specific value. The Flatness value overrides the output device's native setting for reproducing curves. Using the wrong value can lead to disastrous (and expensive!) mistakes.

To activate a path in the Paths panel, click it. You can then see and edit the path in the image window. With the exception of shape layer and vector mask paths, the paths in the Paths panel are independent of any layer. You could create a path with the Background layer active and then later use that path as the basis for some artwork on, for example, Layer 3.

The Paths panel buttons

The seven buttons across the bottom of the Paths panel (refer to Figure 11-17) do more than just simple panel housekeeping. Use them to create artwork from a path and to convert back and forth between paths and selections.

- **Fill Path:** Click a path in the Paths panel and then use this button to fill the area inside the path on the active layer with the foreground color. If you fill an open path (a path with two distinct endpoints), Photoshop pretends that there's a straight path segment between the endpoints. If a shape layer or a type layer is selected in the Layers panel, the Fill Path button isn't available. You can see filled (and stroked) paths in Figure 11-18.

Figure 11-18: Think about whether you want to stroke first (left) or fill first (right).

- **Stroke Path:** Click a path in the Paths panel and then use this button to add a band of the foreground color along the course of the path. Most often, you can think of it as painting the path itself with the Brush tool. If you have a different brush-using tool active in the Toolbox (Clone Stamp, Healing Brush, Dodge, Burn, Eraser, and so on), the path is stroked with that tool. Like a fill, a stroke is added to the currently active layer in the Layers panel. (Remember that you stroke a shape's path in the shape tools Options bar.) Take a look at Figure 11-18 to see how stroking and filling differ.

- **Selection from Path:** When you have a path selected in the Paths panel, you click this button, and *voilà!* An instant — and very precise — selection is at your disposal. You can create a selection from any path. If you want to add feathering to the selection, use the Paths panel menu command Make Selection rather than clicking the Selection from Path button.

- **Path from Selection:** You can create a work path from any selection simply by clicking this button. If the path isn't as accurate as you'd like, or if it's too complex because it's trying to follow the corner of every pixel, use the Paths panel menu command Make Work Path and adjust the Tolerance setting to suit your needs.

- **Vector Layer Mask from Path:** If the layer active in the Layers panel supports transparency and you have a saved or work path selected, you can add a vector layer mask to the layer.

- **Create New Path:** You'll likely use this button primarily to duplicate an existing path. Drag any path to the button, and a copy is instantly available in the Paths panel. When you click this button, you're not creating (or replacing) a work path but rather starting a new saved path.

- **Delete Path:** Drag a path to the Delete Path button or click the path and then click the button. Either way, the path is eliminated from the panel and from your artwork.

The order in which you stroke and fill a path can make a huge difference in the appearance of your artwork. The stroke is centered on the path, half inside and half outside. The fill extends throughout the interior of the path. If you stroke a path and then add a fill, the fill covers that part of your stroke that's inside the path. As you can see in Figure 11-18, that's not always a bad thing. (Both paths are visible for comparison purposes — normally only one path is active at a time.)

Rather than using the buttons at the bottom of the Paths panel to fill and stroke, you can also use the Paths panel menu commands Fill Path and Stroke Path. The commands open dialog boxes that offer more options than simply using the current foreground color. When using the Stroke Path command, you can choose from any of the brush-using tools, which enables you to, for example, very precisely dodge, burn, or clone along a path you create. When using Fill Path, you can add color or a pattern within the path, or fill to a designated state in the History panel.

Keep in mind that Photoshop's Pen tool can now create vector shapes that can be both filled and stroked. That is usually faster, easier, and generally better than creating a path and then filling and stroking on a regular layer.

Sometimes the easiest and fastest way to create a complex path is to make a selection and convert the selection to a path. You might, for example, click once with the Magic Wand and then click the Selection from Path button at the bottom of the Paths panel. Remember to rename the path to save it!

Customizing Any Path

Photoshop gives you a lot of control over your paths, not just when creating them, but afterward, as well. After a path is created, you can edit the path itself. While the path is active in the Paths panel, the Edit⇨Transform Path commands are available, giving you control over size, rotation, perspective, skewing, and even distortion. But there's also much finer control at your fingertips. You can adjust anchor points, change curved path segments, add or delete anchor points, and even combine multiple paths into *compound paths,* in which one path cuts a hole in another. (Think *donut.*)

Adding, deleting, and moving anchor points

Photoshop provides you with a number of tools with which to edit paths although you might never use a couple of them. Consider, for example, the Add Anchor Point and Delete Anchor Point tools shown in Figure 11-19. Now take a look at the Option bar's Auto Add/Delete option. With the Pen tool active, you automatically switch to the Delete Anchor Point tool when over an anchor point, and automatically switch to the Add Anchor Point tool when the cursor is over a path segment. Smart tool, eh? The Convert Point tool, on the other hand, can be invaluable . . . or valuable, at least. Click a smooth anchor point to convert it to a corner anchor point. Click-drag a corner anchor point to convert it to a smooth point.

Figure 11-19: Photoshop gives you every tool you need to edit vector paths.

Nested in the Toolbox with the Path Selection tool (which you use to select and drag a path in its entirety), the Direct Selection tool lets you alter individual path segments, individual anchor points, and even the individual direction lines that control curved path segments. (When you click on a shape with the Direct Selection tool, the Options bar can also be used to change the shape's attributes, including fill, stroke, and size.)

When you click an anchor point with the Direct Selection tool, you can drag it into a new position, altering the shape of the path. If it's a smooth anchor point, clicking it with the Direct Selection tool makes the point's direction lines visible (as well as those of immediately neighboring smooth anchor points). When manipulating paths, the Direct Selection tool follows a few simple rules of behavior (which you can see illustrated by pairs of "before" and "after" paths in Figure 11-20):

✔ **Drag a path segment.** Drag a path segment with two corner anchor points, and you drag those points along with you. If the path segment has one or two smooth points, you drag the segment (reshaping the curve), but the anchor points remain firmly in place. Note in Figure 11-20 (upper left) that when you drag a curved path segment, the adjoining direction lines change length, but they retain their original angles.

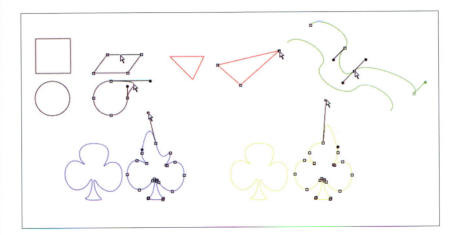

Figure 11-20: The pairs of paths are shown in color for illustrative purposes only — paths are generally black when active.

✔ **Drag a corner anchor point.** Click a corner anchor point and drag, and the Direct Selection tool pulls the two adjoining path segments along with it. As you can see in Figure 11-20 (upper center), the other two anchor points (and the path segment between them) are unchanged.

✔ **Drag a smooth anchor point.** When you drag a smooth anchor point, all four of the direction lines associated with the path segments on either side retain both their lengths and their angles. The direction lines don't change; only the curved path segments connected at the smooth anchor point are altered. In Figure 11-20 (upper right), the path continues to flow smoothly through the anchor point, even as the point moves.

✔ **Drag a smooth point's direction line.** Dragging a direction line changes the curves on either side of the anchor point so that the path still flows smoothly through the point. (Remember that you click the control point at the end of a direction line to drag it.) Figure 11-20 (lower left) illustrates how the path segments on either side of the smooth point adjust as the direction line is changed. However, paths don't always flow smoothly through a smooth anchor point — not if you use the following trick!

✔ **Option+drag/Alt+drag a direction line.** Hold down the Option/Alt key and drag a smooth anchor point's direction line, and you'll break the flow of the path through that point. With the Option/Alt key, you change only the path segment on that side of the anchor point, leaving the adjoining path segment unchanged. In Figure 11-20 to the lower left, the direction line on the left is being dragged without the Option/Alt key (as described in the preceding bullet point). On the lower-right, adding the modifier key preserves the appearance of the adjoining path segment.

You can use the Shift key with the Direct Selection tool to ensure that you're dragging in a straight line. You can also use the Shift key to select multiple anchor points before you drag.

Combining paths

As you've probably noticed through the course of this chapter, some paths are very simple (like the paths in the preceding figure), and some paths are more complex (like the shapes shown earlier in Figure 11-11). Complex paths are often *compound paths:* that is, paths that contain two or more paths (called *subpaths*) that interact with each other. Think about a pair of circles, different sizes, centered on top of each other. What if the smaller circle cut a hole in the middle of the larger circle, creating a wheel (or, depending on how early you're reading this, a bagel)? Take a look at Figure 11-21.

Figure 11-21: Two (or more) paths can interact with each other, creating a compound path, consisting of two or more subpaths.

There are several ways in which two (or more) paths can interact. Complete this sentence with terms from the following list: *"The second path can* (fill in the blank) *the original path."*

✔ **Combine Shapes with:** The areas within the two subpaths are combined as if they were within a single path (although they remain two subpaths).

✔ **Subtract Front Shape from:** The second path is used like a cookie cutter to delete an area from within the first path. (When you need to make a bagel, this is the option!)

✔ **Intersect Shape Areas with:** Only the areas where the two subpaths overlap is retained.

✔ **Exclude Overlapping Shapes from:** All the area within both subpaths is retained *except* where the two paths overlap.

When any shape tool, the Pen tool, the Path Selection tool, or Direct Selection tool is active, the Options bar presents you with four options to determine the behavior of multiple paths. (The first path that you create will always be just a normal path. The options don't come into play until you add additional subpaths.) Figure 11-22 shows you the option name and provides a simple graphic representation to demonstrate the interaction. The upper-left path is the original, with the lower-right path showing how each option controls the interaction between subpaths.

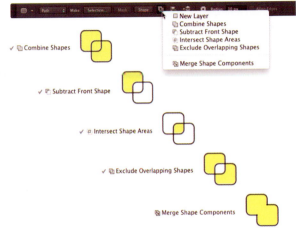

Figure 11-22: The buttons control how a second path (and any subsequent paths) interacts with your original path.

Visible in Figure 11-22 are a couple of new options. When a tool is set to create a shape, the option New Layer is available. Using the Merge Shape Components merges overlapping paths, creating a single path rather than a compound path. (In Figure 11-22, compare the black line to the right of Merge Shape Components to the pair of black lines to the right of Combine Shapes.)

Tweaking type for a custom font

I want to show you one more little thing you can do with vectors in Photoshop, a last bit of fun before this chapter ends. Each individual character in a font consists of paths. You can convert the type to shape layers (or work paths) and change the appearance of the individual characters by editing their paths with the Direct Selection tool.

1. **Open a new document in Photoshop.**

2. **Select 800x600 from the web presets in the Preset menu and then click OK.**

3. **Select the Horizontal Type tool in the Toolbox and set the font.**

   From the Options bar, choose Arial, set the font style to Bold, set the font size to 72, choose Sharp for anti-aliasing, left-align, and click near the lower left of your document.

   Okay, in all honesty, you can use just about any settings you want — but if you use these settings, your image will look a lot like mine.

4. **Type the word Billiards in your image.**

5. **Press ⌘+Return/Ctrl+Enter to end the text editing session.**

6. **Choose Type⇨Convert to Shape.**

   This changes the type layer (editable text on its own layer) to a shape. (Type is its own menu now, not a submenu of the Layers menu.)

7. **Activate the Direct Selection tool.**

8. **Edit the shapes of the *L*s and the *D* to simulate billiard cues.**

   Drag the uppermost anchor points even farther upward to create cue sticks.

   See the result in Figure 11-23.

Figure 11-23: You can convert vector type to shapes and edit the individual character shapes with the Direct Selection tool.

Dressing Up Images with Layer Styles

*I*n artwork and photography, you use shadows and highlights in your image to produce the illusion of depth. Highlights and shadows lead the viewer to imagine that a light is falling on parts of a 3D object. You can also use a shadow or glow to make it appear that some distance exists between one object in the image and another object behind it. Photoshop's built-in layer styles help you add shadows, glows, and other effects almost instantly.

In this chapter, I explain how transparent areas on layers enable lower layers to show through and let your layer styles appear on those lower layers. You get a good look at the Styles panel and how you use it to store and apply layer styles, including your very own custom styles. I then present the all-important (for layer styles) Layer Style dialog box and the various effects that you can add with it. I also show you how to save (and protect) your custom layer styles.

What Are Layer Styles?

A *layer style* comprises one or more effects that surround or are applied to all the pixels on your layer. Effects that surround pixels include strokes (thin or thick outlines of color), shadows (just like the one you're casting right now), and glows (outlines of semi-transparent color). Effects that are applied to pixels include overlays of color, patterns, or even gradients. But Photoshop offers even more, including the ever-popular Bevel and Emboss effect, which does a great job of giving the content of your layer a 3D look. And, of course, effects can be used in combination; check out Figure 12-1 for an example. You can add effects to layers in several ways, including through the Layer Style menu at the bottom of the Layers panel, as shown in Figure 12-2. I explain each of the effects individually later in this chapter in the section on creating your own custom layer styles.

Figure 12-1: Strokes, shadows, and bevels are just some of the effects available.

Just so everyone is on the same sheet of music, when you refer to a drop shadow or an outer glow or a color overlay or any one of the other items shown in the menu in Figure 12-2, call it a *layer effect* or simply an *effect*.

Figure 12-2: You can add a layer style through the Layers panel.

After you apply an effect to a layer or save it in the Styles panel (which I discuss a bit later in this chapter), it becomes a *layer style.* A layer style can include one effect or several effects. The individual layer effects are built into Photoshop, but you can add or delete layer styles and even create your own. By the way, Blending Options, at the top of the list in Figure 12-2, isn't actually a layer effect, but rather it governs how the colors of the pixels on the selected layer interact with pixels on layers below. The checkmarks to the left of some effects listed in Figure 12-2 indicate that those effects are already applied to the layer.

Some layer effects, such as drop shadows and outer glows, appear outside the content of the layer. For those effects to be visible in your artwork, the layer must have at least some area of transparent pixels. If the layer is filled edge to edge, the effect has no place within the image to appear because the glow or shadow would logically be outside the image's canvas. Take a look at a couple of layer style examples in Figure 12-3.

In the sample on the left, you can imagine that the shadow logically also appears to the lower right of the object as a whole (as it does in the sample to the right). However, that's outside the image's canvas, so that part of the shadow doesn't appear in the artwork.

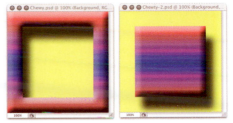

Figure 12-3: Some layer effects need transparent areas on the layer, or they won't appear.

Keep in mind that every layer in an image has the same number of pixels — but some of those pixels can be transparent. When a layer has areas of transparency, layers below in the image can show through. In the two examples in Figure 12-3, the yellow background layer is visible, giving the upper layer's shadows a place to fall. (And remember that a layer named *Background* can't have areas of transparency. Convert it to a regular layer by double-clicking the layer name in the Layers panel and renaming it.) Chapter 10 is full of information on working with layers.

Using the Styles Panel

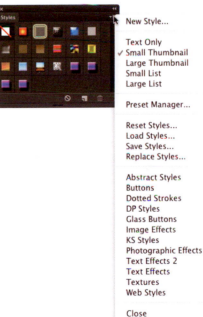

The Styles panel is hidden by default. Choose Window➪Styles to make it visible. This panel, which you see with its menu open in Figure 12-4, is where you find and store layer styles and is the easiest way to apply a layer style to your active layer.

To apply a layer style via the Styles panel, make the target layer active by clicking it in the Layers panel; then click the style that you want to apply. It's truly that simple! To remove a layer style from the active layer, click the leftmost button at the bottom of the Styles panel. You can click the middle button to save a custom layer style (which I explain later in this chapter), and you can drag a layer style to the Trash icon on the right to delete it from the panel.

Figure 12-4: The Styles panel holds your preset and saved layer styles.

Take a look at the Styles panel menu shown in Figure 12-4, starting from the top and making your way down to the bottom. The first command simply adds the style applied to the active layer to the panel (like clicking the Create New Style button).

In the second section of the menu, you can choose from five different ways to view the content of the Styles panel. The Text Only, Small List, and Large List options might come in handy after you create a bunch of custom styles with names you recognize, but until you become familiar with the styles in the panel, their names are pretty much meaningless. The Large Thumbnail option gives you a better view of the effects in the style, but you see fewer styles at a time in the panel than you can with the default Small Thumbnails view.

The Styles panel Preset Manager command opens the same Preset Manager that you access through the Edit⇨Presets menu. Use the Preset Manager (discussed at the end of this chapter) to save custom styles in sets on your hard drive to protect them from accidental loss.

The next four commands in the Styles panel menu are what I call "housekeeping commands" because you use them to control the content of the panel:

- **Reset Styles:** The Reset Styles command returns the content of the panel to its default. You have the option of adding the default set to the current panel content with the Append button or replacing the current content with the selected set by clicking OK.

- **Load Styles:** Use the Load Styles command to add additional styles from your hard drive (or another location). You can download sets from various websites and even purchase prepared sets of layer styles on CD. The set is added to the current content of the panel automatically.

- **Save Styles:** The Save Styles command lets you save the current content of the panel as a set of styles. All the layer styles in the panel at the time are saved in the set.

- **Replace Styles:** Use the Replace Styles command to remove the current content and then add the selected set.

Below in the Styles panel menu, you can find a list of all the layer style sets saved in Photoshop's Presets⇨Styles folder. When you select a set from that list, you have the option once again of appending or replacing the current content of the panel. (The list in your Styles panel menu might differ from what's shown in Figure 12-4.)

The last two commands in the Styles panel menu are used to control the visibility of the panel (Close) and the visibility of the panel and those panels nested with it (Close Tab Group), which depends on how you've arranged Photoshop's panels in your workspace.

Creating Custom Layer Styles

You create a custom layer style by applying one or more layer effects to your active layer. (Once again, remember that you can't apply layer effects or layer styles to a layer named *Background*.) When you have the effects looking just the way you want them, you can add that new style to the Styles panel and even save it for sharing with friends and colleagues. Combining multiple layer effects lets you create complex and beautiful layer styles that change simple shapes and text into art.

Exploring the Layer Style menu

In addition to the pop-up menu at the bottom of the Layers panel (refer to Figure 12-2), you can apply layer effects through the Layer⟹Layer Style menu. As you can see in Figure 12-5, the Layer Style menu has a few more commands than the menu at the bottom of the Layers panel.

The ten items in the Layer Style menu below Blending Options are the actual layer effects. A check mark to the left of the effect indicates that it's currently applied to the active layer. The Copy Layer Style and Paste Layer Style commands come in handy, but if you're more mouse- or stylus-oriented than menu-oriented, you'll find it easier to add the style to the Styles panel and click the style to apply it to other layers. You can also Option/Alt+drag a layer style from layer to layer in the Layers panel to duplicate it. Clear Layer Style is the equivalent of using the leftmost button at the bottom of the Styles panel — it removes all layer effects from the target layer. The four commands at the bottom of the menu are worthy of a little special attention:

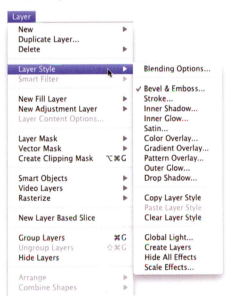

Figure 12-5: You can use the Layer Style menu to apply layer effects and more.

✔ **Global Light:** A number of layer effects are applied at an angle. *Drop shadows,* for example, simulate light coming from a specific angle (which, of course, determines where in your artwork that shadow falls). You use the Global Light command to set the default angle at which your effects are applied. Generally speaking, you want the angle to be consistent from effect to effect and from layer to layer in your artwork. There are exceptions, however, such as the situation shown in Figure 12-6. In that artwork, the two type layers have shadows receding at different angles to simulate a light source positioned immediately in front of and close to the image. (As you can read in the next section of this chapter, when you use layer effects that are

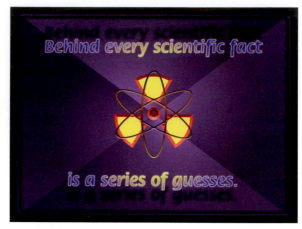

Figure 12-6: Sometimes shadows in your artwork shouldn't all use the Global Light setting.

applied at an angle, you have the option of using or not using the angle in Global Light.)

✔ **Create Layers:** Sometimes you need to edit a layer effect — say, to control where a drop shadow falls on the lower layers in the image. The Create Layers command rasterizes each layer effect (adds it to the image as a separate layer or layers containing pixels). You can then erase portions of the new layers, apply artistic filters, or otherwise customize each effect layer. Remember that after a layer style is rasterized with this command, you can no longer edit it through the Layer Style dialog box, but the original style (if you added it to the Styles panel) is still available.

✔ **Hide All Effects:** You can temporarily hide a layer style with the Hide All Effects command. Alternatively (and more conveniently), you can click the eyeball icon next to the layer style in the Layers panel to hide the effects.

✔ **Scale Effects:** Use the Scale Effects command to uniformly make the layer style larger or smaller.

Exploring the Layer Style dialog box

The first step in creating custom layer styles is to become familiar with the individual layer effects. Each of the ten effects available in the Layer Style dialog box (see Figure 12-7) has its own set of options. Most of the basic default values are very good starting points: You might need to change only a color or perhaps adjust a Size, Distance, or Opacity slider. You can, of course, do lots and lots of customizing for some of the effects.

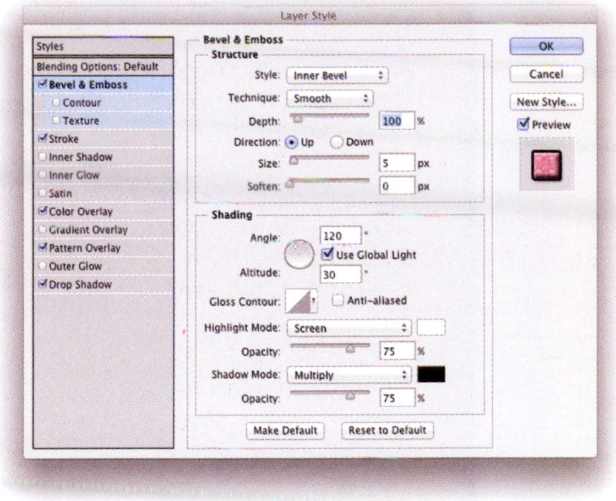

In the column to the left in the Layer Style dialog box, you can select a check box to apply the effect, but you need to click the name of the effect to open that effect's options pane. In Figure 12-7, the check marks show that this particular layer style includes a bevel, a stroke, color and pattern overlays, and a drop shadow. The options pane for Bevel and Emboss is visible, as you can tell by the highlighting in the left column (not to mention the subtle *Bevel and Emboss* in bold at the top-center

Figure 12-7: The Layer Style dialog box has separate options for each layer effect.

of the dialog box). And in the far right of the Layer Style dialog box, note the Preview check box (upper right, which shows what the layer style will look like) and the small sample just below. That sample shows how your style will look when applied to a square about 55x55 pixels.

Take a look at the bottom of the Layer Style dialog box in Figure 12-7 to see the buttons Make Default and Reset to Default. In addition to saving a new layer style every time you hit upon a winning combination of settings, you can make those favorite settings the default. Change your mind later? One click is all it takes to reset to Photoshop's defaults.

As you read the descriptions of the various sets of options, keep in mind some generalities about a few key options that you'll see a number of times:

- ✔ **Color Selection:** When you see a color swatch — a small rectangle or square, usually near the Blending Mode option — you can click it to open the Color Picker and select a different color.

- ✔ **Noise:** When you see the Noise slider, you can add a speckling effect to help diffuse a glow or shadow.

- ✔ **Contour:** Glows, shadows, and the like can be applied linearly, with a steady fade from visible to not visible. Or you can elect to have that transition vary with a nonlinear contour. Generally speaking, nonlinear contours can be great for bevels, but linear is usually best for shadows and glows unless you intend to create concentric halos.

✔ **Angle/Use Global Light:** You can change the angle for several layer effects by entering a specific angle in the numeric field or by dragging in the circular Angle controller. If the Use Global Light check box is selected, you change *all* the angles for that layer style.

Layer effects basics

In this section, I explain the basics of each of the ten layer effects, showing the options available in the Layer Style dialog box for that effect in an insert, as well as one or more examples. And don't forget to take a look at the sidebar, "The four key blending modes." Later in this chapter, you can read about the Opacity and the Fill sliders as well as some other advanced blending options.

Bevel and Emboss

Perhaps the most fun of all the Photoshop layer effects, Bevel and Emboss is a quick and easy way to add a 3D look to your artwork. You can apply a Bevel and Emboss layer effect to text or to buttons for your website. You can also use this effect to create more complex elements in your artwork, examples of which appear in Figure 12-8.

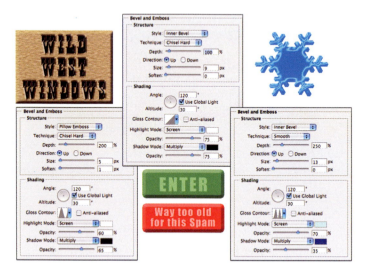

Figure 12-8: The Bevel and Emboss layer effect is very versatile.

When you feel the need and have the time to let your imagination frolic through the fertile fields of Photoshop fun, filters are first, but the Bevel and Emboss layer effect follows fruitfully. Take the time to play with the various settings in the Bevel and Emboss pane of the Layer Style dialog box to see what they do. Add a new layer, create a simple shape (perhaps with one of the shape tools), select Bevel and Emboss from the pop-up menu at the bottom of the Layers panel, and experiment — that's a far more efficient way to get to know this effect than reading technical explanations of each of the options. (One caveat: You won't see any change in your layer with the Stroke Emboss style unless you're also using the Stroke layer effect.) Don't forget to play with the various Gloss Contour presets! Remember, too, that you can add a second contour effect and/or a texture using the two check boxes below Bevel and Emboss in the left column of the Layer Styles dialog box. (As with other effects, click directly on the name Contour or Texture to access the effect's options.)

As you read this book, keep an eye out for the Bevel and Emboss layer effect. When you come across a bevel or emboss effect, such as those shown in Figure 12-9, you might want to take a moment to remember your experimentation and think about what settings I might have used.

Figure 12-9: Many illustrations in this book use the Bevel and Emboss layer effect.

Stroke

As you read this chapter, you'll see the Stroke layer effect often. Each of the insets from the Layer Style dialog box in this section's figures has a one-pixel black Stroke layer effect applied. Adding that tiny stroke helps set off the dialog box from the background.

Not only is Stroke a handy and practical production tool, but it's a wonderful creative effect, too, especially when you use it in conjunction with other layer effects. For example, a stroke of a contrasting color is a great way to redefine the edge of your object when working with an outer glow and an inner shadow. (In the Stroke effect's options, remember that you click the color swatch to open the Color Picker.) A simple stroke can convert even the plainest text into an eye-catching statement. And don't forget that without the Stroke effect, the Bevel and Emboss effect's Stroke Emboss option does nothing for your artwork. Figure 12-10 has a few examples of layer styles that include a Stroke effect.

Figure 12-10: The Stroke effect can stand alone or be used with other layer effects.

Inner Shadow

You can do a couple of things with the Inner Shadow layer effect, as you can see in Figure 12-11. Compare the two sets of options. On the left, a soft, light-colored inner shadow using the Screen blending mode softens edges. On the right, a hard inner shadow, using a dark color and the Multiply blending mode, produces a totally different look. Despite what your eyes might be telling you, the layer effect is applied to the red shape on the *upper* layer.

Figure 12-11: Inner shadows can be soft or hard, light or dark.

The four key blending modes

Photoshop offers over two dozen different blending modes, many of which you see in the Layer Style dialog box. You really need only a few on a regular basis, although it's always fun to experiment with the others, just in case one of them gives you a cool effect.

The *Multiply* blending mode generally darkens. When working with dark shadows or glows, choose the Multiply blending mode so that the layer effect darkens (but doesn't hide completely) the pixels on the layers below. The *Screen* blending mode lightens. Use Screen with light glows and other such effects. The *Overlay* blending mode is a mix of Multiply and Screen. When working with patterns that contain both

dark and light colors, you might opt for Overlay as the blending mode.

Of course you should remember the *Normal* blending mode, too! If you want a glow or shadow to completely block whatever lies below, choose Normal at 100% opacity. You might also want to use Normal with a somewhat lower opacity for a uniform coverage over both dark and light pixels. And don't be afraid to experiment — run through the blending modes (and opacity settings) to see whether you can tweak that custom style just a little more. (For more information on blending modes, see Chapter 10.)

Inner Glow

The Inner Glow effect is much like a non-directional Inner Shadow effect. As you can see in Figure 12-12, an Inner Glow can be the base for a neon glow style. (Add an Outer Glow effect, perhaps a Stroke effect, and there you go!)

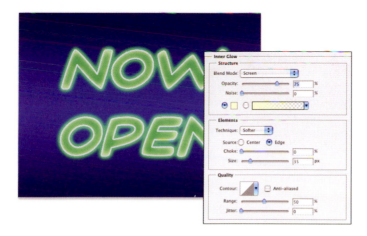

Figure 12-12: Inner Glow offers more control than Inner Shadow.

You can also develop some rather amazing styles by using the Inner Glow and the Inner Shadow in combination. Using similar Size settings and varying the colors and blending modes lets you overlay a pair of effects in combination. And when you play with Inner Glow and Inner Shadow in combination, don't overlook the Contour variations.

Satin

The Satin layer effect uses the shape of the object to produce a wave-like overlay. As you can see in Figure 12-13, it's more effective with type and complex shapes than it is with large plain shapes.

Figure 12-13: The Satin layer effect is very effective with complex shapes.

Color Overlay

The key to using the Color Overlay layer effect is the blending mode. (See the sidebar, "The four key blending modes" elsewhere in this chapter.) When you use Normal, in effect, you paint all the pixels on the layer with the selected color. To blend the color with the original artwork or other effects (such as pattern overlays), choose an appropriate blending mode — Multiply with dark colors, Screen with light colors — or simply experiment with blending modes. However, using the Color Overlay layer effect with the Normal blending mode in a custom layer style is a good way to ensure consistency in artwork, such as buttons and banners for a website. Keep in mind, however, Cover Overlay at 100% opacity and Normal completely hide any Gradient Overlay or Pattern Overlay effect.

Although you'll generally find Color Overlay most useful for simple shapes in artwork and on web pages, you can certainly use it for more exciting effects, such as the effects shown in Figure 12-14. The original is in the upper left, and each example shows the color and blending mode selected. Remember that when you use a layer effect, you can later return and alter or remove that change from your image.

Figure 12-14: Color Overlay can produce subtle or dramatic changes in your artwork.

Gradient Overlay

Unlike the Gradient Map adjustment (see Chapter 6), which applies a gradient to your image according to the tonality of the original, the Gradient Overlay effect simply slaps a gradient over the top of the layer content, using the blending mode and opacity that you select. You also control the shape of the gradient, the angle at which it's applied, and the gradient's scale (see Figure 12-15). And don't forget that a Gradient Overlay using the Normal blending mode and 100% opacity will hide any Pattern Overlay effect.

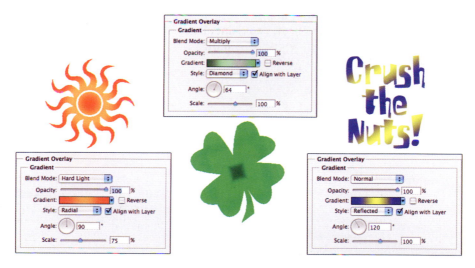

Figure 12-15: In keeping with its name, the Gradient Overlay effect overlays a gradient.

When working with gradients, you click the triangle to the right of the gradient sample to open the Gradient panel. You directly click the gradient sample itself to open the Gradient Editor. (See Chapter 14 for more information on editing and creating gradients.)

Pattern Overlay

Like the Color Overlay layer effect, Pattern Overlay relies on the blending mode and opacity settings to determine how the artwork (pattern) that it overlays interacts with your original artwork. As you see in Figure 12-16, you can scale the pattern, align it to the upper-left corner of your image (with the Snap to Origin button), and link the pattern to your layer so that the appearance of your artwork doesn't change as you drag the layer into position. Click the triangle to the right of the sample pattern to open the Pattern panel and then select a pattern.

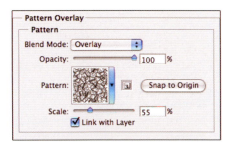

Figure 12-16: The Pattern Overlay layer effect adds texture to your layer's artwork.

Outer Glow

The Outer Glow layer effect is much like a non-directional shadow when applied using a dark color. However, it also has a variety of uses with a light color and the Screen blending mode. As you can see in Figure 12-17, it has practical and whimsical uses. (Please remember that in real life, stars do *not* appear between the horns of a crescent moon!)

In the Structure area at the top of the Outer Glow options, you can select the blending mode and opacity, add noise if desired, and select between a color (click the swatch to open the Color Picker) or a gradient (click the sample to open the Gradient Editor). You define the size and fade of the glow in the Elements area. The Technique pop-up menu offers both Softer and Precise — try them both. And don't overlook the options at the bottom, in the Quality area. Although you use Jitter only with gradients to add some randomness, the Range slider is an excellent way to control the distance at which your glow is offset. When you get a chance, play with different contours for an Outer Glow effect.

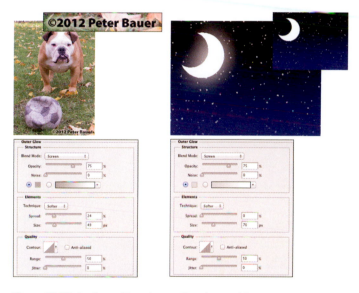

Figure 12-17: An Outer Glow layer effect is a multipurpose layer effect.

Drop Shadow

A drop shadow is a great way to separate the content of one layer from the rest of the image, as you can see by comparing the two versions of the artwork in Figure 12-18. In effect, the content of the target layer is copied, converted to black, and placed behind your layer. The blending mode and opacity determine how the shadow interacts with the layers below. You decide how much to offset and blur the duplicate with the sliders. (Remember that this is a layer style, so no extra layer is actually added to your image.) You'll generally want to leave the Contour option of your drop shadows set to the linear default. As you saw in Figure 12-6, drop shadows are great with type layers!

Figure 12-18: Drop shadows can visually separate the upper layer from the lower layer.

Opacity, fill, and advanced blending

In the Blending Options area of the Layer Style dialog box and the upper-right corner of the Layers panel, you see a pair of adjustments named Opacity and Fill Opacity, as shown in Figure 12-19. Both have an impact on the visibility of the content of your layer.

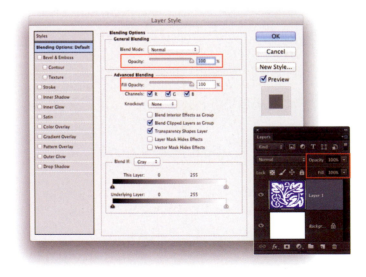

Figure 12-19: The Opacity and Fill Opacity sliders control visibility of a layer.

When you reduce the Opacity setting for the layer, you make the layer content and any layer style partially or completely transparent. Reducing the Fill slider changes the opacity of the pixels on the layer but leaves any layer effects fully visible. When might you want to use the Fill slider? The first thing that comes to mind is when creating the ever-popular Glass Type technique, which produces see-through text that's perfect for your copyright notice on any image:

1. **Add some text to an image with the Type tool.**

   This is a wonderful trick for adding your copyright information to sample images because everyone can see the image, but no one can use it without your permission. Start by adding your copyright information or perhaps the word *Sample.*

2. **Apply a layer style to the type layer.**

   A bevel, a thin black stroke, and perhaps an inner shadow or white outer glow make an excellent combination. (Select the individual effects as described earlier in this chapter.)

3. **Reduce the Fill slider to 0%.**

   Adjust Fill at the top of the Layers panel or in the Layer Style dialog box's Blending Options pane. You can click and type in the Fill field, click the arrow to the right of the field and drag the slider, or simply click the word *Fill* and drag to the left. The type layer disappears, but the layer effect remains.

   You can see all three steps in Figure 12-20.

Figure 12-20: Using the Glass Type effect is a great way to add copyright info to sample images.

The Blending Options pane of the Layer Style dialog box offers you a number of other choices in the Advanced Blending area, as shown in Figure 12-21.

Other than the Fill Opacity slider, you'll probably never change the Advanced Blending options from their default settings, but you might be curious about what they do. Here's a short explanation of each:

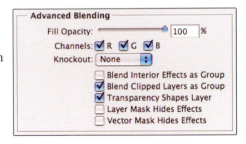

Figure 12-21: You find Advanced Blending options on the Blending Options pane of the Layer Style dialog box.

- **Channels:** Clear one or more of the color check boxes in the Advanced Blending area to hide the layer's content in that color channel. Clear the R check box, for example, and you hide the target layer in the Red channel.

- **Knockout:** You can use the content on the target layer to create transparency on lower layers. The top layer becomes transparent, as do the layers below every place that the upper layer had visible pixels. (I think of it as a "cookie cutter" effect.) If you want to restrict the effect, use the Shallow option, and the knockout extends only to the lowest layer in your layer group. The Deep option knocks out to the *Background* layer (or to transparency if your image doesn't have a background layer).

- **Blend Interior Effects as Group:** You can blend the Inner Glow, Satin, and your overlay effects before the layer as a whole is blended with lower layers. Use this option if it seems your layer effect's blending mode is being canceled out by the layer's own blending mode.

- **Blend Clipped Layers as Group:** If you have layers clipped together (see Chapter 10), you can elect to use the base layer's blending mode for all the layers or let each layer interact independently. You generally want to leave this check box selected.

- **Transparency Shapes Layer:** This is another option that you'll almost always want active. Transparency Shapes Layer restricts the layer style to the visible pixels on the target layer. If, for example, you're working with a small rounded rectangle and a Color Overlay layer effect, deselecting the check box fills the entire layer — not just the rounded rectangle — with color.

- **Layer Mask Hides Effects:** If the target layer's visibility is controlled with a layer mask (see Chapter 8), you can opt to have the layer style hidden by the mask, too. You can also use a layer mask to hide *just* the layer style with this option — say, when you need to make sure that your drop shadow doesn't fall where it shouldn't. Simply create a layer mask that hides those areas where you don't want the style visible and select the Layer Mask Hides Effects check box.

✔ **Vector Mask Hides Effects:** This option uses a layer's vector mask in exactly the same way that the Layer Mask Hides Effects option uses a layer mask. (Remember that a *vector mask* is a path that determines which areas of a layer are visible — see Chapter 11 for information on creating paths.)

If you have an image with a plain white (or plain black) background, you can make that background disappear with the Blend If sliders (see Figure 12-22). In the Layers panel, double-click the layer name *Background* and rename the layer. At the bottom of the Layers panel, click the second button from the right to add a new layer. Move the new layer below the original layer. With the original layer active, open the Blending Options pane of the Layer Style dialog box and drag the upper-right Blend If slider control to the left until the background disappears. As the white background disappears, the checker-board *transparency grid* becomes visible. Press ⌘+E (Mac)/Ctrl+E (Windows) to merge the layers and retain the now-transparent background.

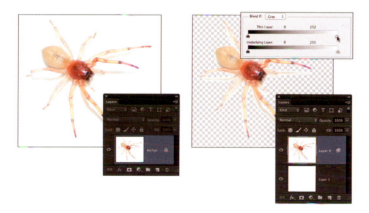

Figure 12-22: Make a white background disappear with the Blend If sliders.

Saving Your Layer Styles

Creating custom styles takes some time and effort. Saving the styles means that you don't have to spend time re-creating the style. Save your styles not only in the Styles panel but also on your hard drive.

Adding styles to the Style panel

After you have your layer style looking just right, you can add it to the Styles panel. From the Styles panel, you can apply your custom style to any layer (except, of course, layers named *Background*) in any image with a single click. You simply make the target layer active in the Layers panel by clicking it; click your custom style in the Styles panel.

To add your style to the Styles panel, you must first create it. Select a layer in the Layers panel, open the Layer Style dialog box, and select the layer effects and options. Click the New Style button to save the style or, after clicking OK in the Layer Style dialog box, click the middle button at the bottom of the Styles panel. Then, in the New Style dialog box that appears, assign your custom style a name and click OK. If desired, you can also elect to save the target layer's blending mode as part of the layer style.

Preserving your layer styles

Adding your custom styles to the Styles panel makes them available day in and day out as you work with Photoshop. However, should you ever need to replace the Preferences file (see Chapter 3) or reinstall the program, all your custom styles are wiped from the Styles panel. To make sure that you don't accidentally lose your custom styles, create and save a set of styles, which you can then reload into the panel whenever necessary.

The Styles panel menu offers the Save Styles command (refer to Figure 12-4), which lets you save all the styles currently in the panel as a set. However, for more control — to actually select which styles you want in your set — use Photoshop's Preset Manager (see Figure 12-23). You can open the Preset Manager from either the Styles panel menu or through the Edit⇨Presets menu. (Make sure that you retain the .asl extension in the filename so that Photoshop recognizes the file as a set of styles!)

As you can see in Figure 12-23, you use Preset Manager to save many kinds of custom bits and pieces. And use it you should! Shift+click to select a series of items or ⌘+click/ Ctrl+click to select individual items; then click the Save Set button. Give the set a name (again, with the .asl file extension), pick a location, and click OK.

Figure 12-23: Use the Preset Manager to make sure your custom styles are safe.

Saving sets of styles, brushes, custom shapes, and the like in the Photoshop Presets folder adds those sets to the various panels' menus. That makes it quite easy to load the set into the panel: Just choose the set from the panel menu. However, you should also save a copy of the set someplace safe, outside the Photoshop folder, so it doesn't accidentally get deleted when you upgrade or (*horror!*) reinstall.

13

Giving Your Images a Text Message

Un croquis vaut mieux qu'un long discours. Or, as folks often paraphrase Napoleon, "A picture is worth a thousand words." But sometimes in your Photoshop artwork, nothing says Bob's Hardware quite like the very words *Bob's Hardware.* A picture of a hammer and a picture of a nail — perhaps toss in some nuts and bolts — all are great symbols for your client's logo. However, you also need to give Bob's customers a name and an address so they can actually spend some money, which goes a long way toward helping Bob pay you.

For a program that's designed to work with photographic images, Photoshop has incredibly powerful text capabilities. Although it's not a page-layout program such as Adobe InDesign or a word-processing program such as Microsoft Word, Photoshop can certainly enable you to add lines, paragraphs, or even columns of text to your images.

Photoshop offers you three categories of text:

✔ **Point type** is one or more lines of text, comparable with the headlines in a newspaper or the text that you add to, say, a Bob's Hardware advertisement. Click with a type tool to add point type.

✔ **Paragraph type** consists of multiple lines of text. Like in a word-processing program, a new line is started whenever your typing reaches the margin. Drag a type tool to create paragraph type.

✔ **Warp type and type on a path** are typically single lines of type that are bent, curved, or otherwise distorted as a special effect. Use the Option bar's Warp Text feature (or Edit⇨Transform⇨Warp), or click with a type tool on a path.

In this chapter, I discuss the tools and panels that you use to add text to an image, how to add paragraphs and columns of text (as you might use in a brochure or booklet), and even how to make your type bend and twist along paths.

Making a Word Worth a Thousand Pixels

To control your basic work with text, Photoshop offers you four type tools, the Options bar, and several options in the Preferences dialog box, both in the Type section, visible in Figure 13-1, and in the Units & Rulers section.

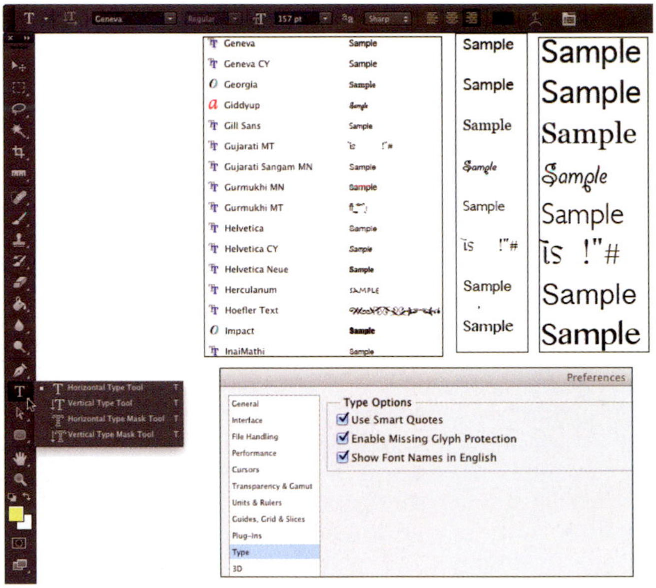

Figure 13-1: Photoshop gives you lots of tools for working with text.

As you can see in Figure 13-1, the Font menus in the Options bar can show a sample of the typeface (using the word Sample) when you click on it. You can activate the preview and choose from five different sizes for the font preview in the Type⇨Font Preview Size menu (shown are Small, Large, and Huge).

Yes, Type has been promoted to a menu, up from a submenu of the Layers menu. You'll also find four panels for more advanced work with text. In addition to the Character and Paragraph panels, Photoshop now offers Character Styles and Paragraph Styles, shown in Figure 13-2. By default, the panels are hidden because you can make the major type-related decisions (such as font style and alignment) right in the Options bar. You might need to show the panels if

Figure 13-2: Use the Character Styles and Paragraph Styles panels to ensure consistency and to make changes quickly.

you're doing some fine-tuning of the text appearance. When you need the panels, you can show them through Photoshop's Window menu.

Type can be informative or decorative or both. You can use the type tools to add paragraphs of text or a single character as an element of your artwork. (In Chapter 11, you can even see how to make custom shapes from your various symbol fonts.) The text can be plain and unadorned or elaborately dressed up with *layer styles,* such as drop shadows, glows, bevel effects, and other effects that you apply to make the layer content fancier. (Layer styles are discussed in Chapter 12.) However you use it, text can be a powerful element of both communication and symbolism. Take a look at Figure 13-3, in which I use the Type tool to add the binary code to the left and even the musical notes below.

Figure 13-3: You can also use type as symbolic or decorative elements.

But before you add any text to your artwork, you need to have a good handle on the various type tools, panels, menus, and options available to you. I start with an introduction to Photoshop's type tools.

A type tool for every season, or reason

Photoshop offers four type tools — or, perhaps more accurately, two pairs of type tools — that assist you with adding text to your images. The Horizontal Type tool and the Vertical Type tool (the first pair) create *type layers*, which show up as special layers in the Layers panel that enable you to later re-edit the text that you put there. The Horizontal Type Mask tool and the Vertical Type Mask tool (the second pair) make selections on the active layer, similar to using the Rectangular Marquee and Lasso tools (as I describe in Chapter 8).

When working with type layers, you can easily make changes to the font, font size, and even the text itself at any time. In addition, you can add layer styles and blend the text with other elements of your artwork using blending mode and reduced opacity.

You can ignore the type mask tools. Instead, use the regular type tools and ⌘+click or Ctrl+click on the layer thumbnail in the Layers panel to load a selection in the shape of the text, and then click the eyeball symbol to the left to hide the type layer. Later, if necessary, you can easily reload the selection — or make changes to the text and load a new selection. When working with a text-shaped selection, add a new empty layer on which you can create a text-shaped stroke or fill, or work with an existing layer's content. You might, for example, make a text-shaped selection to delete an area of another layer, as you can see in Figure 13-4.

Figure 13-4: ⌘+click or Ctrl+click a type layer's thumbnail to make a text-shaped selection for editing other artwork.

Whether working with type layers (or the type mask tools), you have the option of using either horizontal or vertical type. The difference between type that is set vertically and the more common horizontal type rotated 90 degrees is illustrated in Figure 13-5.

You can select type options before adding text to the image, or you can change your options afterward. When you make the type layer active in the Layers panel — but haven't yet selected any text in your image — any changes that you make are applied to all the text on the layer. You can also click and drag to select some of the text on the layer and make changes to only those characters or words.

Figure 13-5: Vertical type stacks the individual characters. You can rotate horizontal type for a different look.

When you're done adding or editing text, you can end the editing session in any of a number of ways:

- ✔ Click the check mark button (or the Cancel button) on the Options bar.
- ✔ Switch to a different tool in the Toolbox.
- ✔ Press ⌘+Return or Ctrl+Enter.
- ✔ ⌘+Shift+click or Ctrl+Shift+click to finish that type layer and start a new type layer.

What are all those options?

Here you are, the proud owner of the world's state-of-the-art image editor, and now you're adding text, setting type, and pecking away on the keyboard. You're faced with a lot of variables. Which options are you going to need all the time? Which ones are you going to need now and then? Which ones can you ignore altogether? Read on as I introduce you to the various text and type variables, and toss in a few general guidelines on which options are most (and least) frequently required.

Take a look at Figure 13-6, in which you can see (in all their glory) the most commonly used text attributes, all of which are available to you from the Options bar whenever a type tool is active.

Tool Presets

Font Family
(Click to open
the font menu.)

Font Size
(Click to select
or click-drag
to scroll.)

Align Right

Align Left

Warp Text

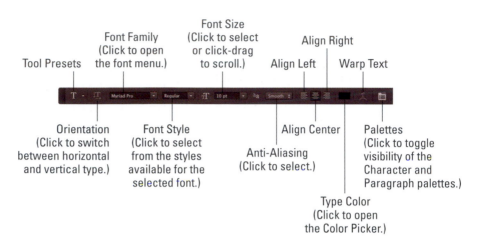

Orientation
(Click to switch
between horizontal
and vertical type.)

Font Style
(Click to select
from the styles
available for the
selected font.)

Anti-Aliasing
(Click to select.)

Align Center

Type Color
(Click to open
the Color Picker.)

Palettes
(Click to toggle
visibility of the
Character and
Paragraph palettes.)

Figure 13-6: Use the Options bar to quickly and easily change the primary attributes of your text.

You can change the following text attributes via the Options bar, which is usually available at the top of your screen:

- ✔ **Tool Presets:** The Tool Presets panel enables you to select a predefined set of options that you've already saved. Set up each as a preset and then activate all the options with a single click. (See Chapter 3 for more detailed information on tool presets.)

- ✔ **Orientation:** The Orientation button toggles existing type layers between horizontal and vertical. Regardless of what type is selected, the entire type layer is flipped when you click this button.

- ✔ **Font menu:** Click the triangle to the right of the Font Family field to open the Font menu, showing all your active fonts in alphabetical order. You can also click in the field itself and use the arrow keys to switch fonts. If you select some type with a type tool first (as shown in Figure 13-7), using an arrow key automatically applies the change to the selected characters. If no characters are selected, you change the entire type layer.

Figure 13-7: Select specific characters, such as the words SELECTING THEM, to change some, or make no selection to change all.

✔ **Font Style:** When a font has
multiple styles built in, you can
choose a variation of the font
from the Font Style menu. Styles
include Regular (or Roman), Bold,
Semibold, Italic, Condensed,
Light, and combinations thereof
(as you see in Figure 13-8). Some
fonts, however, have no built-in
styles.

Figure 13-8: Some fonts have many styles
available.

✔ **Font Size:** You can select a font
size in three ways: by typing a
number in the Font Size field, by
clicking the triangle to the right
of the field and selecting a font
size from the pop-up menu that appears, or by clicking the tT icon to
the left of the Font Size field and then dragging left or right to change
the value in the field. Font size is generally measured in *points* (1 point =
1/72 inch), but you can elect to use pixels or millimeters. Make the
units change in Photoshop's Preferences (choose Preferences⇨Units &
Rulers).

✔ **Anti-Aliasing:** *Anti-aliasing* softens the edges of each character so that
it appears smooth on-screen. As part of this process, anti-aliasing hides
the corners of the individual pixels with which the text is created. When
outputting to a laser printer or other PostScript device, anti-aliasing isn't
required. It is, however, critical when printing to an inkjet or when producing web graphics. Smooth is a good choice unless your text begins
to look blurry, in which case you should switch to Crisp. Use the Strong
option with very large type when the individual character width must be
preserved.

✔ **Alignment:** The three alignment choices on the Options bar determine how lines of type are positioned relative to each other. The buttons do a rather eloquent job of expressing themselves, wouldn't you
say? *Note:* Don't confuse the term *alignment* with *justification,* which
straightens both the left and right margins (and is selected in the
Paragraph panel).

✔ **Type Color:** Click the color swatch on the Options bar to open the Color
Picker and select a type color. You can select a color before adding text,
or you can change the color of the text later. If you start by selecting a
type layer from the Layers panel, you'll change all the characters on that
layer when you select a new color in the Color Picker. Alternatively, use
a type tool to select one or more characters for a color change, as you
can see in Figure 13-9.

Figure 13-9: Select any individual character and change its font, color, size, or any other attribute.

> ✔ **Warp Text:** Warp Text, which I discuss later in this chapter, bends the line of type according to any number of preset shapes, each of which can be customized with sliders. (The text in Figure 13-9 uses the Arc Lower warp style.) Keep in mind, however, that the Warp Text feature isn't available when the Faux Bold style is applied through the Character panel. (I talk about faux styles later in this chapter.)

Each character in a type layer can have its own attributes. Click and drag over one or more characters with a type tool and then use the Options bar or Character panel to change the text attributes. Color, font, style — just about any attribute can be assigned, as you saw in Figure 13-9.

Like many word-processing programs, you can select an entire word in Photoshop by double-clicking the word (with a type tool). Triple-click to select the entire line. Quadruple-click to select the entire paragraph. Click five times very fast to select all the text.

Taking control of your text with panels

For incredible control over the appearance of your text, use the Character and Paragraph panels. In addition to all the text attributes available on the Options bar, the panels provide a wide range of choices. With them, you can customize the general appearance of the text or apply sophisticated typographic styling. The Character and Paragraph panels can be shown and hidden by using the Panels button on the right end of any type tool's Options bar or through the Window menu.

You can use the Character panel to edit a single selected character, a series of selected characters, or the entire content of a type layer. Figure 13-10 shows what you face when "building character" using this panel.

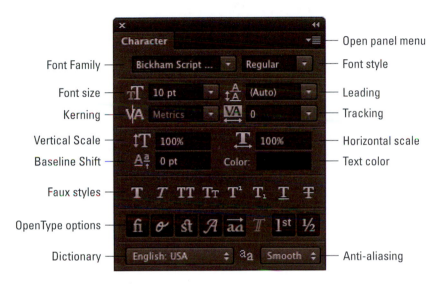

Font Family — Bickham Script ... — Open panel menu
Font style — Regular
Font size — 10 pt — Leading — (Auto)
Kerning — Metrics — Tracking — 0
Vertical Scale — 100% — Horizontal scale — 100%
Baseline Shift — 0 pt — Text color — Color:
Faux styles —
OpenType options —
Dictionary — English: USA — Anti-aliasing — Smooth

Figure 13-10: More choices!

As you can see by comparing Figure 13-10 with Figure 13-7, when an OpenType font is selected in the upper-left field, the Character panel now offers OpenType options as buttons. Which buttons are not grayed out and unavailable depends on which features are built into the OpenType font.

Unless you're a typographer, a number of the fields in the Character panel might require explanation:

✔ **Leading:** Leading (pronounced *LED-ding* rather than *LEED-ing* and which refers to the lead strips of metal that typesetters used to place between lines of type) is the vertical space between lines of text. Generally, you'll leave Leading set to Auto. However, you can select one or more lines of text (select the whole line) and change the spacing. Adding more space gives the text an airy, light appearance. Reducing the leading tightens up the text, which enables you to fit more lines in the same area.

✔ **Kerning:** The space between two characters is determined by the *kerning* built into a font. You can, however, override that spacing. Click with a type tool between two letters and then change the setting in the Kerning field to change the distance between the letters. You might, for example, want to reduce the kerning between a capital *P* and a lowercase *o* to tuck the second character protectively under the overhang of the taller letter. This can produce a cleaner and better-connected relationship between the two characters.

✔ **Scaling:** Vertical and horizontal scaling modifies the height and width of the selected character(s). You'll find this useful primarily for customizing short bits of type rather than long chunks of text.

✔ **Baseline Shift:** Produce subscript and superscript characters, such as those used in H_2O and $E = mc^2$, with the Baseline Shift field. It's generally easier to use the Superscript and Subscript styles (see the next bullet on Faux Styles).

✔ **Faux Styles:** Use faux styles to apply the appearance of a character style, even when they're not built into the font. From the left, as the buttons show, the available faux styles are Bold, Italic, All Caps, Small Caps, Superscript, Subscript, Underline, and Strikethrough. Select the character or characters to which you want to apply the style, and then click the appropriate button or buttons. Generally speaking, if a font offers a specific style in the Font Style menu, you'll use the font's built-in style rather than the faux style. Remember that you can't use Faux Bold when you want to warp text.

✔ **OpenType Options:** OpenType fonts, which can include many more glyphs (characters) than can TrueType or Type 1 fonts, may include a number of special features, including (from left) Standard Ligatures, Contextual Alternates, Discretionary Ligatures, Swashes, Stylistic Alternates, Titling Alternates, Ordinals, and Fractions. If you type certain character combinations, a single character, more visually pleasing, will be substituted. Not all OpenType fonts include all options.

✔ **Dictionary:** Photoshop has more than three dozen dictionaries built in. And, wonderfully or confusingly depending on your personal linguistic talents, you can assign dictionaries on a word-by-word (or even character-by-character) basis. You could, for example, insert a *bon mot* into the middle of your text in the language of your choice, assign the appropriate language dictionary, and not have that phrase trigger an alert when you run a spell check (Edit⇨Check Spelling).

If you click in your image window and start typing but no characters appear, check the Layers panel to make sure no layer is hiding your type layer and verify in the Options bar that your text color isn't the same as the background over which you're typing. If neither of those factors is the problem, it's likely an invalid setting in the Character panel (perhaps Baseline Shift). Press the Escape key, and then right-click on the Type tool icon at the left end of the Options bar and select Reset Tool.

TIP

You'll probably find yourself using certain sets of options pretty regularly in Photoshop. Luckily for you, you don't need to make changes on the Options bar and Character panel every time you want to, for example, add headlines or titles in Minion Bold, 24 pt, no anti-aliasing,

Figure 13-11: Tool presets can save you lots of time.

tracking +180, faux bold, with standard ligatures. Set up the options once and then click the Create New Tool Preset button in the panel at the left end of the Options bar, as shown in Figure 13-11. The next time that you want those specific text attributes, select the preset from that list or the Tool Presets panel, and you're ready to type! (Also take a look at the "Working with Styles" section later in this chapter.)

The Paragraph panel is used, not surprisingly, with paragraph type. The alignment options that you see in the upper left of the Paragraph panel in Figure 13-12 can be applied to both point type and type on a path, but you can usually access your alignment options much more easily from the Options bar.

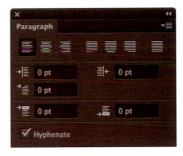

REMEMBER

I use the term *type container* when I discuss the Paragraph panel and paragraph type. Think of it as a rectangular column of text, with the words flowing from line to line, just as they do when you compose e-mail or use a word processor. You drag a type tool to create

Figure 13-12: Most of this panel is only for paragraph type.

the rectangle, and then you type inside that rectangle. In contrast, when you simply click a type tool and start typing, you need to press Return (Mac) or Enter (Windows) at the end of each line.

You can find specific information about some of these options later in the chapter (when I discuss paragraph type), but here's a quick look at the choices in the Paragraph panel:

✔ **Alignment:** As the text flows from line to line in your type container, the *alignment* option determines how the lines will stack. You can align the text for a straight left edge, a straight right edge, or you can have the lines stack centered upon each other.

✔ **Justification:** Unlike *alignment,* which balances one margin of a paragraph, *justification* equalizes both the left and right margins of a paragraph. As you can see by the icons, the difference among the four options is the last line in the paragraph. That last line can be aligned left, centered, aligned right, or stretched to fit from left to right (called *full justification*).

- ✔ **Indent Margins:** Paragraphs of text can be indented from the left margin or the right. Even if you have only a single word selected, the entire paragraph is indented. Harkening back to that last term paper you wrote (whenever that might have been), think in terms of a block quote. You can also use negative numbers in the Indent Margin fields, which extends the paragraph beyond the margin.

- ✔ **Indent First Line:** You can indent the first line of your paragraphs (or extend the first line to the left past the margin with a negative value) without having to press the Tab key. The option can be set before you start adding text and is applied to each paragraph.

- ✔ **Space Before/After:** When your type container includes multiple paragraphs (created by pressing the Return/Enter key), you can specify the distance that's automatically added between them. Rather than pressing the Return/Enter key an extra time between paragraphs, set the spacing in the Paragraph panel.

- ✔ **Hyphenation:** If you're using justification rather than alignment, I recommend keeping the Hyphenate check box marked. When words at the ends of lines of justified type aren't hyphenated, the spacing within the lines can get rather messy. If you don't like the look of hyphens along the right margin, clear the Hyphenate check box or change the hyphenation settings, as described later in this chapter.

Keep in mind that after you drag a type tool to create a type container, you can have as many paragraphs as fit. When you reach the end of a paragraph, press Return/Enter. A new paragraph is created within the type container. Consider the type container to be a column of text, such as you'd see in a newspaper, magazine, or newsletter.

The panel menus — even more options

Like most of Photoshop's panels, clicking the menu button in the upper-right corner of the Character or Paragraph panel opens the Panel menu, which holds a cornucopia of options you probably never need to see. (Consider this: If it were a *really* important option, it would be easier to get to, wouldn't it?)

As you can see in Figure 13-13, not all menu options are available for all fonts. Some of the options are merely command forms of the panel menus (such as the faux styles). A number of the options apply only to *OpenType fonts,* which include a much larger selection of *glyphs* (characters) than do other fonts.

Here are a couple of panel menu options with which you should be familiar:

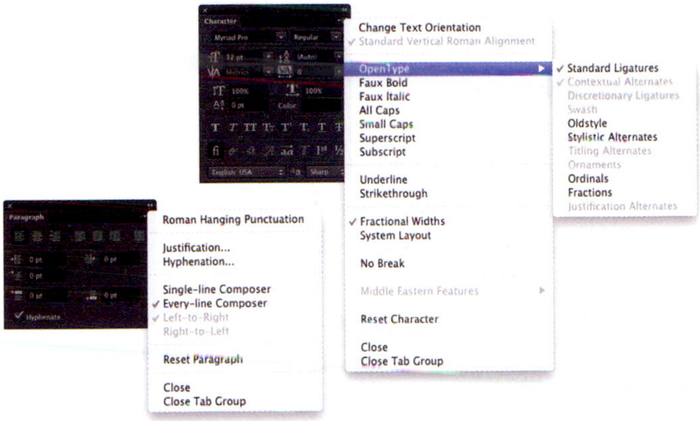

Figure 13-13: Not all options are used with all fonts.

- ✔ **Fractional Widths:** When selected, Photoshop uses this option to adjust the spacing between letters on an individual basis. Will you or I spot the difference? Not with large type, but if you're creating small text (especially for the web), clear this option. How small is small? Generally 10 points or smaller.

- ✔ **System Layout:** Unless you need to match the appearance of text in TextEdit for Mac or Windows Notepad, leave this option deselected. When might you need it? When designing interface items for a program or game.

- ✔ **No Break:** When working with paragraph type, you can select one or more words and choose No Break to prevent them from being hyphenated. You might want to do this with words that are difficult to recognize when split between two lines.

- ✔ **Roman Hanging Punctuation:** Found on the Paragraph panel menu, this option permits the smaller punctuation marks located at the left and right margins of justified text to hang out past the margins. When commas and the like are outside the margin, the margin itself has a cleaner look. Don't use this option if your layout can't handle text that extends past the edges of your column.

- ✔ **Adobe Composer:** This choice is actually quite simple: Single-Line Composer looks at one line of type to determine hyphenation. Every-Line Composer looks at the entire block of text, generally producing a more pleasing appearance.

✔ **Reset (panel name):** If you're seeing some strange behavior from your type tools, you might want to invoke the Reset Character and Reset Paragraph commands. They restore the settings in their respective panels to the defaults, eliminating any errant setting that might be causing the problem.

Remember that you can right-click the tool icon at the left end of the Options bar and select Reset Tool (or Reset All Tools) to immediately return to the tool's default settings. If the Type tool doesn't seem to be working correctly, reset and then reselect your options.

Working with Styles

New in Photoshop are the Character Style and Paragraph Style panels (shown in Figure 13-14). You define a character style based on the character format (font, size, style, and so on), the advanced format (scaling, baseline shift), and OpenType features (when working with an OpenType font, of course). Later, even in another document, you can load and apply the character style and instantly re-format the selected text in the style as defined.

A paragraph style includes all the features found in a character style, plus paragraph-specific options, such as indentation, composition, justification, and hyphenation.

Figure 13-14: Defining a character style (left) and a paragraph style.

After applying a character style or paragraph style, you can select some or all of the text and make changes to any character or paragraph attribute. Keep in mind this hierarchy: Any attribute you define after assigning a style trumps the attribute as defined in that style. If both a paragraph style and a character style are applied to the same text, attributes defined in the character style trump those in the paragraph style. Say, for example, that the paragraph style specifies Minion Pro as the font and the character style specifies Myriad Pro, the text will be Myriad Pro.

You can click the New Style button at the bottom of either panel, and then double-click the style to open a panel in which you manually select each style attribute (see Figure 13-14). Alternatively, create some text and with that text selected, click the New Style button. The new style will use the attributes of the selected text.

If you assign a style and then manually make changes to attributes, a small plus sign appears next to the style name in the panel. Later, if desired, click the left button at the bottom of the panel to restore the attributes with which the style was defined. The second button at the bottom of the panels redefines the style, incorporating those attributes you manually changed.

Styles are stored within a document saved in the PSD (Photoshop) format. If you have styles in, for example, Document-1.psd that you'd like to use in, for example, Document-2.psd, here's what you would do: Open Document-2, open the appropriate styles panel, select the styles panel menu command Load Styles, navigate to and select Document-1, and then click the Open button.

You may never use the Character Styles and Paragraph Styles panels, especially if you already have numerous Type tool presets, but they are a very powerful way to speed formatting of text — and to ensure consistency from word to word, paragraph to paragraph, and project to project.

Putting a picture in your text

Enough of that heavy stuff for now — time to take a look at one of the coolest things that you can do with text. Here's an easy way to create a text-shaped picture, one that's fully editable.

1. **Using File⇨Open, Adobe Bridge, or by double-clicking an image file, open a photo in Photoshop.**

2. **If the Layers panel has a layer named *Background*, double-click the layer name and rename the layer. If the image has multiple layers, choose Layer⇨Merge Visible.**

   You want to work with a single regular (not background) layer for this project. Background layers don't support transparency, and no layers can be placed below a Background layer.

3. **Add your type with the Horizontal Type tool.**

4. **Click the type layer in the Layers panel and drag it below the image layer.**

5. **In the Layers panel, Option+click (Mac) or Alt+click (Windows) the line between the two layers.**

   The two layers are joined together, as shown in Figure 13-15. When you clip two layers, the lower layer serves as a *mask* for the upper layer. The upper layer is visible only where the lower layer has pixels and adopts the opacity of those lower-layer pixels.

Figure 13-15: "Clip" the upper layer to the lower layer.

6. **Finish the image with a layer style (applied to the lower layer) and any other artwork that the project requires.**

   You can click the lower layer in the Layers panel and then click a favorite layer style in the Styles panel. Or, of course, you can create a custom layer style by choosing Layer⇨Layer Style. In Figure 13-16, you see a bevel, a stroke, and a slight inner glow applied to the type layer.

Creating Paragraphs with Type Containers

Although the vast majority of the text that you add to Photoshop artwork is *point* type — that is, type that exists on just one or a couple of lines — you'll certainly find situations in which you need to use paragraph type in a type container. The primary advantage of using paragraph type is *word wrap*. While you type, the text automatically starts a new line every time it reaches the margin.

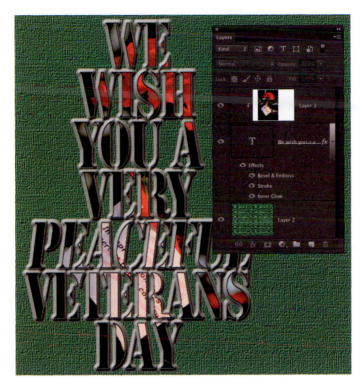

Figure 13-16: Add layer styles to the lower layer so that the effects are visible.

"Why is that a big deal?" you might ask. "I don't mind pressing the Return or Enter key at the end of each line." Ah, but consider the ever-present (when you type like me) typographical error! Or what if the very first sentence of your manual-Return paragraph is missing a word? To insert that word and maintain a visually pleasing right margin, you'd need to go back and redo every line of type. With paragraph type, the content of each line automatically adjusts as you insert that forgotten word.

The difference between point type to create a column of type and paragraph type is comparable with the difference between a typewriter and a word processor. (If you're old enough to remember Wite-Out and Liquid Paper, raise your hand, but not for very long — I don't want to tire you out.)

Adding a type container is simple. Click and drag with the Horizontal Type tool (or, in some rare cases, you might want to use the Vertical Type tool), and then start typing. The type automatically starts the next line as soon as you press enough keys to reach the far margin. You can keep typing until you fill the type container. Press Return or Enter whenever you want to start a new paragraph within your type container.

You can also copy/paste text from a word-processing or text-editing program. You can, for example, open a Microsoft Word document in Word, select the text that you want by clicking and dragging, and then choose Edit➪Copy to place the text into the computer's memory (on the *Clipboard*). Switch to your Photoshop document; select a font, font size, and other attributes (or select a character style or paragraph style after pasting); drag a type container; and then choose Edit➪Paste (or the assigned keyboard shortcut) to place your text inside the container. When the text you need already exists, you not only save time by using copy/paste, but you also eliminate the possibility of introducing typos.

But what if you have more text than fits in the type container? Unlike Illustrator and InDesign, you can't *link* two type containers, enabling the excess text to automatically move to the next container. Photoshop does, however, remind you that your text doesn't fit by showing you a symbol in the lower-right corner of the type container's *bounding box* — the dashed line surrounding the type container. As you can see in Figure 13-17, the lower-right anchor point of the bounding box has a plus sign in it.

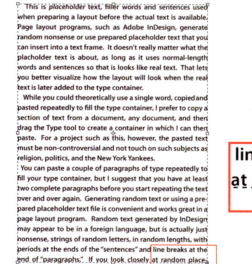

Figure 13-17: A plus sign in the lower-right anchor point warns you that text doesn't fit in the type container.

When you have more text than the type container can hold, you have a number of options:

- ✔ **Enlarge the type container.** Click one of the bounding box's anchor points and drag to increase the size of the type container. Making a type container a little bit wider often gives you an extra line or two of text at the bottom.

- ✔ **Shrink the font.** Select the text with a keyboard shortcut (⌘+A/Ctrl+A) and select a smaller font size on the Options bar.

- ✔ **Decrease the space between lines.** Select the text and decrease the *leading* — the amount of space between lines of type — in the Leading field found in the upper right of the Character panel. By default (the Auto setting in the Leading field), Photoshop uses an amount equal to 120 percent of the font size. You can often reduce the leading to 1 or 2 points larger than the font size before you start overlapping lowercase letters with descenders (*g, j, p, q,* and *y*) and uppercase letters on the line below.

- ✔ **Edit the text.** Rephrase the text, using fewer words to convey the same message. If you're not the author, however, this option might not be available.

Selecting alignment or justification

Photoshop gives you several options for controlling the appearance of your margins. In the "Taking control of your text with panels" section earlier in this chapter, I outline a number of options that you can find on the Paragraph panel menu. But let me go into more detail about a couple of options that you have when adding paragraph type.

Perhaps the most important decision (other than font and font size) that you make when preparing paragraph type is a choice of alignment or justification. When text is *aligned left,* the left margin is perfectly straight, and the right margin is *ragged,* with each line ending where it ends, without any relationship to the lines of type above and below. (The vast majority of the text you see in this book is left-aligned.) A column of text that's *aligned right* has a clean right margin and a ragged left margin. If you choose *center aligned,* the middle of each line of text is centered. Take a look at Figure 13-18 for a visual comparison.

Unlike alignment, justification gives you straight margins on both sides of the column of text. The four justification options at the top of the Paragraph panel differ only in how they treat the last line of a paragraph. As you can see from the Paragraph panel buttons, the last line can be independently aligned left, center, or right; or it can be fully justified, spreading the last line from margin to margin. You shouldn't use the fourth option unless that last line (of every paragraph) is rather full because it looks rather strange when just a couple of words are stretched edge to edge.

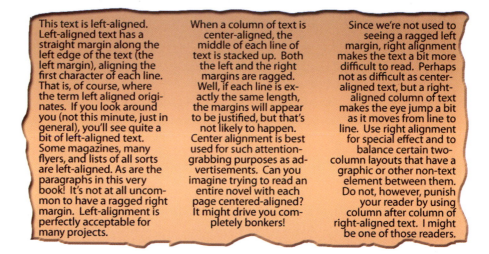

This text is left-aligned. Left-aligned text has a straight margin along the left edge of the text (the left margin), aligning the first character of each line. That is, of course, where the term left aligned originates. If you look around you (not this minute, just in general), you'll see quite a bit of left-aligned text. Some magazines, many flyers, and lists of all sorts are left-aligned. As are the paragraphs in this very book! It's not at all uncommon to have a ragged right margin. Left-alignment is perfectly acceptable for many projects.

When a column of text is center-aligned, the middle of each line of text is stacked up. Both the left and the right margins are ragged. Well, if each line is exactly the same length, the margins will appear to be justified, but that's not likely to happen. Center alignment is best used for such attention-grabbing purposes as advertisements. Can you imagine trying to read an entire novel with each page centered-aligned? It might drive you completely bonkers!

Since we're not used to seeing a ragged left margin, right alignment makes the text a bit more difficult to read. Perhaps not as difficult as center-aligned text, but a right-aligned column of text makes the eye jump a bit as it moves from line to line. Use right alignment for special effect and to balance certain two-column layouts that have a graphic or other non-text element between them. Do not, however, punish your reader by using column after column of right-aligned text. I might be one of those readers.

Figure 13-18: Compare the left and right margins of each column of text.

Ready, BREAK! Hyphenating your text

When a word is too long to fit on the current line of text, either it can be moved to the beginning of the next line (wrapped), or it can be broken into two parts: one finishing the upper line and the other starting the next line (hyphenated).

The hyphenation options are for the truly geeky, *my-typography-is-my-life* types. The defaults are excellent and can suffice for all but the most precise layouts (which you should be doing in InDesign or perhaps Illustrator, anyway).

If you want to fine-tune how hyphenation is applied (or have far too much time on your hands), select Hyphenate from the Paragraph panel menu to open the options shown in Figure 13-19. The Hyphenation check box (upper left) activates/deactivates hyphenation. The top

Figure 13-19: Default hyphenation values give you good results and a pleasing appearance.

three fields govern which words to hyphenate and what limits to place on the hyphenation. (Think of the second and third fields as *Hyphenate or cram into the line without hyphenating.*) The lower two fields control the appearance of the margin, limiting the number of consecutive lines that can be hyphenated and the maximum distance from that margin that a hyphen can be placed.

Shaping Up Your Language with Warp Text and Type on a Path

You can change the line along which your type flows either by using the Warp Text feature or by typing on a path. Type warping uses predefined shapes to which your type is formed (and can be used with both point and paragraph type), and typing on a path uses a custom path (and is used only with point type).

Warping type and placing type along a path are great ways to spice up your message as long as you don't overdo it and make the message illegible or distract from the overall appearance of your artwork. Warp Text is a quick and easy way to bend text, and placing type on a path is a more complex — and more controlled — technique.

Applying the predefined warps

With a type layer active in the Layers panel and a type tool selected, click the button to the right of the color swatch on the Options bar. That opens the Warp Text dialog box, as shown in Figure 13-20, in which you choose both the distortion you want to apply as well as the settings.

Photoshop offers 15 different Warp Text presets, each of which you can customize by dragging any of three sliders. Negative numbers can be used, too, reversing the warp. You can also set the Bend slider to 0 and adjust the lower two sliders to create the appearance of depth or perspective for a type layer, but keep in mind that the Horizontal and Vertical buttons aren't available for some of the styles. Warp Text is one of Photoshop's truly fun features. The best way to become familiar with it is to open the dialog box and test-drive each of the variations. And don't forget to try the Horizontal and Vertical buttons when they're available!

Figure 13-20: The illustration uses two separate type layers, each with its own Warp Text settings.

Customizing the course with paths

You can use the shape tools or the Pen tool to create a custom path along which you add your text. (You find full information about paths and shapes in Chapter 11.) To add type along a path, simply select the Horizontal Type or Vertical Type tool, click the path, and type. The flow of the type from the point on the path where you click is determined by the alignment option that you select from the Options bar or the Paragraph panel. If the text is left-aligned, characters are added to the right of the point where you click (called the *point of origin* for the type). Left alignment is great when adding type along an open path, such as the upper path in Figure 13-21. You might, however, want to choose center alignment when adding type along the top of an arc or circle, so you can click on the top of the arc and not worry about dragging the type later to center it.

If you want type to go in two different directions — say, pointed upward along both the top and the bottom of a circle — and you want the appearance uniform, with the same radius for each arc of text, create two separate paths and two separate type layers, as shown in Figure 13-22.

After you add your type to the path, you can press the ⌘/Ctrl key and reposition the type along the path by dragging. When you press and hold ⌘/Ctrl, the type tool's cursor changes to an I-beam cursor with a heavy black arrow on either side, indicating which way you can drag the type. You see the type's point of origin as a hollow diamond on the path (not to be confused with the hollow squares that represent the path's anchor points). Figure 13-23 gives you a zoomed-in look at the converted cursor and a comparison of the point of origin diamond and the anchor point square. Note, too, that not only can you drag type along a path, but you can also drag it *across* the path, flipping over the type.

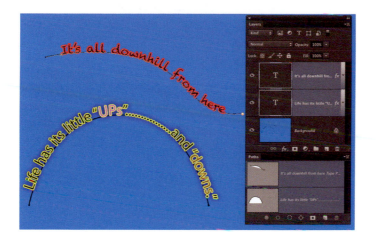

Figure 13-21: Text alignment determines where the text goes from the point where you click on the path.

Figure 13-22: Sometimes you need to create two separate type layers, using two separate paths, to achieve your artistic goals.

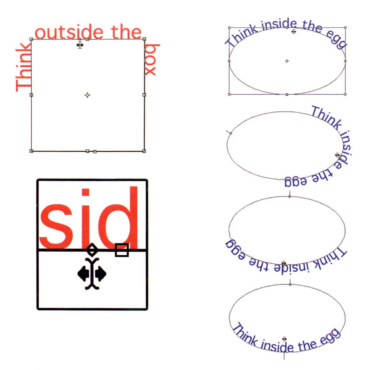

Figure 13-23: When you drag the cursor across the path a short distance, type flips over.

 After flipping type across a path, you might need to adjust the *tracking* (the space between characters), which is the second field from the top on the right in the Character panel. And don't be afraid to click in the type and press the spacebar a few times to adjust the placement of words along the path.

A word about fonts

You already have a nice selection of fonts installed on your computer. Some are installed with the operating system (Windows or Mac), a number of fonts may have been installed with the Adobe Creative Suite, and other programs could have tossed more morsels into the stew. However, you might find that the more you work with text, the more you crave additional fonts.

Although having lots of fonts can stretch your options, too many fonts can lead to slowdowns and other problems. If you do find yourself someday with a massive collection of fonts (I have over 12,000 fonts), none of which you could bear to part with (okay, I *could* part with some of them), use a font management utility. The Mac OS has the built-in Font Book, and Extensis (www.extensis.com/) offers Suitcase Fusion for Mac and Windows (about $100).

14

Painting in Photoshop

*P*ainting. The word evokes images of brushes and palettes and color being precisely applied to canvas. Or, perhaps, images of drop cloths, ladders, rollers, and buckets — color being slopped on a wall and spread around. It doesn't generally bring to mind digital image editing. But painting certainly has a place in your arsenal of Photoshop skills, even if you never create an image from scratch.

In addition to painting landscapes and portraits (which you certainly can do in Photoshop, if you have the talent and training), you can use Photoshop's painting tools for a variety of other tasks. For example, you can paint to create masks, adjust tonality or sharpness in specific areas, repair blemishes and other damage in an image — even to create graphic elements and special effects.

In this chapter, I concentrate on those editing-related painting skills and give you a quick look at painting with the Mixer Brush tool and the airbrush and *erodible* (like a pencil that eventually needs sharpening) brush tips. I introduce you to the basic concepts of painting in Photoshop and also walk you through the basic brush-related tools and the Brush panel, concentrating on those features that you most likely need (as well as a few of the other, more artistic features). To wrap up the chapter, I give you a look at other ways to add areas of color to your images, including the very useful Gradient tool.

Discovering Photoshop's Painting Tools

Nothing in Photoshop gives you more precise control of color in your image than using the Pencil tool with a 1-pixel brush. Remember that your image consists of a whole lot of little colored squares (pixels) and that the color of those individual squares is what produces the appearance of a tree or a sunset or even good ol' Uncle Bob. If you zoom in really close on an image, you can paint pixel by pixel — you could even create an entire image, one pixel at a time! You are, however, much more likely to use the Brush tool with a much larger brush tip to add strokes of color, rather than working one pixel at a time.

As you work in Photoshop, you'll also find many very important roles for the brush-using tools other than painting imagery. From touching up dust and scratches in a scan to removing distant power lines from a photo to perhaps adding wispy hairs to soften the outline of a head, you have lots of reasons to paint in Photoshop (many of which you can read about in Chapters 9 and 10). When you're capable and confident using the Brush tool, you might even find it the best way to make selections in your image. Selections with the Brush tool? That's right — painting in an alpha channel creates or refines a saved selection. (You can read about alpha channels in Chapter 8.) Photoshop even has a brush-using tool that you can use to make selections directly. The Quick Selection tool, like the Magic Wand, selects areas of similar color. However, instead of Shift+clicking in a variety of areas with the Magic Wand to add to your initial selection, you simply drag the Quick Selection tool. The brush diameter, selected in the Options bar, tells Photoshop the size of the area you want to search for similarly colored pixels.

In addition to the Quick Selection tool, you have 19 other tools that use brushes available in Photoshop. Here's a quick look at the various capabilities of those tools:

- **Painting tools:** The Brush, Pencil, and Mixer Brush tools (all discussed a bit later and in more depth) add the selected foreground color to the active layer as you click or drag the tool.

- **Eraser tools:** These tools (also discussed in more depth in pages to come) can make areas of a layer transparent or can paint over pixels with the current background color (if the layer doesn't support transparency).

- **Healing tools:** The Spot Healing Brush and Healing Brush are designed to repair texture, like smoothing wrinkles or adding the appearance of canvas. With the Healing Brush, you designate a *source point* — an area from which you want to copy texture — by Option/Alt+clicking and then dragging over the target area. The Spot Healing Brush, on the other hand, automatically samples the texture around an area and makes the target area match its surroundings. With the Content-Aware option, this tool can better match the healed area to the surrounding image. Quite cool!

- **Color Replacement tool:** Nested with the Brush and Pencil, the Color Replacement tool replaces the color over which you drag with the foreground color. Remember that, by default, the Color Replacement tool alters only the color, not luminosity, so painting with black over pink gives you gray rather than black. From the Options bar, you can set the tool to change luminosity rather than color to darken or lighten, or choose to match hue or saturation.

- **Stamp tools:** The Clone Stamp tool, unlike the Color Replacement tool or the Healing Brush, doesn't copy an attribute (such as color or texture), but actually copies pixels. It's like having copy/paste in a brush. Option/Alt+click a source area and then move the cursor and drag where you want to copy those pixels. It's powerful! The Pattern Stamp tool paints with a selected pattern, using the blending mode and opacity that you designate in the Options bar. The Pattern Stamp tool is sometimes a good way to add texture selectively.

When working with the Clone Stamp tool and the Clone Source panel, you can specify and move between up to five different source points. You also have the option of showing an overlay, which lets you see in advance what dragging the tool will do to your artwork.

- **History brushes:** The History Brush, discussed in Chapter 1, allows you to paint areas of the image to restore them to a previous state in the development process. Nested with the History Brush, the Art History Brush uses the history state selected in the History panel to add an Impressionist look where you paint.

- **Focus tools:** The Blur and Sharpen tools do just what their names say, but you'll likely find the default 50% Strength to be way too powerful for most jobs. Selective sharpening can help bring out details and direct attention in an image. Likewise, selective blurring can hide minor defects and help direct the viewer's eye toward areas of sharpness in the image. If you have avoided the Sharpen tool in the past, give it another chance using the Protect Detail option.

  Tucked in with the focus tools is the Smudge tool. Click and drag to smear pixels along the path. (I find the Smudge tool especially useful for dragging out wispy hairs from heads that appear perhaps too well defined and smooth.)

- **Toning tools:** The Dodge tool lightens, the Burn tool darkens — and if you use the defaults, they do it too much! When using these tools to adjust luminosity in your image, it's best to start with an Exposure setting of about 15% and paint carefully, perhaps repeatedly, rather than making a huge change with Exposure set to 50%.

The Sponge tool is nested with the Dodge and Burn tools. Use it to either increase or decrease saturation as you drag. (Decreasing saturation with the Sponge tool is a great way to create an image that's partially grayscale.)

The Healing Brush and the Clone Stamp tool have a button to the right of the Sample menu in the Options bar. When the Sample pop-up menu is set to All Layers or the new Current & Below option, that button gives you the option of ignoring adjustment layers. You might want to use this option if, for example, you're cloning or healing from multiple layers below an adjustment layer to a new layer that itself would be affected by the adjustment layer. This prevents the adjustment from being applied twice.

Painting with the Brush tool

You control where the Brush tool works by selecting a brush tip of a particular size, shape, and *hardness* (the fuzziness, or lack thereof, along the edges of a round brush tip).

Remember, too, that you can use the Brush and other painting tools to create subtle changes in existing colors. By selecting an appropriate blending mode and opacity, you can mix the painting color into the existing colors in your image. Make these basic decisions from the Options bar, shown for the Brush tool in Figure 14-1.

Figure 14-1: Make the primary decisions about painting tool behavior from the Options bar.

As you see in Figure 14-1, the Options bar gives you access to a miniature Brush panel, from which you can pick a brush tip, change its size, and adjust the hardness of the brush's edges. (Only round brush tips use the Hardness adjustment in the Options bar.) The five sample lines to the right show Hardness, from 0% to 100% in 25% increments, all using a 40-pixel brush. The Brush tool can use any brush tip that you have in the Brush panel — and, as you can read later in this chapter, you can customize the brush tip in a variety of ways.

You're actually ready to paint in Photoshop already! Select a foreground color, select the brush size that you want, decide how hard or fuzzy the edges should be, change the blending mode and opacity (if desired), and drag the tool in your image. (And, perhaps best of all, no turpentine needed for cleaning up — just switch tools in the Toolbox.)

As you work with the brush-using tools, always remember that the selected brush tip is applied as a series of individual impressions, called *instances*. Consider an instance to be a single impression of the brush tip, like tapping a pen once on a piece of paper — it leaves a single dot. Take a look at the outer borders in Figure 14-2. Changing the brush tip's Spacing value (in the main Brush panel, opened through Photoshop's Window menu) shows how instances appear. In the upper left, the spacing is set to the default 25%

Figure 14-2: Changing the Spacing makes the individual brush tip instances visible.

and a continuous line results. To the upper right, Spacing is set to 67%, and the individual brush tip instances are visible as overlapping circles. To the lower left, Spacing is set to 133% — this is a setting that you might use for a dotted or dashed line — and each brush tip instance is visible individually.

If you know you have the cursor set to show the brush tip, but you're seeing the tiny little crosshairs instead, check the Caps Lock key on your keyboard. Caps Lock toggles between precise and brush-size cursors for the brush-using tools. (During the discussion of Photoshop's Preferences in Chapter 3, I show a comparison of the three brush cursor options in Figure 3-11.)

When you change the Brush tool's Opacity setting on the Options bar, you change the appearance of the stroke as a whole. Changing the Flow setting (also on the Options bar), on the other hand, changes the amount of color applied with each instance of the brush tip. When the flow is reduced and the spacing is set to less than 100%, the overlapping area of each brush instance appears darker (or lighter when painting with, for example, white on black). One last item in the Options bar for the Brush tool deserves a quick look. To the right of the Flow field is the Airbrush button. When the Airbrush is on (the button turns dark), the Flow value takes on more meaning. As you paint with the Brush in Airbrush mode with a reduced Flow setting, pausing the cursor with the mouse button down allows color to build up (become more opaque) as if you were using a real airbrush. You can use the Airbrush both as a traditional airbrush artist and to simulate spray paint. You can see both in Figure 14-3.

If your computer has a processor and video card that support OpenGL drawing, you can rotate the image on screen for easier painting. Not rotate the canvas, but rotate the on-screen image! This can be great for fine-tuning a layer mask or doing other

Figure 14-3: Airbrushing and spray painting with the Airbrush option for the Brush tool.

delicate painting tasks. Using the Rotate View tool (nested with the Hand tool) permits you to arrange the artwork for your most comfortable painting stroke. While dragging the Rotate View tool, an on-screen compass's red arrow always orients you to the top of the screen. When you want the image oriented back to the top, simply double-click on the Rotate View tool icon in the Tool panel.

Adding color with the Pencil tool

The Pencil tool differs from the Brush tool in one major respect: Regardless of the Hardness setting in the Brush panel, the Pencil tool always uses a hardness value of 100%. With the Pencil tool active, the Options bar offers the miniature Brush panel, choice of blending mode and opacity, and the somewhat-misnamed Auto Erase option. When selected, Auto Erase lets you paint over areas of the current foreground color using the current background color. Click an area of the foreground color, and the Pencil applies the background color. Click any color other than the foreground color, and the Pencil applies the foreground color. But remember, you're not erasing, just painting with the background color (even on layers with transparency).

Removing color with the Eraser tool

The fourth of your primary painting tools is the Eraser. On a layer that supports transparency, the Eraser tool makes the pixels transparent. On a layer named *Background,* the Eraser paints with the background color. On the Options bar, the Eraser tool's Mode menu doesn't offer blending modes, but rather three behavior choices. When you select Brush (the default), the Options bar offers you the same Opacity, Flow, and Airbrush options as the Brush tool. You can also select Pencil, which offers an Opacity slider, but no Flow or Airbrush option (comparable to the actual Pencil tool). When Mode is set to Block, you have a square Eraser tool that erases at the size of the cursor. Regardless of which mode is selected, the Options bar offers one more important choice: To the right of the Airbrush button, you'll find the Erase to History check box. When selected, the Eraser tool paints over the pixels like the History Brush, restoring the pixels to their appearance at the selected state in the History panel.

A couple of variations on the Eraser tool are tucked away with it in the Toolbox, too. The Background Eraser tool can, in fact, be used to remove a background from your image. However, it's not limited to something in your image that appears to be a background. Remember that digital images don't really have backgrounds and foregrounds or subjects — they just have collections of tiny, colored squares. What does this mean for using the Background Eraser? You can click and drag on any color in the image to erase areas of that color. You can also elect to erase only the current background color and designate the foreground color as protected so that it won't be erased even if you drag over it.

The Magic Eraser, like the Magic Wand selection tool (see Chapter 8), isn't a brush-using tool, but this is a logical place to tell you about it. Click a color with the Magic Eraser tool, and that color is erased, either in a contiguous area or throughout the image, depending on whether you have selected the Contiguous option in the Options bar. And, like the Magic Wand, you can set the tool to work on the active layer or all layers in the Options bar, and you can also set a specific level of sensitivity (Tolerance). Here is the one difference between the two: The Magic Eraser is, in fact, a painting tool in that you can set an opacity percentage, which partially erases the selected pixels.

Working with Panels and Selecting Colors

To select and customize brush tips, Photoshop offers the Brush and the Brush Presets panels (as shown in Figure 14-4). Select a brush tip in the Brush Presets panel (or in the Brush panel or in the Options bar), and then customize it to do your bidding using the options in the Brush panel.

You must have a brush-using tool active to access the Brush panel. If the active tool doesn't use brushes, the entire panel is grayed out and unavailable. If that's the case, simply press B on the keyboard to activate the Brush tool.

An overview of options

The Brush panel, like the Layer Style dialog box, has a column on the left that lists options. Like the Layer Style dialog box, you mark the check box to activate the feature, but you have to click the *name* to open that pane in the panel. As you can see in Figure 14-4, the Brush panel menu offers very few commands, whereas the Brush Presets panel menu includes variations in how to display the panel content, some housekeeping commands for resetting/loading/saving brushes, and a list of brush sets in the bottom half of the menu.

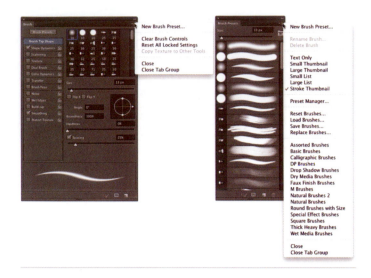

Figure 14-4: The Brush and Brush Presets panels, with their panel menus, provide lots of options.

Don't overlook those little lock icons to the right of the various pane names in the Brush panel. Click the lock to preserve the settings in that pane while you switch among brush tip presets. Any unlocked attributes revert to those with which the brush tip was created. Locking, for example, Shape Dynamics retains those settings even if you switch to a totally different brush tip.

Here, in order, are the Brush panel panes and the options in those panes to which you should pay attention:

- **Brush Presets:** This button opens the Brush Presets panel, where you pick the basic brush tip shape from the brushes loaded in the panel. You can also resize the brush tip, but that's it. (Note that you can also select a brush tip in the Brush Tip Shape panel of the Brush panel.)

- **Brush Tip Shape:** Without a check box to the left or a lock icon to the right, Brush Tip Shape is the pane in which you can select and customize a brush tip. (Refer to the Brush Tip Shape pane in Figure 14-4.) This is perhaps the most important part of the Brush panel. In this pane, you can select a brush tip, change its size, alter the angle at which it's applied, change the height-width relationship (Roundness) of the tip, and adjust the Spacing setting.

- **Shape Dynamics:** Dynamics in the Brush panel add variation as you drag a tool. Say you're working with a round brush tip and choose Size Jitter. As you drag the brush tip, the brush tip instances (the individual marks left by the brush as you drag) will vary in diameter. The Shape Dynamics pane offers Size Jitter, Angle Jitter, and Roundness Jitter. Each of the "jitters" can be set to fade after a certain number of brush tip instances or can be controlled with the stylus that you use with a Wacom tablet. Angle can also be set to Direction, which forces the brush tip to adjust the direction that you drag or the direction of the selection or path you stroke. Use Shape Dynamics to add some variation and randomness to your painting, as shown in Figure 14-5.

Figure 14-5: Use jitter to add variation to the application of your selected brush tip.

✔ **Scattering:** *Scattering* varies the number of brush tip instances as you drag as well as their placement along the path you drag. Like the shape dynamics, scattering can be set to fade or can be controlled with a Wacom tablet.

✔ **Texture:** Use the Texture pane to add a pattern to the brush tip, as shown in Figure 14-5. You can select from among the same patterns that you use to fill a selection. Texture is most evident when Spacing for the brush tip is set to at least 50%.

✔ **Dual Brush:** Using a blending mode you select, the Dual Brush option overlays a second brush tip. You could, for example, add an irregular scatter brush to a round brush tip to break up the outline as you paint.

✔ **Color Dynamics:** Using the Color Dynamics pane, you can vary the color of your stroke as you drag. This comes in most handy for painting images and scenes rather than, say, working on an alpha channel. Just as you might add jitter to the size, shape, and placement of a grass brush while creating a meadow, you might also want to add some differences in color as you drag. You could pick different shades of green for the foreground and background colors and then also add jitter to the hue, saturation, and brightness values as the foreground and background colors are mixed while you drag.

✔ **Transfer:** Think of this pane as Opacity and Flow Jitter. You can add variation to the opacity and flow settings from the Options bar to change the way paint "builds up" in your artwork.

✔ **Brush Pose:** When working with a Wacom tablet (see Chapter 19), this panel enables you to ensure precision by overriding certain stylus-controlled variations in a stroke. If, for example, you want to ensure that the brush tip size doesn't change, regardless of how hard you press on the tablet, open Brush Pose, set Pressure to 100%, and select the Override Pressure check box. You can also override the stylus's rotation and tilt as you paint, setting any value from -100 to +100 for both tilt axis values and 0 to 360 degrees for rotation.

✔ **Other Options:** At the bottom of the left column are five brush options that don't have separate panes in the Brush panel. They're take-it-or-leave-it options — either activated or not.

- *Noise:* Adding Noise to the brush stroke helps produce some texture and breaks up solid areas of color in your stroke.

- *Wet Edges:* Wet Edges simulates paint building up along the edges of your stroke.

- *Build-up:* The Build-up check box simply activates the Airbrush button on the Options bar.

- *Smoothing:* Smoothing helps reduce sharp angles as you drag your mouse or stylus. If the stroke you're painting should indeed have jagged turns and angles, disable Smoothing.

- *Protect Texture:* The Protect Texture option ensures that all the brushes with a defined texture use the *same* texture. Use this option when you want to simulate painting on canvas, for example.

When creating a dashed line or stroking a path with a non-round brush tip, go to the Shape Dynamics pane of the Brush panel and set the Angle Jitter's Control pop-up menu to Direction. That enables the brush tip to rotate as necessary to follow the twists and turns of the selection or path that it's stroking. (You'll generally want to leave Angle Jitter set to 0% so that the stroke follows the selection or path precisely.)

Creating and saving custom brush tips

You can use any artwork as a custom brush tip. With the artwork on a transparent or white background (you don't even need to make a selection), choose Edit➪Define Brush Preset. Type a name and click OK. Your new custom brush is added to the Brush panel. After you define a piece of artwork as a brush, you can add that image to any project with a single click or drag.

Remember that a brush tip is always grayscale, regardless of the color in the artwork from which it was defined and that it will be used to apply the foreground color. Also keep in mind that the maximum size for a brush tip is 5,000 pixels in either dimension.

Picking a color

If you want to apply a specific color to your image with a painting tool, you have to be able to select that color, right? Photoshop provides you with a number of ways to select a color:

- ✔ **Click a saved color swatch in the Swatches panel.**

- ✔ **Enter numeric values or drag sliders in the Color panel.**

- ✔ **Click a color swatch at the bottom of the Toolbox or in the Color panel to open the Color Picker.**

- ✔ **Select a sample size and specify which layers to sample in the Options bar.** When set to Point Size (the default), the eyedropper samples only the one pixel directly under the cursor. You can set the Eyedropper to set the foreground color to an average of a 3x3 sample to avoid having one stray pixel misrepresent the area of the image you want to sample. The sample size average can be as large as 101x101 pixels. (Remember, too, that you can right-click with the Eyedropper to change the sample size without having to visit the Options bar.)

- ✔ **Specify which layers to sample in the Options bar.** When working with layered documents in the past, you could set the Eyedropper to sample either the current layer or all visible layers. The tool's Options bar now offers those two options, as well as Current & Below (the active layer and the layer immediately below it in the Layers panel), and the option to sample the active layer and the next pixel layer below, ignoring any adjustment layers in between, and the option to sample all layers while ignoring adjustment layers.

The Eyedropper's Options bar offers the option Show Sampling Ring. When active and the Eyedropper is in use, the Sampling Ring is a pair of concentric circles (as shown to the right in Figure 14-6). The outer ring is neutral gray to isolate the inner ring from surrounding colors. The bottom half of the inner ring shows the current foreground color, whereas the top half shows the color over which you have dragged the cursor. If you find it distracting, disable it in the Options bar.

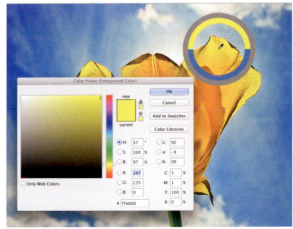

Figure 14-6: Use the Color Picker to define colors with precision. The Eyedropper's Sampling Ring is visible to the right.

In both the Toolbox and the Color panel, the foreground color is shown in the swatch to the upper left, and the background swatch is partially hidden behind it. Swap the foreground and background colors by pressing the X key on your keyboard. Reset them to the default black and white by pressing the D key.

In Chapter 6, I introduce the Color panel and the various ways you can define color with it. Now take a look at the Color panel's big brother, the Color Picker (see Figure 14-6). Note the reminder in the title bar of the Color Picker window that tells you whether you're changing the foreground or background color. (If you find that you're changing the background color when you want to change the foreground color, exit the Color Picker, open the Color panel, and click the foreground swatch.) The best way to get a feel for the incredible versatility of the Color Picker is to open it (click a color swatch at the bottom of the Toolbox or in the Color panel) and click each of the buttons to the left of the numeric fields. Each option changes how the Color Picker appears as well as how it defines color.

The default Color Picker configuration uses the radio button to the left of the H (Hue) field. It presents you with a vertical rainbow slider (the hue) and a square area that defines saturation (left-right) and brightness (up-down). Click or drag in the square area to the left and drag the slider up and down to pick a color. (Compare the two swatches to the left of the Cancel button to see the new color above the previously selected color.) If you click the button to the left of the S field, the slider shows saturation, and hue and brightness are defined in the square area to the left. Starting to see the pattern? Check out the configuration for Brightness (B) as well as the RGB and Lab options. And note that you can type numeric values to define a color as CMYK, but there are no buttons to the left to reconfigure the Color Picker. Likewise, you can type in the # (hexadecimal) field below the B field, but you can't use it to reconfigure the Color Picker. (Hexadecimal color definition is used with HyperText Markup Language [HTML] code in web pages.)

Between the two color swatches in the top center and the buttons to the right are a pair of little icons that aren't always visible. (Check them out in Figure 14-6 if they're not currently showing in your Color Picker.) The top warning triangle tells you that the current color can't be reproduced within your working CMYK color profile. Unless you're preparing artwork for commercial offset press, ignore it — it has nothing to do with your inkjet printer, for example. If, on the other hand, you *are* working on a press-destined project, click the swatch just below the warning triangle to jump to the nearest reproducible color.

The lower icon, a little cube symbol, lets you know that your current color isn't web-safe. *Web-safe colors* are the couple hundred colors that are exactly the same in the base color scheme for both Mac and Windows. If visitors to your website have their monitors — or PDAs — set to show only 256 colors, everyone sees the same thing with web-safe colors. Generally, you can safely ignore the warning because the variation isn't worth worrying about. (If you *do* want to work with web-safe colors, click the swatch below the warning cube icon and then select the Only Web Colors check box in the lower left.)

After you define a custom color with the numeric fields or by clicking in the sample colors to the left, you can easily save the color to the Swatches panel by clicking the Add to Swatches button. Should you need to reselect that specific color later, or even when working on another image, it's right there in the Swatches panel, exactly as originally defined.

Also note the Color Libraries button. Clicking that button swaps the Color Picker for the Color Libraries dialog box, in which you can select spot colors. *Spot colors,* which I explain in Chapter 6, are special premixed inks that can be specially requested when preparing a job for a commercial printing press. Adding a spot color ensures that the color will appear in the final product exactly as expected. However, because they generally require an extra pass through a press, adding spot colors increases the cost of your printing. (Remember that if you want the color to print as a spot color, you don't paint with it, but rather create a *spot channel* to identify where the spot color appears in your artwork.) Spot colors can be used to define colors for nonpress jobs, but the color is converted to your working color mode and printed with a mixture of your regular inks. Return to the Color Picker from Color Libraries by clicking the Picker button.

Integrating Your iPad into Your Painting Workflow

Four iPad apps put Photoshop at your fingertips — literally — and they're each under $3.00! Photoshop Express (free) is an iPad app designed to let you do basic editing of any photo on your iPad, save your changes, and share the image through Photoshop Express's online gallery or Facebook. Adobe Nav ($1.99) connects to Photoshop on your computer and serves as a supplementary screen for activating tools in Photoshop, changing screen mode, swapping colors, and more, just by tapping. Color Lava ($2.99) enables you to use your iPad to create color and color themes to use in Photoshop. Eazel ($2.99) is a gesture-enabled finger painting program, paintings you can then send directly to Photoshop.

 As you read about the Photoshop-related iPad apps, keep in mind that you can use a stylus, such as Wacom's Bamboo Stylus, rather than a fingertip while working on your iPad. Precision, great! No fingerprints, even greater!

Expressing yourself with PS Express

You have Photoshop, so why would you want to monkey around with an app for photo editing? Convenience, speed, showing off on airplanes — those are the first three things that come to mind.

Indeed, Photoshop Express certainly lacks the power of Photoshop, but if it's on your iPad and you need to do a quick edit to an image captured with or downloaded to your iPad, you're all set. You can crop, adjust brightness, sharpen, blur, apply a number of special effects and borders. When done, you can save the image on your iPad (and, of course, send it to yourself or another) and, right from PS Express, share in your personal gallery or post to Facebook.

Using Adobe Nav

Adobe Nav supplements your Photoshop workspace by providing you another screen on which to select tools and more. I like to kick back with my Wacom Cintiq (or, when traveling, a Wacom Intuos tablet) and perhaps even put my feet up while I work. (Take a look at Chapter 19 to learn more about Wacom tablets.) Indeed, those powerful pieces of hardware have programmable controls that reduce my need for poking around in panels and pressing keys on the keyboard. But being able to (without dropping my feet to the floor) tap my iPad to select a different tool is, well, cool! I can determine which tools are shown on the iPad to suit my workflow needs by tapping the Edit button (visible in the lower left corner of the screen to the left in Figure 14-7). To the right in Figure 14-7, you see the tools — click the X to remove a tool, drag a tool to an empty slot, or drag the tools to rearrange their order. (I like to put the tools I use most often at the bottom.) Click the Done button and your tools are set up the way you want them.

Figure 14-7: Activate Photoshop tools (to the left) or edit the available tools (to the right).

In the screen to the left in Figure 14-7, note the three items to the right of the tools. Click the two-headed arrow to swap the foreground and background colors (which update on the iPad as you select new colors in Photoshop), or click the overlapping black and white swatches to the lower-left of the foreground/background colors to revert to black and white. The Screen Mode button rotates through the three screen modes, just like pressing the F key on your keyboard. The Actual Pixels zooms the image in Photoshop to 100% zoom.

In the bottom-center of the screen to the left in Figure 14-7 are two buttons. The button on the left is active in Figure 14-7 and shows the tools and view commands. Click on the button to the right, the four stacked squares, and Adobe Nav switches from a tool navigator to an image navigator. To the left in Figure 14-8, you can see that there are three images currently open in Photoshop. The active image (front-most in Photoshop) shows a flashing blue circle to the left of the file name. Click the New button or tap the Plus symbol

in the image area (when
visible) to open another
image into Photoshop.
As you can see from the
list to the right in Figure
14-8, you can open a new
document, select an image
from any of the groups
of images on the iPad, or
take a photo with the iPad
to open in Photoshop.
(Note, to the left in Figure

Figure 14-8: Switch from one image open in Photoshop to another, or open images into Photoshop.

14-8, that images opened into Photoshop from the iPad become "Untitled"
images and will need to be saved from Photoshop to the local hard drive.)

Getting colorful with Color Lava

Select a color to the left area of the screen shown in Figure 14-9, mix paint in
the middle (the canvas area), click a swatch to the right, and then tap on the
mixed color you want in that swatch. Repeat. Click in the upper-left to "clean"
your finger. Click the X
in the upper-right corner
of the canvas to clear
the paint and prepare to
create more swatches
and themes. Clicking
the smaller set of colors
within the available colors
in the lower-left swaps
between primary colors
and grayscale shades.

Click the right-hand button
in the bottom-center to
select a theme, to select
one of the swatches as
Photoshop's foreground
color (tap the swatch),
to see technical data for
a color theme or send a

Figure 14-9: Mix colors and create color themes to use in Photoshop.

theme to Photoshop or to e-mail a theme (double-tap a swatch), or to rename
or delete a theme (press and hold on a swatch). When you send a theme to
Photoshop, the swatches are automatically added to the Swatches panel.

And here's where Color Lava gets *really* interesting! Take a look at the camera
button in the lower-right corner of the canvas area in the middle of Figure
14-9. Click that button to open (or take) a photo from which to create a
theme. The photo opens in the canvas and you can click to select a swatch

(to the right), and then click anywhere in the photo to set the swatch to that color. (Talk about a great way to create a library of skin tone swatches!) And with a photo open on the canvas, you can drag in the image to blend colors before defining swatches. You can also add any of the colors on the left to the photo and blend it into the existing colors in the image.

Easing your way into Eazel

Of the four Photoshop-related iPad apps, Eazel is, in the beginning, the least intuitive for most Photoshop users. I strongly urge you to watch the demo (at least once) before trying to finger paint with Eazel. To over-simplify, think of using five fingers as "right-clicking" to open a contextual menu. Tap on one of the variables (Color, Size, Opacity for your painting finger, or canvas rotation), and then drag to change the setting. Paint. And when you like what you see on

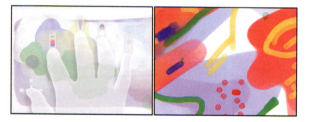

Figure 14-10: Five-finger tapping to open controls (left), and a sample of Eazel art (right).

the canvas, tap with five fingers, select Settings, and save your finger painting or send it to Photoshop. Alternatively (also available in Settings), select Play Demo again.

To the left in Figure 14-10, you see tapping with five fingers to make available (from the lower left) Canvas Rotation, Color, Size, Opacity, and Settings. To the right in Figure 14-10, you see a simple sample of some of the finger painting that changing variables can produce.

Connecting with Photoshop

When working with an iPad in conjunction with Photoshop, you need some secure way to communicate between the devices, right? (You wouldn't want some stranger with an iPad to suddenly send images or swatches to your laptop as you work while enjoying a latte, would you?) In Adobe Nav, Color Lava, and Eazel (the apps that interact directly with Photoshop), there's a Photoshop icon in the lower-right corner of the screen (in Eazel only when Settings is selected). Tap that icon to open a list of available versions of Photoshop running on an available network. Select the "discovered" version of Photoshop with which you want to connect, enter the correct password, click the Connect button, and your iPad is ready to communicate with Photoshop on your computer.

But wait! Before the iPad can communicate with the computer, Photoshop on that computer needs to be made available for that communication. In Photoshop, go to Edit⇨Remote Connections, select the option Enable Remote Connections, input a name for your computer and password of choice in the Service Name and Password fields, and then click OK. When you attempt to connect from the iPad, you'll need to enter that password.

Adobe also offers a number of other tablet apps for iPad (and a number for Android tablets, too). Some extend the capabilities of the programs of the Creative Suite, some are independent creative tools. Check out the Mobile Apps section of Adobe.com.

Fine Art Painting with Specialty Brush Tips and the Mixer Brush

Traditionally-trained artists have a whole load of new options available when using the Brush tool. Depending on what sort of brush tip is selected in the Brush Preset or Brush panel, the Brush panel itself changes configuration. Now available are *erodible* brush tips, and like the pastel and charcoal sticks they represent, they actually wear down as you use them! The profile of the tip changes as you work draw. You'll also find new airbrush and watercolor brush tips with such Brush panel options as Distortion, Granularity, Spatter Size, and Spatter Amount.

As you start to explore the new brush tips and their capabilities, I suggest that you open the Brush Presets panel menu and switch the view to Large (or Small) List. The thumbnails will still be visible, but the actual names of the brush tips will give you more insight into how each behaves before you select one. Brush tip names with the words Stiff or Bristle are designed for use with the Mixer Brush (discussed later in this section).

Exploring erodible brush tips

Brush tips with names such as Square Pastel, Charcoal Pencil, and Round Watercolor are erodible tips. Options in the Brush panel for erodible brush tips are shown in the middle panel in Figure 14-11.

For erodible tips, Size is the brush size before it starts to wear down. The Softness determines how quickly the tip erodes, with zero being the softest and a setting of 100% maintaining the brush tip — no eroding. Preset erodible brush shapes available include point, flat, round, square, and triangle. The Sharpen button resets the brush tip to its default shape.

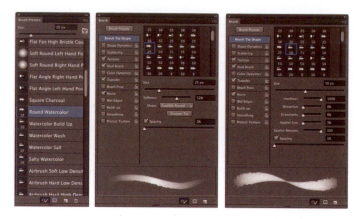

Figure 14-11: Erodible, airbrush, and watercolor tips add fine-art capabilities.

Introducing airbrush and watercolor tips

Airbrush and watercolor brush tips, with names such as Watercolor Build Up, Watercolor Wash, Airbrush Soft Low Density Grainy, and Watercolor Spatter Big Drops, use the options shown in the Brush panel to the right in Figure 14-11.

When working with an airbrush or watercolor tip, the options in the Brush panel include Hardness (think of it as the density of the spray), Distortion (the amount of overspray or spread), Granularity (fine spray or speckles or color), Spatter Size (the size of the droplets), and Spatter Amount (the number of droplets).

Keep in mind that selecting an airbrush brush tip does not activate the Airbrush option in the Options bar. If you want to combine an airbrush tip with airbrush action (so that color builds up when you pause the cursor), click the Airbrush button in the Options bar.

Think about pixel dimensions before selecting these tips — the maximum brush diameter is 50 pixels. You may find times when, to achieve your artistic vision, you need to open a separate document at smaller dimensions, paint in that image, and then use Image Size to scale before copying into your working document. Alternatively, work on a small document, save it, and then use the Place command to add it to your working document as a Smart Object.

Chapter 19 is titled "Ten Reasons to Love Your Wacom Tablet." That chapter is oriented toward general Photoshop users, for the most part. If you're an artist, these new brush tips are more than enough justification to start tablet (or Cintiq) shopping! A mouse or trackpad just can't take advantage of all the new, powerful, *artistically liberating* painting features! Tablets take advantage of not only pen pressure, but also angle and rotation, enabling you to control the shape of the tip as you work with it.

Mixing things up with the Mixer Brush

The Mixer Brush, nested in the Toolbox with the Brush tool, is designed to give traditionally-trained artists a more familiar feel. Also best used with a Wacom tablet or Cintiq and a stylus, this tool takes painting several steps forward. The *bristle tips* available for the Mixer Brush are designed to work more like the physical brushes used to add physical paint to physical canvas, but in a digital sort of way. (The bristle tips can be used with other painting tools, but they pretty much behave like the *static tips*, the brush tips normally used with the other tools.)

The Mixer Brush can apply the foreground color interactively with pixels already on the active layer. Using a "wet" brush (selected in the Options bar) liquefies or melts the existing colors on the layer, pulling them along (with the foreground color) as you drag the tool. To minimize interaction with existing colors, use a "dry" brush or add a layer and paint on the new layer. For a comparison of brushes using the wet (upper stroke) and dry (lower stroke) options, as well as a look at the Mixer Brush Options bar and the Brush Presets panel, see Figure 14-12.

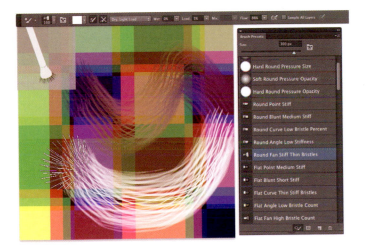

Figure 14-12: The Mixer Brush's Brush Preview in the upper-left can be shown/hidden through the View⇨Show menu.

Some of the options for the Mixer Brush (from the left in Figure 14-12) deserve explanation:

- To the right of the standard tool preset and mini-Brush panel, the color swatch represents the current brush *load*, the paint on the brush. Clicking on the swatch opens the Color Picker; clicking the triangle to the right of the swatch provides an easy way to *clean* the brush (so that it interacts only with existing colors on the layer) or to reload the brush (add color to the mix).

- The two buttons to the right of the color swatch can be used to automatically reload the tool after each stroke and to automatically clean the brush after each stroke. The two buttons can be used together.

- The pop-up menu to the right of the Auto-Load and Auto-Clean buttons provides a list of dry, moist, wet, and very wet presets from which to choose.

- The Wet field controls how the brush interacts with color already on the layer. The wetter the brush, the more it picks up color (and blends with the current brush load) on the layer. A low value overlays the load color without mixing in the existing colors.

- The Load field controls how much "paint" is added to the brush. With a low value, the color runs out quickly and strokes are short. With a high value, the strokes continue to add color. The load settings are most apparent when using a dry brush.

- The Mix field also contributes to how the load color and existing color on the layer interact. A low value uses lots of the load color, whereas a high value uses more of the color already on the layer. Mix isn't used with dry brushes (because they don't interact with the existing colors).

- The Flow field is yet another variable for the amount of color added by the Mixer Brush. Low values result is a more transparent stroke, whereas very high values produce opaque strokes (which tend to be shorter because the brush, you might say, "runs out" of paint).

The Mixer Brush can also interact with strokes applied by the Brush and Pencil tools. And as you fine-tune your masterpiece, remember that you can push this paint around with the Smudge tool and use the Blur, Sharpen, Dodge, Burn, and Sponge tools, too. Sometime when you need a break, open a new empty document, select the Mixer Brush, and explore your inner Rembrandt (or Salvador Dali, perhaps).

Don't forget about the Oil Painting filter, introduced with Photoshop CS6. You'll find it in Photoshop's Filter menu, and you'll find information about using it in Chapter 15.

Filling, Stroking, Dumping, and Blending Colors

You have several more ways to add color to your artwork, none of which use brushes at all. You can, for example, make a selection and fill the selection with color via the Edit⇨Fill command, or you can add a band of color along the edge of the selection with the Edit⇨Stroke command (using the dialog boxes shown to the right in Figure 14-13).

Figure 14-13: Photoshop offers several non-brush ways to add color to your images.

Deleting and dumping to add color

The first time you use the Delete/Backspace key in Photoshop CS6, the keystroke opens the Fill dialog box. The Content-Aware option is sort of a "smart fill." The area surrounding the current selection is analyzed and Photoshop fills to match that surrounding area as seamlessly as possible. If you simply want to delete the current background color, hold down the ⌘/Ctrl key and press Delete/Backspace. You can also fill with the current foreground color by using Option/Alt with Delete/Backspace.

You can also "dump" color into your image with the Paint Bucket tool, nested below the Gradient tool in the Toolbox. Use the Paint Bucket to fill an empty selection with color or to replace the color on which you click with the foreground color. Don't forget vector shapes, either! They're a great way to add perfectly defined areas of solid color to an image. (You can read about working with shapes in Chapter 11.)

Using gradients

You can add *gradients,* which are subtle blends of color, quite easily to your artwork:

1. **Make a selection.**

   Unless you make a selection first, the gradient fills your entire layer. If you want the gradient to fill the entire layer, don't make a selection first.

2. **Select the Gradient tool.**

   Click the Gradient tool in the Toolbox. If you don't see it, look for it nested with the Paint Bucket tool.

3. **Select a gradient.**

   You can open the Gradient panel by clicking the triangle to the right of the sample gradient on the Options bar (see Figure 14-14). You can also click the sample gradient directly to open the Gradient Editor.

4. **Choose a shape.**

   The five buttons to the right of the sample gradient on the Options bar show you the shapes available for the Gradient tool. (From the left, the buttons are Linear, Radial, Angle, Reflected, and Diamond.)

5. **Choose additional options.**

   You can pick a blending mode and opacity, flip the colors in the gradient with the Reverse option, choose Dither to help disguise the transitions between colors, and select the Transparency option to preserve any transparency defined in the gradient.

6. **Drag the Gradient tool.**

   Where you start and in which direction you drag ultimately determine the appearance of the gradient.

The background gradient in Figure 14-14 uses the Angle Gradient option on the Options bar and the gradient that you see in the Gradient Editor. Notice in the Gradient Editor the *Opacity stops* (above the sample being edited) and *Color stops* (below the sample). The *stops* — the squares with points positioned along the sample gradient — determine the color or opacity of the gradient at that particular point. By default, there's a smooth and even blend between neighboring stops, but you can adjust the blend by dragging the small diamonds you see on either side of the opacity and color stops. (**Hint:** The active stops use filled triangles instead of hollow triangles with their little squares.)

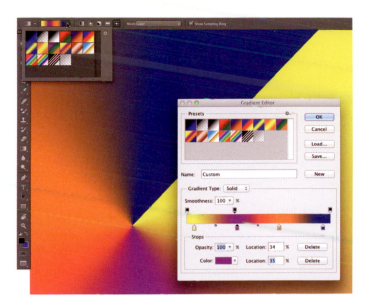

Figure 14-14: Control gradients with the Options bar, Gradient panel, and Gradient Editor.

Click anywhere along the top (opacity) or bottom (color) of the gradient to add a new stop. Drag stops to move them. Option/Alt+drag a stop to duplicate it. Change the attributes of the selected stop with the options just below in the Gradient Editor.

After designing your new gradient, remember to click the New button to add it to the Gradient panel. But keep in mind that custom gradients aren't really saved until you use the Save button or the Preset Manager to create sets on your hard drive. If you don't save your custom gradients, they'll be gone if you need to reset Photoshop's Preferences file (see Chapter 3).

Filters: The Fun Side of Photoshop

The Photoshop Filter menu includes more than 60 commands that you can use to fix, flatter, finesse, and freak out your photos. Open the Filter Gallery to access over 50 additional filters. You can use most of the filters on most of your artwork and some of the filters on some of your artwork, and you probably won't ever use quite a few of the filters.

In this chapter, I start you off with a discussion of the Smart Filters feature, something you should get used to using just about every time you apply a filter. Next, you get a look at what I call the "production" filters, the key filters you use to improve or repair your images, including the new Blur filters. Following that, I show you the basics of two of the most fun features in all of Photoshop: the Filter Gallery and Liquify. Not only are they fun, but you can use them to do wondrous things to your artwork. I wrap up the chapter with a look at several other key filters.

Smart Filters: Your Creative Insurance Policy

One of the most important concepts to keep in mind when working with filters is Smart Filters. When you apply a filter to a pixel layer, that's it — the pixels are changed. But, when you apply a filter to a Smart Object, you create a Smart Filter. With Smart Filters, you can apply one or more filters to a Smart Object and later change your mind about what settings — or even what filters — to use, without reverting to a saved copy of the file or using the History panel. Unlike adjustment layers, which are, in fact, separate layers in the image, Smart Filters work more like layer styles. They appear in the Layers panel below the layer to which they're applied and can be shown or hidden by clicking an eyeball icon (see Figure 15-1). And, like layer styles, you can reopen a Smart Filter by double-clicking it in the Layers panel.

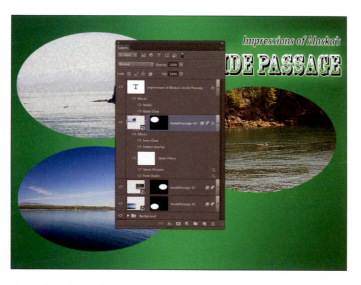

Figure 15-1: Smart Filters are more like layer styles than adjustment layers.

As you can see in Figure 15-1, the layer Inside Passage-02 (the active layer, highlighted in the Layers panel) has both layer effects and Smart Filters applied. The type layer above has only layer effects, whereas the other two Smart Objects, below in the Layers panel, have Smart Filters but no layer effects. Clicking the triangle to the far right of a layer name expands and collapses the list of effects and filters applied. Clicking the eyeball icon to the left of an item hides it without removing it. You can delete a Smart Filter by dragging it to the Trash icon (just as you can with layer effects), which removes its effect from the Smart Object. To reopen a filter's dialog box to change settings, simply double-click the filter name in the Layers panel.

Smart Filters can be applied only to Smart Objects (which are discussed in Chapter 10). Luckily, you can convert any pixel-based layer, even a background layer, to a Smart Object simply by selecting that layer in the Layers panel and choosing Layer⇨Smart Objects⇨Convert to Smart Object. You can even select multiple layers in the Layers panel and create a single Smart Object with that command. You can then apply a Smart Filter to all of the layers in the Smart Object.

Because you can easily remove or change Smart Filters, they provide you with a special sort of creative license: the license to experiment and change your mind. Because they are nondestructive (they don't make permanent changes to the pixels in your image), you can use Smart Filters without fear of damaging your image. Of course that doesn't mean you shouldn't work on a *copy* of your beautiful photo — it's always better to safeguard the original image file and work on a duplicate.

The Filters You Really Need

Photoshop has several filters that you can use on just about any image to improve or finesse it. Most photos, for example, benefit from at least a little bit of sharpening to improve the detail in the image. In some cases, you want to decrease the visible detail in an image in some areas to hide defects, or perhaps you want to blur a background to draw more attention to the subject of your shot. And Photoshop has a couple of filters that you'll find handy for correcting lens distortion and reducing *noise* (specks of red, green, and blue) in digital photos.

Some filters aren't available for images in 16-bit color and some aren't available when you're working in CMYK (cyan/magenta/yellow/black) color mode. Almost all of the filters are available for 8-bit RGB and grayscale images. (No filters are available for GIF or PNG-8 images, which use Indexed Color mode.) And keep in mind that you can apply filters to specific areas of an image by making a selection first. (See Chapter 8 for info on selections and masks.) If you need to use a filter and it's grayed out, head to Image➪Mode and convert to 8-bit/channel RGB mode.

You can instantly reapply the last used filter exactly as it was applied with the keyboard shortcut ⌘+F (Mac)/Ctrl+F (Windows). If you'd like to reopen that last-used filter's dialog box to change settings before reapplying, press Option+⌘+F/Alt+Ctrl+F.

Sharpening to focus the eye

When looking at an image, your eye is naturally drawn to certain areas first. You generally look at bright areas before dark areas and areas of detail before smoother areas in the image. Compare, for example, the three photos in Figure 15-2 (which were taken using different focal lengths and lens apertures). Using Photoshop's sharpen and blur filters enables you to control the amount of detail throughout your image or, when working with selections, in specific areas in order to control the areas to which you want to draw attention.

Figure 15-2: Blurry backgrounds help the subject stand out.

Photoshop offers five sharpen filters, three of which you can ignore. The Sharpen, Sharpen More, and Sharpen Edges filters have no user-definable settings and simply work in accordance with their names. Sure, they do a reasonably good job, but you don't have that all-important control over your images! Skip them in favor of the they-take-some-work-but-they're-worth-it sharpening filters: Unsharp Mask and Smart Sharpen.

Unsharp Mask

The Unsharp Mask filter is, indeed, a sharpening filter, despite the name (which comes from the blurry — *unsharp* — mask created from a copy of the image and used in the sharpening). As you can see in Figure 15-3, Unsharp Mask offers three sliders to adjust the appearance of your image.

Figure 15-3: Despite its name, Unsharp Mask actually sharpens your image.

In the upper left, you see the original image at 100% zoom. The middle image shows the sharpening at 100% zoom. To the right is a 300% zoom in the preview area of Unsharp Mask's dialog box.

Always evaluate your filters at 100% zoom even if you need to shrink the view to only a critical portion of the artwork. Zoomed in or zoomed out views might not accurately reflect the changes that you're making because the image isn't displayed with one screen pixel representing one image pixel. Although video performance is greatly improved in recent versions of Photoshop, 100% zoom is still the safest view in which to make critical decisions. You can, of course, open a second view of the same image with the Window⇨Arrange⇨New Window for [*filename*] command.

Unsharp Mask works by identifying lines of strong contrast — the edges of elements within your image — and increases the contrast along those edges. Along the border of a dark area and a light area, Unsharp Mask uses a thin band of light and a thin band of dark to create a light and dark halo along the edges. That makes the edge appear much more defined. Here's how Unsharp Mask's sliders (as shown in Figure 15-3) work to control the effect.

- **Amount:** The Amount slider determines how much sharpening is actually applied by controlling the brightness and darkness of the halo. An amount of 50% is often suitable for small images that are already in pretty good shape. Use 100% for general photos. Use larger values, up to 500%, for special effects.

- **Radius:** Use the Radius slider to determine the width of the halo. You typically need a value as low as 1 pixel for small images and perhaps as high as 7 for larger images that don't have a lot of tiny detail.

- **Threshold:** The Threshold slider helps you avoid destroying your image by over-sharpening fine details. If the tiniest details in the image get wide, bright halos, they can look garish and unnatural. The higher the Threshold setting, the larger an area must be before sharpening is applied. Typical Threshold settings are 2 for a small image and 5 or 7 for a large image.

Smart Sharpen

The Smart Sharpen filter provides you with an incredible amount of control over the sharpening process. Although it won't (quite) be able to give you a crisp image of that bank robber from the pixelated, blurry surveillance camera (so far, that happens only on TV), it will help you improve just about any image. Those who photograph through microscopes and telescopes might find this filter particularly useful. However, remember that although you might improve an image, some blurs won't be removed by sharpening.

Figure 15-4 shows how well Smart Sharpen works with an appropriate image. (Note that the Preview box is unchecked in order to show the unsharpened original to the right.) In this image, the blurring is consistent throughout the subject of the shot, and there is a reasonable amount of blur. In Figure 15-4, you can see that when you select the Advanced radio button, you get a pair of new tabs in the dialog box: Shadow and Highlight. Use those tabs to control how strongly the effect is applied in the darker and lighter parts of the tonal range.

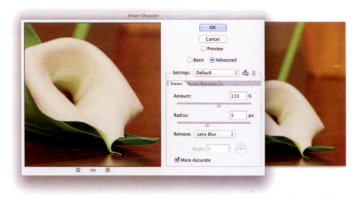

Figure 15-4: Smart Sharpen does a great job with appropriate images.

Smart Sharpen also enables you to specify any of three types of blurring that can be plaguing your image: Gaussian Blur (a uniform blur), Lens Blur (areas of blur beyond the focal distance of the lens), and Motion Blur (the subject or camera moving while the shot was taken). If you don't see distinct evidence of lens blur or motion blur, stick with Gaussian blur.

Blurring images and selections

As you can see in Figure 15-2, blurred areas in an image attract less attention than do the sharper parts of the photo. By making a selection, you can selectively apply Photoshop's blur filters. You can also use the blur filters to hide flaws in an image, including dust, noise, and unwanted little bits and pieces in the picture.

Photoshop CS6 introduces a trio of powerful new blur filters that can be used individually or collectively through the Blur Gallery. In the Filter⇨Blur menu, select Field Blur, Iris Blur, or Tilt-Shift to open the interface shown in Figure 15-5. Click on the box to the right of a field name to add that filter to the image; click on the name of a filter to open that filter's controls and to adjust its blur.

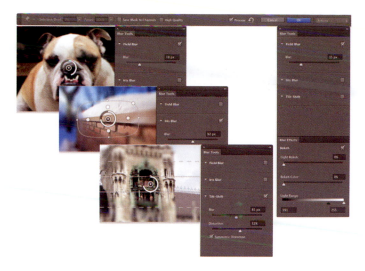

Figure 15-5: The Blur Gallery interface and the three individual blur effects and their sliders.

To the left in the bar across the top, note the Selection Blend slider, which is used to feather the effect along any selection active when the Blur Gallery was opened. The Focus slider, used with Iris Blend and Tilt-Shift, can be used to blur the "in focus" area. When selected, the Save Mask to Channels option creates an alpha of the mask used when applying the blur filters. (Press and hold down the M key to see a preview of the mask.) The High Quality box should generally be selected, unless you are experiencing performance slow-downs. Clicking the button to the right of Preview removes all pins, eliminating the blur and enabling you to start from scratch. Click the Cancel button to cancel; click the OK button to apply the filter(s).

Note that each of the three filters uses "pins" (click in the image window) to control the effect. A pin's amount of blur can be set with the slider in the Blur Tools panel or by dragging along the circle that surrounds the active pin. Click and pin and use the Delete/Backspace key to remove it.

Each of the three Blur Gallery filters uses pins slightly differently:

✔ **Field Blur:** Adjust the blur for the first pin to control blur throughout the image. Add additional pins in other parts of the image with different amounts of blur to create fields of blurring. You might, for example, have a pin to the left in the image with a substantial blur and a pin to the right with a lesser amount of blur to gradually blur the image from one side to the other. Alternatively, you might add a pin to the center of the image with little or no blur, and pins in each corner of the image with a substantial blur, leaving only the center in focus.

✔ **Iris Blur:** Drag the pin (and click to add additional pins), then adjust the inner and outer rings by dragging anchor points. The outer ring represents where the blur is fully applied, while the inner ring controls how much feathering there is between "in focus" and "blurred." Drag the outer ring's anchor points to control both size and shape, and position the cursor outside the ring and drag to rotate. Drag the diamond-shaped anchor point outward to flatten from an ellipse to a rounded rectangle. You'll probably find that you'll most often use a single pin with Iris Blur.

✔ **Tilt-Shift:** Used to simulate the blurring created by a tilt-shift lens, often used in architectural photography. In tilt-shift photography, the lens elements can be manually adjusted to change the angle between the lens and the plane of capture (the sensor in a digital camera), and to change the position of the lens relative to the center of the image plane. This often produces a band of "in focus," with the areas on either side out of focus. When using Tilt-Shift in the Blur Gallery rather than in the field, drag the dashed lines to establish the point where the blur is fully applied, drag the solid line to control feathering between blurred and focused, and drag the control points on the solid line to rotate. Tilt-Shift's distortion slider can be used to introduce distortion of details in one side of the blur (or both sides with Systemic Distortion active). Typically, Tilt-Shift uses one pin.

The Bokeh panel is used to control the quality of the highlights in the blurred area. Use the Light Bokeh slider to control "blooming" of highlights in the blurred area. Use the Bokeh Color slider to manage saturation in the areas around the highlights. Use the Light Range slider to control how much of (or what part of) the tonal range is controlled by the Light Bokeh slider.

While working in the Blur Gallery, you can hide the pins and circles or lines with the shortcut ⌘+H or Ctrl+H to preview without distraction. For precision, you can show/hide the Grid with the shortcut ⌘+' or Ctrl+' (the apostrophe key).

The other Blur filters

Photoshop provides you with almost a dozen blur filters in addition to those of the Blur Gallery. Some of them you're not likely to use at all, such as the Blur and Blur More filters, which give you no control over the process, and Average, which creates a solid color that's an average of all the colors in the image or selection. Some you may use for creative effects, including Box Blur, with which you use a slider to control the vertical and horizontal blurring, and Shape Blur, which blurs based on a custom shape that you select. Motion Blur and the deeply-flawed Radial Blur (it has no preview!) can be useful, especially when used on a selection within a piece of artwork.

The Edit⇨Fade command

Immediately after applying just about any filter or adjustment command and after using many of Photoshop's tools, you can adjust the effect with the Fade command, found under the Edit menu. (Keep in mind that Fade is available only *immediately* after using a filter, adjustment, or tool. You can't even use the Save command in between.)

With Fade, you can reduce the opacity of the previous command or tool, thus reducing its impact on your image. You can also change the *blending mode,* which alters how the command or tool interacts with pixel colors prior to your change. Say, for example, you paint a black stroke with the Brush tool set to Normal and 100% opacity. Immediately afterward, you choose Edit Fade Brush. You can then pick a new blending mode and/or reduce the opacity setting, which changes the painted stroke to appear as if you'd selected the new settings in the Options bar before painting.

You can also apply the Unsharp Mask (or Smart Sharpen) filter and then choose Edit⇨Fade Unsharp Mask, as shown in the figure here. (Yes, the Fade command changes names automatically!) In the Fade dialog box, changing the blending mode from Normal to Luminosity ensures that your Unsharp Mask filter doesn't alter the color of pixels along edges. Using the Fade command this way is the same as if you'd switched to Lab color mode and sharpened only the L channel — without having to switch color modes at all.

Note that the Edit⇨Fade command isn't available when you're working with Smart Filters. If you need to fade the filter, you can first choose Layer⇨Smart Objects⇨Rasterize and then apply the filter. You lose the advantages of working with Smart Objects and Smart Filters, but the Edit⇨Fade command will be available.

The blur filters with which you're most likely to work are

- ✔ **Gaussian Blur:** This filter produces a smoothly blurred version of your image without the distracting artifacts and lines you get by repeatedly applying the Blur More filter. The Radius slider enables you to control the amount of blurring.

- ✔ **Lens Blur:** This filter simulates the effect in which the camera's zoom and aperture create a sharp foreground and a blurry background. You can use an alpha channel (a saved selection) to determine where and how strongly the filter is applied. For a look at the Lens Blur filter in action, see Figure 15-6.

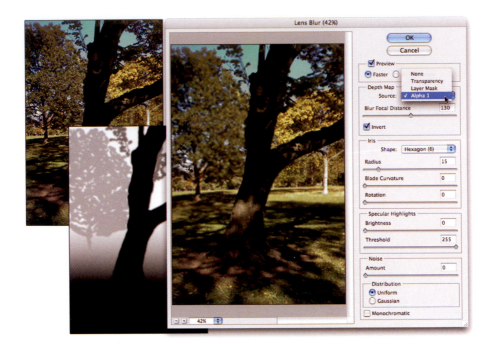

Figure 15-6: Lens Blur can use an alpha channel (mask) to control the blur.

✔ **Smart Blur:** This filter controls the blur by recognizing edges (areas of extreme difference along a line of pixels) and blurring within those areas. You can use Smart Blur in Normal mode to eliminate all fine detail in your image, use it again in Edge Only mode to trace edges in the image, and then use the shortcut ⌘+I/Ctrl+I to invert the image, which produces a black-on-white sketch of your original.

✔ **Surface Blur:** This filter goes beyond Smart Blur in preserving edges. It restricts the blur to large areas of similar color in the image, eliminating the fine detail. It can be very useful for preparing images prior to using the creative filters of the Filter Gallery (about which you can read later in this chapter).

Correcting for the vagaries of lenses

Found near the top of the Filter menu, the Adaptive Wide Angle filter is designed for use with wide angle and fisheye lenses. If a lens profile is available (and the lens data is recorded in the image's metadata), the filter will open up with the Correction menu set to Auto and the lens profile will be applied. If the filter cannot determine what lens was used or if there's no available profile for that lens, select Fisheye or Perspective in the Correction menu and manually adjust the image. (The Correction menu also offers Full Spherical as a correction option.)

Adaptive Wide Angle offers five tools in the upper-left corner (shown in Figure 15-7). Use the Constraint tool to drag between two points in the image that should form a vertical or horizontal line, and then drag to the existing curved line, as shown in Figure 15-7. When you release the mouse button, the filter will straighten the image based on that line. Click the Polygon Constraint tool in the four corners of anything in the image that should be rectangular to help the filter minimize distortion. The Move tool can be used to reposition the image in the canvas, and the Hand and Zoom tools perform their usual tasks. Note, too, the Detail window to the right, which gives you a close-up view of whatever section of the image is under the cursor. If you shot a series of images with the same lens, you can save the constraints you used to correct the first image and later load the constraints for additional corrections to other images. You can access the save and load commands by clicking the button to the right of the Correction menu.

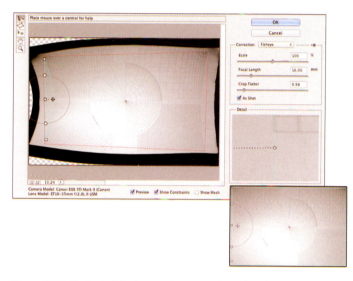

Figure 15-7: To the left in the preview area, dragging the constraint line to the existing curve. In the lower-right, the resulting correction — straight lines!

The Adaptive Wide Angle and Lens Correction filters are dandy, but if you shoot Raw, consider using the Lens Correction tab in Camera Raw instead (see Chapter 7). Working in Camera Raw enables you to make the corrections on unprocessed image data and such corrections can always be tinkered with at a later date.

The Lens Correction filter (Filter⇨Lens Correction) does a wonderful job of cleaning up *pin cushioning* and *barrel distortion* (the outer edges of your image appear to bend inward or outward, respectively). You'll see pin cushioning when shooting with a telephoto lens at its max zoom and barrel distortion at the lens's lower magnification. Both are most obvious when the photo has what should be straight lines at the edges. You can also use Lens Correction to adjust the vertical or horizontal plane of an image, as well as perspective (as discussed in Chapter 9). In Figure 15-8, you see the Lens Correction window's rather complex Custom and Auto Correction panels.

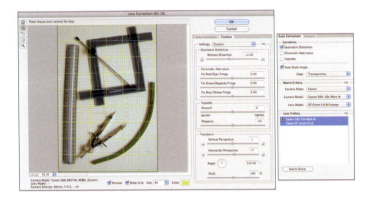

Figure 15-8: In addition to the extensive control in the Custom panel, Lens Correction also offers Auto Correction.

Here's what you have at your disposal in the Lens Correction window:

In the upper-left corner of the window are five tools:

- ✔ **Remove Distortion (top):** Select this tool to drag in the preview area to adjust the distortion factor.

- ✔ **Straighten (second):** This tool is simple: Click and drag along any line in the image that should be straight, and the image is straightened!

- ✔ **Move Grid (middle):** Use this to reposition the grid overlay, aligning it with the content of your image.

- ✔ **Hand and Zoom:** The lower pair of tools should look familiar. The Hand and Zoom tools function as they do anywhere in Photoshop: When the image doesn't fit in the window, click and drag with the Hand tool to reposition; click the Zoom tool to zoom in, or Option/Alt+click to zoom out.

In the Custom panel, you can also find

- ✔ **Remove Distortion slider:** The Remove Distortion slider is the heart of this filter. You use this to compensate for pin cushioning or barrel distortion in the image. Drag it back and forth until your image's vertical and horizontal lines are straight throughout the image.

- **Chromatic Aberration sliders:** Sometimes a photograph shows distorted color along angular lines, such as the branches of trees or latticework. You can minimize these colored halos or fringes with the Chromatic Aberration sliders. Generally speaking, you want to zoom in close on a specific area of detail to make the adjustment.

- **Vignette sliders:** Drag the Amount slider to the left to add a dark *vignette* (fading along the outer edges of the image) or correct a light vignette, drag to the right to add a white vignette or remove a dark vignette. The Midpoint slider increases and decreases the amount of shadowing or highlight along the edges.

- **Transform controls:** Use the Vertical Perspective and Horizontal Perspective sliders to make your image appear parallel to the viewer. Much like using the perspective crop option or the Edit⇨Transform⇨ Perspective command, you're changing the perceived angle of the image to the viewer. (See Figure 9-13 for perspective adjustment in action.)

- **Zoom and grid:** Click the minus and plus buttons in the lower-left corner to zoom out and in, or choose a preset zoom factor from the pop-up menu. Click and drag on the Size field's label (the actual word *Size*) to resize the grid. Click the color swatch to change the color from the default gray. (I liked bright yellow for the image in Figure 15-8.)

- **Saving and loading settings:** From the Lens Correction window's menu (to the right of the Settings pop-up menu), you can save settings and load them later. Because you can name the settings, you can save a set for each of your lenses, at each of their zoom factors, and apply the same correction easily, time after time.

The Auto Corrections panel, shown to the right in Figure 15-8, enables you to apply pre-defined corrections, based on the camera and lens used to capture the image. Most recent model high-end DSLRs from major manufacturers are supported, along with a variety of lenses. If you don't see a preset for your camera/lens combination, click the Search Online button — other photographers using the same gear may have posted a lens profile at Adobe Labs. Remember that Auto Correction is used to compensate for the vagaries of the camera/lens combination — lens distortion, chromatic aberration, and light falloff toward the edges of the image (vignetting). Use the Custom panel to correct for the problems listed earlier in this section.

Cleaning up with Reduce Noise

Digital *noise* — those annoying red, green, and blue specks in your image — can ruin an otherwise lovely picture. (To avoid noise, make sure that your camera is set to shoot at the lowest ISO setting possible.) Photoshop also has a filter for reducing (not necessarily eliminating) digital noise in your images. Found in the Filter⇨Noise menu, Reduce Noise can do an excellent job of minimizing the random red, green, and blue pixels in your image.

When you work with Raw images, do all your noise correction in the Camera Raw plug-in (see Chapter 7). For images in formats other than Raw, use the Reduce Noise filter.

Here are the steps that I recommend when you use the Reduce Noise filter:

1. **Set the details sliders to 0 (zero).**

   In the Reduce Noise dialog box, drag the Preserve Details and Sharpen Details sliders all the way to the left. This eliminates any interference with the actual noise reduction.

2. **Reduce Color Noise.**

   Use the Reduce Color Noise slider to minimize the red, green, and blue specks in your image. Drag the slider slowly to the right until the color noise is gone.

3. **Adjust Sharpen Details.**

   Increase the Sharpen Details slider 1% at a time until the color noise returns; then back off 1%.

4. **Adjust Preserve Details.**

   Drag the Preserve Details slider to the right until you have a good balance between image detail and any luminance noise (bright and dark specks) in the image.

If you see noise of one color considerably longer than the others when dragging the Reduce Color Noise slider, click the Advanced button near the top of the dialog box and work with each channel individually, according to its needs. Also note the Remove JPEG Artifact check box at the bottom of the window. If your image is suffering from JPEG compression problems, selecting that check box might help relieve the effects. (JPEG compression often results in visible borders between 8x8 pixel squares within your image.) Remember, too, that you can use the button to the right of the Settings pop-up menu to save your correction for future use — it will be added to the Setting menu.

Getting Creative and Artistic

Photoshop offers much more than just "fix it" filters. In the Filter menu and the Filter Gallery (opened through the Filter menu), you'll find more than 80 features designed to help you produce creative artwork.

Photo to painting with the Oil Paint filter

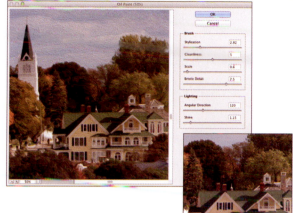

The Oil Paint filter is yet another way to create a painterly effect for a photo. Using the six sliders you see in Figure 15-9, you can create a wide range of looks. Oil Paint is best used with images of larger pixel dimensions — you may find it impossible to reduce the settings enough to present an acceptable result on small images. (You can, of course, use Image Size to increase an image's pixel dimensions, work with Oil Paint, and then use Image Size to reduce the pixel dimensions again.)

Figure 15-9: Oil Paint creates artistic renderings of photographic images. To the lower right, you can see some of the original image.

Oil Paint identifies contiguous areas of similar color in the image and contours the brush strokes to follow the lines of color. The appearance of the individual brush strokes depends primarily on a balance of the four sliders in the Brush section of the dialog box. When first experimenting with Oil Paint, you might find it easiest to drag the Cleanliness slider all the way to the right, the Bristle Detail slider all the way to the left, and then work with the Stylization and Scale brushes to get a good look for the content of the image with which you're working. After you've nailed the general appearance, fine-tune the strokes with Cleanliness and Bristle Detail.

Don't forget to experiment with the Lighting sliders — they can make a *huge* difference in the appearance of the image. Zoom in to 200% and drag the Angular Direction slider slowly back and forth until the detail in the image has the right visual balance between brush strokes and detail. (Think of 90 and 270 degrees as being up/down and zero, 180, and 360 degrees as left/right.) Zoom back out to 100% to fine-tune the Shine setting.

The Oil Paint filter requires that Use Graphic Processor be enabled in Photoshop's Preferences⇨Performance. If your computer's video card doesn't support this feature, Oil Paint won't be available. Keep in mind, too, that Oil Paint is available only for RGB images in either 8-bit or 16-bit color and Smart Objects created from such images.

Working with the Filter Gallery

You can apply and combine lots of Photoshop's creative filters by choosing Filter⇨Filter Gallery. This integrated window lets you use multiple filters at the same time rather than guessing which settings will look good with another filter applied later. Each filter remains *live* (you can change the settings) until you click OK. Check out Figure 15-10.

If Filter Gallery is grayed out and unavailable, head for the Image⇨Mode menu and select 8-Bits/Channel — the Filter Gallery is not available for images in 16-bit color. Keep in mind, too, that the Filter Gallery can be applied as a Smart Filter when working with Smart Objects.

After working with the Filter Gallery for some time you may find that you're only applying one filter at a time. If that's the case, you can open Photoshop's Preferences⇨Plug-Ins and elect to have all of the filters and filter groups shown in the Filter menu. You can then open the Filter Gallery directly to the filter you want to apply.

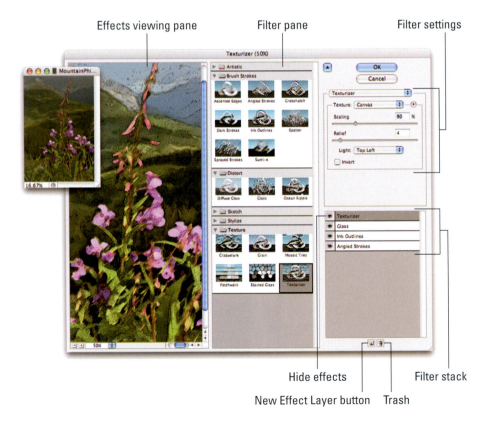

Effects viewing pane   Filter pane   Filter settings

Hide effects   Filter stack

New Effect Layer button   Trash

Figure 15-10: The expansive Filter Gallery interface.

The basic workflow goes like this: Adjust a filter, add a new filter to the stack, select the new filter in the middle pane, adjust the settings to the right, add a new filter to the stack, and so on. If you adjust your first filter settings and then click another filter in the middle column before adding another effect, you replace the first filter rather than adding to it. (If you Option/Alt+click a new filter, it will be added to the stack rather than replace the active filter in the stack.) Here's my step-by-step strategy for working in the Filter Gallery window:

1. **Prepare your image before entering the Filter Gallery.**

   Many of Photoshop's creative filters work best when you prepare the image (or parts of the image) first. You have a couple of key filters that don't appear in Filter Gallery:

   - *Smoothing detail.* Because Photoshop's art-related filters can concentrate on details in your image, too much fine detail can make your filter effects crowded and cruddy. Before working with Ink Outlines, for example, try eliminating the tiny little bits in your image. You could try either Smart Blur or Surface Blur.

   - *Adding detail:* Many of Photoshop's filters don't do anything if the target area doesn't have some texture or detail with which to work. That's where the Add Noise filter comes in handy, adding dark and light specks to the smooth area. Use the Monochromatic and Gaussian options, with an Amount setting from 10% to 15%. After adding noise to the too-smooth area, consider using the Blur⇨Motion Blur filter (to create a linear effect) or the Pixelate⇨Crystallize filter (to make small specks bigger).

2. **Don't forget layers and blending modes.**

   Make a copy of your layer before entering the Filter Gallery so you can later mess around with layer blending modes and opacity to combine the filtered version with the original, which can soften or even enhance the effects you've applied.

3. **Option/Alt+click to add a filter or add to the stack before selecting filters.**

   If you simply click on a different filter, it replaces the filter with which you had been working. Either Option/Alt+click on the new filter or click the New Filter button in the lower-right before clicking on the filter you want to add to the stack.

4. **Play with the stacking order.**

   Drag filters up and down in the stack at the lower right to change their order.

   The order in which the filters are applied often makes a huge difference in the final appearance of your image.

5. **Use the eyeball column.**

It's a good idea sometimes to hide one or more effects in the stack while you fine-tune a filter's settings.

Filters are *cumulative* — changes that you make to one filter can themselves be changed by other filters in the stack.

Not all creative filters are available in the Filter Gallery. Remember that Photoshop has dozens of filters that are available only through the Filter menu, not through Filter Gallery.

Access the online *Photoshop CS6 For Dummies* Cheat Sheet from the link on the inside cover of this book. Among other things, it lists which of Photoshop's creative filters use the current foreground color, background color, or both. Have the correct colors selected before entering the Filter Gallery.

Push, Pull, and Twist with Liquify

Although the Lens Correction and Adaptive Wide Angle filters have added powerful correction tools to your arsenal, you still want to sometimes fix a photograph's perspective or barrel distortion with Liquify. Perhaps. But with Camera Raw's Lens Correction tab and the corrective filters available in Photoshop, Liquify can concentrate on its fun side.

I know of nothing in Photoshop that can bring a smile faster and more easily than creating some strange creature from a friend or loved one in Liquify. I will readily admit that the glow produced by the praise of an art critic is gratifying, but does it compare to, "More, Uncle Pete! Give me *bigger* ears!"? It would certainly be a disservice to the Liquify feature to overlook its powerful image-correction capabilities, so please remember that almost anything you can do to emphasize or enhance an attribute can be done in reverse to minimize that aspect of the image. Make someone short and wide? You can also make them tall and thin. Creating a bulging nose? Create a slim and pert nose. It's all possible with Liquify.

That having been said, examine Figure 15-11, which shows some rather dramatic changes, with the original visible behind and to the left. (This should give you some idea of how useful Liquify can be for more subtle tasks, like trimming tummies, toning arms and legs, thinning noses, and other such work.)

The first thing to note in Liquify's interface is the Advanced Mode option. When deselected, Liquify offers only seven tools, no mask or view options, and only Brush Size, Brush Pressure, and Restore All. If you just need to do a simple bloat or pucker, or perhaps warp a few pixels, deselecting Advanced Mode really simplifies the interface. While the Load Mesh and Save Mesh buttons are available only in Advanced Mode, you will always find commands for those features in the File menu.

Figure 15-11: Liquify gives you unbelievable control over the pixels in your image, especially in Advanced Mode.

Take a look at the tools arrayed along the left edge of the Liquify window in Advanced Mode. Here's what they do, starting at the top:

 Forward Warp tool: Much like Photoshop's Smudge tool, you click and drag the Forward Warp tool to push the pixels around.

 Reconstruct tool: Use the Reconstruct tool as your "undo." Drag over areas that you want to restore to their original appearance. When in Liquify, you can also use the Edit menu's commands Undo, Redo, and Step Backwards and their assigned shortcuts.

Twirl Clockwise tool: (Advanced Mode only.) Click and hold the mouse button down or drag in a circle to spin the pixels within the brush diameter. And if you want to twirl counterclockwise, simply add the Option/Alt key.

Pucker tool: The Pucker tool sucks pixels into the center of the brush. You can click and hold or drag the Pucker tool. Holding down the Option/Alt key toggles you to the Bloat tool's behavior (although you don't actually switch tools).

Bloat tool: The opposite of the Pucker tool, the Bloat tool pushes pixels out from the center. Holding down the Option/Alt key switches to the Pucker tool's behavior.

 Push Left tool: As you drag the Push Left tool, pixels are shifted to the left of the path along which you drag (not necessarily to *your* left). If you drag up, the pixels are shifted to the left on the screen; drag down, and the pixels are shifted to the right on screen. Use the Option/Alt key to reverse the behavior and push pixels to the right of the path.

▶ **Freeze Mask tool:** (Advanced Mode only.) One of the most important tools, the Freeze Mask tool lets you protect areas of your image from change. Paint over an area (you see a red mask) to *freeze* it — to keep it from changing.

▶ **Thaw Mask tool:** (Advanced Mode only.) Unprotect areas with the Thaw Mask tool. It removes the red overlay and lets you liquify the area again.

▶ **Hand tool:** As always, the Hand tool lets you reposition an image in the window when it doesn't all fit. Just click and drag your image to move it in the preview window.

▶ **Zoom tool:** As you might suspect, the Zoom tool functions as it usually does. Click to zoom in, Option/Alt+click to zoom out, and click and drag to zoom in on a specific area.

To the right in the Liquify window are a number of variables and options. Brush Size is the tool brush diameter; Brush Density is comparable to feathering (lower is softer); Brush Pressure controls the strength of the active tool; and Brush Rate controls the speed with which a tool works.

The Reconstruct Options let you restore or partially restore your image to the original appearance. The Reconstruct button opens a slider with which you can back off the changes you've made. Keep in mind that the slider moves from the "Liquified" version to the "pre-Liquify" version of your image. It selectively reverses all of the changes made, not just the previous change. The Restore All button returns your image to its pre-Liquify appearance.

You can make a selection before opening Liquify to work on only a portion of your image. If there's a layer mask on the active layer, you can use it as the basis for a "freeze" in the Mask options (Advanced Mode only). Near the bottom of the right side of the Liquify window (as you can see in Figure 15-11), you can see the View Options, which let you show and hide the *mesh:* the actual distortion you're creating (note the mesh size and color options), as well as view options to show other layers in a layered image.

Do I Need Those Other Filters?

Photoshop has dozens of filters, creative and productive, that you access through the Filter menu rather than through the Filter Gallery. Some do strange and wonderful things to your selection or image, and some just do strange things that you might never need. You can find a description of each of the filters in Photoshop's Help, but a couple of them are worth a bit of attention here.

Adding drama with Lighting Effects

In the Filter⇨Render menu is the powerful Lighting Effects filter, with which you can add spotlights, point lights, and infinite lights. You can choose a preset from the menu in the upper-left (see Figure 15-12) or customize the lights by adding and adjusting the lights of your choice. Click one of the three light buttons in the upper-left, drag the light into position, and then adjust the light with the sliders in the Properties panel. Select which light is active in the Lights panel. In the image window, you can drag to change the angle of a spot light or an infinite light, the scale of a point light, and the shape of a spot light.

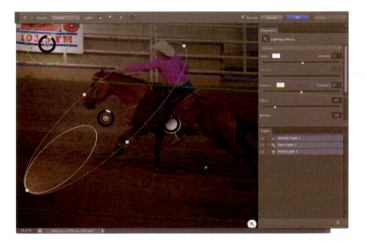

Figure 15-12: A point light in the upper-left, a spot light in the lower-left, and an infinite light in the center.

The Lighting Effects filter is available for RGB images in 8-bit and 16-bit color, and for Smart Objects created from such images. If you want to use Lighting Effects with a grayscale image, you can add a Black & White adjustment or adjustment layer, or head to the Image⇨Mode menu and convert to Grayscale and then convert back to RGB.

Bending and bubbling

In the Filter⇨Distort menu, you find both the Shear and the Spherize filters, both of which are simpler alternatives to Liquify for many projects. Use the Shear filter to bend a selection back and forth, creating curves. Use Spherize to create a bulging, rounded image. Both Shear and Spherize are easiest to control when you make a selection of your target and copy it to a new layer. Shear works only vertically, so you might need to rotate your image before and after using the filter.

Creating clouds

Clouds make lovely, unobtrusive backgrounds (as you see in Figure 15-13) that can be scaled and transformed to produce smoke or steam, and you can even create marbling effects from clouds. In the Filter⇨Render menu, you find Clouds and Difference Clouds. Both filters use a mixture of the foreground and background colors to create a cloud pattern. The Clouds filter replaces the content of the selection or layer (if any), and Difference Clouds interacts with the existing pixels (you can't

Figure 15-13: The Clouds filter produces pleasant backgrounds.

use it on an empty layer) pretty much like Clouds using the Difference blending mode. Apply Difference Clouds several times, perhaps as many as 20, to create abstract backgrounds and marble patterns, or perhaps to simulate microscope slides.

Part IV
Power Photoshop

*T*his part is more specialized than the others in the book. These two chapters cover features of Photoshop that you might never need, but certainly should know about!

Chapter 16 shows you how to streamline some of your work with Photoshop's automation commands. You also read about recording Actions and get a quick look at using scripting to automate Photoshop. Keep in mind that Chapter 16 also includes information on creating your own websites in Adobe Bridge, generating on-screen presentations, creating contact sheets to track your images, and printing multiple copies of an image on a single sheet of paper — saving both time and money!

Video editing is no longer confined to the Extended version of Photoshop! Chapter 17 introduces you to working with video and audio and creating animations in Photoshop. After reading this chapter, you'll have the basic information you need to generate and export video projects. (But it probably won't prepare you to challenge the big Hollywood studios for one of those cute golden statues . . .)

16

Streamlining Your Work in Photoshop

A lot of the work that you do in Photoshop is fun — experimenting with filters, applying creative adjustments, cloning over former in-laws, that sort of thing. A bunch of your work, though, is likely to be repetitive, mundane, and even downright boring. That's where automation comes in. If a task isn't fun to do, if you need to speed things up, or if you need to ensure that the exact same steps are taken time after time, automation is for you.

I begin the chapter with a look at Photoshop's Actions and the Batch command, which enable you to process many files automatically. Next, we welcome back a couple of old (and somewhat dated) friends — Contact Sheet II and PDF Presentation are once again Photoshop features. After that, I give you a quick look at scripts, such as the very powerful Image Processor. *Scripts* are sort of little computer programs that you use to control your computer — Photoshop, other programs, your printer, or even an operating system itself. There's a brief look at extensions and Flash panels. After that, I introduce automation through Bridge's Tools menu and show you the powerful Output panel. Bridge enables you to generate more feature-rich PDF presentations, multi-page PDFs (including amped-up contact sheets and picture packages), and even web galleries of your images.

Ready, Set, Action!

In Photoshop, an *Action* is simply a recorded series of steps that you can play back on another image to replicate an effect or technique. To choose a wild example, say that every image in your new book about Photoshop needs to be submitted at a size of exactly 1,024x768 pixels at 300 ppi, regardless of content. Record an Action that uses the Image Size command to change resolution and then use the Canvas Size command to expand the image to 1,024x768 pixels.

Use that Action (*play* the Action) on each image before submitting it. Better yet, wait until all the images for a chapter are ready and then use the Batch command to play the Action automatically on each of them!

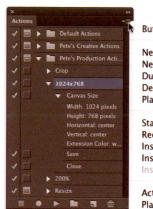

Actions and the Batch command not only streamline repetitive tasks; they also ensure precision — that every one of those images will be *exactly* 1,024x768 pixels, each and every time. But Actions also have a creative side to them. The lower part of the Actions panel's menu (see Figure 16-1) contains Actions sets that you can load into the panel to produce frame and border effects, text effects, and more. (The content of your Actions panel menu might differ from what's shown in Figure 16-1.) You can also purchase collections of Actions from commercial sources.

Figure 16-1: The Actions panel menu includes sets of Actions you can load into the panel.

To work with an Action, open an image, select the Action in the Actions panel, and then click the Play button at the bottom of the panel. As you can see in Figure 16-1, the three buttons to the left use the near-universal symbols for Stop, Record, and Play. The three to the right use the standard Adobe symbols indicating New Set, New Action, and Trash.

Any step in the Actions panel that doesn't have a check mark in the left column is skipped when you play the Action. Any step that has a symbol visible in the second column (the *modal control* column) pauses when you play the Action. Click in the second column when you want the Action to wait for you to do something. Perhaps you'll click in that column next to a Crop step so that you can adjust the Crop tool's bounding box. You might click in the second column next to an Image Size step so that you can input a specific size or choose a resampling algorithm. After you make a change or input a value for that step, press Return/Enter to continue playing the Action.

Notice the grayed-out Save Actions command in the panel's menu in Figure 16-1. Remember that you have to select a set of Actions in the panel, not an individual Action, to use the Save Actions command. If you want to save only one Action, create a new set and Option/Alt+drag the Action to that set to copy it. You can also create a printable text file (`.txt`) of your Actions set by holding down the ⌘+Option/Ctrl+Alt keys when selecting Save Actions. Text versions of your Actions provide an easy reference for what each Action (and step) does to an image.

If you get hooked on Actions, you'll also want to try Button Mode in the Actions panel menu. Each Action appears in the panel as a color-coded button. You don't see the steps of the Action, so you don't know whether an individual step is being skipped and you can't change the modal control column, but you might like the color-coding to sort your Actions.

Recording your own Actions

The real power of Actions comes to you when you record your own. Sure, the sets of Actions included with Photoshop are great, and the commercial packages of Actions have some good stuff too, but it's not *your* stuff. When you record your own Actions, you record the steps that work for your images, your workflow, and your artistic vision.

Actions can't float free in Photoshop's Actions panel: Each Action must be part of a set of Actions. Before beginning to record your Action, you can select an existing set or click the fourth button at the bottom of the panel to create a new set. When you have a set selected, you can then click the New Action button (second from right). Then, in the New Action dialog box that appears (as shown in Figure 16-2), assign a name (and color-code for Button Mode and perhaps an F-key combination) and click the Record button. From that point forward, just about everything you do in Photoshop is recorded as part of the Action until you click the Stop button at the bottom of the Actions panel. No worries, though — you can always delete unwanted steps from a recorded Action by dragging them to the Trash icon at the bottom of the Actions panel. And if you want to change something in the Action, you can double-click a step and rerecord it.

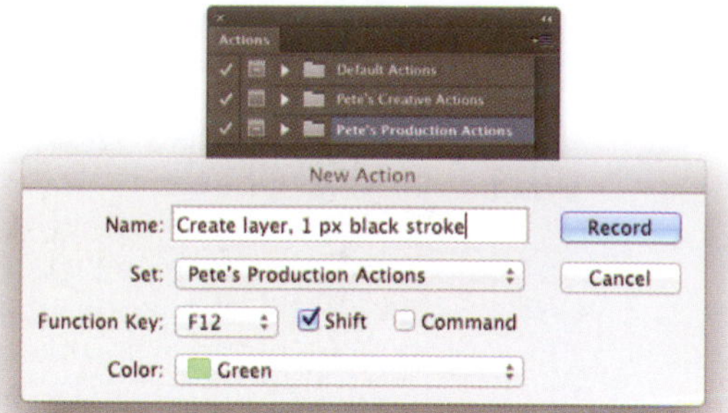

Figure 16-2: After you click the New Action button, you see the New Action dialog box.

You can record most of Photoshop's commands and tools in an Action, but you can't control anything outside of Photoshop. (For that you need *scripting,* introduced later in this chapter.) You can't, for example, use an Action to print (controlling the printer's own print driver), copy a filename from the Mac Finder or Windows Explorer, or open Illustrator and select a path to add to your Photoshop document. Here are some tips about recording your own custom Actions:

- ✔ **Open a file first.** Open the file in which you're going to work *before* you start recording the Action. Otherwise, the Open command becomes part of the Action, and the Action will play on that specific file every time you use it. You can, however, record the Open command within an Action to open a second file — perhaps to copy something from that file.

- ✔ **Record the Close command after Save As.** When you record the Save As command in an Action, you're creating a new file on your hard drive. Follow the Save As command with the File⇨Close command and elect Don't Save when prompted. That closes and preserves the original image.

- ✔ **Use Percent as the unit of measure.** If you need an element in your artwork to be in the same relative spot regardless of file size or shape (like a copyright notice in the lower-right corner), change the unit of measure to Percent in Photoshop's Preferences before recording the Action.

- ✔ **Record/insert menu commands.** When you use a menu command while recording your Action, the actual values that you enter into the dialog box are recorded, too. If you'd rather select the values appropriate for each individual image (perhaps for the Unsharp Mask filter or the Image Size command), insert the command rather than record it. When you reach that specific spot in your process, use the Actions panel menu command Insert Menu Item (refer to Figure 16-1). With the dialog box open, mouse to and select the appropriate menu command; then click OK to continue recording the Action. In Figure 16-3, you see the Insert

Menu Item dialog box when first opened (before a command is selected) and after I used the mouse to select the Image Size command from Photoshop's Image menu.

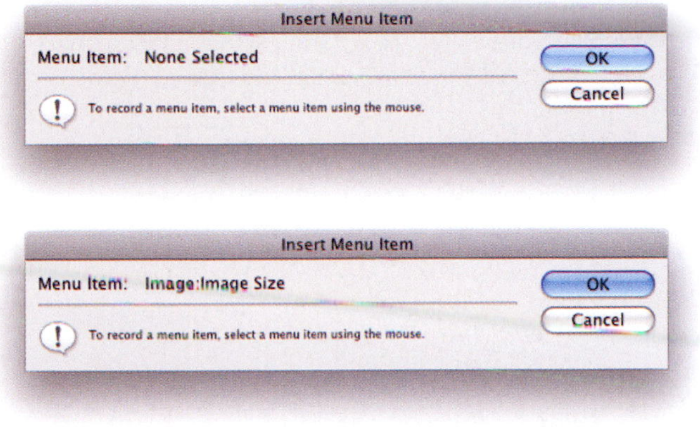

Figure 16-3: Using Insert Menu Item leaves a dialog box open when playing the Action.

✔ **Record multiple versions of a step, but activate one.** Say you want to record an Action that does a lot of stuff to an image, including changing the pixel dimensions with the Image Size command. However, you want to use this Action with a variety of images that require two or three different final sizes. You can record as many Image Size commands as you want in that one Action — just remember to deselect the left column in the Actions panel next to each of the Image Size steps except the one you currently want to use.

✔ **Record Actions inside Actions.** While recording an Action, you can select another Action and click the Actions panel's Play button — the selected Action will be recorded within the new Action.

✔ **Insert a message or warning.** Use the Actions panel menu command Insert Stop to send a message to anyone who plays your Action. The message could be something like "You must have a type layer active in the Layers panel before playing this Action" with buttons for Stop and Continue. Or you could phrase it more specifically: "If you have not selected a type layer in the Layers panel, click Stop. If a type layer is active in the Layers panel, click Continue." The more precise the message, the less confusion later. In Figure 16-4, you see the Record Stop dialog box, where you type your message when recording the Action (top), as well as a look at how the message appears when the Action is played back later (bottom).

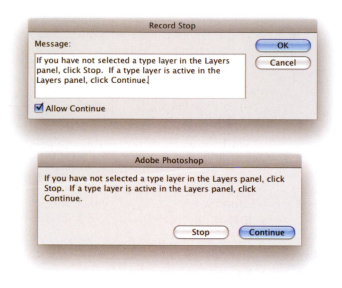

Figure 16-4: Insert a Stop to show a message when the Action is played.

✔ **Remember Conditional Mode Change and Fit Image.** These two commands in the File➪Automate menu are designed to be recorded in an Action that you might later use on a wide variety of images.

• *Conditional Mode Change* is very handy when your Action (or final result) depends on the image being in a specific color mode. When you record Conditional Mode Change in an Action, every image, regardless of its original color mode, is converted to the target color mode (see Figure 16-5). Say, for example, that you need to apply a certain filter in an Action, but that filter is available only for RGB images. If you record Conditional Mode Change before running the filter, the Action will play properly.

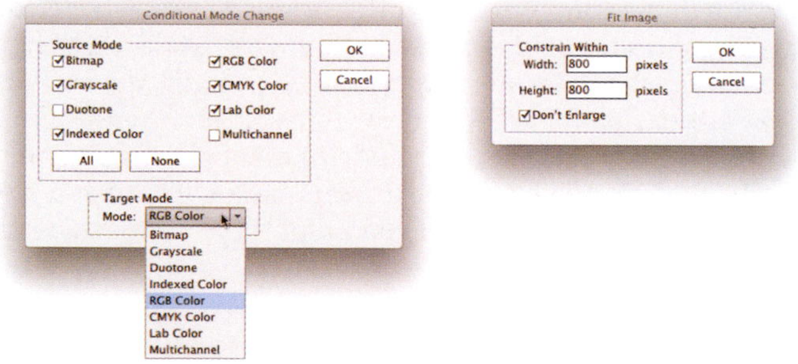

Figure 16-5: Conditional Mode Change and Fit Image are recorded in Actions using the File➪Automate menu.

- *Fit Image* specifies a maximum width and height that the image being processed must not exceed, regardless of size or shape — great for batch-processing images for the web. Fit Image maintains your images' aspect ratios (to avoid distortion) while ensuring that every image processed fits within the parameters you specify (see Figure 16-5). If you need all landscape-oriented images to be 800x600 pixels and all portrait-oriented images to be 600x800 pixels, enter 800 in both the width and the height fields.

Notice the Don't Enlarge check box in the Fit Image dialog box. If you're prepping images for a website and reducing them to a specific size to make them download and display faster, you don't necessarily want to *enlarge* some of the images, making them download *slower*. Disable this option when you're trying to make all the images uniform in size, perhaps for the creation of a PDF presentation (discussed later in this chapter).

✔ **Always record an Action using a copy of your image.** Because the steps that you record in the Action are actually executed on the open file, record your Action using a copy of the original image. That way, if something goes wrong, your original image is protected.

The Actions panel menu also offers the option Allow Tool Recording. This feature enables you to record tools such as the Brush and the Clone Stamp in Actions. However, there are a few limitations. While you can record the tool, you can't record changing its settings. If, for example, you recorded the Action using a feathered 40-pixel brush tip, you'll need to remember to select that brush tip prior to playing the Action. In addition, the data recorded for the tool movement is device-specific. If you record the Action on one computer and play it back on a computer using a different video card and/or monitor, the results may be slightly different. Do not depend on Actions that record tool movement for precision!

Working with the Batch command

Photoshop's File➪Automate➪Batch command plays back an Action on a number of files. You select an Action to play and also a folder of image files to play it on; then you decide what you want to do with the files after the Action finishes with them. You can leave the images open in Photoshop, save and close them, or (much safer) save them to another folder, preserving the originals. Figure 16-6 shows the Batch dialog box and also the pop-up menu for the fields in the File Naming area. (When you select a new folder as the Destination in Batch, you must tell Photoshop how you want the new files to be named.)

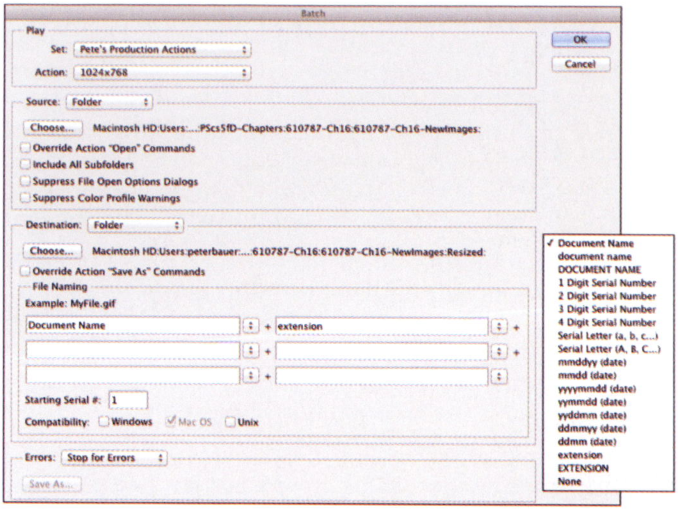

Figure 16-6: The Batch command is much simpler than it looks!

You must remember three things when assigning filenames:

- **Include a variable.** Something must change from filename to filename. Select one of the top nine items in the pop-up menu (some version of the original document name or a serial number or a serial letter). It doesn't have to be in the first field, but one element of the filename must be different from file to file.

- **Don't use a period (.) in any field.** You can type in any of the fields (except the last one you use), but for compatibility, stick with letters, numbers, underscores (_), and hyphens (–).

  Absolutely do not use a period (.) in the filename. The only period that can be used in a filename is the one that's automatically added immediately before the file extension.

- **You have two other decisions of note in the Batch dialog box.** When you elect to suppress any Open commands in the Action, you protect yourself from poorly recorded Actions that start by opening the image with which they were recorded. However, if the Action depends on the content of a second file, you don't want to override that Open command. Generally, you want to override any Save As commands recorded in the Action, relying instead on the decisions that you make in the Batch dialog box to determine the fate of the image.

Keep in mind that you can also select some of the content of a folder in Bridge, and then use Bridge's menu command Tools➪Photoshop➪Batch to run an Action on just those files. The Source menu will be set to Bridge.

Creating contact sheets and presentations

That New Feature icon in the margin is a bit misleading, but I don't have any icons that say "Old" or "Resurrected" or "Back from the Scrapheap." Last seen in Photoshop CS3, Contact Sheet II and PDF Presentation are once again offered in Photoshop's Automate menu (shown in Figure 16-7). Use Contact Sheet to create printable pages of thumbnail-sized images of the files in a folder. PDF Presentation creates very basic on-screen slideshows of the selected images. While convenient (and perhaps familiar), these features lack the polish and versatility of Bridge's Output panel, which is discussed later in this chapter.

File	
New...	⌘N
Open...	⌘O
Browse in Bridge...	⌥⌘O
Browse in Mini Bridge...	
Open as Smart Object...	
Open Recent	▶
Close	⌘W
Close All	⌥⌘W
Close and Go to Bridge...	⇧⌘W
Save	⌘S
Save As...	⇧⌘S
Check In...	
Save for Web...	⌥⇧⌘S
Revert	F12
Place...	
Import	▶
Export	▶
Automate	▶
Scripts	▶
File Info...	⌥⇧⌘I
Print...	⌘P
Print One Copy	⌥⇧⌘P

Automate submenu:
- Batch...
- PDF Presentation...
- Create Droplet...
- Crop and Straighten Photos
- Contact Sheet II...
- Conditional Mode Change...
- Fit Image...
- Lens Correction...
- Merge to HDR Pro...
- Photomerge...

Figure 16-7: Contact Sheet II and PDF Presentation have returned to the Automate menu.

Sticking to the Script

You can use AppleScript (Mac), Visual Basic (Windows), and JavaScript (both) with Photoshop. Scripts are much more powerful than Photoshop's Actions because they can control elements outside of Photoshop itself. AppleScripts and Visual Basic scripts can even run multiple programs and play JavaScripts. If you're interested in scripting, go to the Photoshop folder on your hard drive and explore the content of the Scripting Guide folder. You can find plenty of information to get you started!

You can find more scripts on the Internet, including some at www.adobe.com/cfusion/exchange/index.cfm. Go to the Photoshop exchange and click on Scripts.

If you shoot in your camera's Raw format, perhaps the most useful of the several pre-recorded scripts installed with Photoshop is Image Processor (see Figure 16-8). You can use Image Processor to batch-convert your Raw images to JPEG, PSD, or TIFF — and you can even resize the images automatically while converting! (And while Image Processor is designed to work with Raw files, you can actually convert any file format that Photoshop can open.)

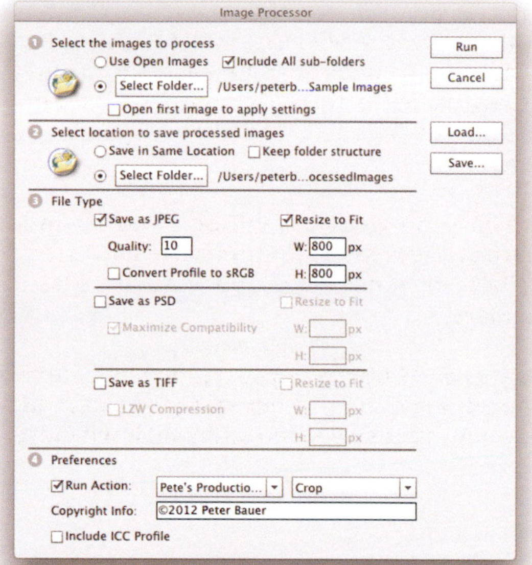

Figure 16-8: Image Processor can batch-convert to speed your workflow.

Image Processor is much simpler than it appears:

- ✔ **Select the images to process.** If the images are already open in Photoshop, great! If not, click the button and select a folder of images. If the source folder has subfolders and you want to process the images in those subfolders, select that option.

- ✔ **Choose a destination.** You can save the files in the folder of origination, or you can click the button and select a different folder in which to save the processed images.

Do not click the Select Folder button and select the source folder. If you want to keep the processed images in the same folder as the unprocessed images, simply click on the Save in Same Location button. Photoshop is smart enough — *most* of the time — to recognize the source folder and avoid re-processing already-processed images in an endless loop, but don't risk it.

✔ **Select the file format and options.** Each of the three file formats offers the option of resizing. JPEG offers options for Quality (the amount of compression — and associated image degradation) and to convert to sRGB (for the web or e-mail). Maximizing compatibility for PSD files ensures the image can be seen and opened by other programs of the Creative Suite and earlier versions of Photoshop. TIFF's LZW compression can significantly reduce file size, without degrading the image at all.

At the bottom of the Image Processor dialog box, you also have the options to run an Action on the images as they're processed, to add your copyright information to the file's metadata (not on the image itself), and to embed the color profile in the image.

Note also the Save and Load buttons. If you set up a couple of folders, one where you dump the originals and another where you save from Image Processor, you can save your usual setup and load it whenever you need to repeat the job.

Adding Extensions to Photoshop

Extensions are custom-made panels that add functionality to Photoshop. Kuler (shown in Figure 16-9), which is installed by default with Photoshop, is used to generate sets of coordinating colors. Other extensions, also called *Flash panels*, are available from a variety of sources, including Adobe Exchange (www.adobe.com/cfusion/exchange/index.cfm).

Extensions can be simple panels that hold a specific set of tools and commands often used together, or complex panels that can runs scripts and access assets outside of Photoshop.

For the adventurous, consider making your own panels using Adobe Configurator, available from Adobe Labs (www.labs.adobe.com). You can, for example, create a custom panel that holds the tools and commands (as buttons) that you use for a particular job.

Figure 16-9: Custom panels can simplify your workspace.

Tooling around in Bridge

The first step in getting familiar with Adobe Bridge's automation options is Bridge's Tools menu (see Figure 16-10). Note that if you have the Adobe Creative Suite installed, you'll also see other programs listed in addition to Photoshop.

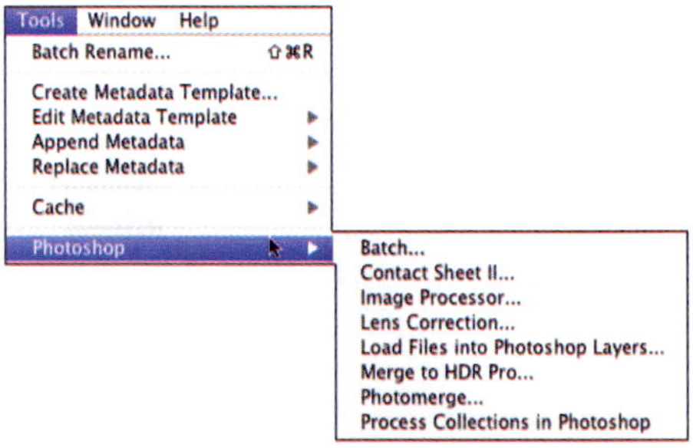

Here's an overview of some of the tasks you can perform through the Tools menu:

Figure 16-10: The Tools commands can make quick work of big jobs.

✔ **Batch Rename.** Rename a whole series of images in a single process! Select the image thumbnails or a folder of images in Bridge, open Batch Rename (see Figure 16-11), construct the new filenames, and click the Rename button.

When building the new file names, use the plus and minus buttons to the right to add or subtract each element. The various choices are shown in the box to the right in Figure 16-11. Each element will have one or two fields or pop-up menus to the right.

Absolutely do not use a period (.) in any text field of the new filename. The only period that can be used in a filename is the one that's automatically added immediately before the file extension. In the text fields, use only letters, numbers, underscores (_), and hyphens (-). To use a period or any other symbol in the new filename risks making the file unrecognizable by Photoshop or any other program. (This means you, too, Mr. & Ms. MacUser!)

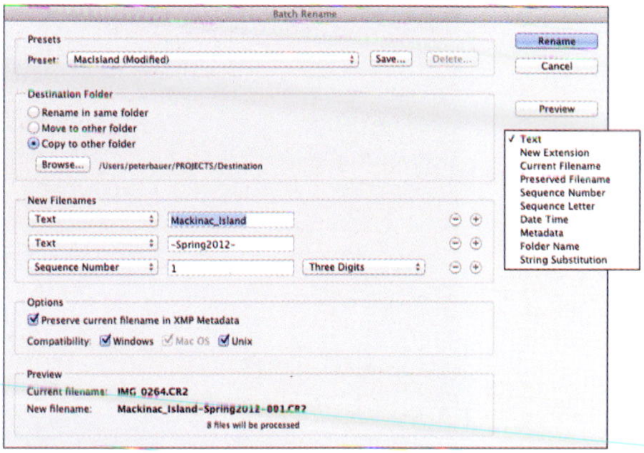

Figure 16-11: Batch Rename enables you to speedily take care of one very important organizational task.

✔ **Work with metadata templates.** Metadata, that useful information about an image stored with the image, often is repeated from file to file. You might, for example, add exactly the same copyright information to each and every image you shoot. Or you might return from a job or trip or vacation with gigabytes of images shot at the same location or of the same subject. Using metadata templates enables you to quickly and easily add metadata to a series of (or even folders of) images, in just a couple of clicks.

✔ **Manage Bridge's cache.** The cache is where Bridge stores thumbnails and metadata of images with which it has already worked. Accessing the cache for a folder (rather than re-processing each image every time you open the folder) can save loads of time. However, sometimes the cache can get corrupted. Should you see, for example, thumbnails of images that have been moved or deleted, go to the Tools⇨Cache menu and elect to purge the cache. You can also build and export the cache for the current folder through this menu, which is a great thing to do just before burning the folder to DVD or CD as a backup!

✔ **Access automation in other programs.** As you can see in Figure 16-10, Bridge's Tools menu also gives you access to a number of Photoshop's automations and scripts. (If you have Illustrator and/or InDesign installed, you'll have access to some of their features as well.)

Creating Fancy PDF Presentations and Multi-Page PDFs

Although you can create basic presentations and contact sheets through Photoshop's File⇨Automate menu, you'll find more powerful capabilities in Bridge, where they are available to all of the programs of the Creative Suite. You can create PDFs, both multi-page and presentations, as well as web galleries, through Bridge's Output panel. Access the Output panel by clicking that workspace's button, selecting Output through the Window⇨Workspace menu, or using the shortcut shown in Figure 16-12.

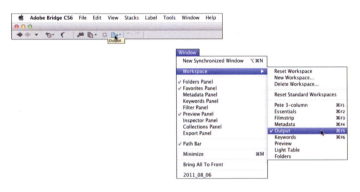

Figure 16-12: You can access Bridge's Output panel in a variety of ways.

Creating a PDF presentation

Portable Document Format (PDF), the native file format of Adobe Acrobat, has become an incredibly useful and near-universal format. It's hard to find a computer that doesn't have Adobe Reader (free software to open and view PDF files) or another program for viewing PDFs, and that helps make PDF a wonderful format for sharing or distributing your images.

In Bridge's Output panel, shown in Figure 16-13, you can quickly and easily create both on-screen presentations (complete with fancy transitions between images) and multi-page PDF documents (suitable for distribution and printing).

To create a PDF Presentation in Bridge, take the following steps:

1. **Select the thumbnails of the images you want to include. You can click and then Shift+click to select a series of images or ⌘+click (Mac)/ Ctrl+click (Windows) to select individual images.**

   Hint: You must select the images; you can't select only the folder. Bridge automatically skips any non-image files that are selected.

Figure 16-13: PDF is a great format for sharing images as presentations or as documents.

2. **In the Document section, choose an appropriate size.**

   Choose one of the web presets, shown in Figure 16-14, rather than a paper size. Adobe Reader can scale the presentation, so 800x600 pixels is a good choice unless you know the presentation will always be played back on a larger monitor. Choose your background color (black is an excellent choice) and determine whether you want to require a password to open the document or to make the presentation non-printable.

3. **Choose a layout of one-by-one.**

   Unless you actually *want* more than one image displayed in each frame of the presentation, use a layout of one column and one row, as you see in Figure 16-15.

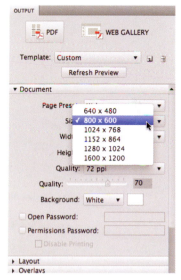

Figure 16-14: Size your presentation for on-screen display rather than print.

4. (Optional.) Add the filename, a header, a footer, or a watermark to each frame.

In the Overlays section (flip ahead to Figure 16-19 if you want to see it), you can elect to add the filename (with or without the file extension) below each image, choosing the font, style, size, and color of your choice. The Header and Footer sections enable you to add a text message (customizable, of course) to the top and/ or bottom of each slide of your presentation. You can also add a watermark, perhaps your copyright information at a reduced opacity, across the center of the image. Your options in the Watermark section (shown in Figure 16-20) include all the font choices, Opacity, and Foreground or Background. (Unless your images include transparency or reduced opacity, select Foreground.)

5. Choose your playback options.

You select whether you want the presentation to fill the screen, how long each frame will be displayed, whether the presentation plays once or continuously, and how it changes from frame to frame. Figure 16-16 shows the layout.

6. Preview your presentation.

Click the Refresh Preview button near the top (shown in Figures 16-14 through 16-16) to make sure you'll get want you want.

7. Save your presentation.

Way down at the bottom of this dialog box (and shown in Figure 16-16), you can choose to view the presentation (or not) when ready with the View PDF After Save option. Click the Save button, name the presentation (Bridge will automatically add the .pdf file extension), choose a location in which to save, and click Save.

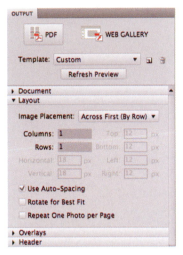

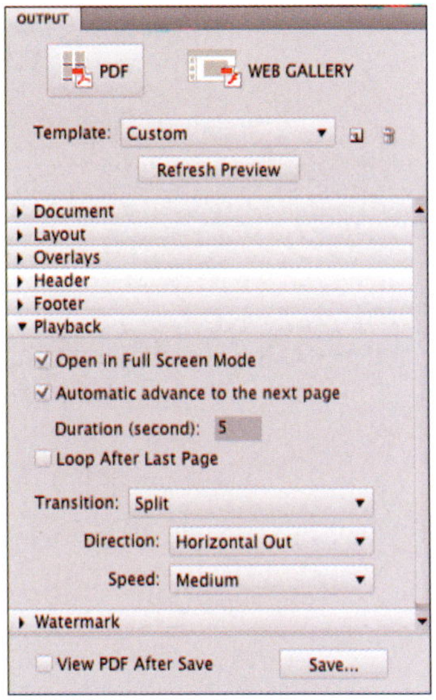

Figure 16-15: It's possible to have multiple images in each frame, but not typical.

Figure 16-16: The options in Playback govern how the presentation will be displayed.

Collecting thumbnails in a contact sheet

In the old Dark(room) Ages, photographers regularly made a record of which images were on which film strips by exposing those strips on a piece of photographic paper, thus creating a *contact sheet.* The contact sheet serves the same purpose as thumbnails or previews in Bridge or the Open dialog box or thumbnail images on a web page — they show which image is which. Hard copy contact sheets are useful to present to a client. Bridge can automate the process for you in the Output panel by generating a PDF that contains small copies of each image in a folder. Here's the procedure:

1. **Select the thumbnails of the images you want to include.**

   Hint: You must select the images; you can't select only the folder. Bridge automatically skips any non-image files that are selected.

2. **Select an appropriate page size in the Document area.**

   Choose from among the presets or define a custom size. If the contact sheets will be printed, use a paper size, as you see in Figure 16-17. If they're intended only for on-screen display, select a size from the web presets (shown in Figure 16-14). Elect to generate high-quality or low-quality thumbnails and pick a background color. (Black is beautiful and makes your images "snap," but also uses a lot more ink when printing.) You can also require a password to open the document or forbid printing the contact sheets.

3. **Define your layout.**

   In the Layout section, you choose how many thumbnails in each row and column (Figure 16-18). You can choose to have the images added to the page row by row (the second image is to the right of the first) or column by column (the second image is directly below the first). You can also define the spacing between thumbnails, but the Use Auto-Spacing option is almost always a safe choice. You can also elect to auto-rotate images so that, regardless of orientation, all the images

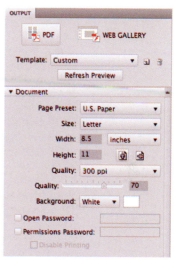

Figure 16-17: Select the size and orientation of the contact sheets in Document.

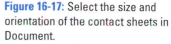

Figure 16-18: Define the number of thumbnails and set the spacing (or use the convenient Auto-Spacing option).

are the same size. Do not select Repeat One Photo per Page when generating contact sheets. (With that option selected, instead of contact sheets you'll have pages with multiple copies of one image).

If your folder is filled with portrait-oriented images, you can certainly have more columns than rows so that each image better fills the area allotted for it. For example, when printing 20 portrait images, using 5 columns and 4 rows produces larger printed images than using 4 columns and 5 rows.

4. **Choose whether to use the filename as a caption.**

   In the Overlays section (shown in Figure 16-19), you can elect to use the filename as a caption, with or without the file extension. If you use this option, be sure not to choose a font size too large to fit within the space allocated for each thumbnail! You can also add a page number in the header or footer of each document.

5. **Add a watermark, header, or footer (or nothing).**

   You also have the option of adding a watermark, as shown in Figure 16-20, but if it's splashed across the middle of the page, it might serve little purpose. You can, however, add a line of text (your copyright info or a logo image, for example) across each image as a bit of protection. More appropriate for a contact sheet might be a header or footer identifying you as the photographer and perhaps mentioning the copyright status of your images, as well as a page number (selected in the Overlay section).

6. **Preview and save.**

   Click the Refresh Preview button (visible in Figure 16-20 near the top) to get a look at what you're creating, make

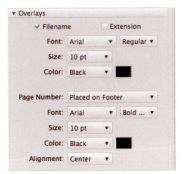

Figure 16-19: Filenames can help your client order prints, but only you might need to see a file extension.

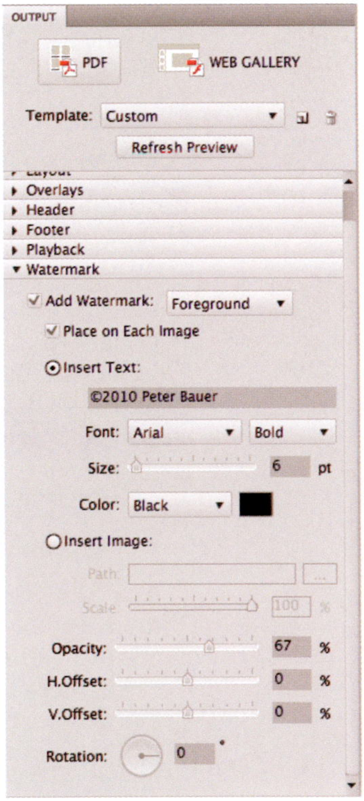

Figure 16-20: Adding a copyright notice across each image can serve as a reminder.

any changes necessary, and then click the Save button. You next see a dialog box in which you name the document (Bridge automatically adds the `.pdf` file extension) and choose a location in which to save. Bridge creates a multi-page PDF, generating as many pages as necessary to hold all of the selected thumbnails.

Saving paper with picture packages

Using Bridge's PDF-generation feature is also a great way to put multiple copies of an image on the same page for printing. Suppose you need to print a dozen copies of an image, each at 4x5 inches. Printing each on a separate sheet of paper takes 12 sheets (oh, the cost!) and 12 print cycles. Define a custom layout in Bridge's Output panel (as shown in Figure 16-21) to put four 4x5 images on a single Letter size page, and you use three sheets of paper and wait through only three print cycles. Um, let's see, which do you want to do?

You have to do the math to get your picture packages to print at the size you want. In this example, I want 4x5 inch prints, so I split the difference between size of the prints and paper in the Top/Bottom and Left/Right margins.

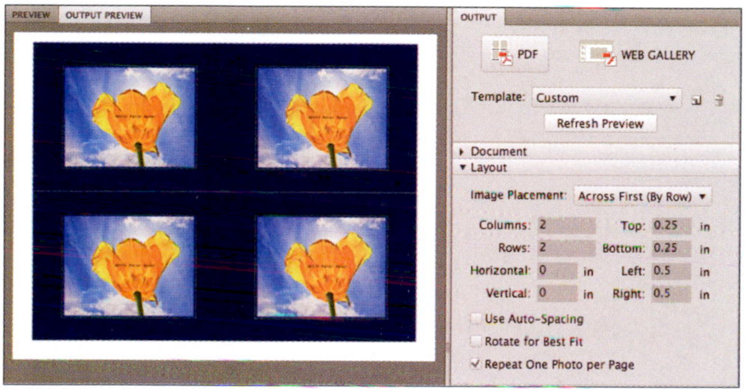

Figure 16-21: Multiple images on a single page to create a picture package.

Creating Web Galleries

In Bridge's Output panel, you can also generate galleries of your photos (see Figure 16-22). Create quick, yet elegant, stand-alone websites of your photos for posting on the Internet.

Figure 16-22: Use Bridge to create websites of your images.

It takes only a few steps (okay, and a lot of experimentation) to create gorgeous galleries to display your photos just the way you want them to be seen. Here's what to do:

1. **Select the thumbnails of the images you want to include.**

   Hint: You must select the images; you can't select only the folder. Bridge automatically skips any non-image files that are selected.

2. **Select a template.**

   To the upper-right in Figure 16-22, you can see the Template menu. Choosing the template that's just right for you might take a number of experiments, but it's certainly worth exploring each of them, one at a time.

3. **Fill out the Site Info.**

   This section is where you name the site, provide your contact info, and list the copyright notice (see Figure 16-23).

4. **Choose colors for the gallery.**

   The options in this section vary, depending on the template selected. Figure 16-24 shows what choices you'll need to make when selecting the Standard template.

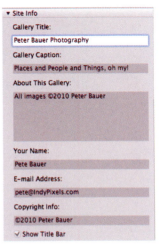

Figure 16-23: The Site Info section provides your visitor with vital information.

5. Fine-tune the appearance.

The content of the Appearance section (Figure 16-25) also varies, depending on the selected template.

6. Preview.

Click the Refresh Preview button (shown in the upper-right in Figure 16-22) to see the fruits of your decision-making process in steps 1–5. You can also preview in your web browsers, which can show you any potential problems with complex templates in certain browsers. It's a great idea, too, to take the time to preview each of the templates, perhaps using the default color schemes and appearance settings, just to get a feel for them.

Bridge saves you time by only processing the first twenty of the selected images when generating a preview. When you finally have the gallery looking *juuuust right* and click the Save button, all of the selected images are processed.

7. Generate the gallery.

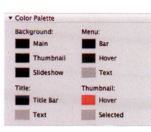

Figure 16-24: Various templates have different components and differing color options.

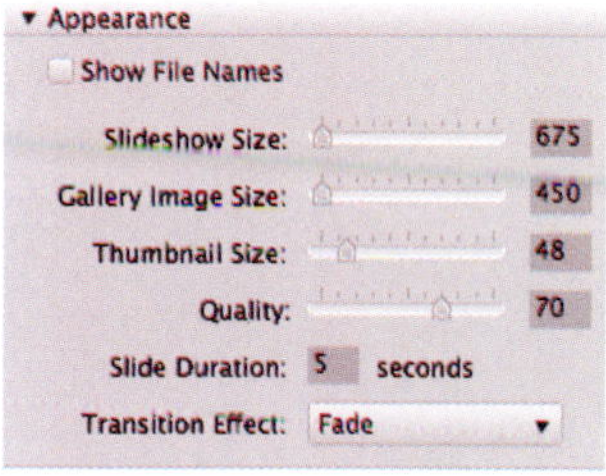

Figure 16-25: The choices you make in Appearance vary from template to template.

Bridge offers you the option to save your gallery to your hard drive or to directly upload it to the host *web server*. The web server is a computer owned by your Internet Service Provider (ISP). (Most Internet service agreements these days include space on the servers for your personal home page.) Check with your ISP for specific upload instructions — the process varies quite a bit from ISP to ISP.

If you'd like to share a gallery with friends or clients but you don't have a web server, save the gallery to your hard drive, send the entire content of the folder you choose as the destination, and instruct the recipient to open the file named index.html using a web browser's File⇨Open command.

17

Working with Video and Animation

In This Chapter

▶ Working with Photoshop's video capabilities

▶ Creating animated GIFs in Photoshop

*W*ith the proliferation of video capture devices, including most new digital cameras and just about every new smart phone, Adobe has extended video editing capabilities to even the non-Extended version of Photoshop. (Prior to the CS6, video editing was available only in the Extended version of Photoshop.) Animation, consisting of a series of frames built one by one, has long been a feature of both versions of Photoshop.

In this chapter, I'll introduce you to the basics of working with imported video. You'll also read about creating animations in Photoshop. But remember that Photoshop is an image editing program and not a full-blown movie-making suite. If you find that your motion picture dreams and aspirations can't be fulfilled by Photoshop, consider Adobe Premiere (or the quite-capable Premiere Elements for those on a budget) and perhaps Adobe After Effects.

Importing and Enhancing Video Clips

The heart of Photoshop's video capabilities is the Timeline panel. You also have the 12 commands of the Layer⇨Video Layers menu, a special Motion workspace, and even a set of Actions named, appropriately, Video Actions, designed to make your work with video both easier and more precise.

Getting video into Photoshop

Getting ready to work with video in Photoshop is as easy as opening any file into Photoshop. Use the File➪Open command, select the video file, click OK, and you're on your way! If you want to restrict the list of files in a folder to only video (or only audio) formats, select Video (or Audio) in the Enable menu at the bottom of the Open dialog box. You can also create a video project starting with one of Photoshop's video presets in the File➪New dialog box, also shown in Figure 17-1. Photoshop supports dozens of video, audio, and still image file formats with which you can create your cinematic masterpieces.

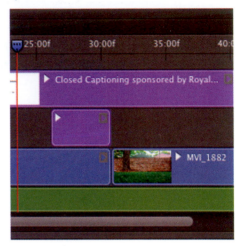

Figure 17-1: You can open a video file or create a new project.

After you have your project started, whether from an existing video file or a new document, you have a couple of options for adding additional clips, tracks, and images:

- ✔ **Click the plus button at the right end of the existing video (or audio) track in the Timeline panel.** You'll add an additional segment to the end of that track. (The plus button is visible at the right end of each track in Figure 17-2.) You'll navigate to and select the file in the Add Media dialog box, comparable to the Open dialog box, and it will be added at the end of the existing segment. (You can easily add transitions between the segments, as described later in this chapter.)

- ✔ **Click the button to the right of the video group name and select Add Media.** This button also opens the Add Media dialog box.

- ✔ **Create a new video layer.** Use the menu command Layer➪Video Layers➪New Video Layer from File, which also opens the Add Video Layer dialog box.

✔ **Copy/paste from another open file.** If you have several segments on a track, the pasted media will be added after the highlighted segment, rather than at the end of the track.

✔ **Place a file.** Use the File➪Place command to add media as a Smart Object to the selected track. If no track is selected, the Smart Object is added outside the existing Video Group.

Figure 17-2: Video groups and layers outside of groups can overlap to play simultaneously.

Using either of the first two techniques or the Place command to add a new segment automatically assigns the added file's name to the segment in the Timeline panel and to the layer in the Layers panel. Creating or pasting media uses the next sequential layer number in both the Layers panel and the Timeline panel.

When you open a video file, Photoshop automatically creates Video Group 1 in both the Layers panel and the Timeline panel, as you can see in Figure 17-2. Video groups not only help keep the content of the panels manageable, they also enable you to work with multiple tracks simultaneously. When you create a new document and paste or place media, you can manually create video groups through the button to the left of a track in the Timeline panel.

As you can see in Figure 17-2, segments in different video groups and layers outside of groups can overlap in the timeline. Much like creating an inanimate image using layers in Photoshop, the position on canvas, along with the layer opacity and blending mode, determine how the elements in the Timeline panel interact. The *playhead*, the blue slider at the top of the timeline whose position is also indicated by the vertical red line, shows what frame of the video is visible on screen at any given moment.

Remember that you can scale the timeline in the Timeline panel using the slider in the middle at the bottom of the Timeline panel. Drag to the left to see more of the timeline; drag to the right to zoom in and work with precision.

Adjusting the length of video and audio clips

After clips are added to the Timeline panel, you can change each segment's length, start point, end point, and the order of play by dragging. Position the cursor in the middle of a clip and drag to re-arrange the order of segments on a track. You can also change the order in which segments play within a video group by changing the stacking order in the Layers panel. Click on the start or end of a segment and drag to "trim," changing what part of the segment plays. The cursor changes to a square bracket with a two-headed arrow when positioned over either end of a segment, as shown in Figure 17-3 on the upper video segment. (The video within the segment to the left of the new start point or, in this example, to the right of the new end point is not deleted — you can later drag the start and end points to change what part of that segment that plays.) For precision, you can also drag the playhead to a specific point on the timeline and right-click on the playhead or use the Timeline panel's menu commands to trim or assign the start or end point for a segment.

Likewise, you can adjust the start and end points of audio tracks and audio segments. Use the Plus button at the right end of the audio track to add another audio segment to that track, or click the musical note button to the left of the track to add another audio track. You can add music and other audio in a variety of formats to Photoshop's Timeline panel. (I don't need to remind you that recorded music, just like your own photographs, is copyrighted material, right?) Click the gray arrow button at the right end of the audio segment to open the Audio fly-out panel (visible in Figurer 17-3), in which you can elect to have the audio fade in and/or out, as well as set the volume for that audio segment.

The start and end of the work area, which determine what part of the entire video will play, can also be set by right-clicking the playhead or through the panel's menu. Alternatively, set the work area by dragging the sliders to the left and right ends of the timeline, visible in Figure 17-3 at the ends of the timeline at 00 and 45:00f.

Figure 17-3: Drag the ends of segments to trim; click the gray arrow at the right end of an audio track to open the Audio fly-out panel.

Adding adjustment layers and painting on video layers

Adjustment layers, not surprisingly, can be added to a video production through the Layers panel or the Layer menu. As with regular layers, an adjustment layer is applied to all video layers below the adjustment layer and within the video group. An adjustment layer can be clipped to a single video layer by Option/Alt-clicking in the Layers panel on the line between the adjustment layer and the video layer immediately below. You might, for example, want one segment of a track to appear as grayscale by adding a Black & White adjustment layer in the Layers panel and clipping it to the video layer below it.

You can use many of Photoshop's painting tools when working with video, including the Brush tool and the Clone Stamp tool. Unless you have a problem on one specific frame of video, you'll want to consider working on a new layer. Keep in mind that there's a major difference between adding a regular layer (Layer⇨New⇨Layer) and adding a new video layer (Layer⇨Video Layers⇨New Blank Video Layer). A video layer has frames, just like a video captured by a camera, whereas a regular layer is static — its appearance remains the same for whatever duration you specify in the Timeline panel.

Say, for example, that you had a dust speck or a water spot on your lens when capturing video (not that *that* ever happens). Working with a still image in Photoshop, you might simply use the Clone Stamp to cover that unsightly set of pixels with other nearby pixels. Say also that you captured, oh, maybe three minutes of high-definition video. At 30 frames per second. For a total of 5,400 frames. That's a *lot* of cloning.

If you clone on the video layer itself or on a new video layer, you'll need to do each frame individually. Instead, if the area is rather similar in each frame, you can add a new regular layer above the problematic video segment and, in the Options bar, set the Clone Stamp tool to sample the current layer and the layer immediately below. Clone once, covering the despicable speck or spot on the new layer, and then in the Timeline panel, drag the "start" and "end" points for that layer to match those of the video segment (see Figure 17-4). When played back or rendered, the cloned area covers the flaw on the video layer — every frame fixed with a single clone! (Remember to set the playhead at the beginning of the video segment that needs fixing before Option/Alt-clicking with the Clone Stamp tool to set the source point.)

Figure 17-4: The "regular" layer will be visible in the video for the entire duration of the video segment below it.

Transitioning, titling, and adding special effects

When working with multiple video segments, you'll generally want your movie to smoothly blend from one clip to another with a *transition*. Photoshop's Timeline panel offers a number of built-in transitions that you can drag between segments on a single track. Click the button immediately to the left of the timeline in the Timeline panel, select the transition, specify the duration for the transition, and then drag the transition onto the track between the two video segments (see Figure 17-5). When played back or rendered, the two video segments blend into each other using the selected transition for the specified duration.

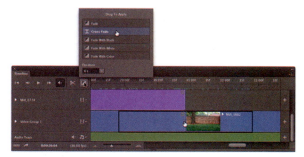

Figure 17-5: Drag transitions to the timeline to blend adjacent video segments.

Adding a title to the beginning of your cinematic extravaganza (and, of course, your name in the Director and Producer credits at the end) is as easy as adding a type layer and specifying the layer's duration in the Timeline panel. You can also add shapes to a video with the various shape tools, just as you would in any other artwork.

To add some spice to your titles and shapes, consider using keyframes to control the opacity, position, and even size of the type layer. A *keyframe* is a marker in the timeline that specifies when a specific event begins and ends. You might, for instance, want the title of your movie to fade in quickly,

remain on screen while
the first frames of the
video play in the back-
ground, and then slowly
fade away, as shown in
Figure 17-6.

Visible in the timeline in
Figure 17-6 are the dia-
monds that represent key-
frames, which I created
using these steps:

Keyframes

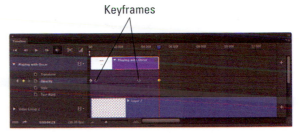

Figure 17-6: Use keyframes to specify start and end points of special effects.

1. **Add the type layer. Select the Type tool, specify the font, size, and other attributes in the Options bar or Character panel, click in the image window and type your text. End the text editing session by clicking the check mark at the right end of the Options bar, by changing tools, or by pressing ⌘+Return or Ctrl+Enter.**

   In the Layers panel, make sure that the type layer is above your video layers and outside any video group.

2. **Position the type layer. Drag the type layer into the position in the image window where you want it to first appear.**

   You'll also want to drag the left edge of the layer in the Timeline panel to the position along the timeline where you first want it to appear.

3. **Specify the duration. Click on the right edge of the type layer segment in the Timeline panel and drag to the point where you want the title completely gone from the screen.**

4. **Expand the options for that track. Click the triangle to the left of the type layer's name in the left column of the Timeline panel.**

   The options are expanded in Figure 17-6.

5. **Add the first opacity keyframe. Position the playhead at the beginning of the title segment, and then click the stopwatch button to the left of the word Opacity.**

   That adds the first keyframe at the playhead position.

6. **Set the opacity in the Layers panel.**

   In this example, because we want the title to fade in, set the layer's Opacity to 0%.

7. **Set the second keyframe. Move the playhead to the point in the timeline where you want the title to be completely visible. Click the**

diamond-shaped button between the arrows to the left of Opacity in the left column of the Timeline panel.

Keep in mind that you can switch the Timeline Unit between Frame Number and Timecode in the Timeline Panel's options, which you access through the panel's menu.

8. **Set the opacity in the Layers panel. So that the type layer is completely visible, set the Opacity to 100%.**

9. **Add the next keyframe. Drag the playhead to the point in the timeline where you want the title to start fading out, and then click the diamond-shaped button to add the keyframe.**

10. **Set the Opacity. Well, okay, we want the opacity still set to 100% at this point, so you don't need to change the Opacity in the Layers panel after all.**

If, however, you want a different opacity value at this keyframe, you can set the opacity as desired in the Layers panel.

11. **Add the last keyframe. Move the playhead to the right end of the title segment and click the diamond-shaped button to add the last keyframe.**

12. **Reduce the opacity. In the Layers panel, set the Opacity field back to zero.**

Drag the playhead to the beginning (or click the button in the upper-left corner of the Timeline panel), and then click the Play button to preview. Your title will fade in between the first pair of keyframes, remain at 100% opacity between the second and third keyframes, and then fade out between the third and fourth keyframes. Whatever other tracks you have in the Timeline continue to play.

Notice that you have several other keyframe-controlled options for the type layer in the left column of the Timeline panel. You could, perhaps, use keyframes to control a text warp, perhaps an arc or bulge. You could also use keyframes in conjunction with Photoshop's Edit⇨Transform commands to control the appearance of the type layer. You might, for example, use the Scale command to make your type layer go from a size of two or three points to filling the entire image window, making it appear to zoom in from a distance. Using keyframes to control the Transform⇨Rotate command can make the type layer spin over time. And, of course, these effects can be used in conjunction with each other, so the title could zoom in from a distance, while spinning and fading in to 100% opacity. (Click the triangle to the left of a video group in the left column of the Timeline panel and you'll see the keyframe-controlled options for video tracks.)

Transforming video layers

So, how about transforming video clips, scaling or rotating a video segment for special effects? Simply convert a video group or video layer to a Smart Object by selecting it in the Layers panel and using the menu command Layer⇨Smart Objects⇨Convert to Smart Object.

Keep in mind, too, that after converting a video group or video layer to a Smart Object, you can work with Smart Filters. Consider, if you will, a video clip captured under low-light conditions at high ISO. After adding your Curves or Levels adjustment layer to lighten up the video segment, you may find an unacceptable amount of digital noise. You *could* use the Reduce Noise filter, click the Next Frame button, use the Reduce Noise filter, click the Next Frame button, and use the — well, you get the idea. Instead, convert the video layer to a Smart Object and apply the Reduce Noise filter as a Smart Filter, reducing noise in all frames of the video segment. (Reduce Noise is just one example of Smart Filters that can be effectively used with video clips.)

The Timeline panel also has some nifty effects built right in, including pan, zoom, rotate, and the combinations Pan & Zoom and Rotate & Zoom. These effects are applied to any video or other layer through the Motion fly-out panel, which you open by clicking the small gray arrow at the right end of a segment in the Timeline Panel.

But what if you want to apply the effect to only a portion of a video segment? Position the playhead at the point where you want to make a change and click the Split at Playhead button (to the left of the Transitions button in the left column of the Timeline panel) or use the panel's menu command of the same name. The segment is divided at that point. If the video layer is within a video group in the Layers panel, it's simply divided into two segments. If the video layer is outside a video group, the portion to the right of the playhead is cut to a separate video track. If you split a Smart Object, you'll create a pair of Smart Objects, both with any Smart Filters that had already been applied.

Rendering and exporting video

You've added all of the video tracks, dragged transitions between segments, created a title with keyframe-controlled special effects, and adjusted your audio to perfection. Now what? Save the file in the PSD file format to preserve all of your editing options, of course. But to actually use the video in any other program, or to share it with others, you'll need to use Photoshop's File⇨Export⇨Render Video command.

You select a filename and location in the top section of the Render Video dialog box. In the middle section, elect to use Adobe Media Encoder to create a video. (You also have the option Photoshop Image Sequence to create a still image from each frame of the video.) Your video file format options include QuickTime (great for video on a variety of platforms), H.264 (a standard for high-definition video), and DPX (digital picture exchange, often used for video that will be further processed in another program). Each format offers a variety of presets. QuickTime, for example, lets you select a compression scheme and enables you to change the dimensions and frame rate of the final video. H.264 presets include device-specific output settings for iPads, iPhones, Android phones and tablets, a variety of high-definition TV standards, NTSC, PAL, and even YouTube.

Near the bottom of the Render Video dialog box, you'll have the option of specifying a range of frames, if you don't want to render the entire video. If your masterpiece includes an alpha channel (QuickTime only) or 3D objects, you'll also be able to specify how those elements are rendered.

After clicking the Render button, Photoshop will export the video in the selected format, with the selected presets, using the selected file name and location. How long it takes to export the video depends on a number of things, including your hardware, the length of the video, and the preset selected.

Creating Animations in Photoshop

In addition to timeline video, Photoshop provides everything you need to create frame-based animation for use on web pages and in presentations.

Building frame-based animations

Although it is certainly possible to start with a video clip or even a photo when creating a frame-based animation, you may find such projects are better suited to shapes and text. You can certainly export a frame-based animation as a QuickTime video, but to post on your website, you're more likely to use Save for Web to generate an animated GIF. (Remember that the GIF file format uses a color table limited to no more than 256 colors, so it's not generally appropriate for photographic or other continuous-tone images.)

Prior to generating the individual frames of your animation, you'll usually want to create all of the elements from which those frames will be created. Keeping each element on a separate layer makes frame creation a very simple process. After you have all of the elements you'll need, open the Timeline panel through Photoshop's Window menu and take a look at the lower-left corner of the panel. If you see the word *Once* or *Forever* with a downward-pointing arrow to the right, you're ready to get started. If you see a button with three little boxes lined up horizontally like (ready for it?) *frames in a movie*, click the button to switch the panel from video timeline to frame animation. (If, for another project, you need to reconfigure the Timeline panel for video timeline, click the button in the lower-left corner.)

In a nutshell, here's how you create a frame-based animation in Photoshop:

1. **Show/hide layers in the Layers panel. Set the Layer panel content to show those elements you want visible in the first frame of the animation.**

   If you want the animation to start with an empty screen, hide all the layers.

2. **Click the New Frame button.**

   Below the frames in the Timeline panel are a number of buttons. The New Frame button is second from the right, next to the Trash icon (which is used, naturally enough, to delete frames).

3. **Rearrange the content of the Layers panel.**

   Show/hide layers, move layer content, and otherwise rearrange the image window to set it the way you want for the second frame.

4. **Repeat as desired.**

   Click the New Frame button, rearrange the items, click the New Frame button, rearrange, and so on until you have all of the frames you want for your animation.

5. **Use Save for Web to create an animated GIF or export as a QuickTime movie.**

   And you're done! (Make sure to save the layered document in the PSD file format, just in case you want to make changes or use some of the elements in another animation down the road.)

Creating frame content

If each frame of the animation was identical, there would be no reason to create an animation — it would appear to be a still image. So, from frame to frame, something is usually different to provide the change-over-time that's the basis for animation. Among the changes you can make in the Layers panel to change the appearance of the animation from frame to frame are

- ✔ **Layer visibility.** You can show or hide the content of a layer.

- ✔ **Layer opacity.** By changing a layer's opacity from frame to frame, you can make the content of the layer fade in or fade out as the animation plays.

 ✔ **Change position.** You can use the Move tool to drag items around on a layer, making them seem to move from frame to frame.

 ✔ **Change blending mode.** Changing a layer's blending mode changes the way that layer's content interacts with the content of layers below from frame to frame.

 ✔ **Add, remove, or change a layer style.** Consider, for example, a round shape with a Bevel layer style that changes, making the object appear to inflate and deflate from frame to frame.

In the Timeline panel shown in Figure 17-7 you can see how a simple animation can be created by adding a frame, moving the content of the two layers, adding another frame, dragging the objects again, and so on.

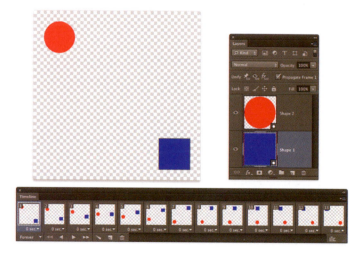

Figure 17-7: Over the course of the animation, the red circle and blue square exchange places on screen.

Tweening to create intermediary frames

To create the animation in Figure 17-7, I actually only create 3 of the 13 frames. I let Photoshop do the other 10 frames, saving me time and ensuring that the animation would play smoothly and precisely. I created the first frame, with the red circle in the upper-left corner and the blue square in the lower-right. I then clicked the New Frame button and dragged the red circle to the lower-left and the blue square to the upper-right. After clicking the New Frame button again, I dragged the red circle to the lower-right (where the blue square started) and dragged the blue square to the upper-left (where the red circle started.)

After creating my three frames, Photoshop *tweened* pair of frames to create the intermediary frames. Tweening creates the frames *in between* two frames in the Timeline panel. I clicked on the first frame, and then opened the Timeline panel menu and selected the Tween command. In the Tween dialog box (see Figure 17-8), you can specify how many frames to generate (I choose five), and what aspects of the frames you want to blend (I only needed to tween for position because there were no changes to opacity or layer styles), and whether to tween between the selected frame and the next frame or the last frame (I chose Next Frame). I then clicked on the second frame I created (frame number seven at that point, second from last) and repeated the Tween process.

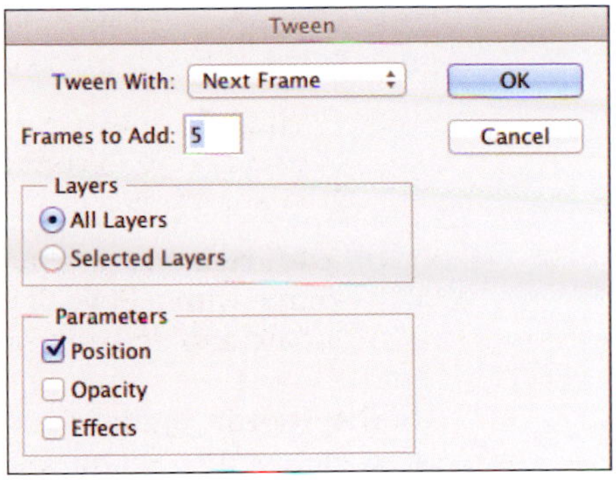

Figure 17-8: Photoshop generated 10 of the 13 frames automatically.

Say that, on your home page, you want a logo to fade out and fade in repeatedly, and you want each fade to be extremely smooth. You could create the logo, set the layer opacity to 100%, add a new frame, reduce the opacity to 99%, add a new frame, reduce the opacity to 98%, and repeat over and over again until you reached 0% opacity. Or you could create the logo at 100% opacity, click the New Frame button, reduce the opacity to 0%, click on the first frame, and use the Tween command to generate 99 more frames, tweening for opacity. Add another frame, return the opacity to 99% (your original first frame is at 100%), and then tween 98 new frames between the second last frame and the newly-created last frame. Your choice . . .

Specifying frame rate

You control how fast (or slowly) your animation plays by specifying a frame rate. Generally, each frame plays for the same amount of time, so you can click on the first frame, Shift-click on the last, and select the frame rate of your choice from the menu below any one of the frames (see Figure 17-9). If you select No delay (0.00 seconds), the animation plays as fast as

Figure 17-9: Select all of the frames and assign a frame rate to control playback speed.

possible. Don't overlook the Other option! You're not restricted to the time delays listed in the menu.

Keep in mind that not all frames need to have the same playback rate. Consider, if you will, the example of the logo that fades in and out on your home page in the previous section of this chapter. There's no reason why the 100% opacity frame couldn't be set to a five or ten second delay, with all of the other frames set to 1/10 of a second.

In the lower-left corner of the Timeline panel, you'll also want to select the repeat for the animation. You can elect to have the animation play once and then stop, to continuously loop (Forever), or you can choose any other number of times for the animation to play in a loop by selecting Other.

Optimizing and saving your animation

If you'll be adding your animation to a web page or a presentation created in Keynote or PowerPoint, you'll want to generate an animated GIF. (Keep in mind that if there's no layer named Background in the Layers panel, your animated GIF can support transparency.) After generating all of the frames, open the Timeline panel menu and select the command Optimize Animation. The default settings, Bounding Box and Redundant Pixel Removal both selected, will generate the smallest file, ensuring smoothest playback. Save the layered and animated file in the PSD file format for future use, and then use File⇨Save for Web to create the animated GIF. (Remember to select the Transparency option in Save for Web if you don't have a background layer.)

If you want to use your animation with devices that don't play animated GIFs, a smart phone, for example, use Photoshop's File⇨Export⇨Render Video command to generate a QuickTime movie.

Part V
The Part of Tens

The 5th Wave By Rich Tennant

"Why, of course! I'd be very interested in seeing this new milestone in the project."

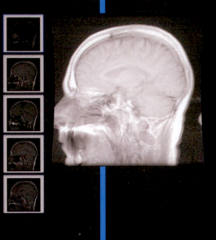

Don't get nervous — this is The Part of Tens and not The Part of Tense!

In Chapter 18, I present you with ten things you may (or may not) want to know about working with the special features of Photoshop CS6 Extended. Perhaps you have the non-extended version and are curious about what you're missing, or perhaps you purchased the extended version as part of a Creative Suite. Or, perhaps, you might skip Chapter 18 and come back at some other time when Photoshop CS6 Extended again appears on your radar screen. Chapter 19 contains a list of a mere ten of the hundreds of reasons why a Wacom tablet can make your work in Photoshop more efficient — and even help you avoid at least one common computer-related disability.

Chapter 20 provides you with ten things you need to know about HDR — high dynamic range photography, which enables you to capture (and reproduce) more of that range from "black" to "white" that we actually see in the natural world.

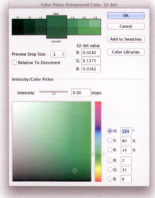

18

Ten (or so) Things to Do with Photoshop CS6 Extended

You might have purchased Photoshop CS6 and are wondering about the additional features of Photoshop CS6 Extended. You might have received Photoshop CS6 Extended as part of a bundle or the Adobe Creative Suite and aren't sure whether you need these features. You might be browsing in the bookstore, trying to determine whether to purchase Photoshop CS6 or Photoshop CS6 Extended. (If this last scenario is the case, my advice to you is this: Purchase this book first and then, with the rest of your money, buy the version of Photoshop that best fits your needs. Read about the Extended features, and if you don't need them, save some money and buy Photoshop CS6. And then use the leftover cash to buy lots more copies of this book to give to friends, family, and co-workers.)

In this chapter, I introduce you to the various special features of Photoshop CS6 Extended. This chapter won't get you fully up-to-speed on how to work with the features; instead, it's meant to quench your curiosity about the difference between Photoshop CS6 and Photoshop CS6 Extended. (For an in-depth look at working with the special features of Photoshop CS6 Extended, see *Photoshop CS6 Bible, Professional Edition* by Lisa DaNae Dayley and Brad Dayley, published by John Wiley & Sons, Inc.)

Understanding Photoshop CS6 Extended

For years, Adobe has heard the pleas of researchers, scientists, and other highly specialized users of Photoshop to include features that fulfill their needs. Adobe provides the tools these specialists need, but rather than just adding them into Photoshop CS6 and making everyone pay the costs for development, Adobe packaged them as a separate, higher-priced version of the software. "Let those who need the new features subsidize their costs!" was the decision. And, in my opinion, it was a fine decision. As I explain, these extended features don't really have a place in the workflow of most Photoshop users. That doesn't mean that if you *do* have Photoshop CS6 Extended that you'll *never* use any of these features! (How do you know which version you have? Watch as Photoshop starts to see which splash screen appears.) Even if you didn't specifically purchase the Extended version (it might have been part of a package deal), you might find a need to calculate a height or a distance using the measuring tools in Vanishing Point, or perhaps use the Count tool. But unless you actually work directly in one of the target fields for the features of Photoshop CS6 Extended, you're not likely to miss the additional capabilities at all. Another clue that you're working in Photoshop CS6 Extended is that you can open the 3D panel and see 3D menu, visible in Figure 18-1, which contains features related to working with three-dimensional objects opened into or created in Photoshop (discussed later in this chapter).

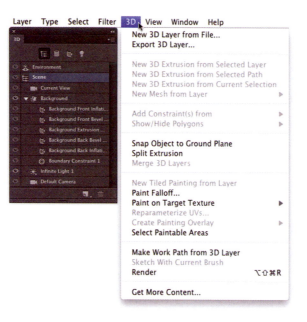

Figure 18-1: Photoshop CS6 Extended includes the 3D capabilities.

Using Smart Object Stack Modes

Working with Photoshop CS6 Extended, you can combine a number of images into a single *stack* as a Smart Object. Within the pile of images, you can determine how the pixels in each interact with those in the others. Select several related or contrasting images and add them as layers to a single image, select the layers, and create a Smart Object by choosing Layer⇨Smart Objects⇨Convert to Smart Object. Return to the Layer⇨Smart Object submenu and take a look at the Stack Modes submenu that's now available. These options determine how the content on the layers within the Smart Object interact to produce the appearance of the Smart Object itself. (Not quite the same, but similar to the way layer blending modes help determine the overall appearance of your artwork.) You can find technical explanations of each option in Photoshop's Help, but I show a couple of stacks as examples. On the left in Figure 18-2, you see a combination of the layers (shown to the left as thumbnails) using the stack mode Summation, which pretty much adds up all the lightness of each pixel in each channel, on each layer. To the right, several images shot for use with Merge to HDR are combined in a Smart Object using the stack mode Mean, which averages the values for each pixel in each channel. Not quite Merge to HDR, but with some planning and prep, it could be a supplemental technique.

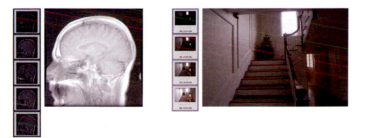

Figure 18-2: A couple of different uses for stack modes.

Working with 3D Artwork

Photoshop CS6 Extended offers lots of 3D capabilities, including 3D extrusions from layers and paths, control over the spatial relationships among objects, improved rendering, and generally improved performance. Figure 18-3 shows many of the features available when working in 3D.

You can use the tools in the 3D Mode section of the Options bar (to the far right) to rotate and roll and drag and slide and scale 3D objects. The 3D panel offers access to each of the materials (think "textures") used with a 3D object, as well as a tab in which you add, subtract, or alter lights used in the 3D scene. (Take a look at the Lighting Effects filter in Chapter 15 for some info on working with lights.)

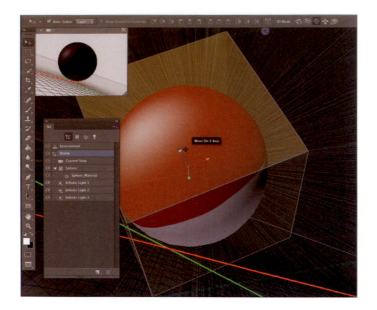

Figure 18-3: Tools, menus, and panels specially for working in 3D.

Creating 3D Objects

Working with a photo or any other 2D artwork, you can create any of a dozen different 3D shapes, from simple spheres, cubes, and cones to donuts, hats, and wine bottles (use the menu command 3D⇨New Mesh from Layer⇨Mesh Preset). Working with a layer that contains areas of transparency, you can extrude shapes as well, stretching the layer content backward into a 3D shape (use the menu command 3D⇨New 3D Extrusion from Selected Layer). Active selections on a layer and even paths can be used to create extruded objects.

Importing 3D Objects

Among the file formats that support 3D that you can open into Photoshop are 3D Studio, Collada DAE, Flash 3D, Google Earth 4 KMZ, U3D, and Wavefront|OBJ. Many ready-made 3D objects can be downloaded or purchased from various websites, including

```
www.turbosquid.com/photoshop-3d
www.daz3d.com/i/3d-models/free-3d-models?cat=382&trid=97319875
www.archive3d.net/
```

And you'll find additional resources by simply using Photoshop's menu command 3D⇨Get More Content. Among the links you'll find are those to Adobe Photoshop 3D Marketplace and Adobe Photoshop 3D Exchange.

You can use Photoshop's File⇨Open command, or add a 3D object to an existing project with 3D⇨New 3D Layer from File.

Rendering and Saving 3D Scenes

After you have your 3D scene looking just the way you want it to appear as a 2D image, use the command 3D⇨Render, followed by File⇨Save As to save in the file format of your choice. Photoshop uses the Shadow Quality and Ray Tracer High Quality Threshold settings set in the program's Preferences⇨3D panel.

You can also use the command 3D⇨Export 3D Layer to save the project in any of five 3D file formats, including Collada DAE, Flash 3D, Google Earth 4 KMZ, U3D, and Wavefront | OBJ.

If you're interested in working with 3D in Photoshop, I highly recommend that you pick up a copy of a book that goes into more detail on the subject. (Let me recommend the *Photoshop CS6 Bible* from John Wiley & Sons, Inc.)

Measuring, Counting, and Analyzing Pixels

Designed for researchers and scientists, the measuring capabilities in Photoshop CS6 Extended are quite powerful. You can measure just about anything and count the number of *whatevers* in a technical image, perhaps from a microscope or telescope.

Measuring Length, Area, and More

If you know the exact size of any element in an image, you can then discover just about anything you want to know about anything else in that image. The key is to set the measurement scale, as shown in Figure 18-4. The Measurement Scale dialog box is opened through the Image⇨Analysis menu or the Measurement Log's panel menu with the command Set Measurement Scale⇨Custom.

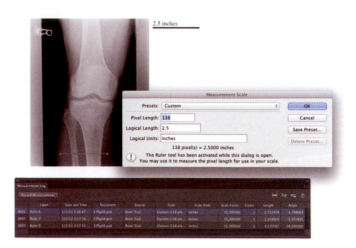

Figure 18-4: Drag a known distance; set the measurement scale.

In this example, we know that the knee is 2.5 inches wide, and that the Ruler tool (nested in the Toolbox with the Eyedropper) was Shift+dragged over 138 pixels. We can, therefore, set the scale to 138 pixels = 2.5 inches. You can add the measurement scale to the image as an editable layer group (visible in the top-center) with the Image⇨Analysis⇨Place Scale Marker command.

Using any selection tool, you can isolate any part of the image, click the Record Measurements button in the Measurement Log panel (which you open, like any panel, through the Window menu), and you'll find out more than you ever wanted to know about that particular selection and its content. In addition to the fields visible in Figure 18-4, the Measurement Log can also track (among other things) the height, width, area, perimeter length of the selection, as well as the minimum, maximum, mean, and median gray values within the selection.

After you have made and recorded all the various measurements you need, you can select all the lines in the Measurement Log (or only a few) and click the third button in the upper-right corner of the panel to export the data for use in a spreadsheet program.

Calculating with Vanishing Point

Photoshop CS6 Extended also offers measurement in perspective through Vanishing Point. Suppose, for example, you need to calculate how much wallpaper to order for the room shown in Figure 18-5. You know the height of the window (70 inches) and, using that as your known measurement, you can have Photoshop calculate the height and length of each wall.

Figure 18-5: Measurements can also be made in perspective with Vanishing Point.

Counting Crows or Maybe Avian Flu

Nested with the Ruler tool and the Eyedroppers in the Toolbox is the Count tool. Zoom in and start clicking on whatever you need to count, whether they're birds in the sky or viruses on a slide. Each item you click is labeled with a number. When you want to record the count, click the Record Measurements button in the Measurement Log. You can also record and work with multiple counts. To the right of the Count Groups menu in the Options bar (see Figure 18-6) are buttons to show/hide the currently-selected count group, to start a new count group, and to delete the current count group. Click the color swatch in the Options bar to select a new color for the count group, and you can customize both the size of the circle that marks the count and the marker number — individually for each count group.

(Don't you love the way that Warning symbol in the margin catches your eye?) Adjust the marker and label sizes *before* you start clicking around in your image with the Count tool — changing the size after placing your count markers can shift them in the image window, destroying your meticulous placement.

Figure 18-6: Click on each item and Photoshop keeps a running tally for you.

Viewing Your DICOM Medical Records

If your doctor's office, hospital, or lab has sent you home with a CD, it probably contains DICOM (Digital Imaging and COmmunication in Medicine) images. It might contain the results of a CAT scan, MRI, ultrasound, or X-rays, and you can open the files and take a look right in Photoshop. Copy the files to your hard drive. (Don't open files into Photoshop directly from CD or DVD.) Choose File⇨Open, and in the Open dialog box, select the frames in which you're interested, and click Open. In the dialog box that opens (shown in Figure 18-7), select the frames, elect to open as layers in an image or in a grid pattern (N-Up), and open. (You can also use Photoshop's File⇨Place command to add a DICOM image to an existing image.)

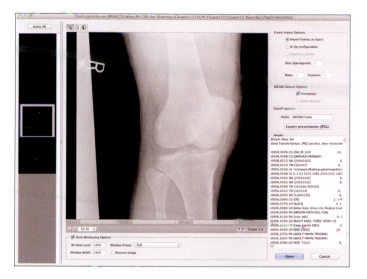

Figure 18-7: Review medical imagery right in Photoshop CS6 Extended.

Ignoring MATLAB

Photoshop CS6 Extended offers all of these interesting features for scientists, researchers, and technicians, so it only makes sense that it should work with some of the file formats they actually use and integrate with their software. When you come across the term MATLAB in Photoshop CS6 Extended, recognize it as a software environment (sort of like a programming language) that speeds calculations and helps coordinate work in various technical programs. Unless you actually work with MATLAB, say in a research lab, you really don't need to know anything else about it. (If you're intrigued by the idea, visit www.mathworks.com.)

19

Ten Reasons to Love Your Wacom Tablet

Drawing tablets from Wacom enable you to use a special stylus, which you hold like a pen or pencil or brush, to move the cursor (rather than using a mouse, track pad, or trackball). Some of Wacom's Bamboo models enable you to control the cursor with Multi-Touch, much like an iPhone or iPad. There are several reasons why using a stylus is a huge improvement over a mouse, and I give you five to start off the chapter. Another five reasons you'll love your Wacom tablet involve maximizing your efficiency; those reasons conclude the chapter.

More Natural Movement

Whether you use a pen only to sign your name or you're a traditionally trained artist, the movement of a stylus is far more natural than pushing a mouse around a desk.

Health and Safety

Use of a drawing tablet instead of a mouse can help avoid repetitive stress injuries and carpal tunnel syndrome, and can be vastly more comfortable for those who suffer from arthritis and tendonitis.

Artistic Control

With up to 2,048 levels of sensitivity, a "click" or a "drag" using a drawing tablet is *far* more versatile than working with a mouse, especially when you're working with the new erodible, airbrush, and watercolor brush tips and the Mixer Brush tool (which are discussed in Chapter 14). Open

the Photoshop Brushes palette and take a look at some of the eight different options that you can control through Pen Pressure, Pen Tilt, or (with the
Wacom Airbrush) Stylus Wheel (see Figure 19-1). And don't forget about tools
that can be directly controlled with pen pressure, such as the Quick Selection
tool, which can use pen pressure to adjust the brush diameter.

Figure 19-1: Scattering, Color Dynamics, and
Transfer also have pen-controlled options.

Extended Comfort

You can lean back and relax or sit up straight: With fingers poised over the
keyboard or hand grasping mouse, you're pretty much locked into a single
position, often for hours at a time. With the long cord of a Wacom tablet
plugged into a handy USB port or connected wirelessly using Bluetooth
technology, you have the flexibility to change positions, move back from the
monitor, even slouch in a way that would make Mom turn pale — all while
still sending input to the computer. Whether you work with the tablet on the
desk or on your lap, it doesn't matter; do whatever is most comfortable and
efficient for you. (And now you can integrate your iPad into your workflow —
perfect for use with a Cintiq. See Chapter 14.)

Programmable ExpressKeys, Touch Rings, and Touch Strips

How about convenient controls, right on the tablet, that let you access modifier keys, keyboard shortcuts, and even brush sizes and tool selection? No need to lean back in toward the desk to press a key or two; just program your most-needed keystrokes to the tablet. Keep in mind, too, that the Intuos line is southpaw-friendly — switch the USB cord and all the labels and controls conveniently flip over for lefties.

The Optimal Tablet

The inexpensive Bamboo series come in several sizes and in Multi-Touch and pen models (as well as Multi-Touch *and* pen). The professional Intuos line includes four different sizes, with working areas (the *active area*) ranging from about 4x6 to more than 12x19 inches and 2,048 levels of sensitivity, and don't overlook the wireless model. The Cintiq line, which combines a pressure-sensitive tablet into a flat screen monitor, comes in 12-inch and 21-inch models, and the new 24-inch HD Cintiq. (Visit www.wacom.com to see the full line of products — and don't overlook the numerous other products available, including the Bamboo Stylus for iPad, which not only ensures accuracy, but also minimizes fingerprints, and the free Bamboo Paper iPad app, which captures your notes, doodles, and sketches.)

If you have a fine-arts background, you might want a larger tablet. If you are not a traditionally-trained artist, you might be more comfortable with a smaller tablet, on which you can make smaller strokes. Regardless of what size tablet you have, don't forget that you can zoom in on a specific area of your image while you work. (And keep in mind that you might also want to have a smaller tablet to slide right into your laptop case, too.)

The Pen's Switch

Most (but not all) Wacom pens have a switch, called the DuoSwitch, right on the side that (by default) lets you right-click or double-click simply by rocking the switch. Rather than tapping the pen twice on the tablet to double-click (which could leave two spots of color if the Brush tool is active), simply press the DuoSwitch's upper rocker. And, of course, you can program the DuoSwitch to other functions as well, such as a specific keystroke, a modifier key, even panning and scrolling.

Setting Preferences

After downloading and installing the latest version of the Wacom driver for your tablet, open the Control Panel and customize your tablet. (On a Mac, choose System Preferences⇨Wacom Tablet. In Windows, choose Start⇨All Programs⇨Wacom Tablet⇨Wacom Tablet Properties.) The Control Panel (see Figure 19-2) enables you to assign a specific function or keystroke to each of the ExpressKeys, Touch Ring, and Touch Strips, as well as program your various pens and mouse. (Options vary for Bamboo and Cintiq models.) Settings can be customized for Photoshop, Bridge, and even iTunes. You can share saved Preferences settings with friends and co-workers.

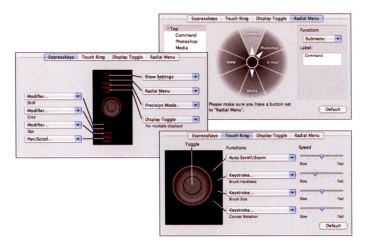

Figure 19-2: Think about what keystrokes and functions are best assigned to the Intuos 4's easy-to-reach ExpressKeys and Touch Ring.

The Accessories

Wacom offers a variety of pens, an airbrush, a five-button mouse, and even a CAD-friendly lens cursor to help you get the very most out of your tablet. Choose the input device that's best for you — or switch among several, using the one that's most appropriate for the specific job at hand.

Cintiq for the Ultimate Control

The ultimate tablets are, of course, the Cintiq tablets, which integrate a monitor into the tablet, enabling you to paint or draw directly on your image. Wacom offers Cintiqs in both 12" ($999) and 21" ($1,999), and a new 24" HD model ($2,599). And although the prices may seem like a *lot* of money for a tablet, it's not too extreme if you consider the money you may save by not purchasing a monitor. Whether you use the integrated stand and paint on your Cintiq on your desk (see Figure 19-3) or take advantage of the long cable and work with the display in your lap, you're bound to find increased accuracy and productivity at your fingertips — literally!

Figure 19-3: Consider using a Cintiq in place of a standard monitor.

Until you're perfectly comfortable using a stylus and tablet, the Cintiq line might be a bit of a stretch. But after you've worked with the more affordable lines of tablets (Intuos and the entry-level Bamboo pen models), you may develop a craving for a Cintiq!

Ten Things to Know about HDR

*T*he world of photography continues to evolve at an amazing pace! Not only has digital photography pretty much replaced film, the various Raw file formats are more and more common in both professional and high-end hobbyist photography. A typical camera phone now captures as many or more pixels than did an expensive pocket camera just a few years ago. My iPhone even offers an "HDR" option, which does help some in challenging lighting conditions, such as a photo of a dark room with the bright outdoors in the windows. But the iPhone HDR option doesn't hold a candle to the high dynamic range images you can produce with a good camera and Photoshop's Merge to HDR Pro.

I begin this chapter with an explanation of high dynamic range photography, give you some pointers for capturing the images that you'll use in an HDR image, and then explain how you actually combine and use HDR photos.

Understanding What HDR Is

HDR stands for *high dynamic range*. The dynamic range is the visual "distance" from black to white. By making that visual distance greater, you create a wider tonal range in the image. The world we see around us contains far more range than can be reproduced on a monitor, printed to paper, or even saved in a 16-bit image. (See Chapter 6 for an explanation of 8-bit, 16-bit, and 32-bit color.)

Consider, for example, shooting an image in a room with windows on a sunny day. If you expose your image for the content of the room, whatever is outside is blown out and completely white (see the examples in Figure 20-1). If you expose for the outside, the content of the room is in shadow. So, why not create an image in which the content of the room *and* the world outside the windows are *both* properly exposed?

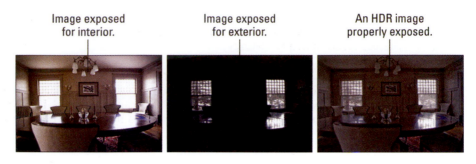

Image exposed for interior. Image exposed for exterior. An HDR image properly exposed.

Figure 20-1: You can expose for the room and lose the highlights, you can expose for the highlights and lose the room, or you can have both with HDR.

Is HDR "the future" of photography, the way digital has supplanted film? Probably not, until we have cameras that can capture true HDR images natively, as well as a way to better take advantage of the enhanced tonal range when printing. (If you're a camera engineer, I might have a way to handle the first problem. Look me up, eh?) Is HDR something about which you should be aware, so that you can take advantage of its potential to meet difficult challenges in your own photography? Absolutely!

Capturing for Merge to HDR Pro

To merge several exposures into an HDR image, you need to have several exposures with which to work. There are two ways to meet the challenge: You can shoot a series of exposures, or shoot one Raw image and make several copies with different Exposure values.

If you want the absolutely best results from Merge to HDR Pro, keep two words to keep in mind: *manual* and *tripod*. Those are the keys to capturing multiple exposures for use with Merge to HDR Pro. The only variable you want to change from shot to shot is the camera's shutter speed — everything else, including focus, should remain the same. Your tripod should be sturdy and level, and a cable release is a good idea. You can use auto focus and auto exposure to set the lens and get an exposure recommendation from the camera. But then switch the lens to manual focus and set the camera to manual exposure. Before each exposure, adjust only the shutter speed.

How many exposures do you need? I recommend a minimum of three (the best exposure possible for the scene's midtones, one "overexposed" for detail in the shadows, one "underexposed" for detail in the highlights). Each scene differs to some degree, but you'll want to capture as much of the tonal range as possible. It is better, however, to use seven separate exposures with Merge to HDR Pro. More than that is rarely necessary, and most scenes can be captured in five exposures.

If you are familiar with *exposure values*, try for a range of perhaps seven, including three below and three above the "optimal" exposure. If that's unfamiliar territory, try shooting the optimal exposure, a shot at 1/4 the shutter speed of the first shot, and a shot at four times the original shutter speed.

Okay, so say that you don't have a tripod and there's a shot that's just crying for HDR. Set your camera to auto-bracket at the largest increment possible, set the camera to "burst" mode, get as settled as possible, frame the shot, focus, take a deep breath, let the breath out halfway, pause, press and hold the shutter button. In burst mode, three (or more, depending on your camera) shots are taken as quickly as the camera can operate. In auto-bracket mode, the exposure is automatically changed for each shot. (Note that you need to set the camera to auto exposure bracketing, sometimes seen as AEB, not white balance bracketing. Check your camera's User Guide.)

Preparing Raw "Exposures" in Camera Raw

Alternatively, and usually with quite good results, you can change the exposure after the fact using Camera Raw. (You'll want to use a Raw image, not a JPEG image, for this technique.) Here's how:

1. **Shoot the best exposure possible.**

2. **Transfer the image to your computer.**

3. **Open the image into Camera Raw.**

   Make sure that Camera Raw's Workflow Options — click the blue line of info below the preview — are set to 16-bit color.

4. **Adjust the image until it looks perfect.**

5. **Click the Open Image button to open from Camera Raw into Photoshop.**

6. **Copy the image into a new file and save in the TIFF format.**

   Select⇨All. Choose Edit⇨Copy followed by File⇨Close (don't save), and then File⇨New. (The preset will be Clipboard, so just set Background Contents to Transparent and click OK.) Choose Edit⇨Paste followed by File⇨Save As, choose TIFF as the file format, and save. Using this procedure strips out the EXIF data, making sure Merge to HDR Pro doesn't use the wrong exposure value.

7. **Reopen the original Raw file into Camera Raw.**

8. **Drag the Exposure slider to the left to reduce the exposure by 2.**

   Two is just a general guideline — watch for maximum detail in the highlights.

9. **Hold down the Option/Alt key and click Open Copy.**

   This prevents Camera Raw from overwriting the earlier adjustment in the file's metadata.

10. **Copy the image into a new file and save in the TIFF format.** (Repeat Step 6, using a sequence number or other change to the filename to differentiate from the first Tiff.)

11. **Reopen the Raw file into Camera Raw a third time.**

12. **Drag the Exposure slider to the right to increase the exposure by 2.**

    Again, two is just a starting point — you want to see maximum detail in the shadows.

13. **Hold down the Option/Alt button and click Open Copy.**

14. **Copy the image into a new file and save in the TIFF format (repeat Step 6, using a third filename.)**

You can now use these three adjusted images in Merge to HDR, as described in the following section. The results likely won't be as great as using a series of separate exposures, but should be better than a single exposure.

Working with Merge to HDR Pro

After you have the exposures from which you want to create your HDR masterpiece, you need to put them together using Photoshop's Merge to HDR Pro.

You can open Merge to HDR Pro either through Photoshop's File⇨Automate menu or you can select the images to use in Bridge and use Bridge's menu command Tools⇨Photoshop⇨Merge to HDR Pro. (If you open through Photoshop, you'll either need to open the images into Photoshop first, or navigate to and select the images to use. If you browse, the files must all be in the same folder on your hard drive.)

Be patient with Merge to HDR Pro — it has a lot of work to do before you get to play with the combined exposures. When the calculations are done, the Merge to HDR Pro window opens (as shown in Figure 20-2).

Each of the images in the merge is shown as a thumbnail below the preview. You can deselect each image to see what impact it has on the combined exposure. (After you click on the green checkmark, give Merge to HDR Pro a couple of moments to redraw the preview.) If you're working with seven exposures and one seems to degrade from the overall appearance, leave that thumbnail's box deselected.

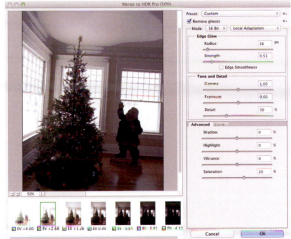

Figure 20-2: Merge to HDR opens after the images have been processed.

By default, Merge to HDR Pro assumes that you want control over the image right away and sets the Mode menu to 16-bit color. You then have the options shown in Figure 20-2, as well as a few others, including the Curves panel (as shown in Figure 20-3).

So, what are all those options you see in Figure 20-2 and Figure 20-3?

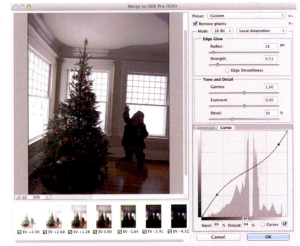

Figure 20-3: In 16-bit mode with Local Adaption, you have quite a bit of control.

- ✔ **Preset:** If you have a series of similar images that require the same adjustments, you can save and load presets.

- ✔ **Remove Ghosts:** When you're capturing multiple exposures, especially outdoors, moving objects in your image may have left "ghosts" behind. This option helps minimize those moving objects.

✔ **Edge Glow:** Use the Radius and Strength sliders in combination to increase the perceived sharpness of the image.

✔ **Tone and Detail:** Think of the Gamma slider as your contrast control. Dragging to the right flattens the contrast between highlights and shadows; dragging to the left increases the contrast. The Exposure slider controls the overall lightness (to the right) or darkness (to the left) of the image, just like Exposure slider in Camera Raw. The Detail slider sharpens the smallest bits in the image. The Shadow and Highlight sliders control the lower and upper parts of the image's tonal range. For both sliders, dragging left darkens and dragging right lightens.

✔ **Color:** Visible in Figure 20-2, the Advanced tab shares space with Curve in Local Adaptation. The Vibrance slider controls the saturation of the near-neutral colors and Saturation controls all of the colors in the image. (These sliders, too, are comparable to their counterparts in Camera Raw and are discussed in more detail in Chapter 7.)

✔ **Curve:** Click on the curve to add an anchor point and drag up/down or enter numeric values to adjust the tonality of the image. The Corner option produces a sharp change in the angle of the curve, which is generally not desirable. The button to the right of Corner resets the curve.

Switching the Mode menu to 32-bit color restricts you to adjusting the preview — anything else will be done in Photoshop after you click Merge to HDR Pro's OK button. (The entire expanded tonal range is still in the 32-bit image, it's just the preview that you're adjusting.) Using options other than Localized Adaptation in 16-bit mode give you less (or no) control over the conversion from 32-bit color.

In 32-bit mode, you have a simple slider to adjust the preview; 16-bit mode's Exposure and Gamma sliders control the overall tonal range and the contrast between shadows and highlights.

Note that 16-bit and 8-bit offer the same options, but I don't recommend converting from 32-bit to 8-bit in Merge to HDR Pro. If you need an 8-bit version of the image, work in16-bit, and then after perfecting the image in Photoshop and saving as 16-bit, use the command Image⇨Mode⇨8-Bits/Channel to convert and Save As (or Save for Web and Devices) to save the 8-bit copy.

Remember that when the changes you make in Merge to HDR's 16-bit mode are finalized, the unused parts of the 32-bit tonal range are discarded. Working in 16-bit mode in Merge to HDR Pro can be convenient, but you can also stay in 32-bit mode, open into Photoshop with the OK button, save the 32-bit image, and then do all the adjusting available in Merge to HDR Pro — and *much* more — in Photoshop. Want to fine-tune or change the image sometime down the road? Sure, why not? Simply reopen the saved 32-bit image and re-adjust, paint, filter, whatever, and then save again. Need a 16-bit copy to share or print? Save first as 32-bit, adjust, and then use Save As to create the 16-bit copy.

Saving 32-Bit HDR Images

A 32-bit image can be saved in a number of file formats, including Photoshop's PSD and Large Document Format (PSB), as well as TIFF and some specialized formats. Unless you're sending the image to another program (perhaps when working with computer animation) or a client who has requested a specific format, stick with PSD, PSB, or TIFF.

HDR Toning

Found in the Image⇨Adjustments menu, HDR Toning (see Figure 20-4) is your 32-bit image adjustment master tool. It offers the same Local Adaptation, Equalize Histogram, Exposure and Gamma, and Highlight Compression options found in Merge to HDR Pro. (Each of the options is described in the "Working with Merge to HDR Pro" section of this chapter.) Although it's also available for 16-bit and 8-bit images, HDR Toning is designed to work with the 32-bit images you create with Merge to HDR Pro. You'll also see HDR Toning when you convert to 16-bit or 8-bit color through the Image⇨Mode menu.

Figure 20-4: HDR Toning offers the same options as Merge to HDR Pro's 16-bit mode, but in 32-bit color.

Painting and the Color Picker in 32-Bit

If you have Photoshop CS6 Extended, you can paint in 32-bit color. The Brush, Pencil, and Mixer Brush tools (but not Color Replacement) are available. The Blur, Sharpen, Smudge, and Eraser tools are also available in 32-bit color, but not Dodge, Burn, Sponge, Background Eraser, or Magic Eraser. Type layers, shapes, and paths are also at your command. You can add color to a 32-bit image with the Gradient tool, but not the Paint Bucket. And although the History Brush is available, the Art History Brush is not. The Content-Aware Move, Patch, Healing Brush, Spot Healing Brush, and the Red Eye tool are disabled. 32-bit images can have multiple layers and layer styles, too. Be aware, too, that not all blending modes are available in 32-bit color. Normal, Darken, Multiply, Lighten, Difference, and about a dozen less commonly used blending modes are enabled for tools and layers.

Working with painting tools and gradients requires a way to define color in 32-bits. When you open the Color Picker while working with a 32-bit image, you'll see something different. In Figure 20-5, the 32-bit Color Picker shows some additional features. In addition to working with HSB and RGB fields, color is defined with the Intensity slider. Think of "intensity" as "exposure." It permits color values that go beyond RGB's 255/255/255. Define the color *and* choose how light or dark the exposure is — it's sort of a fourth dimension of color definition.

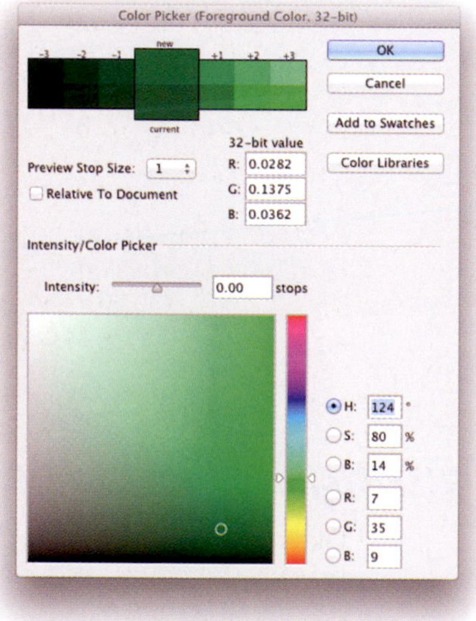

The bar at the top shows the last-selected color below and the current selection above. You can click on any of the size previews to the left or the six to the right to jump to that color. You control how different each of the 12 previews is from the current color with Preview Stop Size.

Figure 20-5: The incredible range of 32-bit color requires a new way to define "color."

Filters and Adjustments in 32-Bit

The list of filters available in 32-bit color is even shorter than the list for 16-bit color. The Filter Gallery, Adaptive Wide Angle, Lens Correction, Liquify, Oil Paint, and Vanishing Point won't work in 32-bit color, but you do have the key Blur and Sharpen filters, as well as Add Noise, Clouds and Difference Clouds, Lens Flare, Emboss, Lighting Effects, High Pass, Maximum, Minimum, and Offset. Don't forget that 32-bit images can be converted to Smart Objects to apply Smart Filters!

The only adjustment layers that can be added to 32-bit images are Levels, Exposure, Hue/Saturation, Photo Filter, Channel Mixer, and Color Lookup, along with Solid Color, Gradient, and Pattern fill layers. In the Adjustments menu, you'll also find HDR Toning and Desaturate at your service.

Selections and Editing in 32-Bit

Not surprisingly, the Rectangular Marquee, Elliptical Marquee, Single Row, Single Column, Lasso, and Polygon Lasso tools are available when working in 32-bit color because they simply create selections around pixels. Also not surprising is the unavailability of the Magnetic Lasso tool because it works its magic based on identifying differences between neighboring colors. And, on the subject of magic, the Magic Wand is also out of commission when working in 32-bit color, but you can work with the Quick Selection tool in your HDR image.

And after you have made your initial selection, you'll find that Refine Edge is fully functional in 32-bit color, as are the Select⇨Modify commands and Transform Selection. You can also save and load selections (alpha channels) and work in Quick Mask mode in 32-bit images.

Printing HDR Images

Okay, well, you can't really print the entire tonal range of a 32-bit image — no printer (or paper) can handle the range. In fact, you can't print an image in 32-bit color at all from Photoshop (the Print and Print One Copy commands are disabled). What you *can* do is print a 16-bit (or 8-bit) image that has outstanding highlights, outstanding shadows, and outstanding midtones.

After saving the 32-bit original, use Photoshop's Image⇨Mode⇨16-Bits/ Channel command to convert to 16-bit color (using Local Adaptation, as described earlier in this chapter). After changing the color depth, use Image⇨ Image Size to set your desired print size. You can either uncheck the Resample box and enter your desired print dimensions, letting Photoshop calculate the new resolution, or you can use the Resample option and input both the print dimensions and resolution. The resampling algorithm should be set to Bicubic Automatic, not Nearest Neighbor or Bilinear, neither of which is appropriate for most photos. (Those are your only three options when resampling a 32-bit image.)

When the image is ready, open Photoshop's File⇨Print window. Choose the printer and click the Print Settings button to set up the printer. Choose the specific paper on which you will be printing and disable the printer's color management. Choose the printer's resolution and — if your printer has the capability — select 16-Bit Output.

To the right in Photoshop's Print dialog box (as shown way back in Figure 4-11), make sure that Photoshop is managing colors and that you have selected the printer's own profile for the specific paper on which you are printing. Generally you should use the Relative Colorimetric rendering intent and Black Point Compensation. (Note that if your print is *way* too dark, Black Point Compensation should be disabled.)

You need to make all of the printer-specific choices by clicking the Print Settings button before clicking the Print button. If you want to save this 16-bit version of the image, use Save As to create a new file. Using the Save command would overwrite the 32-bit original HDR image.

And there you have it — ten things you should know about HDR. You're now ahead of the curve and ready for the Next Big Thing in digital photography!

On behalf of everyone involved with the production of this book, let me say thanks for coming along for the ride. We wish you peace, love, health, and happiness!

Index